MARX
AND
MARXISM

MARX
AND
MARXISM

GREGORY CLAEYS

NATION
BOOKS
New York

Nation Books
116 East 16th Street, 8th Floor New York, NY 10003
www.nationbooks.org
@NationBooks

Printed in the United States of America

First Edition: April 2018

Originally published in 2018 by Penguin Random House UK in Great Britain

Published by Nation Books, an imprint of Perseus Books, LLC, a subsidiary of Hachette Book Group, Inc. Nation Books is a co-publishing venture of the Nation Institute and the Perseus Books.

The Hachette Speakers Bureau provides a wide range of authors for speaking events. To find out more, go to www.hachettespeakersbureau.com or call (866) 376-6591.

The publisher is not responsible for websites (or their content) that are not owned by the publisher.

Library of Congress Control Number: 2017963877

ISBNs: 978-1-56858-897-1 (hardcover), 978-1-56858-896-4 (e-book)

LSC-C

10 9 8 7 6 5 4 3 2 1

Contents

Many Marxes

Karl Marx was the Jesus Christ of the twentieth century. On Easter Day, 1918, Russian newspapers which had previously announced, 'Christ is Risen', replaced this with 'One Hundred Years Ago To-day Karl Marx was Born'.[1] If they had then claimed he had walked on water or had awakened from the dead, few would have been surprised. He looked the part of the Father, too. The old man with the grey beard and shaggy hair – the portrait most know of Marx – bears more than a passing resemblance to the grumpy patriarch many Christians envision on his heavenly throne. We can see Cecil B. DeMille or Steven Spielberg casting him in the part.

So why, and how, did history nominate Marx for this role? Marx may have been 'the Prophet Himself', as his friend the Thuringian tailor Johann Georg Eccarius put it.[2] However, unlike Christ, he was never content only to console the poor: he wanted, more ambitiously, to end poverty instead, and thus the need for consolation. Yet it is not even clear whether Marx became 'great' because his works were so popular, or because he stood for an idea whose time had come. At his death much of his writing (perhaps three-quarters) was still unknown.[3] Few now read the early polemics, *The Holy Family* (1845) or *The Poverty of Philosophy* (1847), much less *The Cologne Communist Trial* (1852) or the tedious diatribe against Max Stirner in *The German Ideology* (1845–6). By the time he died in 1883, *A Contribution to the Critique of Political Economy* (1859) and volume one of *Capital* (1867) had appeared. *The Eighteenth Brumaire of Louis Napoleon* (1852) and *The Civil War in France* (1871) told

1

something of Marx's politics and historical analysis. And of course *The Communist Manifesto* (1848) represented Marx's programme as a whole.

By the early twentieth century this inheritance had grown. Editions of Marx and commentaries on his writings produced in the USSR and East Germany in particular were always selective. By the 1920s many of his manuscripts had been assembled in Moscow by the first great Marxologist, David Riazanov, who was later shot by Stalin. Correspondence appeared in dribs and drabs. A key early text, Marx's 'Critique of Hegel's *Philosophy of Right*' (1843), was published in 1927.[4] In 1932 came the 'Paris Manuscripts' (1844), whose theory of alienation seemingly offered a 'humanist' critique of Stalinism which might free Marx from the taint of totalitarianism. By 1968 this was widely regarded outside the communist bloc as Marx's main work, and it is often treated today as second only to *Capital*. Yet the question remains as to whether he abandoned it as inadequate or superseded.

Discerning what Marx 'really meant' has always been a function of the times as well as of the texts available. Interpretations accordingly have proliferated. Shelves of books on Marx entice, beg, berate and intimidate the potential reader. Blowing the dust off these volumes we quickly discover that there is not one Marx or one Marxism: there are many. Privileging one view of either above the rest across a range of complex issues is bound to be contentious. But some readings have proven historically more influential than others, largely because they answer more of our questions. Later readers are prone to ask: Why was Marx so successful as a thinker? Did he have a 'system' and, if so, what does it consist of? Does Marx take us to Lenin? To Stalin? To the revisionist Eduard Bernstein or the 'renegade' Karl Kautsky? Is Marx's theory of alienation still relevant? Was Marx an economic determinist? Did he regard the end of capitalism as inevitable? Is class the most important category of social analysis? Did Marx deny a role to individuals in history? Was he a democrat or a totalitarian? To complicate matters, Marx answered many of these questions in different ways as the circumstances around him altered. The first testing ground for his theory of communism, Europe in 1848, had altered greatly by his death in 1883. Now too Russia loomed not solely as the epitome of reaction, but as potentially a revolutionary venue.

Yet in other respects not only Europe, but the world, was exactly what Marx had predicted by the time he died. He prophesied an evangelical, crusading capitalism which aimed to conquer the globe. His understanding of this process remains amongst the most compelling explanations ever offered. The great secret of Marx's success, it is argued in this book, lay in his ability to synthesize this vision into a few simple formulae which the masses could easily digest, while presenting a complex and all-encompassing worldview which was captivating and intellectually stimulating to the well-educated. No competitor succeeded in achieving this degree of comprehensiveness, or in provoking the extraordinary intellectual ecstasy and moral fervency that Marxism has often induced.

The line between the popular and elite readings of Marx has often been deliberately maintained. Many Marxist intellectuals have strained to make Marx and his 'system' as unintelligible as possible, if only to justify their leadership of the inchoate masses in the correct direction. This is usually achieved by adopting tortuously obscure, convoluted Hegelian phraseology which renders Marxism a kind of gnostic, secret science accessible to only the few. It is analogous to the medieval church's insistence on using Latin to exclude the masses from accessing the sacred texts. The seductiveness of incomprehensibility here has proven extraordinarily powerful. Words like 'dialectic' and 'negation' may pierce the veils of ignorance and dispel the superstitions of the many, but can also become weapons that defend unintelligibility. In its simplest form official Marxism–Leninism, or 'Diamat' (dialectical materialism), became a bland, formulaic dogma. Here complex theory is reduced to a few ritualistic and easily parroted phrases. This world view purports to answer every question, and is invoked ever more shrilly and insistently in response to any query or doubt. Most later readers bolt quickly when confronted with either of these discourses. But hundreds of thousands have become 'Marxists' – some of the most dogmatic sort – without having read a line of Marx, indeed without being able to read at all. And some have found this to be a virtue rather than an anomaly.

Those who do read Marx carefully view him variously as a philosopher, an economist, a historian, a sociologist, a political theorist, even a literary craftsman. The approach to Marx adopted in this book is chiefly through the history of socialism. Like many other disappointed nineteenth-century radicals, Marx thought communism – a variety of socialism – answered the most burning issue of the time: the rapid spread of capitalism. There were (and are) many socialisms on offer. Just which one(s) Marx adopted, and why, and with what consequences, are the most important questions we may ask of his writings today. But we must treat Marx as critically as we would any other thinker: not reverently, but giving credit where credit is due.

If this approach makes Marx appear less original than is sometimes presumed, it also portrays him as more practical and less wedded to metaphysical schemas. It depicts him navigating a complex field of alternatives to capitalism in a peculiarly compelling way, while still making mistakes, and sometimes overstating his own accomplishments. It makes him seem less Hegelian, and in later life less philosophically oriented. Marx is not portrayed here as either a genius or a scoundrel. The movements associated with his name have lent hope to hundreds of millions of victims of tyranny and aggression, but have also proven disastrous in practice, and resulted in the deaths of millions. Part of this failure, doubtless, was Marx's doing, but most of it was not, simply because Marx never had the power to put his ideas into practice and thus was never forced to compromise with historical necessity. Of all the great critics of modern society, however, Marx is the one we most need to confront, to question, to engage with. Both his critique of capitalism and his vision of the future, we will see, speak across the centuries to our times, even if the questions he poses are more difficult to answer than ever, and his answers are sometimes simply wrong.

As Marx is the central figure in this book, so the Bolshevik Revolution of November 1917 is its key historical event. Few communists have emulated Marx. Many more have followed Lenin's revolutionary course. Part Two here considers how Marx's ideas evolved through to the present, and how they relate to his original outlook.

PART ONE

Marx

CHAPTER 1

The Young Karl

Karl Marx was born on 5 May 1818 in the small Rhineland city of Trier, near the French border, which then had about 12,000 inhabitants.[1] Until recently the largely Catholic, liberal-leaning town had lived quite happily under twenty years of French occupation. Many of its citizens, including Marx's future father-in-law, Ludwig von Westphalen, harboured sympathies for revolutionary principles and even, in the 1830s, for the socialist schemes of Henri de Saint-Simon's followers. Marx's father, born Hirschel ha-Levi Marx, came from a long line of rabbis; but, renamed Heinrich Marx, he practised law as a Protestant convert (from around 1817), after the kingdom of Prussia, in which Trier was then located, forced Jews out of such professions. He too had liberal sympathies, urged wider political representation and assisted in local poor-relief schemes. His wife, Henrietta, came from a family of Dutch rabbis.

The young Karl spent most of his schooldays with classical authors like Homer and Ovid. He was not a particularly distinguished student. His school director was a republican who sympathized with Rousseau and Kant and saw the French Revolution of 1789 as extending Enlightenment principles of liberty and equality. Marx imbibed such principles, one of his first essays (1835) insisting that choosing a profession should be guided by 'the welfare of mankind and of our own perfection', the happiest person being 'the man who has made the greatest number of people happy' (1:8). We witness here, at the age of seventeen, a desire to define 'the nature of man' by 'the spark of divinity in his breast, a passion for what is good, a striving for knowledge, a yearning for truth' (1:637)[2] – as good a definition of himself throughout his life as any Marx ever provided. Thirty-five years later he wrote to his daughter Laura respecting the Irish question that while he desired to accelerate the class struggle he was also 'acted upon by feelings of humanity' (43:449). The latter thus remained a dominant motif in his life. 'Those who have the good fortune to be able to devote themselves to scientific pursuits must be the first to place their knowledge at the service of humanity. One of his favourite sayings was: "Work for humanity"', recalled his son-in-law Paul Lafargue.[3] To term him a 'cosmopolitan humanitarian' would not be a misnomer. Yet he always fought shy of the romantic implications of such sentimentalism.

In October 1835 Marx left Trier to study law in Bonn. Seemingly destined for an academic post, he led the traditional riotous student life, drinking to excess, duelling and spending a night in gaol for rowdiness. In October 1836 he moved to Berlin, where his focus shifted from law to philosophy. Nine days after submitting his dissertation on 'The Difference between the Democritean and Epicurean Philosophy of Nature', Marx was awarded his doctorate of philosophy in 1841 (by the University of Jena, after he had grown disenchanted with Berlin). Epicurus was regarded as a forefather of Enlightenment French materialism, though Marx also portrayed him as anticipating a Hegelian idea of self-consciousness, which his preface termed 'the highest divinity' (1:30).

Hegel and the Young Hegelians

The newly minted doctor viewed the world as an oyster to crack. In these years Marx saw himself as at the cutting edge of modern philosophical development, and capable of reconciling the most radical paradoxes that had been created by the Enlightenment collision with what he would soon term 'bourgeois society'.[4] This confidence resulted most directly from his confrontation with the greatest German philosopher of the age, Georg Wilhelm Friedrich Hegel (1770–1831), and his followers.

Approaching Hegel via Marx we need to know something about four themes in particular: Hegel's metaphysics; his philosophy of history; his political theory; and his method, the famous 'dialectic'. Following Plato, Hegel's philosophical starting point was pure Idealism: only the world of Spirit or Mind (*Geist*), or self-conscious reason, was real. 'Things' did not exist, 'for "thing" is only a thought'.[5] Hegel's chief concern was to define both human nature and history in terms of mankind's desire for freedom. This he portrayed partly in terms of Spirit's coming to awareness of its own free nature. As Hegel's *The Phenomenology of Spirit* (1807) plotted it, humanity progressed from naïve empiricism, knowing only what our senses present to us, to its logical end, an eventual stage of knowing the Absolute (or God, or Mind's own nature). Spirit's progress towards self-consciousness was 'dialectical' insofar as every stage constantly evolved into the next through a process of contradiction, by negating the previous stage while preserving something of it, a process Hegel called *Aufhebung*, or 'sublation'. Each stage involved self-consciousness 'alienating' itself in nature, developing in history and emerging again in the self-consciousness of humanity, in a progression from lower to higher.

Few modern readers find this scheme comprehensible in such abstract terms. If we see Mind as a metaphor for progressive human development, and as describing an empirically verifiable desire for freedom occurring through real social institutions and relations, however, the theory makes more sense. Hegel's goal, Charles Taylor writes, was thus to define 'a whole, integrated life in which man was at one with himself, and men were at one with each other in society'.[6] No small ambition! In the former sense, this meant unifying our own alienated souls with God, the Absolute, as well as recognizing the world as our own creation, and thus overcoming 'alienation' (*Entfremdung*), the failure to achieve such recognition. In the latter, it meant achieving 'consciousness of belonging to a community'.[7] Here the ideal was Periclean Athens, whose 'spontaneous harmony' has been called Hegel's 'utopia'.[8]

Hegel's philosophy of history attracted many by explaining how subsequent stages embodied Spirit's growing self-consciousness. History, in a word, possessed 'meaning'. 'What distinguished Hegel's mode of

thinking from that of all other philosophers was the exceptional historical sense underlying it', thought Friedrich Engels (1820–95), Marx's
lifelong intellectual partner, recalling that Hegel had first posited
'that there is development, an intrinsic coherence in history' (16:474).
Commencing with Persian despotism, where only the monarch is free,
humanity passed through the Greek *polis*, where consciousness of freedom (for the few) first arose; to Rome, where slavery still shows that
not all are free; to Christianity, and the recognition of mankind as spiritual beings; thence to the Germanic world, where after the Reformation it became clear that 'the human being as such is free'.[9] But how
could the moderns hope to emulate the achievements of the ancients?
Whereas virtue was civic, not merely private, in classical Greece, now
there was no turning back. Modern individuality had staked its claims
against ancient republicanism. The young Hegel was greatly impressed
by the French Revolution. He had glimpsed the 'world soul' on horse-
back as Napoleon entered Jena in October 1806. Hegel's glorification of
reason has been seen as having its counterpart in attempts to found a
Cult of Reason during the revolution.[10] The older Hegel, however, believed that modern Prussia might exemplify the further progress of
Spirit.

Nonetheless a major hitch in this otherwise soothing narrative was
posed by the profound disharmony which potentially characterized
the age of commerce and industry. Hegel was the first significant modern German philosopher to confront the reality of commercial society.
Civil society, he thought, now recognized the positive value of individualism, as well as the growth of mutual dependency through the
operation of 'the system of needs and wants'. But its flip side posed a
peculiar threat to any dreams of abolishing servitude and achieving
freedom. This would become Marx's starting point.

This threat first became evident to Hegel around 1793, when he began
studying the chief eighteenth-century Scottish political economists,
Sir James Steuart, Adam Ferguson and Adam Smith.[11] What he discovered was potentially very disturbing. These writers broadly defined humanity's progress from 'rudeness' or 'simplicity' to 'refinement'. The
newly emerging international market, new forms of machinery, an increasingly specialized division of labour and concentrated production

in workshops – of which they were the first witnesses – were well designed to meet the growing demand for commodities and the limitless proliferation of needs generally. It was much less clear that the workers themselves actually benefited from these developments. Smith in particular would be associated with an ideal of increasing economic freedom and minimizing state interference. But he too was aware that great wealth might be created while the workforce became increasingly degraded. Specialization and poverty seemed paradoxically interwoven in commercial society. In 1803–4 Hegel lectured, paraphrasing Smith, that 'in the same ratio that the number produced rises, the value of the labor falls; the labor becomes that much deader, it becomes machine work, the skill of the single laborer is infinitely limited, and the consciousness of the factory laborer is impoverished to the last extreme of dullness'. 'Factories and workshops', he added, 'based their existence on the misery of a class'.[12] If this class were to become sufficiently large it would surely threaten any presumption that increasing freedom was humanity's destiny.

Hegel did worry about this prospect. But he cannot be blamed for failing to foresee capitalism's future course. The universal and explosive nature of the factory system was not yet obvious. Some thought it might be confined to Britain, the 'workshop of the world'. Hegel also regarded inequality of wealth as 'absolutely necessary'. Work might become 'more mechanical, dull, spiritless'. But that was the price of progress.[13] Classical Athens had after all been based on slavery, and surely the modern system was less oppressive. There was still the danger that the rabble might revolt. But there was no question here of challenging the right to property. This Hegel regarded as sacrosanct, as the offspring of appropriation. It was indeed the very 'embodiment of personality', 'the first embodiment of freedom'. Modern selfhood was freed from earlier religious and personal obligations and focused instead chiefly on objective relations framed by property.[14] The means by which individuality was realized was through such rights, implying that those without property were in effect not even human. In any case machinery might well replace mechanical human labour and 'through the consummation of mechanical progress, human freedom is restored'. 'Human beings are accordingly first sacrificed', but afterwards 'they emerge through the more highly mechanized condition as free once more'.[15] This anticipates strikingly some of Marx's later reflections on the problem.

Nonetheless spiritual freedom (Spirit's self-knowledge) and social freedom (in society, at work and politically) now seemed poles apart. Indeed applied to a model of universal industrialization the freedom of the few seems contingent on the degradation of the many. Hegel's chief political work, the *Philosophy of Right* (1821), purportedly resolved this problem. It assumed that the modern division of labour fulfilled demands both for individual freedom and for satisfying needs through exchange, thus substantially producing the common good through individuals pursuing their own private interest. But the state still needed to mediate between conflicting strands in civil society and tensions produced by the market, a view Marx upheld until 1843. To this end certain restraints on wealth accumulation were required. Social harmony would be safeguarded if the state used its bureaucracy as a 'universal class', protected by its own sense of *Standesehre* (collective sense of honour), to uphold 'the universal interests of the community'. But could the bureaucracy live up to such expectations? And would the state tolerate growing demands for political representation and freedom of speech and assembly, or prove repressive instead?

Hegel's later system of thought could be taken to imply that the most rational state was modern Prussia. His more conservative followers, and the bureaucracy of this very state, were smugly satisfied with this conclusion. They were however confronted by a more radical group, the Young or Left Hegelians, who felt that the dialectic of thesis, antithesis and higher synthesis implied further progressive movement, chiefly by advances in theological and political criticism, with the first necessarily preceding the second, since religion provided crucial support for the established order.[16] Though initially lukewarm about Hegel's system, Marx encountered their views in 1837, at the Young Hegelians' Berlin watering hole, the Doctors' Club, where philosophy and drink intermingled freely. Exulting in their own cleverness and cocky in the extreme, the Young Hegelians agreed that reason could march still further onwards, and was quite possibly embodied in one or other of their group, who were all desperately keen to excel. 'Young' to them meant feisty, radical, sceptical, practical. Philosophy, they hoped, could now become 'realized', meaning that all thought was meaningful only if it eventuated in action, or 'praxis…*truth in concrete activity*'.[17] This would be a central principle for Marx, who became an exuberant member of the group before breaking with them around 1845.

At this point theology became a key sticking point dividing Hegel's followers. The Young Hegelians were all interested in engaging with Hegel's account of religion. The Right Hegelians were chiefly intent on defending it, seeing Hegel's system as proving the truths of Christianity. The book which finally led Engels to shed his religious beliefs, the theologian David Strauss's *Life of Jesus Critically Examined* (1835), also helped to shift other Young Hegelians further from orthodoxy by suggesting that much of early Christianity was mythological and, like all religions, reflected the community from which it sprang. Soon it became clear that criticizing religion was tantamount to undermining the state itself. When Prussia appeared increasingly reactionary after Friedrich Wilhelm IV's ascent to the throne in 1840, and after the philosopher Friedrich Schelling, who opposed Hegel, began lecturing at the University of Berlin in 1841, three Young Hegelians – Bruno Bauer (1809–82), Ludwig Feuerbach (1804–72) and Max Stirner (1806–56) – took up this line of criticism.[18]

Hegel's erstwhile most accomplished student, and Marx's close confidant at this point, Bauer considered Prussia as a key obstacle to freedom. He urged that Hegel's political ideal should be replaced by a new republican ethos of civic duty which would negate the egoism of civil society. Bauer also regarded atheism as the logical terminus of Hegel's system, a point he drove home in a savagely satirical pamphlet.[19] He had already suggested that human self-consciousness was all that 'God' or 'Absolute Spirit' meant. His attack on the illusion, false appearance or self-deception created by religion, and his insistence on dispelling it, were soon central to Marx's outlook. Bauer also thought egoism could be overcome through collective identification with self-consciousness. Going beyond Strauss he now denied the historical existence of Jesus Christ (although he admired the practical religion of the ancient Greeks). Then he plumped openly for atheism, and promptly lost his job. Bauer's idea that religion represented an inverted reality was appealing to Marx, who had little respect for Christianity or Judaism. Marx now concluded that no philosophy was worth discussing unless it was atheistic, and planned with Bauer to found a journal called *The Archives of Atheism*. In 1844, following the same trajectory as Marx, Bauer attacked the division of labour and emphasized its interference with recognizing the collective nature of labour. But Bauer then turned against socialism and communism, warning that here the state would govern every detail of life and abolish 'freedom in the smallest things' by subjecting all to a dogmatic principle of absolute equality.[20] So he too would soon incur Marx's wrath.

The idea that the biblical image of God was only human consciousness externalized, 'the moral nature of man taken for absolute being', became the great theme promoted by Ludwig Feuerbach.[21] His *Essence of Christianity* (1841) portrayed God as a projection of human desires and denounced Hegelian philosophy as the last stage of religion. In 1843 Feuerbach criticized Hegel in two short articles, insisting that the attributes Hegel associated with Spirit were in fact only human. Theology was not about discovering God, Spirit or the divine element in the human, but about human self-understanding. This implied that philosophy must study humanity in its real, concrete relations. 'The secret of theology is anthropology' became the flattering slogan of the new view.[22] Humanity was now at the centre of the universe, defined by *Gattungswesen* – 'species-being', 'species essence' or 'species existence' – a term adopted from Strauss.[23]

There was sufficient ambiguity in this key term to allow it to perform many functions. To Feuerbach it meant identifying with the species, 'the absolute unity of humanity', knowing our true nature as that of the species, and subsequently actualizing human capacities within it, where this was alone possible. It implied overcoming subjective individuality and, through education (*Bildung*), achieving a kind of self-renunciation. It was at once a principle both of religion and of sociability. 'All aspects of life that expressed man's activity as a "species being" were "sacred": marriage, love, friendship, labor, knowledge', writes John Toews.[24] Here a sense of community also entailed a duty towards it in support of these activities and relations. Bauer also used 'species-being' to describe the content of the Hegelian Absolute and the activity of self-consciousness. But he accused Feuerbach of limiting humanity's capacities by defining human nature too abstractly. Instead he thought people were infinitely capable of self-development because this was in fact their species essence.

The acceleration of this train of thought now appears astonishing. In the Italian Marxist Antonio Labriola's later formulation, Feuerbach 'gave a final blow to the theological explanation of history (man makes religion and not religion man)'.[25] To Engels the 'spell was broken; the "system" was exploded and cast aside…Enthusiasm was universal: we were all Feuerbachians for a moment' (26:364). To Feuerbach, alienation had nothing to do with Spirit and everything to do with social relations, the 'essence of man' being 'contained only in the community, in the unity of Man with Man'.[26] But this is clearly an ideal community, or utopia, not any real society. Species-consciousness is an ethical standpoint to be aspired to, more than a description of existing unity based on similarity. On this 'concept of society', Marx wrote to Feuerbach in August 1844, 'a philosophical basis for socialism' could rest. The progression of humanity was thus towards species-being, also construed as 'conscious life activity', thought Marx: 'free, conscious activity is man's species character' (3:276). Man was a species-being 'because he treats himself as the actual, living species; because he treats himself as a *universal* and therefore a free being' (3:275). (We see how much of Hegel remains here.) Ideas of love, justice and mercy, associated with the divine, were thus really attributes of human society. These alienated qualities moreover could be reclaimed by humanity, as Hegel too had maintained. Feuerbach had discovered that 'the social relationship of "man to man"' could become the principle of 'true materialism' and 'real science' (3:328).

Nonetheless this was still a very abstract and ethereal 'materialism'. Its core concept, humanity's species-being or communal essence, explained why God and heaven were attributes of an ideal human community and why Feuerbach called his philosophy 'humanism'. But Feuerbach still embraced a principle of love, which he called 'nothing else than the realisation of the unity of the species through the medium of moral sentiment'.[27] His ideas thus appeared suspiciously like an atheistic version of Christianity. Marx agreed that 'criticism of religion is the premise of all criticism' (3:175), religion being the basis of the state (as Hegel maintained) and the critique of the imaginary arbitrary sovereign being the prelude to the critique of real ones. But Marx was propelled at this crucial point beyond philosophy to history, and to a new form of materialism which apparently broke from humanism entirely.

Marx's dramatic split from Feuerbach resulted partly from two other responses to the latter by Young Hegelians. Both queried how the ideal of a communal 'species-being' could be reconciled with the reality of an increasingly egotistical civil society. First, Bruno Bauer's brother Edgar suggested that the state only epitomized this egoism, and should be abolished by those who were propertyless. For this Edgar was convicted of sedition and spent four years in prison. Marx seized on the idea, however, although it implied that human fulfilment could now be found in neither the state nor civil society.[28] Second, projecting the intellectual fantasy of self-empowerment to its logical extreme, Max Stirner in *The Ego and Its Own* (1845) dissolved civil society into an egoism driven by sensuous desire, thereby destroying every apparent defence of sociability, or morality generally, not based on pure self-interest and need. But Stirner then also contended that Feuerbach's concept of 'humanity' itself still possessed (as Engels put it) 'the theological halo of abstraction' and was thus 'thoroughly theological' and idealistic (38:12). It too posited, essentially, a religion of man. (Bruno Bauer agreed.) So if Hegel had been slain 'by way of the Feuerbachian dissolution of Hegelian speculation' (4:303), this in turn was the final nail in Feuerbach's theological coffin.

Stirner seemingly made every kind of altruistic humanism just another variant on religion. If 'species-being' was a merely theological concept, then 'Man' now stood like the naked emperor, stripped of his theological garb, with Marx poised to ridicule his embarrassment. And if 'Man' and 'species-being' were theological concepts, what could 'criticism' recover, or promote, as the alternative to egoism? What moral standpoint now existed if all moral standpoints were religious in origin and thus untenable? Was the 'unity of man' a theological postulate? Was 'society' too?

At one level this boils down to a simple question: if we are critical of 'egoism', why should we love or even merely assist others, especially strangers? The traditional answer, that God commands us to do so on the basis of our common humanity, was no longer an option. Neither Marx nor Engels wanted to proclaim a new religion, or a variation on an old one, like the British socialist Robert Owen or the Saint-Simonians. Stirner seemingly provided one answer by simply glorifying actual egoism, thus sidestepping the problem. But Stirner too would soon fall victim to the same logic, his 'egoistic man' denounced as just another abstract category and idealized human essence. To Engels the 'love of humanity' was, after Stirner, left with no other basis than a vague and undefined 'unselfish' 'egoism of the heart', a dead-end formulation that Marx wisely failed to take up. This alone, Engels thought, 'is the point of departure for our love of humanity, which otherwise is left hanging in the air'. Stirner needed to be informed, insisted Engels, that 'his egoistic man is bound to become communist out of sheer egoism. That's the way to answer the fellow. In the second place he must be told that in its egoism the human heart is of itself, from the very outset, unselfish and self-sacrificing, so that he finally ends up with what he is combating' (38:12) – which is clearly having one's cake and eating it too. Again Marx seems to have been unconvinced by these arguments.

Another possibility at this point, however, was offered by Moses Hess (discussed below) and also by Eduard Gans (1797–1839), one of Marx's lecturers in 1836–8 who espoused Saint-Simonian ideas. They suggested that the progress of association in modern society was superseding antagonism, including 'the exploitation of man by man', a 'complete end' to which would be achieved by one 'inevitable' revolution.[29] Gans had visited factories in England in 1830–31 and concluded that workers there were no better off than slaves or feudal vassals. He even wrote of 'the struggle of the proletariat against the middle class' and suggested that 'free corporation' or 'association' (*Vergesellschaftung*) was the workers' necessary response. Unlike Hegel, Gans suggested that poverty was not inevitable but might be abolished. But he also warned that a society based on the Saint-Simonian slogan, 'to each according to their capacities', might well end up as a 'slavery of surveillance'.[30] This revealed tensions in broader socialist ideas in this period, which we must now briefly consider.

The Jacobin and Socialist Background, 1789–1842

Socialists seek to reorganize society to satisfy the needs of the majority without the poverty, inequality, competition and waste associated with capitalism. Like many of their utopian predecessors they imagine ways of belonging to groups and of relating to other people which are more generous, kind and peaceful, and which minimize or abolish exploitation and oppression. They embrace values like friendship, trust, harmony, fraternity, unity and solidarity, which seem to be waning in modern society, but which might be recaptured or created anew. Their principal problem has always been how to sustain these bonds, which can be easily achieved in short bursts of enthusiasm, over a lengthy period of time and a considerable expanse of space. From the early nineteenth century many schemes have been hatched to answer these ends, from mixtures of public and private ownership through to various types of co-operation, community living and communism. Marx remains first and foremost a socialist who aimed to provide a framework that makes possible human self-development on the largest scale and in a collective setting where fulfilment for the few does not require exploiting the many. A theory of sociability necessarily lies at the heart of his system. What compelled him to choose the particular system he did, and to imagine that it would answer these ends, are key questions we will address here.

Throughout the ages many attempts have been made to share property communally, usually in small societies, or religious associations like monasteries, and often with considerable success. Thomas More's *Utopia* (1516) defines the literary expression of this idea, which some suppose aspires to return to that original Golden Age of plenty and equality which was the Greek image of humanity's origins, and others link to Christian ideas of heaven on earth. In *Utopia* property is common, luxury is held in contempt, rotation between rural and urban work occurs regularly, and equality and transparency prevail. Equality is a recurrent theme in most subsequent radical reform movements, and has often been linked to ideas of crisis, the millennium, redemption and the apocalypse. In the modern era the French Revolution was the chief attempt to end inequality and the vestiges of feudal privilege. Marx and most Marxists viewed the revolution of 1789 and subsequent overthrow of Louis XVI as paving the way for a 'bourgeois' or middle-class revolution which was in turn succeeded by the plebeian revolt of the Jacobins (1792) and the dictatorship of Robespierre (1793–4). The revolution proved that despotic monarchies could (and should) be overthrown, and established the pattern of upheaval often emulated thereafter. But it had not gone far enough. The abortive uprising of Gracchus Babeuf's Conspiracy of the Equals (1796) represents the communist wing of the revolution. Its principles, as defined by Sylvain Maréchal, author of the *Manifeste des Égaux* (1796), centred on abolishing distinctions between masters and servants, poor and rich, by eliminating inheritance and private property and mandating compulsory labour, overseen by a revolutionary committee. All produce would be placed in a common store, and education and health care would be free and universal.[31] Babouvism, defined chiefly as equality of incomes introduced by a minority revolutionary dictatorship, was continued by Philippe Buonarroti, and then Auguste Blanqui (1805–81), who insisted on the need for small groups of conspirators to seize power violently and oversee the progress of revolution through dictatorship. Blanqui's legacy remained vital to Marxism, but more, we will see, to Lenin than to Marx.

The leading early socialists became active following the monarchy's restoration in France in 1814. Most opposed violence, and some even 'politics' as such, as creating unnecessary disharmony. Political struggles, they agreed, were really 'knife-and-fork' matters. Overthrowing kings or gaining the vote did not feed the poor or mitigate harsh conditions in the new factories. In Britain the term 'socialism' was linked in particular to Robert Owen (1771–1858). A wealthy cotton spinner who was also deeply concerned about his workers' well-being, Owen had successfully improved their situation at his mill at New Lanark in Scotland. Thereafter he laboured incessantly to pass factory acts to raise the age of employment, reduce hours of labour and educate the young. In 1817, amidst national economic crisis, he proposed that unemployed workers be rehoused in rural communities or 'Villages of Co-operation' of 500–1,500 inhabitants. Here work would alternate between agriculture and manufactures, competition would end and property would be shared in common. Owen hoped that this 'social system', soon shortened to 'socialism', would eventually supplant entire existing forms of organization, with great cities and centralized industry being abandoned. His followers, notably George Mudie, William Thompson and John Gray, became the earliest critics of the new science of modernity, liberal political economy, from a socialist viewpoint. They propounded a rudimentary theory of crisis (the first occurring in 1825) which would become the basis for Marx's later conception, as well as an account of why wages fell short of the value of labour, and how labour could be justly rewarded.[32]

The need for such proposals was driven by the increasingly obvious deterioration in the well-being of those who worked with the new machines. Like Marx in 1844, as we will see, Owen took as his starting point the corrosive effects of the division of labour described by Adam Smith in his famous passages on 'mental mutilation' in Book 5 of *The Wealth of Nations* (1776). Having proclaimed in Book 1 how efficient specialization in workshops was for making commodities like pins, because each individual was more productive when devoted to only one part of the task, Smith now turned to the adverse effects that resulted. Alarmingly he noted that narrow specialization and constant repetition might make the workforce 'as stupid and ignorant as it is possible for a human creature to become'.[33] The case for capitalism was potentially fatally undermined.

Smith's solution to this problem was more education for the labourers. Owen's was much more radical. Marx admired much that he had achieved at New Lanark, including reducing working hours and introducing infant education. Owen helped commence the profit-sharing system of workers' ownership, later known as 'co-operation' (although New Lanark was not run this way). This idea became central to Marx's vision of communism, as we shall see, though not until the later 1850s. Well before Marx, too, Owen was a materialist and atheist who opposed both religion, which he publicly denounced in 1817 as the chief barrier to social progress, and traditional marriage, at least so far as favouring ease of divorce. His insistence that human character resulted from the environment, and was not impaired by any original sin, was also critical to Marx's outlook. And also like Marx, Owen did not court public opinion; what Marx 'especially praised in Robert Owen was that whenever any of his ideas became popular he would come forth with a new demand making him unpopular'.[34]

In France socialism was promoted in particular by Charles Fourier (1772–1837), who like Owen rejected the existing system of commerce as morally degrading. His idea of the small-scale community or *phalanstère*, again limited to a few thousand, was not communist. Land, buildings and machinery were to be owned in common, but profits were to be shared according to capital invested (four-twelfths), labour performed (five-twelfths) and talent (three-twelfths). In his regime, which was much more psychologically sophisticated and elaborate than Owen's, Fourier proposed adapting tasks to each individual's passions and frequently alternating between roles; a great abundance and variety of food; and a sexually satisfying communal life. Marx shared this vision of labour as ideally a creative reflection of inner capacities and inclinations.

The last influential communitarian was Étienne Cabet (1788–1856), who also inspired a national political movement around his schemes, which were given early expression in the novel *A Voyage to Icaria* (1840). His proposals for an American communist colony were discussed by the German communists in London for an entire week in 1847, only to be rejected (partly through Marx's and Engels' influence) on the grounds that emigration meant deserting the cause, and that communism could not be established on a small scale 'without its acquiring a completely exclusive and sectarian character'.[35] However, Cabet did found a short-lived colony near what is now Dallas, Texas, one offshoot of which lasted for half a century.

More influential on Marx were the followers of Henri de Saint-Simon (1760–1825), who was not himself a socialist but a visionary who foresaw the future of industrial society chiefly in terms of a scientific and technocratic 'administration of things' superseding the 'government of persons'. This assumption was adopted by Marx and Engels with a view to proving that industrial progress implied abolishing the state.[36] The Saint-Simonians also promoted a new religion to facilitate group cohesion (like Owen), and imitated Catholicism in their attempt to fuse church and society. Having coined the phrase 'the organization of labour', the Saint-Simonians in the late 1820s championed the idea of the national regulation of industry rather than workers' co-operation. Their aim, however, was not community of goods, but a system in which 'each one will be classified according to his ability and remunerated according to his work'.[37] This influenced the socialist Louis Blanc's *Organization of Labour* (1839), which anticipated Marx's later views on co-operation.[38] It was also a source for Thomas Carlyle's proposals for militarized state industrial management in *Past and Present* (1843), whose feudal and paternalist cast Marx and Engels rejected, but which in some respects remarkably foreshadowed Soviet economic organization a century later. All these plans nonetheless favoured concentrated industry over the balance between rural and urban preferred by Owen and Fourier, and by some later socialists, like William Morris.

In the German states a small socialist movement had also emerged by the late 1830s.[39] Its leading intellectual exponent was a Cologne sugar-merchant's son, Moses Hess (1812–75). Hess became perhaps the single most important influence on the young Marx, and for several vital years (1843–5), when Marx saw him regularly in Paris, Hess was often one or even several steps ahead of him intellectually. Initially inspired by Babeuf, Hess's *The Holy History of Mankind* (1837) used Hegelian categories to describe the reconciliation, through communism and by returning to the original state of humanity, of humanity's alienation from itself and from God. In the future the state would disappear and the people would form a perfect community, with marriage based solely on affection, and the family becoming the focus of social bonding. Hess also prophesied an imminent workers' revolution, and by 1847 had described this in terms strikingly similar to those Marx would use in *The Communist Manifesto*. In *The European Triarchy* (1841) Hess foresaw industrialization in Britain underpinning a new communist society – a 'New Jerusalem' – at the heart of Europe, also led by France and Germany, where exploitation would end and machines would free mankind from drudgery and allow complete social equality. Following another Young Hegelian, August Cieszkowski, Hess insisted that Hegel's philosophy now dictated action (or 'practice') in order to create a new future, rather than merely speculating on what history meant.[40]

By 1843 Hess was 'exclusively engaged in the philosophical development of communism'.[41] He now prophesied that the state would be replaced by a 'unified social life' defined by co-operation between individuals. In an essay on money (1845) he described existing commerce as an expression of alienated humanity. After a lively conversation with Hess in October 1842, Friedrich Engels – not yet Marx's intellectual partner – emerged a 'very eager communist'. Marx himself encountered Hess in the Doctors' Club in Berlin in mid-1841. Though Marx was only twenty-three, six years his junior, Hess found him enormously stimulating. Hess called him *'perhaps the one genuine philosopher* now alive', writing that he 'combines a biting wit with deeply serious philosophical thinking'. He believed Marx would 'give medieval religion and politics their last blow', and stated: 'Imagine Rousseau, Voltaire, Holbach, Lessing, Heine and Hegel united in one person. I say *united*, not thrown together – and you have Dr. Marx.'[42] Hess broke from Marx in May 1846, however, thinking him too harsh with his fellow communists. He later accused Marx of seeing 'the misery of the workers and the hunger of the poor' as 'only of scientific and doctrinal interest', adding: 'You are above such miseries…You are not gripped by that which moves the hearts of men'.[43]

The second German communist of note was a genuine plebeian, the tailor Wilhelm Weitling (1808–71). His vision, however, was of the quasi-millennial, evangelical sort that Marx despised. Like Thomas More, Weitling advocated uniform clothing and communal eating, which Marx contemptuously dismissed as 'barracks communism'.[44] Inspired by Saint-Simon, Weitling thought three wise men should govern the future commonwealth: a physician, a scientist and an engineer; and he even suggested a new Messiah might also arise. Encountering Marx in Brussels in March 1846 at a meeting of a small circle of communist enthusiasts, Weitling disdained the study of economics, and suggested Marx knew little of the real working classes. Marx promptly upbraided him like an errant schoolchild, and rejected moralistic plati- tudes which lacked a firm strategy as useless. He caustically hinted that Russia, with its 'associations of nonsensical prophets and nonsensical followers', was the best place for Weitling. Finally Marx 'in extreme anger and irritation' banged on the table, making the lamp totter, and insisted that 'ignorance has never yet helped anybody'.[45]

This was Marx's first major attack on a fellow communist. It was soon followed by another against the 'fantastic emotionalism' and 'am- orous slobberings' of Hermann Kriege, a Weitlingian living in New York who preached a 'love-imbued opposite of selfishness' and thought communism meant emigrants to America should receive 160 acres of free land (6:35, 41–2, 46). A much heavier assault was mounted on Marx's chief contemporary competitor, the French mutualist anarchist Pierre-Joseph Proudhon (1809–65), who was skewered in *The Poverty of Philosophy* (1847) after many nights' heated conversation had revealed, as Engels later put it, 'an unbridgeable gap between them' (26:278).[46] Did these outbursts indicate a pattern of purging or splitting which would bedevil later communist movements? Did Marx desire personal dictatorship based on a 'new intolerance' rooted in 'the religion of rea- son', as Proudhon feared?[47]

CHAPTER 2

Marx's Conversion to Communism

Rebellious youth often sinks into staid respectability. Marx could easily have become a solidly loyal if liberal professor or bureaucrat in due course, held close to the bosom of the Prussian state, as enemies should be. He would remain, in many respects, bourgeois and even aristocratic in his personal tastes. But a conventional career was not an option. Nothing less than changing the world entirely was Marx's goal. Indisputably he came to see himself as a modern Prometheus, taking on both the heavenly powers and the lords of the earth to save mankind. Never before, perhaps, had one man set himself the task of establishing complete justice for humanity without the gods' assistance. That was Marx.

Journalism was the first port of call in this quest. Here Marx had great talents. He began working for the Cologne newspaper, the *Rheinische Zeitung*, in 1842. Becoming its editor later that year, he rapidly expanded its circulation and soon made it the most important opposition journal in the German states. Politically Marx was now a radical democrat, regarding republicanism as the natural ally of atheism. His first major publication (in May 1842) was an impassioned defence of press freedom which condemned 'the censored press as a bad press' (1:159).[1] Here we glimpse Marx's ideal: 'Freedom is so much the essence of man that even its opponents implement it while combating its reality...No man combats freedom; at most he combats the freedom of others' (1:155). A vindication of the peasants' right to gather fallen wood ensued, based on 'a customary right of the poor in all countries', their 'right of property' and their 'feeling of kinship' with the wealthy (1:230, 234). (A large portion of penal offences in Prussia at this time concerned this issue.) There followed another piece, on the plight of the distressed Moselle winegrowers. Marx condemned the 'always cowardly' nature of private interest and the 'inhuman' bent of selfish legislators who had 'an alien material essence' as their 'supreme essence' (1:236). This indeed was 'bound to degrade' the 'state into a means operating for the benefit of private interest' (1:241).

To Marx the Hegelian possibility of a neutral state arbitrating between selfish interests and upholding 'humane and rightful motives' (1:248) was clearly slipping away. Indeed he was rapidly concluding that we cannot be free in a 'state' at all, if governments usually sided with the propertied few against the impoverished multitude. In broaching these issues Marx constantly skirted the line between what was permissible and what might be suppressed. A censor was even despatched to try to entice him to take up a career in the Prussian civil service in Berlin – the antithesis of radical democracy. Of course he refused. When Marx published an article criticizing the Russian Tsar, the newspaper's licence was revoked.

These concerns, Engels later recalled, led Marx 'from politics pure and simple to economic conditions and thus to socialism' (50:497). Marx's was the cause of the *free human being* (1:306). He deployed (and deplored) the contrast between man's 'material nature' and his 'ideal nature' (1:310). He sought a new definition of the common good, and constantly equated private property with selfish and inhuman interests. Communism – the term was publicized chiefly by Cabet at this point, and identified as 'the most truly religious' of doctrines – was one way of representing universal humanity against selfish interests.[2] The term did not yet for Marx describe the antidote to capitalism's inadequacies.[3] Accused in October 1842 of embracing communism, Marx thus wrote that his paper 'does not admit that communist ideas in their present form possess even theoretical reality, and therefore can still less desire their practical realisation, or even consider it possible' (1:220).

In 1842 Marx still seemingly accepted the possibility that the state might be an 'association of free human beings who educate one another', so long as it was 'built on the basis of free reason, and not of religion' (1:193, 200). In 1843, however, he began to question this assumption. He followed Hegel in presuming that history's progress indicated the growth of freedom, and later interpreted both the 1861 ending of serfdom in Russia and the abolition of slavery in the USA in these terms. But what role did or ought the state to play in this process? Marx's main work in 1843, the 'Critique of Hegel's *Philosophy of Right*', exposed the limits of 'political emancipation', and concluded, as he later recalled, that legal and political relations were only comprehensible by viewing 'the anatomy of this civil society' in 'political economy' (29:262). The state rested on civil society and had no existence outside it. 'Just as it is not religion which creates man but man who creates religion', Marx insisted, 'so it is not the constitution which creates the people but the people which creates the constitution' (3:29). The problem of the state was not soluble unless collisions of class interests in civil society were eradicated. This meant that

> The immediate *task of philosophy*, which is at the service of history, once the *holy form* of human self-estrangement has been unmasked, is to unmask self-estrangement in its *unholy forms*. Thus the criticism of heaven turns into the criticism of the earth, the *criticism of religion* into the *criticism of law* and the *criticism of theology* into the *criticism of politics*. (3:176)

Thus would the 'entire mystery' (3:9) of Hegel's philosophy be solved.

As a radical reformer Marx regarded democracy as the only constitutional form that united 'the general and the particular'. He even insisted that, from a French viewpoint, 'in true democracy the *political state is annihilated*' (3:30), echoing Hess and perhaps Proudhon.[4] The basic problem, as Marx was now beginning to conceive it, was, what state or community corresponded to the purest idea of the general interest, or species-being? Hegel's bureaucracy dealt with private interests only insofar as they appeared as corporations or estates (*Stände*). It could not, Marx insisted, represent a general interest, which required the particular 'becoming the *general* interest' (3:48). Marx now linked 'the dependence of man on man' with private property, and suggested that 'No matter how this dependence may be constituted in and for itself, it is *human* over against the slave' (3:102). This suggests that overcoming such dependence by ending private property was now looming as Marx's goal. Capitalism simply generated the last form of mass servitude. But this was not yet clearly stated.

Such a conclusion hinted at the limits of political radicalism. Demands for universal male suffrage had been central to reform movements since 1789. Germany needed to follow this route, and, thought Marx, 'The emancipation of Germany means the emancipation of mankind', with philosophy leading the proletariat. The socialist critique of democratic radicalism was generally that gaining the suffrage under capitalism would leave the condition of the working classes fundamentally unaltered. Marx agreed that making men citizens by giving them the vote did not alter their economic relations one iota – it merely offered political leverage for discussing such issues. This did not mean that 'democracy' and the franchise were useless. Elections were 'the chief political interest of actual civil society' (3:121). But Marx now saw their limits as goals of social improvement. It now seemed that 'activity, work, content, etc.' were a mere means to the end of individual existence, rather than realizing 'socialized man', that is, man's communal or communist essence.[5] This could only be attained by 'true democracy' overcoming the contradiction between state and civil society. Marx may have taken these thoughts further, but his extant notes are incomplete.[6]

Democracy, then, was not an end in itself for the working classes. Their emancipation implied the 'emancipation of humanity as a whole', meaning, apparently, abolishing all servitude. To claim with Robert Payne that Marx's 'aim was to destroy democracy' is simplistic.[7] He increasingly sought to eradicate the state as an alienated entity separate from civil society, acting as an instrument of class oppression or possessing an interest of its own – for example through the bureaucracy – against the majority. These 'alienated' powers needed to be returned to their source, and any imaginary or fictitious independence of the state or monarch destroyed. For the rest of Marx's life his political thought would remain dominated by this quest.

What did Marx envision would replace this system and animate the new post-political or post-statist ethos? This is a puzzling question.

Some socialists were democrats; others were not. Many were hostile to politics as such. Communitarianism implied a greater stress on duty to the collective, although like enhanced sociability or expanded friendship, this was clearly more viable amongst a few thousand people living together who knew and trusted one another.[8] But at no point do we find Marx (unlike Engels) expressing strong support for small-scale socialist communities. Moreover, pleas for mutual assistance often involved appeals to fellow feeling, love or sympathy, a strategy which Marx sought to avoid. Socialists often imagined that a pre- or anti-commercial 'natural' sociability might simply bounce back once the egoism fuelled by trade and competition ended. But this presumes an underlying suppressed sociability and natural affection for others, the existence of which remains unproven. And it does not answer the question as to why 'communism', yet to be defined, might remedy the deficiencies of radical democracy, or best fuel this sociability.

Nonetheless Marx was beginning to believe that communism meant 'true democracy' insofar as the 'communist essence' of civil society (or the joint interest of all its members *qua* humans) could only be realized by abolishing private property, which invariably divided this interest and rendered it particular. In May 1843, writing to the Young Hegelian Arnold Ruge, he still hoped that the sense of freedom which 'vanished from the world with the Greeks' could again be embodied in 'a community of human beings united for their highest aims…a democratic state' (3:137). But his movement from radical democracy or 'political emancipation' to communism as 'a special expression of the humanistic principle' (3:143) was now astonishingly swift. The former might be realized in a state based on the universal rights of man, as Bruno Bauer proposed. How the latter might be ordered was still unclear.

Marx at this point greatly admired Bauer, and indeed their tracks, like Marx's and Hess's, ran parallel for about a year. Bauer's essay 'On the Jewish Question' (late 1842–early 1843) linked religious and commercial prejudice and contended that the Jews required political emancipation.[9] Marx thought he had not gone far enough. His own 'On the Jewish Question' (late 1843) demanded 'human emancipation', and described the 'rights of man' as essentially the 'rights of property', of enjoying one's possessions 'without regard to other men, independently of society, the right of selfishness'. The 'so-called *rights of man*, the *droits de l'homme* as distinct from the *droits du citoyen*,' he insisted, 'are nothing but the rights of a *member of civil society*, i.e., the rights of egoistic man, of man separated from other men and from the community' (3:162). The 'right of liberty' in particular was 'based not on the association of man with man, but on the separation of man from man', especially through private property (3:162–3). Within the state men supposedly considered themselves as communal beings, by contrast to their private lives in civil society. Marx now saw this as a spurious, ersatz communality. Men's 'species-being, in community with other men', could not be expressed in the state because communal being there was only illusory. 'The perfect political state is, by its nature, man's *species-life*, as *opposed* to his material life', he now insisted (3:153–5). A real species existence had to be sought beyond the state, indeed beyond 'politics'. Marx had reached the limits of political emancipation. At this point, in a crucial passage, he summarized his argument, and indeed his goals for the rest of his life:

> Only when the real, individual man re-absorbs in himself the abstract citizen, and as an individual human being has become a *species-being* in his everyday life, in his particular work, and in his particular situation, only when man has recognised and organised his '*forces propres*' as *social* forces, and consequently no longer separates social power from himself in the shape of *political* power, only then will human emancipation have been accomplished. (3:168)

Yet the problem remained as to how this ideal community was to be defined. Socialist schemes were a penny a dozen by this point, and the public was already weary with competing plans and proposals. Marx was reluctant to confront religion and politics with a 'ready-made system' like Cabet's (3:143). The point was not 'constructing the future and settling everything for all times' but rather the '*ruthless criticism of all that exists*' (3:142). (Criticism, however, always implies an imagined alternative.) The stage was set for Marx's rejection of 'utopian' socialism.

The final turning-point in Marx's formulation as to how human emancipation would be achieved came swiftly thereafter. The key passage, written in late 1843 or early 1844, is replete with the sort of paradox that he loved, based on contradiction and opposites appearing to merge into one another. Marx now proclaimed that the solution lay in

> the formation of a class with *radical chains,* a class of civil society which is not a class of civil society, an estate which is the dissolution of all estates, a sphere which has a universal character by its universal suffering and claims no *particular right* because no *particular wrong* but *wrong generally* is perpetrated against it; which can no longer invoke a *historical* but only a *human* title; which does not stand in any one-sided antithesis to the consequences but in an all-round antithesis to the premises of the German state. (3:186)[10]

In negating private property, the proletariat would negate the principle of existing society too. Communism would become the proletariat's mode of redemption, indeed, in a considerable logical leap, 'the total redemption of humanity',[11] abolishing servitude as such, which seemingly defines Marx's goal, the social realization of 'species-being'. Philosophy would be the 'head' of this emancipation and the proletariat its 'heart', with philosophy being realized only by abolishing the proletariat, and the proletariat being abolished only with the 'realisation of philosophy' (3:187). This is a pleasingly symmetrical if anatomically puzzling image, hinting at secular salvation, redemption through suffering, and the vindication of wounded innocence; audacious in its assumption that the world's problems might be solved by the practical unity of concepts; suggestive too of a split between intellect and emotions which hinted that the former should guide the latter. The proletariat, the new universal class, thus epitomized the 'communist essence' of civil society as well as of human nature.

Marx was now poised for the final break from Hegel. At this very moment, however, he can be understood as seeing the proletariat as a Hegelian category in order to assign it universality, as embodying Feuerbach's species-being, and possibly also – adapting a

Judaeo-Christian idea of universal salvation – even as seeking 'divine perfection without a transcendental divinity'.[12] He accepted the tripartite scheme adopted from Hess whereby 'the German proletariat is the *theoretician* of the European proletariat, just as the English proletariat is its *economist*, and the French proletariat its *politician*' (3:202). But 'the proletariat' was for Marx still more a concept than a reality. Its great numbers in countries like Britain, where the peasantry was not the largest class, might qualify it as 'universal'. But in Germany it was tiny, perhaps 4 per cent of the male population. Nonetheless, with a nod to Hess in particular, Marx proposed a sharp break from existing discourses about 'the social problem' and 'the poor'. Marx gave the working class agency, a goal and the guidance to fulfil its own destiny, albeit as a 'heart' led by the 'head' of philosophy. No longer is the opposition an undifferentiated 'people'. Now it is more clearly (if still abstractly) defined by class and economic position. Spirit could no longer guide humanity forwards: the proletariat would do so, assisted by its friends. At this moment, in 1843–4, the Marx the world came to know first emerges.

In October 1843 Marx moved to Paris to edit a new journal, the *Deutsch-Französische Jahrbücher*, with Ruge. The following summer a true partner arrived on the scene. Having been unimpressed at a brief, 'distinctly chilly' encounter with Engels in Cologne in 1842 (as Engels recalled; 50:503), Marx met him again in Paris at the Café de la Régence near the Louvre on 28 August 1844. This time they hit it off. A few drinks turned into a few more drinks and a ten-day conversation. Together, now best of friends, they contemplated a joint break from Young Hegelianism. This was mostly accomplished in an assault on the entire school entitled *The Holy Family* (1845) – 'holy' because, in their view, all still remained trapped within theological categories. Its tone of vituperative contempt would linger in many of Marx's more polemical works and often pass down to later Marxists.

Engels brought to the partnership a deeper knowledge of socialism than Marx. Living in Manchester since late 1842, he mingled frequently with Owen's followers and had seen factories at first-hand; indeed he helped to manage one. He was already a convert to communism too. He and Marx were at one in seeing the French Revolution and overthrow of monarchies as only foreshadowing further forms of liberation. Both thought old forms of serfdom and slavery were being replaced by the new servitude of factory labour – where was progress here? The plot of modernity, then, was established. But the mysteries of its unfolding still needed to be revealed to a dormant, ignorant and confused world. To explain, and then to help overthrow, this world, via the proletariat, now became their lives' work.

The crucial move was to define just what 'the proletariat' actually was and where it was going. By July 1844 Marx had settled upon the English working class as the clearest example of modern developments, and on political economy as 'the scientific reflection of English economic conditions' (3:192). Both, he thought, would set the pattern for the rest of the world. To confront the emerging master science of modernity was the only logical step forwards. But this in turn meant identifying its deficiencies vis-à-vis the necessary course of humanity's emancipation, which meant its antagonism to humanist politics. In his first substantial encounter with political economy, an essay he wrote on the utilitarian economist and historian James Mill, Marx proclaimed that the existence of money led man to regard 'his will, his activity and his relation to other men as a power independent of him and them'. In exchanges men did not relate to each other as men, so 'things lose the significance of human, personal property' (3:212–13). Exchange, however, ought to be 'equivalent to *species-activity* and species-spirit, the real, conscious and true mode of existence which is *social* activity and social enjoyment' (3:216–17).[13] Again the demands of an ideal species-life were central:

> the *community* from which the worker is *isolated* is a community the
> real character and scope of which is quite different from that of the
> *political* community. The community from which the worker is isolated
> by *his own labour* is *life* itself, physical and mental life, human morality,
> human activity, human enjoyment, *human* nature. *Human nature* is the
> *true community* of men. The disastrous isolation from this essential

nature is incomparably more universal, more intolerable, more dreadful, and more contradictory, than isolation from the political community. (3:204–5)

At this point communism to Marx was still essentially a 'humanistic principle'. Unlike Engels he knew little about real experiments involving community of goods. Theoretically, though, he had made some headway. He had read Cabet, Victor Considérant, Fourier, Pierre Leroux and Proudhon by late 1842. Leroux had juxtaposed the two great classes in society – the bourgeoisie and the proletariat – as by 1832 had his friend Jean Reynaud, though neither saw their interests as irreconcilable. Marx probably encountered Lorenz von Stein's *Der Sozialismus und Kommunismus des heutigen Frankreichs* (1842) – which described the proletariat as the modern class of industrial workers – through Engels, who mentioned the 'dull, miserable' book in June 1843 (3:388). Marx also read the former Fourierist Constantin Pecqueur, who advocated collective property ownership, and described the process of concentration of capital. As late as September 1843, in a letter to Ruge, Marx still called communism 'a dogmatic abstraction' which was 'itself only a special expression of the humanistic principle' (3:143).

Then, in early 1844, Marx read Engels' Owenite-inspired essay entitled 'Outlines of a Critique of Political Economy', written in late 1843. This condemned political economy as springing from 'the most detestable selfishness' and urged its criticism from 'a purely human, universal basis' (3:418, 421). Like a good Hegelian, Engels maintained that 'free trade must produce the restoration of monopolies on the one hand and the abolition of private property on the other' (3:424). He hinted that ultimately modern industry would bring about 'the reconciliation of mankind with nature and with itself', and insisted that only communism could abolish coerced exchange (3:426). He made it clear that this perspective alone – humanism applied to political economy – could be the starting point for a new critique of society. Marx called the essay a 'sketch of genius'.[14]

Moses Hess was another obvious inspiration for Marx at this point. Marx called religion 'the *opium* of the people' (3:175). So did Hess. Marx wanted to reconcile spiritual and social freedom. So did Hess.[15]

Before Marx, Hess insisted that communism would best fulfil human-ity's communal nature. He conceded the limitations of the 'raw' form of 'unified social life' expressed by Babeuf, but agreed with Proudhon that communism also implied 'the negation of all political domination, the negation of the concept of the state or politics', which was also Marx's conclusion. To Hess the 'principle of the new age – the absolute unity of all life' (no principle was adequate which was not 'absolute') made possible 'scientific communism'. Hess provided a contrast be-tween 'community' (*Gemeinschaft*) and 'alienated labour' which Marx clearly found compelling. He saw money as a new form of alienation, succeeding theology in disguising the human nature of exchange. One of the great benefits of communism, Hess believed, was that it would return control over economic life to the entire community. It could only arise from the abundance which modern production permitted. In 'community', he wrote in 1843, labour would not be 'organized', but people would simply do what was required. Where 'labour takes place out of an inner drive, it is a passion which promotes the enjoyment of life, a virtue which carries its own reward in itself'. Where, however, it was 'brought about through an external drive, then it becomes a bur-den which degrades human nature and oppresses it, a vice which can be carried out only for the vile wages of sin: it is wage or slave labour'. This was in keeping with the idea that the new society would avoid coercion at all costs. But by 1844 Hess insisted that 'Social wealth must not be acquired by individuals and left to chance – it must be man-aged and organized so that each gets apportioned his own.' This clearly clashed with any thought of relying on 'inner desires' to perform la-bour voluntarily. Hess's vision also remained ethereal and speculative, a grand march of 'absolute' philosophical categories towards the fulfil-ment of Christianity, with little historical underpinning.[16]

Marx now began to link communism to the proletariat's revolution-ary prospects. Yet to Marx, as we have seen, embracing communism was initially a philosophical move, not an economic one. Communism was the dialectical negation, contradiction or opposite of private prop-erty, its categorical or philosophical 'humanist' antithesis. Philoso-phy necessarily progressed through such contradictions. At this point Marx became a communist chiefly because of his dialectical approach, rather than any knowledge of communist experiments or any sense of how they might solve capitalism's most pressing problems. Hess in particular showed how 'having' – the obsession with possession – alienated the physical and intellectual senses, such that communism implied 'the true resolution of the strife between existence and essence, between objectification and self-confirmation, between freedom and necessity, between the individual and the species', the 'gaining of ultimate unity here on this earth' (3:296).[17] This indicates a desire to solve Hegel's main problem. Marx's entire project until 1845–6, then, involved philosophical criticism, and superseding philosophical antitheses in the search for higher unity, not yet engagement with real economic relations. Nowhere is this clearer than in his great work of 1844.

CHAPTER 3

The 'Paris Manuscripts', Alienation and Humanism

Unpublished until 1932, the 'Economic and Philosophic Manuscripts' or 'Paris Manuscripts' of 1844 (he never gave it a title) is Marx's most controversial work.[1] It plays little or no role in early accounts of his thought.[2] By the 1960s, however, its theory of alienation became the starting point for most analyses of his philosophy, and particularly those critical of Stalinism. The text, indeed, was regarded as so subversive of orthodox Marxism that initially it was not printed in the first major German edition of Marx's writings, the *Werke* (1957–68), and was only added in a supplementary volume in 1985. (A Russian edition appeared in 1956.) As late as 1961 Henri Lefebvre described the 'deep mistrust' prevailing officially towards it.[3] It represents Marx's first engagement with political economy (crucially through Engels' 'Outlines of a Critique of Political Economy'), as well as the working out of Feuerbach's critique of Hegel, of his own critique of radical democracy and of his embrace of communism. However, there are real problems in reading the work, notably its confused, fragmentary form, Marx's playful obtuseness, and the abstractness, ambiguity and complexity of the philosophical context and background. The published editions are, to an important degree, manufactured texts, and suggestive rather than definitive.[4] Since Marx did not publish it we also do not know whether he came to reject some or even all of its central theses as naïve or ill-conceived.

Nonetheless to many readers the 'Paris Manuscripts' is the most attractive and compelling of Marx's writings, and indicates his final goal more clearly than any other. It advocates a humanist ideal with freedom as the object of life. Exploitation is replaced by freely chosen creative activity which aims to maximize 'species-being', viewed chiefly as a kind of sociability or community – Marx uses the word 'trust' frequently. Many see this as an appealing foundation for Marx's system, from which the rest, even *Capital*, is deduced, and view Marx as promoting 'a kind of social living which is *really* social, where egoism and competitiveness are things of the past'.[5] Few readers fail to identify with its aspirations.

Marx's starting point in the 'Paris Manuscripts' is mankind's stunted desire to attain freedom. Political economy is now the entry point into this discussion. 'Alienation' is seen as the main barrier to freedom, which is conceived chiefly in terms of our need to realize our 'species-being'. Marx acknowledges the 'real theoretical revolution' begun by Feuerbach, who alone had made '*positive*, humanistic and naturalistic criticism' possible, and later credits him with having established 'true materialism' and 'real science, by making the social relationship of "man to man" the basic principle of the theory' (3:232, 328). He then begins his engagement with political economy. Wages are defined as the outcome of struggles between labour and capital, and tend normally to the level of bare subsistence. To raise them, labourers must 'sacrifice their time and carry out slave-labour, completely losing their freedom, in the service of greed'. With the progress of the division of labour, work becomes increasingly 'very one-sided, machine-like' and the labourer 'from being a man becomes an abstract activity and a belly', resulting in 'overwork and premature death' and 'decline to a mere machine' (3:237–8). The progress of society, meanwhile, ensures an increasing concentration of wealth amongst ever fewer capitalists. There are lengthy excerpts, mostly from Adam Smith, as to what profit is; how capital accumulates and competition, defined as '*war amongst the greedy*' (3:271), operates; and how it leads to the displacement of landowners by capitalists. Romantics nostalgic about the pre-capitalist era who assail this transition are dismissed; 'filthy self-interest' is also 'the root of landed property' (3:267). This system is contrasted with 'association', which, as applied to land, re-establishes 'the intimate ties of man with the earth, since the earth ceases to be an object of huckstering, and through free labour and free enjoyment becomes once more a true personal property of man' (3:268).[6]

Central here is Marx's account of 'estranged labour'. He wants to explain not only how the worker becomes poorer as the capitalist becomes richer, but how the *devaluation* of the world of men is in direct proportion to the *increasing value* of the world of things', a fact which is explained by the 'objectification of labour', its production as an alien object. This *'loss of the object and bondage to it'* represents a 'loss of realisation' (*Verwirklichung*) of the workers. The parallel with religion is obvious: 'The more man puts into God, the less he retains in himself. The worker puts his life into the object, but now his life no longer belongs to him but to the object' (3:272). 'Alienation' involves two terms, *Entfremdung* (estrangement or alienation) and *Entäusserung* (externalization). While we objectify ourselves in creating material objects, this does not mean we are 'alienated' from them, only that we necessarily externalize ourselves in them. The former is a condition of our existence, the latter a mere side effect.[7]

Marx then describes four types of alienation: (1) of the worker from the product of labour as an alien object; (2) of the worker from himself during the 'alien activity' of production; (3) of the worker from his 'species-being', or his social essence, which demands that he 'treats himself as a *universal* and therefore a free being' engaged in 'free, conscious activity'; and (4) of the worker from other workers. In all of these, 'alienation' means a lack of self-realization or a collective failure to attain levels of sociability and mutual recognition appropriate to our essence and capabilities.[8] The defining feature of the entire process, it appears, is that alienated labour is 'not voluntary, but coerced; it is *forced labour*', and as the product of another, 'it is the loss of his self' (3:274).[9] For Hegel private property made and defined the modern self. For Marx its absence implies the opposite. Private property is 'the product, the result, the necessary consequence, of *alienated labour*', as well as its cause (3:279).

This theory is often understood as a general analysis of work under capitalism, though Marx had not yet seen a factory, and Engels'

Condition of the Working Class in England in 1844 was not yet published. Some also see it as exploring a wider problem of meaninglessness or worthlessness, and thus as foreshadowing existentialism.[10] It is certainly a theory of sociability. Marx states that 'The estrangement of man, and in fact every relationship in which man [stands] to himself, is realised and expressed only in the relationship in which a man stands to other men' (3:277). (Elsewhere he hints at how we can measure this: the 'direct, natural, and necessary relation of person to person is the *relation of man to woman*'; 3:295.[11]) Marx aims to work out Hegel's theory of alienation, by applying this to real civil society as understood by political economy, which thus reunites the philosophical and the historical aspects of Hegel. But Marx is also moving beyond Hegel at the same time. In modern society, Marx writes, man is a 'debased, enslaved, forsaken, despicable being' (3:182). Hegel believed that alienation resulted from a failure to comprehend our unity with God and/ or nature, and to recognize our unity with the infinite. Marx now proposes seeing these relationships as social rather than metaphysical, and defined by work rather than thought. Hegel had grasped '*labour* as the *essence* of man', but meant only abstract mental labour (3:333). Considering real work done by real people, we reach a different conclusion: humanity constantly re-creates itself through conscious activity. It does so collectively, through 'the co-operative endeavours of mankind'; a gloss on Hegel which precisely suited Marx's own philosophical needs, and probably also on Gans's 'association', as an ethical ideal as well as a practical ongoing development, and on various socialist writers.

The goal is now to take back communally that which has become alienated through 'forced labour', and thus to establish its opposite, 'free labour and free enjoyment' (3:268).[12] We are told that 'the emancipation of the workers contains universal human emancipation...because the whole of human servitude is involved in the relation of the worker to production, and all relations of servitude are but modifications and consequences of this relation' (3:280). Just how this is to be achieved is not spelt out. It clearly means eliminating coerced labour as such. We know that it will involve communism. But in fact even more is implied: Marx aspires to recapture our social nature. 'Species-being' is the central concept here; it is the fulcrum on which all else rests.

Private property causes self-estrangement because it makes labour forced rather than voluntary, and whatever is coerced is wrong. We see how far the issue of free choice or will sits behind this argument, which is perhaps one of Marx's foundational principles, and a deduction from seeing freedom as our 'essence'. Private property perverts our senses by commodifying them, which leads us to treat other people as means to accumulate objects. Marx goes on, hinting at his later account of the 'fetishism of commodities':

> The abolition of private property is therefore the complete *emancipation* of all human senses and qualities, but it is this emancipation precisely because these senses and attributes have become, subjectively and objectively, *human*. The eye has become a *human* eye, just as its *object* has become a social, *human* object – an object made by man for man. (3:300)

We will need to consider in due course how far this position, articulating a radical liberation of the senses by prioritizing experience over possession and by creating the *'rich human being* and the rich *human need'* (3:304), survives in Marx's later writings, especially the *Grundrisse* and *Capital*. But Marx clearly provides us here with an extraordinary account of why communism solves Hegel's main problems. Private property prevents us from realizing our species-being, defined as humanist sociability. Communism is 'the vindication of real human life as man's possession' (3:341). A contemporaneous note on James Mill explored just what this alternative form of production might entail. This passage is vital to understanding Marx, for it gives us an excellent sense of what he thought 'unalienated' labour might entail:

> Let us suppose that we had carried out production as human beings. Each of us would have *in two ways affirmed* himself and the other person. 1) In my *production* I would have objectified my *individuality*, its *specific character*, and therefore enjoyed not only an individual *manifestation of my life* during the activity, but also when looking at the object I would have the individual pleasure of knowing my personality to be *objective, visible to the senses* and hence a power *beyond all doubt*.

2) In your enjoyment or use of my product I would have the *direct* enjoyment both of being conscious of having satisfied a *human* need by my work, that is, of having objectified *man's* essential nature, and of having thus created an object corresponding to the need of another *man's* essential nature. 3) I would have been for you the *mediator* between you and the species, and therefore would become recognised and felt by you yourself as a completion of your own essential nature and as a necessary part of yourself, and consequently would know myself to be confirmed both in your thought and your love. 4) In the individual expression of my life I would have directly created your expression of your life, and therefore in my individual activity I would have directly *confirmed* and *realised* my true nature, my *human* nature, my *communal nature*. (3:227–8)

Here Marx builds a bridge between the two potentially conflicting aims of seeing the overcoming of alienation through each individual's fullest expression of their own powers and capacities, and understanding the process in social terms as a collective activity and end. Work would become a '*free manifestation of life*, hence an *enjoyment of life*', rather than 'an alienation of life' (3:228). This sounds like Fourier and Hess, in the sense that 'free' here means 'voluntary'. But Marx wants to stress that this could only be accomplished collectively. Alienation could not be overcome solely on an individual basis because our wholeness cannot be recognized except in the eyes of others (partly expressed, we note, through love) and when conceived as a species or collective activity. But this also meant, as Hess had realized, that decisions about work would have to be taken. The possibility of coercion, or at least of restricting consent (even if democratically), appears.

In another passage – one of the most extraordinary of this period – Marx toys with a much more elaborate theory of social reciprocity, specifically one not perverted by money or commodification, which hinted at a general theory of ideal human relations. Here he asserts:

Assume *man* to be *man* and his relationship to the world to be a human one: then you can exchange love only for love, trust for trust, etc. If you want to enjoy art, you must be an artistically cultivated person; if you want to exercise influence over other people, you must be a person with a stimulating and encouraging effect on other people. Every one of your relations to man and to nature must be a *specific expression*, corresponding to the object of your will, of your *real individual* life. If you love without evoking love in return – that is, if your loving as loving does not produce reciprocal love; if through a *living expression* of yourself as a loving person you do not make yourself a *beloved one*, then your love is impotent – a misfortune. (3:326)

This may be demanding the impossible, or at least the implausible. One may, for example, enjoy art aesthetically and emotionally without having greatly refined taste or remarkable artistic abilities. This is a different, and doubtless less rarefied, form of enjoyment, but potentially highly rewarding nonetheless. And love is, alas, often unrequited. Sometimes we must give more, and sometimes take more, in the hope that eventually we come out even. At the very least we are being set up here for a great deal of sorrow by way of failed reciprocity. But the superiority of social interaction based on at least attempting reciprocity is clearly implied, as is avoiding having our relationships commodified or corrupted by money. So wanting a 'human' relationship with others implies, first of all, the need for *reciprocity* in our social relations. As in exchange, we must offer real equivalents, like for like, even if only symbolically. Second, it implies the Hegelian reclaiming of the artificial world as our own, conceived both individually and collectively. Here the sense of 'having' represents the 'sheer estrangement' of all the senses: 'The less you *are*, the less you express your own life, the more you *have*, i.e., the greater is your alienated life' (3:309). 'All passions and all activity must therefore be consumed in *avarice*' (3:309). The obsession with possession is the most dangerous and distorting of all psychological tendencies.

Here too we see illuminated another of Marx's more profound but otherwise opaque musings, when he describes the type of communism he finds appealing. Marx dismisses every form of communism which involves levelling down, which is based on envy and merely annuls private property. This 'negates the *personality* of man in every sphere' as well as 'the entire world of culture and civilisation', and produces instead a 'community of labour' with the 'community as universal cap-italist'. Rather than the *'positive community system'* of shared property, he wants

> *Communism* as the *positive* transcendence of *private property as human self-estrangement,* and therefore as the real *appropriation* of the *human* essence by and for man; communism therefore as the complete return of man to himself as a *social* (i.e., human) being – a return accomplished consciously and embracing the entire wealth of previous development. This communism, as fully developed naturalism, equals humanism, and as fully developed humanism equals naturalism. It is the genuine resolution of the conflict between man and nature and between man and man – the true resolution of the strife between existence and essence, between objectification and self-confirmation, between freedom and necessity, between the individual and the species. Communism is the riddle of history solved, and it knows itself to be this solution. (3:295-7)

This is very playful, but not very helpful. The conceptual footwork is dazzling, but what lies behind the concepts is less clear. By returning all previously alienated private property to the community we com-mence, with communism, human history proper, defined as 'human-ism' or 'social existence'. This is a theory of sociability which has 'grasped the positive essence of private property' (3:296), namely its collective nature. But what does this mean in practical terms? How do we express this sociability? Marx clearly believes that societies which resist egoism are better than those corroded by it. This follows Hess, who supported a principle of love to dispel egoism. Marx was wary of such quasi-religious language. He wanted reciprocity, but not via moral exhortation. But he notes that the 'smoking, eating, drinking' of the French artisans had 'association' as their purpose, and that here 'the brotherhood of man is no empty phrase with them, but a fact of life, and the nobility of man shines upon us from their work-hardened bod-ies' (3:313). So a fundamental aspect of 'human' relationships is socia-bility itself.

Indeed it is more. Sociability is both an end and a new need, and a core component in self-realization, without which all-roundedness is incomplete. As a need it is utterly separate from our relations with objects or commodities, which may and do interfere with its fulfilment, by diverting us from people to things and thus leading us to fail to recognize the social essence of things. Equality is central to this sociability. It is synonymous with 'species-being'. *The Holy Family* would add that equality is 'man's consciousness of…other men as his equals and man's attitude to other men as his equals. Equality is the French expression for the unity of human essence, for man's consciousness of his species and his attitude towards his species, for the practical identity of man with man'. The *'objective being of man'* is thus 'the *existence of man for other men*, his *human relation to other men*, the *social behaviour of man to man'* (4:39, 43).[13]

'Communism' here thus chiefly meant 'recapturing species-being'. It was not the answer to an oppressive division of labour – as a new approach to specialization would be. It was not yet a system of organizing production, or of satisfying collective needs. These are not implied by the dialectical demand to treat categories in terms of opposites which progress by contradiction. But at this stage Marx, in Hegelian fashion, regarded the logical step of negating private property as answering the problem of alienation. 'Socialism', apparently including the cruder forms of communism, provided the first step in this negation, being 'man's positive self-consciousness'. Communism was 'the negation of the negation', the *'actual* phase necessary for the next stage of historical development in the process of human emancipation' and 'the necessary form and the dynamic principle of the immediate future'. But even it was 'not the goal of human development' (3:306). Philosophically, communism was a humanist category of unalienated sociability rather than a way of producing or of organizing society.

In 1845 Marx still asserted that the proletariat was 'compelled as proletariat to abolish itself and thereby its opposite, private property, which determines its existence, and which makes it proletariat. It is the *negative* side of the antithesis, its restlessness within its very self, dissolved and self-dissolving private property'. We are still on categorical ground here, even if the key question was now what the proletariat 'will historically be compelled to do' (4:36–7). In this manner Hegel, rather than Hess, Engels or Feuerbach, made Marx a communist. But if communism was now the categorical antithesis of private property, Marx's categorical inflexibility cut him off from other solutions to the problems of poverty and alienation. Indeed it encouraged the suppression of such solutions, including mixed forms of ownership and management like those Fourier proposed. Hegelian communism logically cut off alternatives which history might have permitted.

Various difficulties stem from Marx's position at this point. The first may be termed 'ethical'. It is usually assumed that in 1844 Marx posited an essentialist view of human nature rooted in a Hegelian conception of self-actualization, as modified by Feuerbach, which makes developing basic human powers our purpose or end in life, the good or ideal. Our desire for freedom lay at the core of this proposition. But this was not egotistical freedom, or a liberty defined by either juridical or commercial relations. Self-actualization could not be achieved individually, but required a communal context, here defined by 'species-being'. This in turn could only be realized if private property was abolished and communism introduced.

It is sometimes thus contended that Marx's idea of 'essence', meaning chiefly our desire to be free in this social context, is 'the foundation of his ethics'.[14] Alienation – forced labour – prevents us from realizing our 'essence' while communism – voluntary labour – seemingly expresses it. But at some levels this 'essence' is elusive. Marx offers no particular proof that it exists. His theory of alienation clearly implies that society could be defined by an unalienated sociability which embodies species-being. 'The motive of those who exchange is not *humanity* but *egoism*', Marx asserted, paraphrasing Adam Smith (3:320).[15] 'Greed' was often Marx's target. The modern world 'put egoism and selfish need in the place of these species-ties', and dissolved 'the human world into a world of atomistic individuals who are inimically opposed to one another' (3:173). There was the problem in a nutshell.

But reversing this process could not be done with a magic wand, for example by demanding a principle of love. Marx was wary of idealist solutions, and soon felt compelled to resolve the problem very differently. Let us jump ahead a moment in our narrative. Replying to Max Stirner about a year later, Marx insisted that the contradiction between society and individual 'disappears' when the form of society which creates it ends. The communists thus 'do not put to people the moral demand: love one another, do not be egoists, etc.' (5:247). They did not have to preach self-sacrifice. Instead their new social ideal would emerge from actual economic developments, rather than being introduced arbitrarily and unhistorically as a deus ex machina or idealist impetus external to them. In an ingenious logical shift, history steps in where philosophy falters. This implies that we do not seek a particular end for humanity against which present deficiencies are to be compared and judged: history provides this end for us. The idealist problem is evidently solved.

The 'Paris Manuscripts', however, provides just such an apparently idealistic comparison. Economics and ethics are at opposite poles. Political economy is juxtaposed with humanism: the purpose of production is profit, and not human well-being. Thus 'the existence of the human being' may be *indifferent* and even *harmful* to the capitalist (3:284): that is the logic of the system. But if political economy inverted humanity's true aims, how should the latter be defined? The increasingly specialized division of labour described by Steuart, Ferguson and Smith stunted human capacities.[16] By contrast Marx deployed an ideal of all-round development or many-sidedness to define his humanism, and to describe the unalienated life. He was in good company here. Besides Hegel, various Enlightenment thinkers had stressed that modern life lacked wholeness because specialization allowed some faculties and capacities to develop while impeding others. Friedrich Schiller, for example, compared the 'all-unifying Nature' of the Greeks to the 'one-sidedness' and 'fragmentary specialization of human powers' of the moderns. Moses Hess accepted the same ideal.[17]

To Marx this wholeness seemingly implied maximum control over one's destiny and circumstances, including command over the process of work. 'Voluntariness' captures part of this ideal, though the concept is hardly unproblematic. Unresolved tensions remain between the individualistic and social components of the theory of alienation. Must all-roundedness be conceived as a social rather than an individual problem or aspiration? Why should my development be contingent on yours, or hindered by its absence? What if only the few were capable of being all-rounded? In 1845 Stirner's absolute 'egoist' autonomy would express the individualistic extreme of this possibility.[18] Marx resolutely wanted to preserve the communal context of self-realization, and to reconcile all-roundedness and species-being. In 1844 his concern was centrally with *work* rather than society as such, and work is mostly a collective activity. But even activity which was not '*directly* communal activity…affirmed in *actual* direct *association* with other men' could be understood as 'social':

> when I am active scientifically, etc. – an activity which I can seldom perform in direct community with others – then my activity is social, because I perform it as a man. Not only is the material of my activity given to me as a social product (as is even the language in which the thinker is active): my own existence is social activity, and therefore that which I make of myself, I make of myself for society and with the consciousness of myself as a social being. (3:298)

All-round development thus stood in stark contrast to humanity's existing alienated condition. Applying this concept today, however, readers might still be perplexed at the difficulty of imagining a condition of not being alienated at all. Much of life lies outside the sphere of work, and alienation and domination persist outside relationships generated by the social division of labour. Existential questions return: tensions within ourselves, with our families and groups and with nature are seemingly inevitable. Inequality, anxiety, boredom and fear similarly arise outside work. A state of complete as opposed to partial non-alienation thus seems to be essentially a (Hegelian) theological concept, like 'perfection'. Still, we can imagine societies that facilitate our satisfaction, assist well-being, encourage creativity, reduce anxiety and grant more free time from drudgery. All of these qualities lend meaning to life and promote happiness and a sense of self-fulfilment. In addition, conceiving our happiness as interwoven with that of others, and defining it as 'sociability', we rise above the implication that minimizing alienation is an isolated and solitary affair and see co-operation as essential to it. This much Gans, Hess and Feuerbach had pointed to, and was also implied in the concept of species-being. Indeed, as we will see, this seems to have been the course plotted by the later Marx, who sought not to abolish alienation utterly but only to mitigate its worst effects, and to define its supersession more politically in terms of control over the labour process. This makes his concerns seem accordingly much less 'existentialist' than in the 1840s.

Marx never published the 'Paris Manuscripts'. Still mired in a Hegelian problematic, and still perilously close to Feuerbach, he was most likely unwilling to proceed further with its narrative, and within a year probably realized that the project of attacking egoism from the perspective of species-being was futile. Instead, in *The Holy Family*, he saw off most of his former Young Hegelian associates, especially Bruno Bauer, with a tedious vengefulness. Here too he acknowledged that Proudhon had 'done all that criticism of political economy from the standpoint of political economy can do' (4:33).[19] It followed, he thought, that the point was to 'rise above the level of political economy' via 'the critique of political economy'.

This became Marx's lifelong ambition. But rise to what standpoint? What level lay 'above' political economy, if 'humanism' now looked suspiciously like another incarnation of idealism? 'Political economy', Marx wrote, '*defines* the *estranged* form of social intercourse as the *essential* and *original* form corresponding to man's nature' (3:217). So whatever lay 'above' it still required a description of an unestranged or original nature, or some variant on species-being. Private property was the cause of alienation, so Marx's goal was now communism. His new method, the critique of political economy, now seemingly demanded a novel critical moral standpoint, whose defence would conclude by championing communism. This required an entirely new approach to the subject. Marx's erstwhile comrades were now left behind in the mists of abstract theory, grappling with ethereal idealism, bogged down in the swamps of theology. Marx saw a way out of these problems. Young Hegelianism had to be abandoned, and the ladder to emancipation kicked away. As Engels later wrote, the 'cult of abstract man' was about to be 'replaced by the science of real men and of their historical development' (26:381).

In the 'Paris Manuscripts' Marx hints repeatedly that he wants to deal with the 'real' estrangement of 'real' human beings, the recapturing of whose species powers is 'only possible through the co-operative action of all of mankind, only as the result of history' (3:333). Yet even in *The Holy Family* the proletariat still often appears as the abstract antithesis of private property, a Hegelian category rather than a real class of people. At this point Engels published *The Condition of the Working Class in England in 1844* (1845), which laid forth in provocative detail the proletariat's sufferings and the dissolution of society into competition, atomism and selfishness. Reading this book is essential for those who confront Marx today, seeking answers to philosophical questions. It explains why Marx and Engels became communists. Here was all the cruelty of modernity exposed. Marx now planned a 'Critique of Politics and Political Economy', which was to appear in mid-1845. In the event the latter section only was published in 1859. The former was never written.

The problem in part was defining the new starting point and reaching beyond Hegel and all his acolytes. O brave new world! To solve this task Marx and Engels embarked on a six-week research trip to England in July–August 1845. In London and Manchester they met leading Chartists and socialists. They read a great deal, often sitting in an alcove at a great bowed stained-glass window in Chetham's Library in Manchester, founded in the seventeenth century. Marx took extensive notes on the Owenite William Thompson's books in particular. They probably met members of the thriving Owenite branch in Manchester. They also became acquainted with German emigrant workers in London. Here too Marx was probably aware of a special congress of Owen's Rational Society, convened to oversee the winding up of the Queenwood community and with it Owenism in general.[20] If further evidence were required, this would have driven home the failure of communitarianism. But as one epoch in the history of socialism came to an end, Marx and Engels began to labour intensively on a work that would define a new one.

CHAPTER 4

The German Ideology, History and Production

The text today called *The German Ideology* was written with Engels in Brussels over the winter of 1845–6 but printed only in 1932. Conceived in an atmosphere of mirth and hilarity which kept Marx's family awake, it was long abandoned to what he called the 'gnawing criticism of the mice' after its main purpose, 'self-clarification', was achieved (29:264). All that most modern readers want to know about Marx's argument is contained in the part now labelled 'I. Feuerbach', which was not originally a coherent chapter. The lengthy sections that follow on Bauer, Stirner and the so-called True Socialists, who were heavily influenced by Feuerbach, and behind them Hess, now interest few. They are often petty, vindictive and splenetic, indeed tedious in the extreme.

Considerable controversy exists as to how we should view the currently printed text.[1] Some 300 pages of the original manuscript are missing, others are incomplete or crossed out (some are used elsewhere), or mixed up like puzzle pieces thrown up in the air. Even the title is absent. Much of what remains is tentative, experimental, even contradictory. Marx may have abandoned the prospect of publishing it because the substantial proportion devoted to attacking Max Stirner was soon irrelevant, for Stirner's star burnt out rapidly.[2] By the 1860s too the anarchism with which Marx had to engage was not Stirnerian individualism, but Bakuninist and Proudhonist collectivism. So there was no reason to publish the Stirner section later either. Feuerbach too fell out of popularity quickly. What was useable was eventually presented anew by Marx in the 1859 preface to *A Contribution to the Critique of Political Economy*.[3] So here again we have another major text which was potentially consciously abandoned. Nonetheless it became amongst the most famous of Marx's and Engels' writings.

'Stirner is right in rejecting Feuerbach's "man"', Engels had written in a letter to Marx in November 1844: 'Feuerbach deduces his "man" from God, it is from God that he arrives at "man"'. He concluded that 'The true way to arrive at "man" is the other way about. We must take our departure from the Ego, the empirical, flesh-and-blood individual... We must take our departure from empiricism and materialism' (38:12). But what kind of materialism? If, as the tenth of the famous 'Theses on Feuerbach' – written in 1845–6 to summarize Marx's main principles – expressed it, the standpoint of the old materialism was bourgeois society, that of the new was 'human society or social humanity'. Marx no longer viewed the essence of man as an 'abstraction inherent in each individual' (as the sixth 'Thesis' put it), but as 'the ensemble of the social relations' (5:4).[4] This was the definitive response to Feuerbach.

More than any other formulation, therefore, this sixth 'Thesis' marks the transition from the young to the older Marx. But what is this mysterious 'ensemble', upon the interpretation of which so much now hinged? Does it imply that all idealistic descriptions of human nature are 'theological'? Marx denied that either Feuerbach's account of 'species-being' or Stirner's 'ego' could be an abstract 'essence' of the self. The former, however, had been the chief basis of his plea for communism in 1844. Now the humanist 'Man' was revealed as just wishful thinking about the need for human sociability. But abandoning it might imply that 'flesh and blood' humans had no communal essence at all, or had lost what they once had, even if they lamented its absence. Still, if sociability was not derived from an abstract 'essence', it might be a long-lost ethos, or something to be created out of existing communal practices. Appealing to an 'ensemble' of social relations apparently resolves most questions about human nature into issues concerning 'observable behaviour', albeit without denying that an essential though evolving nature rooted in needs underlies such behaviour and provides historical continuity.[5]

Feuerbach's 'essence' was an idealist, even religious, premise. Marx now wanted to describe actual social relations. At another level he was also grappling with Owen's dictum that character results from 'circumstances', or the environment. (This is the subject of the third 'Thesis'.) At yet another he was merely asserting the group character of much of our basic identity. 'Essence', Marx wrote, 'can only be regarded as "species", as an inner, mute, general character which unites the many individuals *in a natural way*' (5:4). But how did the new 'ensemble' reflect real society, rather than itself remaining an abstraction? For if 'social humanity' is just 'species-being' recast, we have not passed beyond Feuerbach at all, but are only playing with terms. Had Marx jettisoned Feuerbach's concept, but not its substance? What happens to the idea of freedom as humanity's 'essence'? Or humanism? What happens to the catalogue of human needs defined as human nature in 1844 (3:336)?

Stirner had nonetheless dealt Feuerbach a fatal blow, as Feuerbach had done to Hegel. Marx now proceeded to bury what remained of Feuerbach, along with Stirner and the 'whole Young Hegelian movement' – 'the German ideologists' (philosophers had a short shelf-life at this point).[6] Replacing one form of idealism (Hegel's) with another (Feuerbach's), Marx conceived, was a mistake: one must transcend all forms of idealism. The 'entire body of German philosophical criticism from Strauss to Stirner', he claimed, had been 'confined to criticism of religious conceptions'. Even 'the political, juridical, moral "Man", in the last resort – was religious'. This viewpoint 'Saint Max' Stirner had been able to 'dispose of...once for all' (5:29). He had revealed that 'the predicates of God handed down by Feuerbach' were still 'holy'. But this implied that the communism to which Marx had converted in 1843–4 was itself essentially 'holy', or Hegelian. (This is probably why Marx renounced any hope of publishing the 'Paris Manuscripts'.) Forced to reject part if not all of his own standpoint, Marx clung onto the critique of political economy, which condemned private property as the chief cause of alienation. But his perspective possessed as yet no historical or practical dimension. It was still the ideal standing in judgement over the real.

And so Marx discovered history. Although the new standpoint was political economy, behind it lay history.[7] In a passage crossed out in the manuscript of *The German Ideology*, Marx wrote: 'We know only a single science, the science of history' (5:28). (We recall that Marx wrote earlier that philosophy was 'at the service of history'; 3:176.) Its first premises were 'real individuals, their activity and the material conditions of their life' (5:31). Individuals are no longer 'consciousness', as Hegel imagined. Mental labour was secondary to the fact that they produced their means of subsistence and material life. 'Civil society' was now the 'true focus and theatre of all history', whose prior concentration on 'spectacular historical events' was thus 'absurd' (5:50). All else follows from this assertion.

One of Marx's most famous propositions states that all forms of consciousness, and 'Morality, religion, metaphysics and all the rest of ideology', now 'no longer retain the semblance of independence. They have no history, no development; but men, developing their material production and their material intercourse, alter, along with this their actual world, also their thinking and the products of their thinking. It is not consciousness that determines life, but life that determines consciousness' (5:36–7). The forceful conclusion is that 'liberation' is 'a historical and not a mental act', which requires 'food and drink, housing and clothing in adequate quantity and quality' (5:38). These needs represent the 'enduring facts of human nature' (in G. A. Cohen's phrase)[8] which for some Marxists underpin the 'ensemble' of social relations. From this follows the famous, dramatic deduction of the eleventh of the 'Theses on Feuerbach' – later emblazoned on the statue over Marx's grave in London, and echoing Hess and Cieszkowski – that while philosophers had hitherto interpreted the world, the point was 'to change it' (5:5).[9] The abstract self's return to a condition of harmony achieved by philosophical reconciliation no longer interested Marx: he sought instead to maximize human control over life itself. The difference between the two is the distance between thought and action, and between an abstract ideal of being unalienated and a real condition of self-controlled labour. This was indeed a turning point of great significance.

Now viewed as the chief cause of alienation, the division of labour occupies centre stage in Marx's and Engels' new approach.[10] The separation of material and mental labour resulted in consciousness feeling 'that it is something other than the consciousness of existing practice', and ensured a juxtaposition of 'enjoyment and labour, production and consumption'. Marx concluded that 'the only possibility of their not coming into contradiction lies in negating in its turn the division of labour' (5:45), which made the worker 'one-sided, cripples and determines him', but which was itself 'determined by the development of intercourse and productive forces to such a degree of universality that private property and division of labour become fetters on them' (5:437–9).

One crucial passage defines the transition from 1844 to 1845–6, and demonstrates that 'all-round development' would be the concept linking the earlier and later writings, and the single most important idea in Marx's system. Marx announced that

> the real intellectual wealth of the individual depends entirely on the wealth of his real connections. Only this will liberate the separate individuals from the various national and local barriers, bring them into practical connection with the production (including intellectual production) of the whole world and make it possible for them to acquire the capacity to enjoy this all-sided production of the whole earth (the creations of man). *All-round* dependence, this primary natural form of the *world-historical* co-operation of individuals, will be transformed by this communist revolution into the control and conscious mastery of these powers, which, born of the action of men on one another, have till now overawed and ruled men as powers completely alien to them. (5:51–2)

Thus would alienation be solved in practice. Thus too 'private property can be abolished only on condition of an all-round development of individuals precisely because the existing form of intercourse and the existing productive forces are all-embracing and only individuals that are developing in an all-round fashion can appropriate them, i.e., can turn them into free manifestations of their own lives' (5:438–9).[11] Thus 'the workers assert in their communist propaganda that the vocation, designation, task of every person is to achieve all-round development of all his abilities' (5:292). So the communist revolution both 'removes the division of labour' and 'ultimately abolishes political institutions' (5:380).

Such a progression would only be possible, however, if productive forces continued developing. Communism would build on capitalism's achievements. Small-scale experiments too were now ruled out.

'Empirically', Marx deduced, 'communism is only possible as the act of dominant peoples "all at once" and simultaneously, which presupposes the universal development of productive forces and the world intercourse bound up with them.' The proletariat would become 'world-historical' as this market extended and so would communism, 'its activity' (5:49). Hegel's historical scheme was thus secularized, with 'proletariat' supplanting 'Spirit'. In a wonderfully satirical inversion of Hegel, Marx declared that the 'world-spirit' 'turns out to be the world market' (5:51). It now appeared that no ideal, such as species-being, needed to be followed. Communism was not 'a *state of affairs* which is to be established, an *ideal* to which reality [will] have to adjust itself. We call communism the *real* movement which abolishes the present state of things' (5:49). This was *the* definitive statement of Marx's break from utopianism. It was intended to mark a decisive rupture from Hegelian and Feuerbachian idealism. It would be repeated, with the emphasis that communism was not 'invented' or 'discovered', in *The Communist Manifesto* (6:448). But it left many questions unanswered. And ultimately, as we will see, it was very misleading insofar as it disguised Marx's own aims for the future. For the communist propagandists too, as we have seen, had an aim or ideal. So Marx had not abandoned all ideals, only the description of communism as one.

In projecting how the division of labour would be surpassed Marx and Engels, in a famously controversial passage, evidently invoked Fourier in describing the future communist society as one where

> nobody has one exclusive sphere of activity but each can become
> accomplished in any branch he wishes, society regulates the general
> production and thus makes it possible for me to do one thing today
> and another tomorrow, to hunt in the morning, fish in the afternoon,
> rear cattle in the evening, criticise after dinner, just as I have a mind,
> without ever becoming hunter, fisherman, shepherd or critic. (5:47)

Yet this extremely vivid image, so evidently unsuited to that modern urban, industrial vision of communism implied elsewhere here and in *The Communist Manifesto*, has puzzled many commentators, most of whom (like Marx himself) would probably be categorized as more skilled in after-dinner criticism than hunting or fishing. Later on, admittedly, Marx wrote that 'labour cannot become a game, as desired by Fourier' (29:97). The whole original passage may in any case have been meant satirically – one of the jokes which kept the family awake.[12] Yet Marx underscored the point by remarking that since individuals would no longer be subordinated to the division of labour, 'In a communist society there are no painters but only people who engage in painting among other activities' (5:394). This was *the* definitive description of 'all-roundedness'. In retrospect, for a man whose life was a study in specialization (in study), it is an odd remark. But it may clarify Marx's otherwise startling later comment that he could not actually envision himself living in the future society. For there would be no professional 'critics' then either. And Marx was not much good at anything else.

Despite the new standpoint, a Hegelian conception of freedom as expressed in labour is still present here, as is the concept of alienation. Marx notes that as 'long as man remains in naturally evolved society, that is, as long as a cleavage exists between the particular and the common interest, as long, therefore, as activity is not voluntarily, but naturally, divided, man's own deed becomes an alien power opposed to him, which enslaves him instead of being controlled by him' (5:47). Passing from 'natural' to 'voluntary' activity, however, 'men once more gain control of exchange, production and the way they behave to one another' and possess 'control and conscious mastery' of powers which 'have till now overawed and ruled men as powers completely alien to them' (5:48, 51–2).

'Voluntary' and 'control' are the operative words here. Though consciousness plays a key role, since we need to know what 'control' means, collective organization for the common good is crucial, much more than in 1844. This defines humanity's future ambitions. Freedom is now conceived as 'only possible within the community', where each individual has 'the means of cultivating his gifts in all directions'. By contrast, at present, while 'individuals seem freer under the dominance of the bourgeoisie than before, because their conditions of life seem accidental; in reality, of course, they are less free, because they are to a greater extent governed by material forces' (5:78–9). Communism, however, 'for the first time consciously treats all naturally evolved premises as the creations of hitherto existing men, strips them of their natural character and subjugates them to the power of the united individuals' (5:81). The 'appropriation of the totality of the instruments of production' is equated with 'the development of a totality of capacities in the individuals themselves' (5:87).

Mankind could thus guide its own destiny through 'a general plan of freely combined individuals'. The proletariat, not Spirit, becomes aware that it creates the world, which is therefore only an alien entity when it is not brought under communal control. The central premise here is 'free combination'. But details as to what this means are lacking. Coercion would ruin this scheme, by overthrowing its key presumption. Having a plan formulated by the few while leaving the many only to implement it also contradicts its spirit.

The focus of Marx's analysis now was termed the 'mode of production', which (as described in 1859) 'conditions the general process of social, political and intellectual life' (29:263). This had already been partly suggested in 1844, when Marx wrote that 'Religion, family, state, law, morality, science, art, etc., are only *particular* modes of production [of private property], and fall under its general law' (3:297). In the new schema, if human beings were broadly products of their environment (which all materialists posited), the economic realm, or forces and relations of production, was crucial amongst the factors shaping their behaviour. Social, political, legal and religious power flowed from property ownership. Central to this process was the way the division of labour had developed, notably between town and country.

The new theory was summarized in 1846:

Social relations are closely bound up with productive forces.
In acquiring new productive forces men change their mode of
production; and in changing their mode of production, in changing
the way of earning their living, they change all their social relations.
The hand-mill gives you society with the feudal lord; the steam-mill,
society with the industrial capitalist. (6:166)

Engels later stated that before Marx the causes of historical change were 'to be sought in the changing ideas of human beings, and that of all historical changes political changes are the most important and dominate the whole of history'. That view was now supplanted by the idea that all history 'revolved around class antagonisms and class struggles' (24:191–3), a conclusion Marx and Engels reached independently in 1844–5. It represented the viewpoint of political economy.[13]

There are more or less technologically determinist readings of the new theory. Marx of course wanted communism to emerge from capitalism. A common interpretation is that 'Marx proved that the economic structure of society is the foundation whose evolution explains all other aspects of social evolution.'[14] But did he believe that these developments were inevitable? We might plausibly say that on this account technology and economic development will take us most of the way towards communist society by themselves, if we have the patience to wait it out: the factory system creates the proletariat, which inevitably overthrows capitalism. We might also say that class consciousness is extremely important in achieving the final goal, particularly if sooner seems better than later in terms of the pain endured getting there (the proletariat might not get the message quickly). Both propositions might thus depend on how long we are willing to wait. Either way, technology and other productive forces shape society fundamentally, and class is the central category of social analysis. Economics is primary, and politics derivative, though much hinges on how reductionist this assertion becomes, and often class struggle is of course also 'political'. Either way, much of historical development results not from conscious decision-making but the working out of a vast and diverse network of causes, motives, actions and counter-actions. But it is one thing to say that we desire a particular historical outcome, and quite another to say that it is inevitable.

Here as elsewhere we should be wary of reading Marx dogmatically. 'Productive forces' and 'social relations' are roughly things and people, but organizations, technology and processes are intertwined in various ways. Science requires scientists, for instance, but the way they are organized or not will have a direct bearing on how discovery, invention and production proceed. The theory is only very tentatively explored here, and is meant to be indicative, an initial stab at, rather than the last word on, a very large subject. The method was meant to be historical and self-reflexive, and itself subject to change; indeed even self-subversive if the facts demanded it. Many later Marxists would forget this. Marx's schema, and especially its prophetic dimensions, was also meant specifically to empower humanity, and by cutting through ideology to reveal that mankind *could* control its fate if only it *would*. Our behaviour is only determined insofar as we do not understand in what degree it is determined, which is invariably less than we imagine, once we know. A key message now, as later, was that history was constantly in flux. There were no 'eternal categories', but 'the moment you present men as the actors and authors of their own history', which was the point of the critique of ideology, 'you arrive...at the real starting point' (6:170) – which is clearly a dig at Hegel. Now history ceases to be wholly determined and the first moment of the self-conscious control of humanity's destiny begins. This is akin to proclaiming a new stage in humanity's enlightenment.

So for Marx the terminus of Hegel's scheme of Spirit's progressive self-consciousness was not even yet the beginning of humanity's true self-consciousness. This was also the answer to theories of historical determinism generally, as well as to Owen's conundrum, addressed in the third of the 'Theses on Feuerbach', reminding us that the 'educator must himself be educated' (5:4). (But if character is created by circumstances who changes these?) We see through the veil of illusion woven from economic and philosophical categories, and particularly the primary misconception, more important than all the rest, that relations of bourgeois production are 'natural' (6:174). Now people begin to make their own history, though, as *The Eighteenth Brumaire of Louis Bonaparte* (1852) says, 'they do not make it just as they please; they do not make it under circumstances chosen by themselves, but under circumstances directly encountered, given and transmitted from the past' (11:103). This limits, but does not eliminate, our flexibility in shaping history to our own purposes. This is a startling, brilliant and empowering insight. But ironically it also prioritizes consciousness and ideas to an astonishing degree.

The central analytical section of *The German Ideology* describes the historical evolution of forms of property. The main forms of production are (1) tribal; (2) ancient communal and state ownership, where slavery exists and private property begins; (3) feudal or estate property, where landed property is maintained by serf labour, and craftsmen and traders emerge to prominence in towns; and (4) modern capitalism. Each type of economic organization gives rise to a specific superstructure of law, government, religion, and so on, corresponding to the mode of property ownership and dominance of particular classes. Class struggle occurs in each stage, and is a key cause of social and political transformation and historical progression. Thus 'all collisions in history have their origin, according to our view, in the contradiction between the productive forces and the forms of intercourse' (5:74–5). So instead of stages in Spirit's unfolding self-awareness and its movement towards freedom, we have stages in the development of property, with communist freedom emerging at the end. Just how detached from the base the superstructure was remained controversial, however. Engels would later describe the 'relative independence' of the state (49:60). But this tells us little.

Detail is lacking too as to how revolution is the 'driving force' of history (5:54). Much may happen between great historical developments in which class struggle as such need not be predominant. Marx's premise is not that *all* history is class struggle, only that the latter expresses the most important transformations in accordance with economic development. There is a sense that class struggle sharpens after the transition from feudalism to capitalism, as exploitation intensifies and conditions of work in factories deteriorate. Consciousness of class struggle and of class itself also expand now, as class interests become more antagonistic, and with the rise of socialism.

Class consciousness for Marx means not only an awareness of what we share with others who occupy similar productive roles. We also need to understand how classes contribute to what for Marx is the necessary or inevitable path of historical progress. Classes are defined by their relation to the mode of production, but may be more or less conscious of their collective role as a class. Class interests are assumed to be more or less rational calculations defined by this role. In industrial societies the main classes are the bourgeoisie and the proletariat. Prior to this, however, the landed elite, or aristocracy, small producers and a large peasantry or class of slaves or serfs were prominent. Most persist under capitalism, but decline in importance as the bourgeoisie relentlessly destroys the old aristocracy, industry breeds urbanization and progressive crises drive small producers and peasants into the proletariat and enrich the bourgeoisie at the same time. So only the grand, titanic struggle between the two great modern classes at the apex of modernity really interested Marx.

The meaning of history is thus defined in terms of class struggle, and an end or telos of the final stage of communist equality. But not all phenomena are reducible to class conflict. Many other social divisions besides class – gender, race, ethnicity, religion, nationality – interact with both class and each other. They may also hinder what Marx regards as the optimal outcome of capitalism's development, namely a class-conscious proletariat's insistence that communism must replace it. (This is the main reason why Marx undertheorized them.) Besides the bourgeoisie, other classes, notably the petty bourgeoisie (small shopkeepers, tradesmen and small-scale producers) and the peasantry, may oppose Marx's ideal of the future society. Within classes, individuals carry or embody the attributes of that class in their social relationships, though they can depart from the determined character of their class, and have their behaviour shaped by other phenomena (religion, nationalism, etc.). Just how this extremely complex process develops we are not told. But we may belong to the bourgeoisie, for instance, yet like Marx and Engels renounce its interests because we see the rectitude of the proletariat's cause. This too dilutes the determinist implications of the theory, and potentially gives a crucial role to the intelligentsia.

How original was the general hypothesis of *The German Ideology*? The idea that 'power follows property' had been prominent in seventeenth- and eighteenth-century history writing in Britain. It was expressed most notably by the Scottish school of conjectural history, which included David Hume, Adam Ferguson, John Millar and Adam Smith, out of which political economy emerged. Building on a tradition associated with the seventeenth-century republican James Harrington, the Scots described the famous 'four stages' theory of progressive, universal forms of society (hunting/gathering, pastoral, agricultural, commercial), and defended 'commercial society' as the freest and wealthiest of all.[15] Here we witness the first accounts of the emergence of urban commercial wealth as challenging, and then displacing, landed power. Around 1800 'capitalism' came increasingly to describe the new system.[16] Here too the notion that government was, in Smith's words, 'instituted for the defence of the rich against the poor, of or those who have some property against those who have none at all', was a commonplace.[17]

The Scottish writers, while well aware that the rich often abused their power, did not assume class struggle to be the motor force of historical development. Instead they preferred to assess the effects of population growth and a natural desire to better our condition. As we have seen vis-à-vis Hegel, some acknowledged the devastating effects of the new 'mechanical arts' on the workforce. Ferguson in particular in 1767, in a passage quoted by Marx in 1847 and again in 1861, noted that manufactures 'prosper most, where the mind is least consulted, and where the workshop may, without any great effort of imagination, be considered as an engine, the parts of which are men' (6:181; 30:275). (Here Ferguson is praised for bringing 'out more sharply and emphatically the negative aspects of the division of labour'.) This is Marx's starting point: the division of labour in increasingly automated workshops means that 'the human being has been further dismembered' (6:188).

Nonetheless the 'materialist conception of history' (a phrase introduced by Engels in 1859, which appears only in title headings in the printed *German Ideology*), or 'historical materialism', which Engels used, sharpened the perception that *primacy* must be given to economic factors in historical interpretation, and that class struggle resulted from their development.[18] This might be regarded as Marx's most substantial and important lifelong claim. Though Marxism would often be called 'scientific socialism' (*wissenschaftlicher Sozialismus*), Marx himself disliked the phrase, which Proudhon and Karl Grün had used. But *Wissenschaft* in German merely means 'methodical and systematic study'. The implications of linking the 'materialist conception of history' and the natural sciences, which were not explored here, were embraced enthusiastically by later followers.[19] This is discussed further below.

The German Ideology was also centrally about 'ideology'.[20] This term has three main meanings: to denote an idealistic worldview, which Marx rejects; to describe 'influential beliefs and forms of social consciousness'; and to indicate 'false consciousness or illusion'.[21] The latter hints at a 'true', 'scientific' understanding which trumps all others – namely one generated by using Marx's own theory, which pierces through 'ideological' illusions. Most ideology is regarded as class propaganda and thus as 'false' – at least in the sense of being limited, or not universal – except for ideas which support a 'proletarian outlook', which are 'true' because they represent or emanate from the most virtuous and 'universal class', and are forecast to be exonerated by history. This reduces the truth content of ideas – at least social and political ideas – to a sociology of knowledge, as well as a moral essentialism (proletarian ideas alone are 'true'). It roughly corresponds to the juxtaposition of utopia with science, and of the ignorant mass with their 'educators'. In its most complete and reductive form it also hints at the hypothesis that 'might is right'.

This line of thinking has little intellectual purchase today, though it remains common in popular culture. In studying ideas nowadays we are more careful, as Leszek Kolakowski stresses, to distinguish between ideological content, or function, and cognitive value, or scientific legitimacy. The mere fact that large numbers of people believe something has no bearing on its truth or moral superiority as such. For Marx, however, any proposition's truth value was intertwined with its emancipatory potential, and thus 'Marx's epistemology is part of his social utopia'.[22] This resulted in the conviction that Marxism was an epistemologically sealed universe where only Marxists were, indeed could be, right.

Only with Karl Mannheim's *Ideology and Utopia* (1936) would Marxism too be accorded the status of ideology. The history of philosophy from Plato onwards, however, is littered with accounts of human stupidity and wishful thinking and the inability of the many to transcend both. Marx's view differs in part in the majority being truth incarnate, so to speak, even though only the few may at first be aware of this. But it also differs in one later form (the 'fetishism of commodities') in explaining the core of modern illusion in terms of a relationship between things and social relations. Here the majority may be wrong most of the time. This ties at least some forms of 'false consciousness'[23] to historical and economic relationships rather than explaining them through deficiencies of education, intelligence or understanding. This challenges the truth content of all social ideas, most of which seemingly express class interest as such, and thus an inevitable bias. It also implies that 'propaganda' or untruth can as well serve the interests of the cause as truth itself, indeed that 'objective truth' does not exist, except as proletarian class consciousness; or even if it did it would have to take a distant second place to promoting the cause, the end thus justifying the means, and might thus becoming right.[24] Similar claims have recently emerged in the idea of a 'post-truth' society, and in some theories of 'post-modernism'.

Marx's main proposition here, however, respects how ideas emerge and why some predominate. *Geist* is dethroned, and with 'the putrescence of absolute spirit' (5:27) the final break from Hegel occurs. The class which dominates material production also dominates mental production: 'The ideas of the ruling class are in every epoch the ruling ideas, i.e., the class which is the ruling *material* force of society is at the same time its ruling *intellectual* force...The ruling ideas are nothing more than the ideal expression of the dominant material relationships, the dominant material relationships grasped as ideas' (5:59).

Here 'ideology' raises a second major problem. As with the question of the 'truth' of ideas, the assertion of their transience and class dependency makes it difficult if not impossible for us to speak of 'ethics' as anything other than impermanent, historically conditioned and rooted in class perspective. This implies that no transhistorical or universal model of ideal human behaviour, no 'best practice' or 'model' of sociability (or relating to others), exists to be emulated. 'Good' and 'evil' are relative to time and place. All morality is simply 'ideology' or 'a superstructure of economic relations'.[25] The loudest voice at any given point reflects the values of the dominant class, and is doomed to fall silent when that class expires. The morality of the coming dominant class, the proletariat, was in the process of emerging, and to bring its victory about might justify any means. But it seems now, quite dramatically, that this end could not be defined as it had been in 1844 by the humanism of the 'Paris Manuscripts' – what later generations would often find most valuable in Marx. But did Marx really believe that religion (an illusion) and morality (a class-based practice) should be treated similarly? What happens to 'all-round development' as an ideal of human development? Are the communist propagandists who demand it also deluded? What happens to 'freedom' as the end point of 'all-round development'? Aren't all these also 'ideology' or reflections of class interest? Perhaps they are not when they are sufficiently universalized. Thus, some suggest, Marx based his idea of all-roundedness on a concept of human needs which was not subject to historical malleability in the same way morality or ideology were. Instead his 'morality of emancipation', in the political theorist Steven Lukes's phrase, rejected the dominant-morality paradigm of rights in particular, and was based not on assumptions rooted in bourgeois society but on permanent if evolving human needs.[26]

These remain perplexing questions not least because, as we will see shortly, the ideals of free activity and self-development persist in Marx's later works. In 1845–6, however, the key issue was whether humanism could still be seen as the goal of history, or whether it too now had to be seen as originating in and limited by a given stage. Marx wanted a critical standpoint on capitalism which was neither idealistic nor moralistic. He sought to create a society which eliminated greed, but without defining its opposite as an ideal to be followed because this would make him an idealist. He now particularly wished to move beyond, or to transcend, Hess's 'love' and Stirner's 'egoism'. Thus, as we have seen, he insisted that 'communists do not oppose egoism to selflessness or selflessness to egoism…they rather demonstrate its material source, with which it disappears of itself…communists do not preach *morality* at all…They do not put to people the moral demand: love one another, do not be egoists, etc.' (5:247). In communist society 'the genuine and free development of individuals' would be 'determined precisely by the connection of individuals, a connection which consists partly in the economic prerequisites and partly in the necessary solidarity [*Solidarität*] of the free development of all, and finally in the universal character of the activity of individuals on the basis of the existing productive forces' (5:439).[27] Here 'individuals' consciousness of their mutual relations will, of course, likewise be completely changed, and, therefore, will no more be the "principle of love" or *dévoûment* [devotion] than it will be egoism' (5:439). And so Hess and Stirner, love and egoism, were disposed of. A new mode of production would give rise to a new mode of sociability.

Nonetheless we will see that the future would still be defined by relations of solidarity and all-roundedness. The communist propagandists were not deluded. Morality based on class antagonism would end; when in 1877 Engels spoke of the 'proletarian morality of the future' (25:86) this is what he meant. Its seeds lie in the present. So morality is 'always a class morality' (25:87). Yet both 'solidarity' and 'all-round development' remain *as ideals of human behaviour*, even if Marx rather speciously refuses to call them this, or to view them as 'morality'. Delineating the 'connection' which will exist in communist society implies that we ought to identify and encourage whatever 'solidarity' we discover in existing productive relations. For example, communist propaganda might stress – as Marx himself later would – that a new co-operative ethos emerging within capitalism would and should eventually dominate. This again implies that the communists do preach 'morality', and flies in the face of the objection that there was no possibility of a Marxist ethics now, under capitalism. It also implies that the new society still commences from small-scale beginnings or so-called heterotopian spaces where critical morality becomes possible, even if this is not an intentional community.

Very different and quite contradictory views have emerged on this vital and complex issue. Some see Marx as consistently 'committed to the moral superiority of socialism over preceding systems'.[28] Others stress 'the profound commitment to humanist and egalitarian values that remained throughout as the ethical foundation of Classical Marxism', and indeed base Marx's entire system on an ethical starting point.[29] In this interpretation Marx retained freedom as his central goal. But that freedom was always conceived in a social context, where my development is part of – and contingent in turn on – yours. Without the mutual support or solidarity that allow this to happen, no freedom is meaningful.

Yet others assert that, in *The German Ideology*, Marx 'rejects the possibility of ethics altogether', though in his later writings he introduces a new ethical standpoint.[30] Another well-known account insists that 'Marx did not have an ethical theory'.[31] To some this leaves a palpable void which could be filled by a morality of pure expediency justifying anything that promised to advance the communist cause. If morality was completely abolished, nothing was left 'but simply power'.[32] Marx was 'supremely indifferent to morality; everything that favored the revolution was right, everything that worked against the revolution was wrong'.[33] In this vein Lenin wrote in 1920 that 'to a Communist all morality lies in this united discipline and conscious mass struggle against the exploiters. We do not believe in an eternal morality, and we expose the falseness of all the fables about morality'.[34]

Some however see Marx as asserting that moral standards will be 'higher' in communist society not because 'they approach more closely to some timeless moral ideal, but only that they belong to a society which as a whole is higher as measured by its productive powers and the non-moral goods they furnish to people'.[35] Jon Elster assumes that 'communism will be a society beyond justice', and that Marx specifically rejected the idea that 'communism substitutes altruist motivations for selfish ones', which is exactly what many presume it does.[36] The Russian Marxist Vera Zasulich (the assassin of the governor of St Petersburg in 1878), however, while denying that Marxism possessed an 'official system of morality', stressed that all Social Democrats sought solidarity. This consisted minimally in not 'doing anything contrary to the general good', and maximally in 'doing everything one can for the general good'; a view she described, partly under John Stuart Mill's influence, as 'utilitarian morality'.[37] Marx would later be combined with Kant, Darwin and other writers in order to fill an apparent gap.

We can resolve some of these issues by proposing that Marx can be understood as rejecting moral claims which served as apologies for the ruling class while upholding others which were genuinely human or universal. His approach to solidarity (later described as 'co-operation') and to all-roundedness clearly challenges the view that he had no 'ideal'. He had one, consisting of these two components. But it was also growing out of existing productive relations. It was not timeless, or superhistorical, precisely because it could only emerge out of capitalism and modern industry; and it was not beyond or above class, because it would emanate from the proletariat, the only universal class. But an ideal it was, nonetheless, and in this sense Marx remained an 'idealist' who aimed to fulfil the 'vocation, designation, task of every person'.[38] In 1845 he clearly viewed relationships between people – or sociability – as a key measure of humanity's progress. The aim was to 'free [man] from the filth of gain' and end the slavery 'of labour for gain and of his own as well as other men's *selfish* need' (4:113). He also asserted that 'If correctly understood interest is the principle of all morality, man's private interest must be made to coincide with the interest of humanity'. This could be accomplished by ensuring that 'each man must be given social scope for the vital manifestation of his being. If man is shaped by environment, his environment must be made human' (4:130–31). This was Owen's key point. *The German Ideology* did not supersede these assumptions.

So if a Marxist ethics is possible in principle, then the twin ideals of solidarity and all-round development are surely its basis. Such an ethics cannot be deduced if we regard human nature as simply the 'ensemble of social relations'. This means merely that human behaviour is not informed by Spirit, but is shaped by the environment, and comprises a huge range of outlooks and activities, morally good, bad and indifferent. An ideal of human behaviour and aspiration had been provided in 1844. Alienation is a condition of fragmented disunity caused chiefly by dividing labour. The opposite of the fragmented person is the whole person, and for Marx the best type of whole person was all-rounded; that is to say, not only not alienated (negatively), but fully developed (positively). And the best all-round person possessed a sense of species-identity and solidarity, for 'free, conscious activity' (the definition of 'species-being') was only possible collectively. These aims rested in turn on a theory of needs in which adequate food, clothing, housing, clean air and water, free time, self-development towards all-roundedness, and so on, define the good life. These needs were not 'ideological' and not susceptible to class interpretation. Fulfilling them remained an ideal which Marx never abandoned, as we will see. To the contrary, his life's work was to universalize them.

It is a moot point, however, as to how far we can speak of Marx having a theory of justice as part of his ethics, at least separate from the system of production, the chief means of realizing human aims. Exploitation – or 'theft' of surplus value – leaving the worker desolate, can be described in Marxian terms as 'unjust'; Marx would later call 'a relationship imposed by force' 'an injustice' (34:246). Some, like the Russian philosopher Nikolai Berdyaev, indeed simply assume that the theory of surplus value is 'primarily an ethical doctrine'.[39] But capitalism is not *as such* unjust for Marx: on its own terms, its purpose is chiefly to exploit labour and this is exactly what it does. Hence Marx at one point describes the leading political economist David Ricardo as being 'great' and 'important' precisely because he ignored 'human beings' and keeps in view 'the development of productive forces alone' (33:114, 36:258). Marx's acuity too lay partly in not moralizing about this process. But he did commonly use terms like 'robbery', 'theft' and 'coercion' to describe the extraction of surplus value under capitalism, implying an accusation of injustice – for example writing about the *'theft of alien labour time, which is the basis of present wealth'* (29:91). To deny that this implies a moral standpoint defined by justice would be fatuous. 'Theft' is an overt and incontrovertibly moral category: it implies a right and a wrong, and a right to justice to boot.

The last substantial achievement of *The German Ideology* lay in its account of politics. In 1843 Marx decided that existing states merely reflected class conflicts in civil society. No real human emancipation could thus occur in the political sphere. He also rejected Hegel's idea that a neutral bureaucracy could arbitrate between class struggles. Coercive states were required chiefly to suppress the working classes. Now it is emphasized that, once the latter realized that 'they must overthrow the state' (5:80), private property and social classes would end and the state would, as Engels later put it, 'die out' (24:321).[40] Instead of an alien entity juxtaposed with civil society, the democratic management or administration of economic affairs would prevail. Thus 'there will be no more political power properly so-called, since political power is precisely the official expression of antagonism in civil society' (6:212).

This description, perhaps more than any other, and the assumption of finality which underpins it, makes communist society appear like a secular version of the millennium. This resolution of the problem begged several questions, however. Only if we reduce politics to class conflict can we whisk it away so easily. Divisions of opinion not rooted in class exist in all societies, and might even be expected to increase as societies became more complex. Some tribal peoples are constantly at war. Moreover, 'democracy' was clearly presumed to persist as the mode of administration. But if political parties merely expressed class interests, could more than one party exist in future if only one class existed? And what did 'democracy' mean if only one party existed? Could factions or tendencies or other divisions of opinion still be legitimate? Lenin, as we will see, was sometimes assumed to have suggested that every cook could govern the state. (He had no experience of reality-TV stars.) But even master chefs might be dismayed by the vast details to be mastered in 'the administration of things', as might politicians by the challenges of gourmet cookery.

Despite these difficulties, the revolution in thought which *The German Ideology* represents is incontestable. We can no longer imagine studying any society without first asking about its system of production, its property ownership and its dominant class. Marx shows us that the world, having surrendered its divine character, is humanity's creation. He says, in effect: 'Close your eyes, stick your finger on the globe and choose a nation. Tell me what its mode of production is and I will tell you what its legal, religious and philosophical systems are, even what it thinks.' These are amongst the most substantial achievements of modern historic insight. The view that there is no abstract 'human nature' as such, only an unfolding, self-made ensemble of social relations underpinned by a bedrock of real needs, magnifies the value of the perception, despite the problems it introduces. We also see that history only makes sense when it is conceived as having a rational point or aim, namely ending exploitation.

The perspectives established here remained the basis for the rest of Marx's life work. After 1846 the main statement of his historical theory came in the 1859 preface to *A Contribution to the Critique of Political Economy*. There he returned to his earlier manuscript to see what could be useful in it. In a lengthy paragraph he summed up his early insights and described the 'guiding principle of my studies'. His reckoning with Hegel in 1844 had brought the conclusion that 'the anatomy of civil society must be sought in political economy'. The totality of the relations of production – the 'mode of production of material life' – 'conditions the general process of social, political, and intellectual life. It is not the consciousness of men that determines their existence, but their social existence that determines their consciousness' (29:262–3). So much for Hegel. Class struggle, curiously, is not mentioned as such. Instead, conflicts between material productive forces and relations of production, or the existing relations of production with the 'property relations', are described as resulting in 'social revolution'. That is to say, technological development indicates that a different form of society is possible, or inevitable, which corresponds to new productive forces and their implications for property ownership. Marx also insisted, rather oddly, it would transpire, that

> A form of society never breaks down until all the productive forces are developed for which it affords room. New and higher relations of production are never established, until the material conditions of life to support them have been prepared in the lap of the old society. Therefore mankind always sets for itself only such tasks as it is able to perform. (29:264)

Thus 'the productive forces developing within bourgeois society create also the material conditions for a solution of this antagonism. The prehistory of human society accordingly closes with this social formation' (29:264).

CHAPTER 5

Socialism, the Revolutions of 1848 and *The Communist Manifesto*

The moment when it seemed real history might actually commence occurred in 1847–8, when Europe was convulsed by a 'colossal eruption of the revolutionary volcano' (38:199), instigated by commercial crisis, poor harvests and food riots. January brought insurrection in Sicily. Then constitutions were proclaimed in Naples, Florence and Turin. In February King Louis-Philippe abdicated after revolution broke out in Paris. A provisional republican government was instituted, and national workshop schemes began aiding the unemployed. Revolt then spread to Austro-Hungary, Poland, Italy and Germany. Constituent assemblies met in Frankfurt and Berlin. Across Europe radicals toasted the final downfall of despotisms near and far. In the heat of the moment it was easy to believe that this was 1789 all over again, except bigger and better. 'In the realm of ideas', the Russian socialist Alexander Herzen, then an émigré in Paris, exulted, 'the exploitation of man by man is over, because no one any longer considers this relation to be just.'[1]

Such expectations proved sadly premature. By June the tide was turning towards reaction. A newly elected assembly in France closed the workshops and thousands of workers died in street fighting. The corps of 'barricades professors' – in the poet Georg Herwegh's term – who left Paris to liberate Germany, were trounced at their first encounter with regular troops, as Marx had warned. Then Russian troops rescued Austro-Hungary and Prussia, and crushed the Poles and Hungarians. Neither Germany nor Italy succeeded in achieving unity. In Britain the Chartist movement declined rapidly. In France universal suffrage was repealed in May 1850 in what Marx condemned as an overt act of bourgeois dictatorship.[2] Then, on 2 December 1851, the president, Louis-Napoléon Bonaparte, staged a coup. The National Assembly was dissolved and the empire restored in 1852. Severe repression lasted until 1859, and censorship until 1862.

Despite such defeats, these upheavals for the first time publicized socialist alternatives to liberal ideologies of freedom of trade, industrialization, rights and constitutionalism.[3] The communists were now organized in various groups, with Marx having founded a correspondence committee in 1845 which included the most radical Chartists, the Fraternal Democrats. In 1847, pursuing another strategy, the chief French communist, Cabet, sought to found a new community in the USA – this was what probably led Engels to downplay the value of communitarianism from this time onwards. ('Who in France believes in Icarie, who in England believes in the plans of Owen', the final section of The German Ideology had asked; 5:461.) In London the German Workers' Educational Association, founded in 1840, was led by Karl Schapper, Heinrich Bauer and Joseph Moll. They also headed the secret League of the Just, which emerged in 1836 amongst German artisans in Paris from the Outlaws' League, and which sought violent revolution to achieve equality through community of goods. Schapper, however, worried that Marx aimed 'to establish some kind of aristocracy of intellectuals and rule over the people from your new godly thrones'.[4] In June 1847 the League renamed itself the Communist League, and in September it announced a new slogan, 'Workers of the World, Unite'. This displaced 'All Men Are Brothers', whose religious implications Marx disliked intensely. Marx was later accused of supporting Blanquist minority putschism. But the League's officials were democratically elected and always subject to removal, which, Engels later wrote, 'alone barred all hankering after conspiracy, which requires dictatorship' (26:322). And Marx recalled that he and Engels only joined the League 'on the condition that anything conducive to a superstitious belief in authority be eliminated from the Rules' (45:288).[5]

In late 1847 Marx and Engels set out the League's first principles in a new programme. This was adopted at its second congress, held above the Red Lion pub in Soho. Marx was instructed to write it up. What became *The Communist Manifesto* was preceded by three earlier drafts: a seventeen-point list of the 'Demands of the Communist Party in Germany'; a summary by Engels entitled 'Draft of a Communist Confession of Faith'; and a later revision entitled 'Principles of Communism', where Hess's influence lingered.[6] The last of these is much closer to the *Manifesto*'s final text, though it mentions constructing 'large palaces' for workers in the countryside, in an Owenite or Fourierist fashion, which combine 'the advantages of both urban and rural life without the one-sidedness and disadvantages of either' (6:351), a proposal rarely mentioned thereafter. It also insists that the new social order 'will have to take the running of industry and all branches of production in general out of the hands of separate individuals competing with each other'. Instead it would 'ensure that all these branches of production are run by society as a whole, i.e., for the social good, according to a social plan and with the participation of all members of society. It will therefore do away with competition and replace it by association.' Moreover, 'the division of labour making one man a peasant, another a shoemaker, a third a factory worker, a fourth a stockjobber' would 'completely disappear' (6.348). Instead

> Education will enable young people quickly to go through the whole
> system of production…to pass from one branch of industry to
> another according to the needs of society or their own inclinations.
> It will therefore free them from that one-sidedness which the present
> division of labour stamps on each one of them. Thus the communist
> organisation of society will give its members the chance of an all-round
> exercise of abilities that have received all-round development. (6:353)

This was evidently a mixture of Fourier's and Owen's schemes.[7]

Then came Marx's take on the revolutionary moment. 'A spectre is haunting Europe – the spectre of communism' is the resounding phrase which opens *The Communist Manifesto*. It would ring immortally across the next century. Completed in January and published in London in February 1848, it is justly accounted as Marx's most accessible work. The 'most revolutionary document ever given to the world' (39:60), as the Chartist George Julian Harney termed it, had little immediate impact in England, where it was largely unknown until the 1890s.[8] Elsewhere the story was different, and Engels in 1888 called it 'undoubtedly the most wide-spread, the most international production of all Socialist Literature' (26:516). Eventually it appeared in some 200 languages. Its programme was imitated by many later Marxists, and its insistence on centralizing state power, we will see, was closely followed by Lenin and Stalin. The 'party' in its title, however, was the entire progressive working-class movement, 'the party in the broad historical sense' (41:87), not a coterie of Blanquist closet conspirators 'who accomplished the coup and who themselves are, at first, organised under the dictatorship of one or several individuals', as Engels put it in 1875, terming the strategy 'obsolete' (24:13). The later shift from communist party to Communist Party is thus a critical one.

The *Manifesto* succinctly summarizes Marx's and Engels' joint efforts up to 1848, especially the historical sections of *The German Ideology*. Its central theme is the development of modern capitalism, its ruthless overthrow of older social and economic systems and its inevitable tendency to ever greater crises, the last of which would usher in – after revolution and a prolonged interim period – the final stage of communism. Class war, it contends, would reveal the necessity for workers to rise above national identity and antagonism, which are viewed as fast disappearing, and to embrace internationalism. First the bourgeoisie would destroy the last vestiges of feudalism. Then, standing behind it, the proletariat would push forwards to create its own society. The critical point would come when centralization of the means of production 'became incompatible with' the progressive socialization of labour, for example large numbers of concentrated industrial workers. In other words, the individual nature of ownership and the small number of owners would collide with the social nature of production and the huge proletariat, implying the need to socialize ownership too.

The *Manifesto* trumpeted Marx's distance from all preceding schools of socialism and communism. 'Communism' was now juxtaposed with 'capitalism'. The proclamation that 'the history of all hitherto existing society is the history of class struggles' (6:482) placed revolution at the centre of Marx's narrative. Modern capitalism displaced feudal relations with the most 'naked, shameless, direct, brutal exploitation' (6:487). (Note the moralistic language, which clearly implies a counter-ideal.) All social relations were reduced to one financial connection, the 'cash nexus'. With utter unsentimentality capitalism transformed both the inner and outer worlds in the image of universal commodity production and consumption, and swept aside everything which preceded it. 'All that is solid melts into air', Marx observed. But while remaking the world, capitalism also created its own gravediggers. The dreams and experiments of the 'utopian' socialists, as they are termed here – chiefly Fourier, Owen and Saint-Simon – are supplanted by 'actual relations springing from an existing class struggle' (6:498).[9] Communism, we are told, 'abolishes eternal truths, it abolishes all religion and all morality, instead of constituting them on a new basis; it therefore acts in contradiction to all past historical experience' (6:504). A hint of secular millenarianism thus remains here too, as well as an obsession with novelty and originality, especially vis-à-vis the Young Hegelians and all other socialists.

Following the historical section a communist programme is presented. This consists of ten points:

1. Abolition of property in land and application of all rents of land to public purposes.
2. A heavy progressive or graduated income tax.
3. Abolition of all right of inheritance.
4. Confiscation of the property of all emigrants and rebels.
5. Centralisation of credit in the hands of the State, by means of a national bank with State capital and an exclusive monopoly.

6. Centralisation of the means of communication and transport in the hands of the State.

7. Extension of factories and instruments of production owned by the State; the bringing into cultivation of waste-lands, and the improvement of the soil generally in accordance with a common plan.

8. Equal liability of all to labour. Establishment of industrial armies, especially for agriculture.

9. Combination of agriculture with manufacturing industries; gradual abolition of the distinction between town and country, by a more equable distribution of the population over the country.

10. Free education for all children in public schools. Abolition of children's factory labour in its present form. Combination of education with industrial production, &c., &c. (6:505).

It is notable that nationalizing industry is absent from this list. Private ownership of industry and other enterprises seems to continue (albeit hemmed in by regulation), with its gradual extinction rather than immediate abolition envisaged. A clear vision of the future is proposed 'in which the free development of each is the condition for the free development of all' (6:506), a catchy slogan whose meaning echoes Marx's earlier claim that 'In the individual expression of my life I would have directly created your expression of your life, and therefore in my individual activity I would have directly *confirmed* and *realised* my true nature, my *human* nature, my *communal nature*' (3:227–8). There is no discussion of alienation or invocation of 'species-being' here. Some child labour remains, evidently permanently.[10] It should be noted too that while the bourgeoisie would be swept away eventually, at least through abolishing inheritance, Marx did not oppose compensating property owners; respecting rural estate holders, at least, Engels recalled in 1894 that 'Marx told me (and how many times!) that in his opinion we would get off cheapest if we could buy out the whole lot of them' (27:500).

How original were the *Manifesto*'s ten proposals? Obvious debts exist to Thomas Carlyle in the notion of conscripted 'industrial armies', and to Louis Blanc, the Saint-Simonians and Gans, in the organization of labour. There is also a deeper sense of a modern apocalypse, of a theologically inspired drama played out on the barricades in which the original Golden Age would be restored and mankind assume its innocence anew as revolution assured humanity's redemption from its original sin, private property. *The German Ideology* had insisted that the 'abolition of the contradiction between town and country is one of the first conditions of communal life' (5:64). It had still adverted to the 'setting up of a communal domestic economy' (this was clearly Engels) where 'the supersession of individual economy is inseparable from the supersession of the family' (5:76). But small-scale communities could not organize themselves vis-à-vis the international market. Although one sentence in the *Manifesto*'s programme proposed redistributing population to end distinctions between town and country, the communitarian socialism of Owen and Fourier essentially has been abandoned here. From now on, following Saint-Simon and Hess, both Marx and Engels and most later Marxists treated the centralized state as the appropriate scope for thinking about socialism. Combining education and production, as the programme propounded, was Owenite and Fourierist, however, as was the standpoint of the critique of political economy. Advocating co-operative production was still to come. The abolition of inheritance and the statist scheme of industrial management were Saint-Simonian, and Hess was still a presence here too.

The *Manifesto*'s programme implies that Marx thought that urban, technologically dominated modernity promised a vastly superior form of human existence compared to that of preceding societies. Communism was possible at lower stages of productive development. But introducing it in primitive circumstances – 'barracks communism' – implied reducing all to the lowest standard of living. All the benefits of relative abundance promised in the *Manifesto* would be lost, as well as the potential for all-roundedness. In the cases of Stalin and Mao in particular, as we will see, embracing Marxism necessitated a breakneck race to industrialize. Marx asserts in the *Manifesto* that the end point of modern existence is a high standard of living relatively equally divided, not reducing work time or making labour satisfying or creative. What, then, has happened to Fourier's vision, touched on in *The German Ideology*? Has a technology- and commodity-centred vision prevailed over one devoted to overcoming the division of labour? In communist society, we are told, accumulated labour will be 'but a means to widen, to enrich, to promote the existence of the labourer', instead of labour being as at present 'but a means to increase accumulated labour' (6:499). These tensions remained in Marx's thought.

The *Manifesto*'s main development is that centralized states are now tasked with superintending production. What was called 'communal management' in earlier texts (e.g., 6:305, 353) now became the state's responsibility. As the 'Principles of Communism' expressed it, 'the proletariat will see itself compelled to go always further, to concentrate all capital, all agriculture, all industry, all transport, and all exchange more and more in the hands of the State' (6:351). But the *existing* state is also termed 'a committee for managing the common affairs of the whole bourgeoisie' (6:486). Elsewhere Marx recognized that not all states could be characterized this way. Even in the modern world power was often shared with the landed aristocracy, indeed deliberately to shift the burdens of power and to avoid being associated with the naked armed power of the state, which if fused with resentment of exploitation could instigate revolt.[11]

This reveals a contradiction in Marx's system which would dog all forms of Marxism subsequently. To manage entire economies the state needs to be strengthened immensely. Yet eventually this state, as an agency of class oppression and as an alien body separated from civil society, was to disappear. So what should we call the remaining administrative bodies? It is unclear why Marx's emphasis upon centralization did not imply further discussion of bureaucracy. The new apparatus or interim state, after all, would be vastly more complex than that it replaced. Was Marx so blinded by his critique of Hegel that he could not envision such a scenario? Clearly he presumed that only administrators of production would remain, namely workers paid a plebeian wage, not an independent bureaucracy in the Hegelian sense. Yet national planned production would require large numbers of such administrators, many of whom would have to be specialists. Engels later wrote, 'If we had to start wielding power tomorrow we should need engineers, chemists, agronomists' (27:548). Marx's reluctance to countenance persistent specialization, or to reconcile this with all-round development, failed him at this point.

Highly centralized states posed other dangers too. In March 1850 Marx was linked with a document, later famous for its extremism, which insisted that German workers accept 'the task of the really revolutionary party to carry through the strictest centralisation', and urged them not to 'allow themselves to be misguided by the democratic talk of freedom for the communities, of self-government, etc.' (10:285). Possibly, however, this circular to Communist League branches 'seriously distorts Marx and Engels' views on both the timing of revolutionary developments and the use of terror'.[12] It was not signed by Marx, and its Blanquist overtones were probably anathema to him, despite the need for alliances with Blanquist exiles after 1849. They wanted to establish communism immediately after the revolution. Marx resisted this idea, and especially the former Prussian officer and Communist League leader August Willich's hint that the guillotine could hasten the process, insisting instead that 'a series of years' of 'education and gradual development' might be required.[13]

Marx's hope in the *Manifesto* that nationalism would disappear proved equally overoptimistic. 'The working class knows no country', he proclaimed, echoing *The German Ideology*'s observation that in the proletariat 'nationality is already dead' (5:73) and Engels' insistence that nationalities would 'merge with one another and thereby supersede themselves' (6:103). Proletarian internationalism and cosmopolitanism would erode previous forms of national chauvinism as class consciousness succeeded that of nationhood. Marx did not imagine that nationalism would remain a powerful focus of group, ethnic, religious and linguistic identity, and for aspirations for freedom for the next century and more, or that economic competition as well as reaction to conquest and empire might indeed intensify national loyalties. To Isaiah Berlin this was a key weakness in his thought.[14] (Mikhail Bakunin and some of his followers, like James Guillaume, also accused

Marx of being a German nationalist in the chauvinistic sense.[15]) Nor did Marx perceive the limitations of a Eurocentric vision for liberation movements elsewhere. He may have inherited some of this inability to appraise nationalism clearly from Hegel. But this blindness is of a piece with his incapacity to theorize adequately other forms of group identity, like race and ethnicity. There was some evidence here of what we might today term a 'republican' ethos, though Marx assumed that patriotism would be supplanted by internationalism, presumably without the loss of love of place. Thus in 1850 Marx apparently commended the idea that the Universal Society of Revolutionary Communists would 'form ties of solidarity between all sections of the revolutionary communist party, causing national divisions to disappear according to the principle of republican fraternity' (10:614).[16]

Marx's views on these matters, however, did alter gradually. Most importantly, he came to see Ireland's claim to nationhood as just. In 1867 he wrote that he had 'sought by every means at my disposal to incite the English workers to demonstrate in favour of FENIANISM' and now regarded Ireland's separation from England as 'inevitable', having once thought it 'impossible' (42:460).[17] By 1869 he insisted English workers had to 'separate their attitude towards Ireland quite definitely from that of the ruling classes' and ally with the Irish, forming a 'free federal relationship', before they could make any progress themselves (43:390). England would *'never accomplish anything* BEFORE IT HAS GOT RID OF IRELAND', he emphasized to Engels (43:398), adding some months later that promoting this was the International Working Men's Association's 'most important object' (43:475). Imperialism, in other words, was a major barrier to radical political consciousness. Crucially, too, by the 1860s Marx regarded the 'rights of self-determination of nations' as the chief means of curbing 'Muscovite influence in Europe' (42:204). Here Polish independence was key.

Amidst collapse, chaos, the revolutionaries' defeat and their flight into exile, reckoning on the failures of 1848 took many forms. Two of Marx's subsequent works from this period, *The Class Struggles in France* (1850) and *The Eighteenth Brumaire of Louis Bonaparte*, apply the new historical method and its class analysis to current events. For Marx 1848 proved first and foremost that the idea that republican states stood above class and represented the common interest was illusory. Parliamentarism had failed the proletariat. The peasantry and petty bourgeois in particular had rallied to the forces of order and tradition. They were blinded: Marx constantly uses the language of mystery and illusion. By 1852 the *Manifesto*'s short-term optimism had evaporated. The world was not yet modern enough to fulfil its predictions. For a time, at least, the scene shifted back to the prospect of revolution in Britain, the most advanced industrial nation and thus the prototype of capitalist development.

Marx's analysis now revealed the limitations of the theories and strategies of 1848. The first problem was forming a successful revolutionary coalition. The *Manifesto* introduces the proletariat as the modern working class. Though a majority of Europe's population, peasants were to Marx essentially reactionary, and obstructed progress. They suffered from what he contemptuously condemned here as 'the idiocy of rural life' (6:488). They were fast disappearing in Britain, converted into hired labourers or proletarians. Such would be their fate elsewhere.[18] Marx has been accused of having an in-built bias against peasants which would eventually spell disaster for millions.[19] In 1872 he reiterated his belief in the superior efficiency of large-scale cultivation (23:132). Three years later he warned that peasants would oppose any revolution unless they were won over by measures which both improved their condition and assisted the transformation from private to collective land ownership 'so that the peasant arrives at this economically of his own accord' (24:517). At the very least it is clear that he thought small-scale peasant proprietorship was doomed to disappear, following the same rules which governed the concentration of industrial production in the hands of a few large enterprises. The prospect of a co-operative socialist agricultural policy rested on this premise. Yet even in Western Europe small farms actually proliferated with the growth of capitalism in the nineteenth century. There was moreover no evidence they were less productive. So on this vital question Marx was simply wrong. Yet he still imagined generations would pass before collectivization could be achieved on the land, or so Engels later stated. This implies that Marx thought persuasion and material incentives, rather than force, were preferable means of achieving this vital end.

The second problem was more narrowly political. In 1850, *Class Struggles in France* developed for the first time the later key concept of the 'dictatorship of the proletariat', describing 'the *class dictatorship of the proletariat as the necessary transit point to the abolition of class distinctions generally*' (10:127).[20] Marx also termed this the 'dictatorship of the working class' (10:69). In April 1850, and again in June, the short-lived Universal Society of Revolutionary Communists used 'dictatorship of the proletariat'. Other hands were at work in these documents, however, so we cannot be sure that this was Marx's phrasing. Though it was later central to Leninism, Marx and Engels only used the term some eleven times in total.[21] They never meant it to imply the dictatorship of one individual, a view Weitling had mooted, which Marx rejected as 'nonsensical', urging instead that the provisional government 'must consist of the most heterogeneous elements, which by means of an exchange of views have to agree on the most appropriate mode of administration' (7:556–7).[22] Nor did they mean Blanqui's dictatorship of a small revolutionary group.

So what did the phrase imply? Did it mean a Roman-style institution, limited in duration, with a fixed purpose, and accountable to some other group, thus not a despotism? Or was it akin to the 'dictatorship of the bourgeoisie', the normal, coercive rule of the middle class over the workers, however spuriously 'democratic'? Did it imply what would later be called 'totalitarian democracy'?[23] Contextual study of the term and related expressions reveals that for Marx it meant little more than an interim, post-revolutionary, temporarily extra-legal mechanism to be succeeded by a new legal order. We get no sense, however, of what kind of constitution might follow. This dictatorship would be by a democratic majority: it was a class dictatorship of the largest class. Dictatorship of the *proletariat* – this is where the emphasis lies – was thus meant to be *juxtaposed* with Blanquist ideas of dictatorship by a small group. It meant class rule, as opposed to personal or minority rule.[24]

Nonetheless the concept confirms Marx's new political strategy in light of the defeats of 1848. Writing in March 1852 to Joseph

Weydemeyer, he explained what was novel in his new perspective. He had not discovered class struggle, rather

> My own contribution was 1. to show that the *existence of classes* is merely bound up with *certain historical phases in the development of production*; 2. that the class struggle necessarily leads to the *dictatorship of the proletariat*; 3. that this dictatorship itself constitutes no more than a transition to the *abolition of all classes* and to a *classless society*. (39:62–5)[25]

Marx did not use the phrase again for over twenty years, until the *Critique of the Gotha Programme* (1875) defined the 'revolutionary dictatorship of the proletariat' as the 'political transition period' between capitalism and communism (24:95). It was Engels, not Marx, who stated baldly in 1891, 'Look at the Paris Commune. That was the Dictatorship of the Proletariat', and reiterated that 'our party and the working class can only come to power under the form of a democratic republic. This is even the specific form for the dictatorship of the proletariat' (27:191, 227).

It seems clear then that by 1850 neither Marx nor Engels accepted Blanqui's idea of 'the small number of those who accomplished the coup and who themselves are, at first, organised under the dictatorship of one or several individuals' (24:13).[26] Marx wanted a dictatorship not of minority conspirators, but of the proletariat as far and away the largest class in society. This was crucial to its self-emancipation. 'Dictatorship' referred to a mode of proceeding, not a constitution. In 1849 Marx stressed that for the will of the majority to be 'one and the same' this majority had to consist of '*one single class*' with the same interests (8:272). (But the problem of the peasantry remains: is the 'single class' the 'working class', which might include it, or the 'proletariat', which did not?) In 1852, at least, Marx regarded universal suffrage as the '*political supremacy of the working class*' (11:336). Responding to Bakunin later, Marx insisted that elections were determined by the economic interrelations of the voters, such that 'as soon as the functions have ceased to be political, 1) government functions no longer exist; 2) the distribution of general functions has become a routine matter which entails no domination; 3) elections lose their present political character' (24:519). In the changed circumstances of 1895 Engels again reiterated the centrality of universal suffrage in a new introduction to *The Class Struggles in France*. Once a 'means of deception', universal suffrage was now 'an instrument of emancipation'. This meant that 'The time of surprise attacks, of revolutions carried through by small conscious minorities at the head of masses lacking consciousness is past' (27:520). And so, until 1917, it might have seemed.

CHAPTER 6

Exile, 1850s–1880s

Condemned by the Cologne police as 'politically unreliable', Marx had been forced into exile in Brussels in early 1845. When revolution broke out his wife Jenny was arrested and interrogated, but failed to divulge that Karl had donated a substantial sum of money to the German workers in Brussels to purchase arms. Here, in 1848, he too was arrested, confined with a *'raving madman*, whom he was obliged to fight every moment' (6:562), and expelled to Paris on a charge of 'vagabondage'. In April 1848 Marx returned to Cologne to edit the *Neue Rheinische Zeitung*, its title echoing his earlier platform, which was soon the leading advocate of 'red republicanism'. In February 1849 Marx stood trial for inciting rebellion. He was acquitted following a vigorous defence of a free press, and even thanked by the jury for his informative analysis of events. But the journal was banned in May, and Marx was exiled to Britain, arriving in London in early June.

Here he remained the rest of his life, for the next thirty-four years, often sequestered in the great domed British Museum Reading Room after it opened in 1857 (seat G7 was his reputed favourite). Early on he sank into wretched poverty, and he was frequently heavily in debt. In desperation Marx even applied for a job as a railway clerk in 1862, but was rejected because of his illegible handwriting. For some time in the early years he could hardly work. Then his projects proceeded by fits and starts. He was frequently diverted to new and complex subjects – learning Danish and Russian, for example – then, when he disliked the results, recommencing his earlier studies; then diverted again by the

need for paid journalistic employment; then again by irritating polemics against him. He found it hard to concentrate on one task, and
was never happy with anything he regarded as imperfect. Engels complained that so long as Marx had not read a book he felt was important
'you won't be able to settle down to writing' (38:330) – a well-known
cause of writer's block, and clearly the flip side of Marx's enormous
self-confidence. Chronic illness exacerbated all these tendencies. So
publishers' deadlines came and went, and eventually most of a lifetime would be swallowed by one great work. Thankfully, however, he
could rely for financial support upon Engels, who had returned from
Germany in 1850, having experienced combat under Willich during the
revolution. Engels spent most of the next twenty years at his father's
firm in Manchester, starting at £100 a year plus 10 per cent of the profits, which allowed him to support Marx regularly. (No evidence exists
of any effort to improve the lot of the workers there.) And, not opposed
to inheritance in practice, Marx used several to help stave off the debt
collectors.

In early exile in London a steady stream of visitors made their way
to Marx's humble abode. Later the crowds grew even larger, and sometimes Marx's resourceful housekeeper, Helene Demuth, had to bring
them to order. Many evenings were spent, the exiled journalist Wilhelm Liebknecht later recalled, at the German Workers' Educational
Association, a microcosm of socialist sociability, whose 'massive ma-
hogany table, the shining pewter-pots, the foaming stout, the prospect
of a genuine English beefsteak with accessories, the long clay pipes in-
viting to a smoke', made a home away from home. Here by day, in 1850–
51, Marx lectured the workers on political economy, writing formulae
on the blackboard and quizzing them after his exposition if they failed
to query him. He played chess with some, like Liebknecht, who judged
him a poor strategist. But 'when he loses the game, he is most disagree-
able', Demuth once complained, having borne a note from Jenny im-
ploring him not to play.[1] For Marx was indeed a sore loser.

Marx was speedily dragged down into the poisonous swamp of refu-
gee squabbles, which were riven with 'petty jealousies, intrigues, base-
nesses and rivalries', not to mention police spies. The only thing that
united many was their 'common and fanatical hatred of Marx...their

bête noir' (38:431–2). He offered some account of these in the characteristically satirical, sarcastic *The Great Men of the Exile*, which however fell into the hands of the Prussian police and was not printed until 1930.[2] (Don't 'write with too much rancour and irritation', Jenny advised him in 1844, but the advice fell on deaf ears; 3:579.) Despite close personal friendships with some workers, Marx often found real proletarians disappointing. 'Voila our Straubingers [travelling journeymen], it's tough that world history should have to be made with people such as these', he wrote of some Cologne workers in 1852 (39:137). He fell out with many associates, including Willich, who challenged Marx to a duel which his friend Conrad Schramm accepted in his stead, receiving a bullet in the head for his troubles (he survived). Willich's chief associate in the Communist League, Karl Schapper, was also soon *persona non grata*, along with a host of exiled bourgeois democrats. In September 1850 the League split, the vast majority, mainly workers, siding with Willich and Schapper, a rump of mostly more educated artisans with Marx. The former expelled Marx from the League, and continued to plot insurrection in Germany. Resentful that Marx headed a party of intellectuals, they saw themselves as the true proletarian heirs of the movement. Emigration soon sapped their numbers, however, especially after the 1849 California Gold Rush. Even Marx considered heading for America. (We can imagine him as a prospector peering into his gold pan high in the Sierra Nevada, musing about surplus value.) By early 1853 the League ceased to exist.[3]

In the 1860s Marx was again caught up in a lengthy and vituperative controversy when he accused a former radical, Karl Vogt, of being in the pay of Napoleon III. Again he squandered valuable time in a tedious polemic. Bakunin thought petty spite was an alarmingly large motive for Marx, who in turn felt compelled to defend himself. But he remained close to the more left-wing Chartists, notably Ernest Jones and George Julian Harney, though the latter transferred his support to Willich and Schapper in 1851, while Jones was excoriated for countenancing alliances with the middle class. But isolation was also a tonic to Marx. 'I am a *critic*', he insisted to the poet Ferdinand Freiligrath in 1860.[4] Criticism one could do alone, or at least with an Engels to lean on.

Marx's friends and acquaintances, as well as his enemies, have left some telling sketches of his character in these years. Like everyone he had failings and strengths. Marx's virtues and vices as a man were closely allied. He was hypersensitive and easily wounded by criticism, yet caustic and merciless with opponents. Prone to overconfidence, perhaps possessed of a bit of a messiah complex, he was overly keen to assert his own superiority and originality, which meant disparaging others. Though he despised pomposity he often appeared haughty and imperious. In the right cause these were all useful qualities. Many who encountered Marx felt that anyone so clever and self-assured must surely be right. But Marx was not always right, and never gave ground to an opponent easily, even over a game of chess. He had many of the prejudices of his age, and could appear racist and anti-Semitic, for he could not resist any opportunity to insult an opponent.[5] His contempt for the smaller Slavic peoples echoed his ethnic pride as a German. Curiously, he also thought phrenology a useful way of assessing people.

Amongst his associates, the Saxon radical F. A. Sorge later recalled, Marx was often viewed as a 'friendly, pleasant, likable man'. He was genial, liked a glass or three of beer and good company, and could tell jokes, laugh heartily and recite poetry better than most, thanks to an excellent memory. He could be harsh with critics (once, when a gentleman pointedly asked Marx who would clean shoes in the future society, he replied sharply, 'You should').[6] But he was kind, helpful and hospitable to several generations of fellow refugees and socialists who made their way to his various London homes. Wilhelm Liebknecht saw him almost daily for some twelve years, and praised his 'generous heart that throbbed so warmly for everything human and for everything bearing human features'. He remembered, too, that Marx could 'stand opposition, although not unfrequently he flew into a passion over it'.[7] Another confidant, the tailor Friedrich Lessner, emphasized that 'Marx always attached an extreme importance to meeting and talking with working men', and recalled that his 'humour was irrepressible, his laugh a very hearty one'. Lessner met him first in early 1848, and left this portrait:

Marx was still a young man, being about 28 years old; nevertheless he strongly impressed all of us. Marx was of middle height, broad-shouldered, and of an energetic bearing. The forehead was high and beautifully moulded, the hair was thick and jet-black, his look penetrating, his mouth already showed that sarcastic trait so dreaded by his opponents. His words were short and concise; he did not utter superfluous words, each sentence was a thought, and each thought a necessary link in his argument. He spoke with a convincing logic; there was nothing dreamy about him.[8]

Then there were his enemies. The radical journalist Karl Heinzen called Marx 'a cross between a cat and an ape', and remembered him thundering at opponents in an argument, 'I will annihilate you!' The revolutionary émigré Carl Schurz, a Union general during the American Civil War, recalled having 'never seen a man whose bearing was so provoking and intolerable', and recollected his 'biting scorn' for all who crossed him. 'To no opinion which differed from his own', Schurz added, 'did he accord the honour of even condescending consideration. Every one who contradicted him he treated with abject contempt'.[9] A police spy who met Marx around 1852 defined the 'dominating trait of his character' as 'a limitless ambition and love of power'. A sometime friend, Gustav Techow, wrote that 'this man with his fine intellect is lacking in nobility of soul. *I am convinced that a most dangerous personal ambition has eaten away all the good in him.*'[10] The Russian intellectual Pavel Annenkov, too, said he was 'the embodiment of a democratic dictator', and described him in detail in 1846:

Marx himself was a man of the type made up of energy, will power, and invincible conviction – a type of man extremely remarkable also in outward appearance. With a thick mop of black hair on his head, his hairy hands, dressed in a coat buttoned diagonally across his chest, he maintained the appearance of a man with the right and authority to command respect, whatever guise he took and whatever he did. All his motions were awkward but vigorous and self-confident, all his manners ran athwart conventional usages in social intercourse but were proud and somehow guarded, and his shrill voice with its metallic ring marvelously suited the radical pronouncements over things and people which he uttered. Marx was now in the habit of speaking no other way than in such categorical pronouncements over which still reigned, it should be added, a certain shrill note superimposed on everything he said. This note expressed his firm conviction that it was his mission to control minds, to legislate over them and to lead them in his train. Before me stood the figure of the democratic dictator incarnate, just as it might be pictured in one's imagination during times devoted to fantasy.[11]

Finally, in 1879, the liberal-minded Crown Princess Victoria asked the Scottish MP Mountstuart Elphinstone Grant Duff to make Marx's acquaintance. He found 'a short, rather small man with grey hair and beard which contrast strangely with a still dark moustache'. The face 'somewhat round, the forehead well shaped and filled up – the eye rather hard but the whole expression rather pleasant than not, by no means that of a gentleman who is in the habit of eating babies in their cradles'. He thought Marx a 'well-informed nay learned man', if 'slightly cynical' – as well he might appear when quizzed in such company (24:580).

Marx was of course also a husband and father. In 1843 he married his childhood sweetheart, Jenny von Westphalen (1814–81), a beautiful, much-courted baron's daughter four years his senior, who used the title of 'baroness' on the visiting cards she had printed in London.[12] Little good it did her, though a German paper when reporting a recitation by Mrs Marx at its New Year's Eve banquet found it 'very impressive to watch exceptionally gifted ladies trying to improve the intellectual faculties of the proletariat'.[13] Lessner described her as 'the excellent Mrs. Marx, a tall, very beautiful woman, and of noble bearing, but for all that so extremely good-natured, amiable, spiritual, and so free from any pride and stiffness, that she seemed like one's own mother or sister'.[14] But though she and 'the Moor' (as Jenny and Engels called Marx, on account of his swarthy appearance) were deeply attached, and she bore him eight children, their family life suffered from the strain of dire poverty. In later years they grew apart, and she was often angry and irritable at him and the children. Marx's personality was often an obstacle. Even when young he was no good with money. As a student he borrowed frequently from his father. Mastering the intricacies of capitalism did nothing to assist managing his own household. Jenny shared from youth his sympathy with the poor, however. She trudged in the footsteps of his intellectual odyssey, reading Feuerbach in 1843, and later transcribing many drafts of Marx's works. When they married that year Marx took forty-five volumes of books with him on the honeymoon, and filled 250 pages of notes. But Jenny was soon pregnant anyway.

In exile in Paris in 1843–4 the Marxes lived a normal bourgeois lifestyle. Their friends included the poets Heinrich Heine and Georg Herwegh, the Young Hegelian Arnold Ruge and Marx's future great antagonist, Bakunin. The latter found Marx's conversation 'always instructive and witty, when it was not inspired by petty hate, which alas! was only too often the case'.[15] In Brussels in 1845 Marx had to swear off political activities and relied on loans from Engels, who appeared for a time with an Irish working-class girl from Manchester whom Jenny refused to meet formally (class prejudices died hard). Jenny's mother sent her faithful maid Helene Demuth, 'Lenchen', to help the Marxes. She remained with the family until 1883, when she became Engels' housekeeper, and she was eventually buried in Highgate cemetery beside Karl and Jenny. It is generally accepted that she bore a child by Marx in 1851, Frederick Demuth, who was given up for adoption to an English working-class family after Marx asked Engels to declare himself the father. 'Freddy' became a machinist and a close friend of his half-sister Eleanor, notwithstanding her great shock when, at Engels' deathbed, she discovered the secret of his paternity.[16]

Jenny was indeed long-suffering. Her first child, also Jenny, was born in 1844. In Brussels a second daughter, Laura, followed in 1845. A boy, Edgar or 'Musch', appeared in December 1846. The 'living soul' of the house, he died of gastric fever in Marx's arms in April 1855. Marx, whose love of the young was often remarked on by visitors – he would even play with stray children he met on walks – wrote that 'only now do I know what real unhappiness is' (39:533). Jenny bore a fourth child, Heinrich, in November 1849, but he was sickly and the bailiffs even impounded the dying child's cradle. Another daughter, Franziska, also lived only a short time (1851–2), and Jenny had to beg money for her coffin. Eleanor was born in 1855. Another child died in 1857 before being named. In 1860 Jenny contracted smallpox, and the children had to be quickly removed from the house. She wrote that Marx nursed her with 'the utmost tenderness' (41:573). 'The devil alone knows what misfortunes we suffer', he lamented to Engels (41:216).

From 1850 to 1856 the Marxes lived in near-squalor in Dean Street, Soho, where sometimes eight people inhabited two rooms and had only bread and potatoes to eat. Prussian police agents observed them closely, noting visitors, riding near them on omnibuses, sitting in cafés beside them. Marx later admitted that 'GENERALLY SPEAKING I am not good at detecting spies', but once became so fed up with one he 'turned round and stared at him with my notorious EYEGLASS' (monocle), at which he 'doffed his hat' and disappeared. (44:206). One even entered the household, where he found, at the centre of world revolution, 'not one clean or decent piece of furniture in either room, but everything is broken, tattered and torn, with thick dust over everything and the greatest untidiness everywhere'. The only table was littered with 'manuscripts, books and newspapers, besides the children's toys, bits and pieces from his wife's sewing basket, and cups with broken rims, dirty spoons, knives, forks, candle-sticks, an inkpot, tumblers, Dutch clay pipes, tobacco ash'. In addition the whole flat was befogged by tobacco and coal smoke.[17] It was no place for a family, or for emancipating humanity.

Crises in the Marx household finances were more regular than those in the capitalist system. In these years creditors and pawnbrokers became intimates; one of the latter was even known as 'Uncle'. Once Marx tried to pawn Jenny's family silver and was arrested on suspicion of stealing it; he spent a day and a half in gaol. In the winter of 1852 he could not even go out: his coat had been pawned. Another time, just as *Capital* was ready for the publisher, both his clothes and watch were at the pawnbroker's. When he could Marx fled home, leaving at 9 a.m. for the ethereal realms of the British Museum Reading Room (the coolest place in London on a hot summer's day, he proclaimed), lunching at the Museum Tavern, and returning late, often via the pubs on Tottenham Court Road. One night, after a crawl through eighteen such establishments, Marx, Edgar Bauer and Liebknecht broke some street lamps and were hotly pursued for a time by three or four policemen.

Earlier that evening a very drunken Marx had assured a group of English Oddfellows that Germany would eventually triumph over all other nations. He often worked through the night, getting by on a few hours' sleep and endangering his health. Occasionally he picked up small pieces of journalism, chiefly for the *New-York Daily Tribune*. His health was not improved by constantly smoking the cheapest cigars. His eyes often troubled him owing to so much late-night work. So did his haemorrhoids, his liver and rheumatism in his back and right arm. Then a painful skin disease brought recurrent boils or carbuncles (his 'monsters'), which meant he often could only write standing up. Insomnia plagued him recurrently. Yet his children remembered many happy times, too, not least when clambering on their father's back when he obligingly played donkey with them, or when he read out loud the whole of Homer, Shakespeare and much more.

An inheritance in 1856 stayed the misery, allowing the family to rent a small house near Hampstead Heath and permitting what Marx called 'the SHOW OF RESPECTABILITY' (40:331), which included educating his girls at the South Hampstead College for Ladies. But many more crises awaited. Marx considered declaring bankruptcy, even as his carbuncles attacked again. But from 1864 onwards the family were able to move to larger premises, and finally, following several more inheritances, to free themselves from debt. They even gave a ball in 1864. With a capital of £1,500 Marx made (some suppose) more than £400 speculating on the stock market and revelled in being able to 'relieve the enemy of his money'.[18] But two years later he was again begging Engels for rent money.

When volume one of the 'Bible of the working classes', as Engels called *Capital* (35:35), finally appeared in 1867, it found few readers and brought no financial respite. Marx ruefully recalled his mother's sarcastic aside: 'How right my mother was: "If only Karell had made capital instead of etc."' (43:25). He found it difficult to return to the topic, and made hardly any headway with volume two. By 1868, though, he had achieved sufficient respectability to be named 'Constable of the Vestry of St. Pancras', a minor and mainly honorific office, though the British government refused him citizenship. (A confidential letter from Scotland Yard stated that he had 'not been loyal to his own

King and Country'.[19]) Then in 1869 Engels sold his father's cotton factory, which had brought him an income of as much as £1,000 a year (equivalent to perhaps £400,000 today), and provided Marx with a regular stipend of around £350 annually, typically sent weekly in £5 or £10 notes cut in half. This helped, amongst other things, to provide for the crowd of destitute political and other refugees who converged on Marx's house in the late 1870s and early 1880s. These were kept at bay in part by Lenchen, now described as 'an ancient German woman', who demanded letters of introduction from all Germans seeking entry (24:568–9). The many British visitors included the stockbroker-turned-communist H. M. Hyndman, who praised Marx as 'undoubtedly a genius'.[20] Hyndman wanted to form a working-class political party and his own works, especially *England for All* (1881), adapted parts of *Capital* without permission, predictably producing a rift with Marx. But Hyndman's Democratic Federation, founded in 1881 and renamed the Social Democratic Federation in 1884, became Britain's first substantial Marxist-leaning organization.

Marx's wife died of cancer on 2 December 1881. Their daughters' subsequent fate was not happy.[21] All adored their father, and possessed his impossibly high standards and expectations. Marx's daughter Jenny married a French revolutionary journalist, Charles Longuet, but died, also of cancer, in early 1883. Eleanor Marx ('Tussy') moved in with the writer Edward Aveling in 1872, although he was married, and played a leading role in the Social Democratic Federation and then the breakaway Socialist League, where William Morris was active. An indefatigable activist, organizer and trade union leader, she was her father's true political heir, even travelling to the USA to lecture for the cause. Alone in the family she identified herself as Jewish. She learned Yiddish, and said her 'happiest moments' were spent amongst East End Jewish workpeople. Aveling was often attached to Engels' purse-strings, however, and had many other female admirers. Notwithstanding her free-love principles, Eleanor poisoned herself in March 1898 after he married a young actress.[22] Despite Marx's initial disapproval, Laura Marx married the Cuban-born French socialist Paul Lafargue. They both killed themselves in 1911 after concluding that they could no longer serve the communist movement.[23] Marx found his legal sons-in-law disappointing: Longuet was 'the last of the Proudhonists' and Lafargue 'the last of the Bakunists', Marx complained to Engels, adding 'may the devil take them!' (46:375).[24] Marx once lamented that his great regret in life was not that he had sacrificed his fortune for the cause of revolution. That, he insisted, he would gladly do over again. It was rather that, in marrying, he had brought so much suffering to others, and by that more upon himself. Though Marx loved his children dearly, this was too true.

CHAPTER 7

Political Economy

Most readers who approach Marx's economic writings are more concerned with the fact that capitalism generates exploitation and inequality, injustice and poverty, misery and chronic crises than explaining precisely how it does all this.[1] Nonetheless we must have some sense of why Marx felt his theory of surplus value was such a vital discovery. We also need to know whether Marx in his later works retained the theory of alienation, the critique of the division of labour and the goal of all-roundedness elaborated in 1844, and how he envisioned a socialist system of production and exchange operating. Finally, we need to assess how far co-operation now served as the means of unifying these themes for Marx, and how its political character addressed the theory of alienation. To answer these questions we must consider in particular the *Grundrisse* or *Outlines of the Critique of Political Economy* – the 'completest' of Marx's works, as McLellan calls it[2] – which was written in 1857–8 as a first draft of *Capital*, but not published until 1939. When composing it Marx referred to his 1843–5 notebooks, which helps account for elements of continuity between the two periods. Let us first, however, briefly introduce Marx's magnum opus.[3]

'It seems as though the wretched book will never get finished. It weighs like a nightmare on us all', complained Marx's wife Jenny in November 1863 (41:585). But the first volume of the 'LEVIATHAN' (41:585), *Capital: A Critique of Political Economy*, finally reached the light of day in Hamburg in 1867. The English translation had to wait another twenty years. What distinguishes *Capital* from Marx's other (draft) economic writings of this period is its polished style, rigorous organization and relentless pace. Marx also uses a vast array of evidence – often drawn from factory inspectors' reports ('Blue Books') – to detail just what capital is and does, and to reach the inescapable conclusion that people under capitalism are of little or no worth at all compared with profit.

Few readers, however, ever penetrate the great text very far. Reading *Capital* has for many been like hacking a trail through the jungle. Marx described his masterpiece as 'the most terrible missile that has ever been hurled at the bourgeoisie' (42:358). That we can concede. Readers journeying into the text, however, often feel exhausted by the mass of complex detail, even before reaching the mathematical formulae. Though Marx said he only 'coquetted' with Hegel's method in *Capital* (35:19), his language is often obtuse. Many have lost their bearings early on in the journey, and quickly retreated. William Morris began the attempt around 1883 and later recalled suffering 'agonies of confusion of the brain over reading the pure economics of that great work'.[4] The great German Social Democratic leader August Bebel barely got past the beginning. Fidel Castro boasted of reaching page 370, about halfway.[5] On first encountering the book Ho Chi Minh used it as a pillow, perhaps hoping to gain by osmosis what close study failed to yield.[6] Most later non-economists shy away from a full-scale confrontation.

Yet occasionally we emerge upon vistas of startling beauty and grandeur, and see why Marx termed his great endeavour 'a work of art' (42:174). It revels in irony and satire, and is rich in literary allusion, leading us sometimes to wonder whether this is economic theory at all. And indeed in some ways it is not: it is a book about humanity and inhumanity, liberation and slavery, on a grand, indeed apocalyptic, scale. It is a biting, compelling work, drawing the reader in time after time with vignettes of the suffering of individual workers and the savage brutality of factory life. We stand amazed, too, at the astonishing effrontery of capital, Genghis Khan–like, sweeping across the panorama of all previous history and laying waste to all before it on an epochal scale. The book remains a classic of modern social history long after its economics have ceased to interest most.

Capital is also a moral fable which promises a redemptive happy ending to the titanic struggle of the virtuous poor against the nefarious rich. At one level it is one long moralistic declamation against a system fuelled by sordid greed. 'We should be appalled', Marx wrote in the first German edition, 'at the state of things at home' if conditions there were akin to England, as he declaimed against 'the most violent, mean and malignant passions of the human breast, the Furies of private interest'. Capitalism existed in 'a form more brutal or more humane, according to the degree of development of the working class itself' (35:9). Marx's chief concern was not to declaim, however, but to portray individuals 'only in so far as they are the personifications of economic categories, embodiments of particular class relations and class interests' (35:9–10). Yet a yardstick against which their actions are judged is constantly before us. Marx often compares what ought to be 'normal' with what capitalism does. This is clearest when discussing the working day:

> The capitalistic mode of production (essentially the production
> of surplus value, the absorption of surplus labour) produces thus,
> with the extension of the working day, not only the deterioration of
> human labour power by robbing it of its normal, moral and physical,
> conditions of development and function. It produces also the
> premature exhaustion and death of this labour power itself. It extends
> the labourer's time of production during a given period by shortening
> his actual lifetime. (35:271)

And again:

> The capitalist maintains his rights as a purchaser when he tries to
> make the working day as long as possible, and to make, whenever
> possible, two working days out of one. On the other hand, the peculiar
> nature of the commodity sold implies a limit to its consumption by
> the purchaser, and the labourer maintains his right as seller when he
> wishes to reduce the working day to one of definite normal duration.
> There is here, therefore, an antinomy, right against right, both equally
> bearing the seal of the law of exchanges. Between equal rights force
> decides. (35:243)[7]

Capitalism aims to maximize exploitation of the worker, principally by prolonging the working day, producing what Marx called 'absolute' surplus value, and through intensifying and rationalizing labour to increase output, which generated 'relative' surplus value. Only 'compulsion from society' could inhibit these processes and ensure a 'normal' working day. This campaign had begun with Owen's first efforts to limit working hours, which, once denounced as a 'communistic Utopia', were now ensconced as Factory Acts (35:304).[8] Such legislation proved, of course, that the supposedly 'natural laws' of capitalism could be altered as consciousness of their inhumanity expanded.

The central aim of *Capital* is 'to lay bare the economic law of motion of modern society' (35:10). Volume one commences by analysing commodities and their use and exchange value. The latter is determined by the quantity of abstract labour or 'socially necessary labour time' (35:12) it represents, which is the amount of labour normally required to produce it under average conditions. Unpaid labour accrued by the employer as capital is the basis of modern accumulation and industry. The relentless search for profit in turn is explained as necessarily holding down the workers' standard of living. Volumes two and three, published by Engels in 1885 and 1894, examine circulating capital, dividing this into three aspects, money capital, commodity capital and productive capital, all of which follow the general principle of needing to increase value. But the course of accumulation does not run smoothly. The *Grundrisse* terms the declining rate of profit the 'most important law of political economy'. This might be mitigated by other factors, such as the growing absolute mass of profit as the system expanded, or the possibility of exploitation intensifying, or higher rates of profit being achieved in foreign trade. So this declining rate is also a 'tendency', if nonetheless a key cause of the recurrent crises which proved the system's basic instability. Marx also offers an account of rent. Volume three summarizes capitalism's distinctiveness in two features: the fact that it produces goods as commodities; and the fact that generating surplus value is its chief aim and determining motive.

One of *Capital*'s great themes is that the 'absolute general law of capitalist accumulation', the desire to derive profit from wealth, means that the more wealth, capital, the proletariat and productivity grow, the greater is the pauperism of the many. This echoes the 1844 formulation that 'the worker becomes all the poorer the more wealth he produces' (3:271). But here it is an empirical description of a class rather than a philosophical proposition respecting alienated workers. Economists have been vexed as to whether by 1867 Marx meant absolute immiseration – falling into deep poverty – or relative impoverishment – the gap between rich and poor increasing, but the latter's standard of living possibly increasing. Marx himself later altered his view somewhat, and Engels said Marx assumed that wages were 'extremely elastic' (24:69). Real wages have risen at various stages since the mid-nineteenth century, but have also fallen at times, as in the past decade. The general process by which all this took place was governed by market competition, which Marx regarded not as a 'natural law', but a process which could be historically superseded. Marx was thus highly critical of the German socialist Ferdinand Lassalle's account of the 'iron law of wages', which implied their inevitable decline on Malthusian grounds, rises in wages being negated by growth in family size. He was equally scathing about John Stuart Mill's assumption that the laws of production were 'governed by eternal natural laws independent of history' (28:25), and were rooted in a 'science' of 'facts'.[9] The accumulation of capital also ensured, however, that the average rate of profit tended to decline. Meanwhile both mechanization and competition produced crises of overproduction of goods.

Though we recognize it today as derived from his 1844 perspective, Marx's account of 'The Fetishism of Commodities and Its Secret' is usually regarded as among *Capital*'s key revelations.[10] The leading Bolshevik Nikolai Bukharin described it simply: 'Relations between men present themselves as relations between commodities.' Marx had earlier claimed that 'Money is not a thing, it is a social relation' (6:145). Now he wrote that 'the social character of men's labour appears to them as an objective character stamped upon the product of that labour; because the relation of the producers to the sum total of their own labour is presented to them as a social relation, existing not between themselves, but between the products of their labour'. By a process of reification (*Verdinglichung*, or 'thing-making'), therefore, 'a definite social relation between men…assumes, in their eyes, the fantastic form of a relation between things.' This was analogous to the religious world, where 'the productions of the human brain appear as independent beings endowed with life' (35:83).

We are back on Feuerbach's ground, except that commodities are not wholly imaginary, like the gods, but symbolize real social relations. Think of the phrases often reported in the news, 'In the markets today…' or 'The economy grew this month…' where we imagine something impersonal rather than real people. 'The economy is fine' means 'companies are making good profits' and 'stocks are booming', but it does not follow that 'wages are good and rising'.

Money is a special form of 'universal commodity' which plays a key role in disguising these relations. Hegel's theory of alienation had posited that we need to recognize ourselves in those things outside us which are our own creation. Marx develops this insight substantially here. The social world, technology and economic relations all emanate from combined human effort. To see ourselves in them renders them part of the public sphere, and the product of human will, and awakens the realization that we are public, collective, human beings rather than merely exploited workers. This is crucially a *political* process. Marx now stresses that 'The life-process of society, which is based on the process of material production, does not strip off its mystical veil until it is treated as production by freely associated men, and is consciously regulated by them in accordance with a settled plan' (35:90). Thus the problem of alienation is solved: only the democratic organization of labour can dispel ideology and fetishism by substituting conscious will for supposed 'natural laws'.

Volume one of *Capital* ends with a famous passage respecting the eventual incompatibility of the centralization of capital and socialization of labour. 'Accumulation of wealth at one pole' is 'at the same time accumulation of misery, agony of toil, slavery, ignorance, brutality, mental degradation, at the opposite pole' (35:640). Capitalism arose 'under the stimulus of passions the most infamous, the most sordid, the pettiest, the most meanly odious' (35:749). It would end with 'the revolt of the labouring class, a class always increasing in numbers, and disciplined, united, organised by the very mechanism of the process of capitalist production itself.' Eventually

> The monopoly of capital becomes a fetter upon the mode of production which has sprung up…Centralisation of the means of production and socialisation of labour at least reach a point where they become incompatible with their capitalist integument. The framework is burst asunder. The knell of capitalist private property sounds. The expropriators are expropriated.

And so 'the expropriation of a few usurpers by the mass of the people' completes 'the negation of the negation' (35:750–51).

Sadly for Marx, *Capital* fell stillborn from the press, despite various anonymous and pseudonymous reviews which he and Engels composed to 'bang the drum' (42:427). Engels planned to appear to attack the book *'from the bourgeois point of view'*, but his 'recipes' (as Marx called them) did little to puff up sales (42:445, 449). Just how much good Engels did the cause may indeed be doubted; one of his appraisals began, 'This book will disappoint many a reader' (20:216). He complained, too, that Marx was as 'bashful as a young girl' when it came to promoting his work (42:467).

Marx's theory of surplus value is the best-known theme in his mature economic theory. Devotees regard it as one of Marx's greatest achievements. Others take a very different view. 'I understand nothing of the theory of surplus value', wrote the Austrian socialist leader Victor Adler to Karl Kautsky, adding, 'and, frankly, I don't give a damn.'[11] G. D. H. Cole thought that 'what is novel is the use to which he [Marx] puts the theory, and not the theory itself'.[12] Louis Althusser called it 'the woolly and literally untenable labour theory of value which Marx claimed as his one genuinely personal discovery'.[13] Some have found the proposition as metaphysical as the physiocratic insistence that land produced all value.[14]

The originality of Marx's theory can also be challenged. The Owenites had maintained that 'unequal exchange' occurred when wages were less than the value of what the labourer produced. To John

Francis Bray, 'capitalists and proprietors do no more than give the working man, for his labour of one week, a part of the wealth which they obtained from him the week before!'[15] William Thompson said 'pretended exchanges' were 'made without full and satisfactory equivalents'.[16] Marx agreed that when money was paid as a wage, the difference between this and the product's value was the capitalist's gain. In 1853 he described 'the *fraudulent* exchange of past for present labour' as meaning that past labour (capital) was not exchanged for 'an equal quantity of present labour' (39:381). He also wrote that the 'exchange between labour and capital, the result of which is the price of labour, even though for the worker it is a simple exchange, must for the capitalist be not-exchange. He must receive more value than he has given' (28:247). But he insisted that surplus value was generated within production itself. 'Necessary labour' was the amount of labour required to sustain the workman at a minimal level of subsistence. Value created beyond this was stolen by the capitalist.

Following Malthus, political economists from Ricardo onwards insisted that the average wage always tended to subsistence level, given competition for jobs from too many workers. But in proportion to the product's value the actual input of physical labour (as opposed to abstract labour power) might be enormous – many workers and little or no machinery – or relatively little – much machinery and a few workers. This altered what Marx called 'the organic composition' of capital, and made calculating averages difficult. Nonetheless Marx, like Thompson, regarded the illusion that wages represented a fair exchange 'freely' agreed on by contract as one of capitalism's central mystifications, the 'appropriation of alien labour *without exchange*' passing for 'the semblance of exchange' (28:233, 513). (Anyone who has ever worked for a low wage and watched the boss pocket the profits gets the point immediately.) Some later socialists assumed there was little difference between earlier accounts of unequal exchange and Marx's theory. The Fabian Beatrice Webb, for example, thought Thompson's view was 'afterwards incorporated by Karl Marx in his work on Capital'.[17]

To Marx, then, surplus value was the value of 'surplus labour', the unrewarded portion of the working day which went to the capitalist after a subsistence wage was paid. So if the worker was employed for six hours making something which was sold at the value of twelve hours' labour, the difference, as realized in the price when the product was sold, was the surplus. Beyond discussing the length of the workday Marx did not explain how surplus value might be reduced in socialism or communism. He did describe how it was augmented under capitalism, for instance by technological innovation which lowered production costs and/or increased output for the same or less labour cost. But the possibility of increasing surplus value was also limited, and thus profits faltered. Yet, paradoxically, the more relative surplus value increased, the more the rate of profit tended to fall. Marx regarded this as a key discovery. For it seemingly guaranteed that capitalism was not only prone to crisis, but would inevitably expire.

Machinery merely exacerbated the process of exploitation, hastening in addition the further 'moral degradation' and 'intellectual desolation' of women and children (35:403). The working day was prolonged to ensure maximum use of machines. Labour was intensified partly by increasing their speed and rendering the work simpler and more uniform. Finally 'factory work exhausts the nervous system to the uttermost, it does away with the many-sided play of the muscles, and confiscates every atom of freedom, both in bodily and intellectual activity'. A 'barrack-discipline' governs the 'industrial army', and the 'place of the slave-driver's whip is taken by the overlooker's book of penalties' (35:425–7). The results were devastating. The factory became a veritable death camp *avant la lettre*. Just one of Marx's statistics: in Manchester in 1875 the average age of death in the upper middle class was thirty-five. For labourers it was seventeen (35:636). But even worse than work was no work, for 'barbarity in the treatment of paupers' was the lot of the 'industrial reserve army' (35:647).

Buried within this narrative, however, is a utopian vision. Technology might eventually 'free everyone's time for their own development' and create 'an abundance of disposable time' (29:93). The *Grundrisse*'s now-famous section entitled the 'Fragment on Machines' (29:80–98) echoes Hegel and Hess in envisioning technology dominating production and workers merely supervising it. The information required to create and operate this technology eventually predominates even over

the machines themselves. This knowledge Marx characterized as social in nature, and based on 'general intellect'.[18] These comments retain a striking relevance today, as we emerge into an age of artificial
intelligence, robotics and driverless cars.

The question of how socialist exchange might function in the future
is also addressed in the *Grundrisse*. Here Marx responded to a Proudhonist who wanted to define value in order to provide a theory of just
exchange while retaining private ownership of the means of production.[19] Like some Owenites, Proudhon proposed that workers exchange
produce using notes based on hours of labour. This scheme was conceived by Josiah Warren in 1827 and practised in Owenite labour exchanges in the mid-1830s.[20] It was expounded in John Gray's 'labour
money exchange utopia', as Engels called it (26:291), and would be
picked up again by the economist Johann Karl Rodbertus. In *The Poverty of Philosophy*, responding to Proudhon's *The System of Economic
Contradictions or the Philosophy of Poverty* (1846), Marx treated this
'utopian' deduction from Ricardo by opposing all individual exchange,
even on the basis of embodied labour time (6:124–8). In 1844 he had
rejected both a general increase in wages, as not giving 'labour their
human status and dignity', and equality of wages, which would make
society as a whole 'an abstract capitalist' (3:280). In 1857–9 he reiterated that such schemes faced the same difficulties as other market-
based systems of exchange, namely that supply and demand would
alter the value of goods, and labour notes would become a new form
of money (28:73–7, 29:320–23). Wages would also vary according to the
work done and the labourer's productivity. Marx agreed, however, that
labour time was still 'real value', by contrast to which price was only
'nominal value'. But labour time could not serve as the basis of price.
This was the function of money, which Marx called the condition 'for
the development of all forces of production'. In the short-term labour-
note schemes nonetheless retained some value. Notwithstanding some
critics' insistence on Marx's 'aversion to the idea of justice',[21] his *Critique of the Gotha Programme* proposed that 'a given amount of labour
in one form is exchanged for an equal amount of labour in another

form' (24:86). But there was no question of applying this principle in the eventual, higher stage of communism.[22]

Marx's vision of machinery and attitude towards free time for self-development are central to the controversies respecting the relationship between his earlier and later works. For some, his growing emphasis on greater free time implies a significant shift in strategy respecting social goals compared to the 'Paris Manuscripts'. Around 1861–3 Marx began defining free time as a key end of production. Commenting on an obscure 1821 pamphlet, *The Source and Remedy of the National Difficulties*, he noted that 'there remains the fine statement: "A nation is really rich if the working day is 6 hours rather than twelve. WEALTH IS DISPOSABLE TIME, AND NOTHING MORE."' He now agreed that 'FREE TIME, DISPOSABLE TIME, is wealth itself, partly for the enjoyment of the product, partly for FREE ACTIVITY, which, unlike LABOUR, is not determined by a compelling extraneous purpose which must be fulfilled, and the fulfilment of which is regarded as a natural necessity or social duty, according to one's inclination' (32:391).[23]

Within the sphere of labour, Marx now increasingly perceived 'the emancipation of the workers' (3:280) in terms of democratic control over production. But compared to 1844 'emancipation' was now also understood as occurring substantially outside work. This implies a less ambitious, more realistic and more overtly political scheme than the position sketched in 1844. Gone is the language of the 'complete emancipation of all human senses', and the promise of 'the total redemption of humanity'. Even 'attractive labour' now seems in retreat, where 'individual self-realisation' is chiefly enabled by a balance of socially necessary labour in the 'realm of necessity' on one hand, and increased free time in the 'realm of freedom' on the other (37:807), a dichotomy not present in the early writings, where alienated labour is central. So Alfred Schmidt describes 'the attitude of the mature Marx' as 'sceptical', having in it 'nothing of the exuberance and unlimited optimism that is found in the idea of the future society presented in the Paris Manuscripts' because 'Men cannot in the last resort be emancipated from the necessities imposed by nature.' 'The problem of human freedom is reduced by Marx to the problem of free time', and that is that.[24]

Besides ignoring the political control of the labour process, this exaggerated description neglects recurrent comments on overcoming the division of labour. It implies that Marx retreated substantially on the question of how far necessary labour could be rendered 'attractive'. In 1857 he described Fourier's 'great merit' as being 'to have stated that the ULTIMATE OBJECT is the raising of the mode of production itself, not [that] of distribution, to a higher form'. But he immediately added: 'Free time – which is both leisure and time for higher activity – has naturally transformed its possessor into another subject; and it is then as this other subject that he enters into the immediate production process' (29:97). Marx conceded that 'for work to become *travail attractif*, to be the self-realisation of the individual…in no way implies that work is pure fun, pure amusement, as in Fourier's childishly naïve conception. Really free work, e.g., the composition of music, is also the most damnably difficult, demanding the most intensive effort.' He added:

> Work involved in material production can achieve this character only if (1) its social character is posited; (2) if it is of a scientific character and simultaneously general [in its application], and not the exertion of the worker as a natural force drilled in a particular way, but as a subject, which appears in the production process not in a merely natural, spontaneous form, but as an activity controlling all natural forces. (28:530)

Though he used the phrase '*travail attractif*', Marx was now less concerned with alienated labour and more with life outside work. Only in communist society, it appears, did the prospect exist of abolishing 'alien labour' as such and replacing it by 'attractive labour'.

In *Capital* 'attractive labour' is thus absent. We search in vain too for the language of human emancipation.[25] Its place is taken, as Marx put it in 1865, by 'the final emancipation of the working class, that is to say, the ultimate abolition of the wages system' (20:149). The burden has shifted from improving the realm of necessity to developing the realm of freedom, a prospect which was simply not present in 1844. In volume three of *Capital* Marx insisted that the realm of freedom actually begins only where labour which is determined by necessity and mundane considerations ceases; thus in the very nature of things it lies beyond the sphere of actual material production. Freedom in this field can only consist in socialised man, the associated producers, rationally regulating their interchange with Nature, bringing it under their common control, instead of being ruled by it as by the blind forces of Nature; and achieving this with the least expenditure of energy and under conditions most favourable to, and worthy of, their human nature. But it nonetheless still remains a realm of necessity. Beyond it begins that development of human energy which is an end in itself, the true realm of freedom, which, however, can blossom forth only with this realm of necessity as its basis. The shortening of the working day is its basic prerequisite. (37:807)

This implies that the future society would not renounce the division of labour to supersede alienation, but would reduce working time instead, introduce machinery to perform the most unpleasant tasks and educate labourers to a much higher standard. Marx said relatively little about superseding the division of labour in later life, though it remained a vague and distant goal. His focus was more upon narrowing if not eliminating the gap between intellectual and manual labour than ending specialization as such. Engels, however, reverted to his youthful utopianism in reiterating in 1872 that to solve the housing question it was necessary to consider Fourier and Owen, in whose 'model plans the antithesis between town and country no longer exists'. This would involve abolishing 'modern big cities' and allowing 'industry to be distributed over the whole country' (23:347–8, 282).[26] *Anti-Dühring* also suggested that when the division of labour was replaced 'productive labour will become a pleasure instead of a burden' (25:283).

Marx's mature economic writings also retain the 1844 goal of allroundedness. Shortening the workday to enlarge the realm of freedom would enable 'the development of the rich individuality, which is as varied and comprehensive in its production as it is in its consumption' (28:251).[27] The end-product would be 'Universally developed individuals, whose social relationships are their own communal relations and therefore subjected to their own communal control…not the products of nature but of history' (28:99). This required 'producing man as the most total and universal social product possible (for in order to enjoy many different kinds of things he must be capable of enjoyment, that is he must be cultivated to a high degree)', which Marx conceded required 'conditions of production based on capital' (28:336). The stage Marx characterized in terms of 'Personal independence based upon dependence *mediated by things*' gives way to 'Free individuality, based on the universal development of individuals and the subordination of their communal, social productivity, which is their social possession' (28:95). This is hardly a case of simply saying that the germs of the future society lie in the present. Marx clearly states what the future orientation of society should be. The goal is 'a community of free individuals, carrying on their work with the means of production in common, in which the labour power of all the different individuals is consciously applied as the combined labour power of the community' (35:89). Elsewhere this is described as 'the free exchange of individuals who are associated on the basis of common appropriation and control of the means of production' (28:96). Only here would the 'mystical veil' of society's 'life-process' be stripped off.

The *Grundrisse* defined three stages of freedom, moving from personal dependence to personal independence to free individuality. Here Marx dismissed the idea that 'free competition is the ultimate development of human freedom', terming it instead 'the most sweeping abolition of all individual freedom and the complete subjugation of individuality' (29:40). Both freedom and individuality thus remain the central goals of his system, as in 1844. Both would be achieved, however, by integrating education and production. *Capital* insisted that Owen, 'the father of co-operative Factories and Stores', had 'shown us in detail' how the factory system exhibited the 'germ of the education of the future' in combining productive labour with instruction and gymnastics, this being 'the only method of producing fully developed human beings' (35:486). Owen had also shown that a 'superior character' for all could be formed in the new factories (29:99).

Avoiding the language of 'attractive labour' did not mean that Marx retreated from the concept of alienation. To the contrary, he now emphasized that, with the need for exchange and the growth in the power of money, 'the exchange relationship establishes itself as a power external to and independent of the producers. What originally appeared as a means to promote production turns into a relationship alien to the producers' (28:84). Thus the 'general exchange of activities and products…appears to the individuals themselves alien, independent, as a thing' (28:92). And so the product of labour also appeared

> as a combination of alien material, alien instrument and alien labour – as *alien property*, and after production it has become poorer by the life force expended, and it begins the DRUDGERY anew as labour capacity EMPLOYED by the *conditions of labour*. The recognition of the product as its own, and its awareness that its separation from the conditions of its realisation is an injustice – *a relationship imposed by force* – is an enormous consciousness, *itself the product* of the capitalist mode of production and just as much the knell to its DOOM as the consciousness of the slave that he *could not be* the *property of another* reduced slavery to an artificial, lingering existence, and made it impossible for it to continue to provide the basis of production. (34:245–6)

Besides 'force', or lack of consent, which we have earlier described as Marx's central principle, the dominant image here is that of being 'crippled'. Developing 'one single faculty at the expense of all other faculties' made the labourer 'a crippled monstrosity, by forcing his detail dexterity at the expense of a world of productive capabilities and instincts' (35:359, 365). Workers 'crippled by lifelong repetition of one and the same trivial operation' were 'thus reduced to a mere fragment of a man' (35:490). Marx reiterated that

> within the capitalist system all methods for raising the social productiveness of labour are brought about at the cost of the individual labourer; all means for the development of production transform themselves into means of domination over, and exploitation of, the producers; they mutilate the labourer into a fragment of a man, degrade him to the level of an appendage of a machine, destroy every remnant of charm in his work and turn it into a hated toil; they estrange from

him the intellectual potentialities of the labour process in the same proportion as science is incorporated in it as an independent power; they distort the conditions under which he works, subject him during the labour process to a despotism the more hateful for its meanness; they transform his lifetime into working time, and drag his wife and child beneath the wheels of the Juggernaut of capital. (35:639)

But surprisingly Marx also concedes that 'Some crippling of body and mind is inseparable even from division of labour in society as a whole' (35:368). It is unclear, then, as to how relevant the 1845–6 passage on days filled successively with hunting, fishing, cattle-raising and criticism (presuming they were serious) now were. Marx envisioned communist society as highly complex, industrial, and subject to much of the same economic rationale as capitalism, albeit with the crucial difference that the workers are in control and may maximize their free time as well as ease the strain of labour.[28] Private property disappears as a source of alienation. But whatever division of labour and work discipline industry requires remain. There is no hint of returning to workshop production, to smaller-scale activities or arts and crafts, or to enhancing creativity within the labour process. Only the prospect of machinery finally making much free time possible renders a vision of greater all-roundedness realistic.

The language of alienation, then, is indisputably present in Marx's later works. But this does not mean that the concepts mean what they did in 1844. Three main positions have emerged respecting the degree of consistency between 1844–5 and 1857–67.[29] The first sees no important change. To McLellan, alienation is the theme most obviously 'running through the whole of Marx's writings' and remains 'central to Marx's whole thought, including *Capital*'.[30] István Mészáros insists that '*none* of the meanings of alienation as used by Marx in the *Manuscripts of 1844* dropped out of his later writings'.[31] Kolakowski agrees that the theory of alienation 'is present in Marx's social philosophy until the end of his life; "commodity fetishism" in *Capital* is nothing but a particularization of it'.[32]

The second position sees the 'Paris Manuscripts' as offering a fuller theory of alienation, but one nonetheless present in the later works.[33]

A variation on this, we have seen, is that the later writings shift from overcoming alienated labour towards viewing all-round development as occurring mostly in free time. Alienation is a central category in the *Grundrisse* and *Capital*, but not as conceived in 1844, for now the exploitation of labour and the related question of free time are more important. Here Marx's later concern with surplus value appears much more practical than the earlier stress on alienation. It is the 'theft' of free time which prevents the worker's self-development and capacity for species-life, rather than alienation as such. While Marx still notes 'the alienation of the individual from himself and from others', there are key differences from the account offered in 1844. The abstract Feuerbachian humanist conception of human nature Marx had relied on in 1844 is missing. 'Species-being' is not entirely absent – *Gattungswesen* appears twice in the *Grundrisse* (W42:168, 404) – but it plays no systematic role, and there is no quest for 'ultimate unity'. Instead, as we will see shortly, it is replaced in the chief development of Marx's thought in the late 1850s by a concept of free, co-operative labour, which as an ongoing process has subsumed the normative implications of species-being. This, it now appears, is the only form of association (at least prior to communist society) which might embody our communal potential. It is not indebted to Hegel moreover but represents an extension of Marx's critique of the *Philosophy of Right* into the sphere of economic organization, as well as providing a political solution to the problem of alienation.

The third position sees the early writings as more or less an obstacle to the mature economic thought, and especially the theory of value, with some (notably Althusser) asserting that alienation was essentially a 'pre-Marxist' concept and that Marx indeed progressed to an 'anti-humanist' perspective through an epistemological 'break' 'with all previous ideological conceptions of history', which were replaced by the 'science' of the materialist conception of history.[34] Thus 'In 1845, Marx broke radically with every theory that based history and politics on an essence of man.'[35] This implies, we have seen, that sociability is not 'man's essence', but something which needs to be created out of existing conditions.[36] A variant of this (as expressed by Sidney Hook) is that 'the central notion of "self-alienation" is foreign to the historical, naturalistic humanism' of the later Marx, being 'a concept which is originally and primarily religious in nature, and derivatively, metaphysical.' All that remains of the earlier notion, in this view, is the theory of the 'fetishism of commodities', by which we fail to discern in alien material things the social relationships they actually represent.[37] Some also conclude that Marx now 'felt that there was no solution to the loss of "self" in work inherent in technology', which meant accepting 'not only the division of labour but hierarchical organization as well'.[38] Another variation on the third theory is that the later writings exhibit a 'radical change of emphasis' because Marx shifted his focus from realizing human nature to developing technology.[39] And another is that Marx abandoned his early perfectionism, but still allowed his theory of alienation to provide the moral standpoint for criticizing capitalism. Here 'human emancipation' was transformed into the 'emancipation of the proletariat', a much less ambitious concept than that of 1844. Now it meant abolishing the wages system, not ending alienation. In this view much of the Hegelian and Feuerbachian philosophical baggage of the 1840s, and especially the desire to resolve Hegel's theory of alienation, was dumped unceremoniously overboard in the 1850s. Some of the language of 1844 remains. But it was now attached to a firm, historically grounded foundation – the free association of co-operative producers – rather than to any abstract humanism.

By the late 1850s Marx's description of the goals of communism became more political than philosophical.[40] This is indeed the chief shift in his thought in this period. Alienation was now less a state of being than a condition of lacking political control. Alienated labour had been defined as 'forced labour', as contrasted with 'voluntary' labour. 'Voluntary' now came to mean 'democratically organized', with consent thus conceived collectively. This becomes clear when we consider how and why the concept of co-operation moved to centre stage in Marx's thought. Existing accounts seriously underplay the extent to which Marx's account of co-operation distinguished his later economic and political writings from the perspectives of 1844.[41] Terrell Carver rightly contends that the idea that Marx was somehow always first and foremost a philosopher is misleading, if not simply mistaken.[42] We can concede that his mature system rested on a theory of organization as much as, if not more than, a philosophical framework.

To clarify this we need to appraise the shifts in Marx's use of the term 'co-operation'. Originally meaning a description of many workers labouring side by side, 'simple co-operation' implied 'the social productive power of labour': 'When the labourer co-operates systematically with others, he strips off the fetters of his individuality, and develops the capabilities of his species'. The very fact of co-operating, their 'union into one single productive body', is instigated by the capital which brings workers together (35:334–6). From this they learn how to use co-operation to attain what in 1844 had been conceived as species-identity. *The German Ideology* had insisted that co-operation in the existing division of labour 'appears to these individuals, since their co-operation is not voluntary but natural, not as their own united power but as an alien force existing outside them, of the origin and end of which they are ignorant, which they thus cannot control' (5:48). Under capitalism, co-operation for the workers was 'not a relation which belongs to them' and not a 'reciprocal association, but rather a unity which rules over them, and of which the vehicle and director is capital itself'. Yet this process promoted their *'interconnection and their unity'* while also demanding superintendence and 'the need for command' (30:261–2). Conscious, voluntary co-operation, however, is the opposite of alienation. Here we see the distance between 'natural' co-operation and 'voluntary' co-operation as democratic control over production, where we are alienated when the division of labour allows the capitalist to rule us, but submit cheerfully to the will of the majority in guiding production when we elect those who control us.

Some complain that Marx 'never explained how this control was to be organised'.[43] To contemporaries the evidence was abundant: British workers, and some elsewhere, had discovered the advantages of co-operative production. This only really became clear to Marx by the late 1850s. His most important programmatic statement of the period, the 1864 Inaugural Address of the International Working Men's Association (IWMA), proclaimed that the 'political economy of the working class', defined as 'social production controlled by social foresight', had enjoyed two signal victories since 1847, both originating in Owenism.

The first was the Ten Hours' Act limiting the workday, which proved the falsity of the 'blind rule of the supply and demand laws' on which the 'political economy of property' was based. In 1865 Marx declared that Owen's move in this direction in 1815 was 'the first preparatory step to the emancipation of the working class' (20:110). In 1866 Marx then urged that the working day be reduced to eight hours in order to ensure to labourers 'intellectual development, sociable intercourse, social and political action' (20:187).

The second victory lay in the evident viability of co-operative production, which we must now briefly consider. In the mid-1860s Marx termed 'co-operative labour' the first of all the great 'social questions' of the day (42:200). He pushed the theme constantly in the IWMA, asking for a debate on it in 1865 and including it in the 1869 programme (20:386; 21:143). The *Critique of the Gotha Programme* (1875) urged establishing 'the conditions for co-operative production on a social scale, and first of all on a national scale', not, as Lassalle proposed, through state aid and guidance (in keeping with Lassalle's Hegelianism). Such co-operatives were 'of value only insofar as they are independent creations of the workers and not protégés either of the government or the bourgeoisie' (24:93–4). 'Co-operative factories', Marx wrote, 'furnish proof that the capitalist has become no less redundant as a functionary in production as he himself, looking down from his high perch, finds the landowner redundant'. These even enjoyed a higher rate of profit than average, and every crisis brought more former managers willing to work at their old posts 'for low wages'. In 'a cooperative factory the antagonistic nature of the labour of supervision disappears, because the manager is paid by the labourers instead of representing capital counterposed to them' (37:385–6). Following 'the English socialists', co-operation would supersede the existing structure of capitalist management:

> the office of manager, the LABOUR OF SUPERINTENDENCE, can now be bought on the market in the same way as any other kind of labour capacity…It has become quite unnecessary for *capitalists* to perform this LABOUR OF DIRECTION…The best demonstration of this are the cooperative factories built by the workers themselves. They are proof

that the capitalist as functionary of production has become just as superfluous to the workers as the LANDLORD appears to the capitalist with regard to bourgeois production. (32:497)[44]

So an alienated relationship is replaced by democratic political control. Now, Marx insisted,

The cooperative factories of the labourers themselves represent within the old form the first sprouts of the new, although they naturally reproduce, and must reproduce, everywhere in their actual organisation all the shortcomings of the prevailing system. But the antithesis between capital and labour is overcome within them, if at first only by way of making the associated labourers into their own capitalist, i.e., by enabling them to use the means of production for the employment of their own labour. They show how a new mode of production naturally grows out of an old one, when the development of the material forces of production and of the corresponding forms of social production have reached a particular stage. (37:438)

'Co-operation' would become the bridge from capitalism to communism, where democracy goes beyond politics to economics. The oft-quoted (and much puzzled over) statement in *The German Ideology* that 'Communism is not for us a state of affairs which is to be established...We call communism the real movement which abolishes the present state of things' (5:49), which in 1845–6 was a vague assertion, and a means of evading the charge of idealism, now precisely described co-operation's emergence within capitalism. This is also what Marx meant when he famously insisted that the communists had no 'plan' and hence were not utopians, but merely developed existing trends in capitalism. Co-operation proved that production was possible 'without the existence of a class of masters employing a class of hands'. Owen had commenced this scheme, and some contend that Marx thus came to prefer his federated township model over other 'utopian' proposals.[45] But Marx insisted that co-operation needed to be 'developed to national dimensions, and, consequently, to be fostered by national means' (20:10–12) – something Owen would not contemplate (although Thompson, Mudie and Gray all did). Co-operation was now defined as 'the republican and beneficent system of *the association of free and equal producers*', which demanded 'one large and harmonious system of free and cooperative labour' (20:190).[46] It alone could ensure the 'abolition of the wages system'. So communism alone would not end alienation. Workers' control was required:

> the labourer looks at the social nature of his labour, at its combination
> with the labour of others for a common purpose, as he would at
> an alien power; the condition of realising this combination is alien
> property, whose dissipation would be totally indifferent to him if
> he were not compelled to economise with it. The situation is quite
> different in factories owned by the labourers themselves, as in
> Rochdale, for instance. (37:89)[47]

This then was the model Marx continued to promote, where managers in 'co-operative factories' were paid as salaried workers, rather than as capitalists extracting surplus value (32:504). It was more indebted to Owenism than to any other form of early socialism. As in the case of self-imposed discipline, it also meant that co-ops controlled their own work, so that even harsh norms were still voluntary and thus un-alienated. But this was only possible where property in the means of production was publicly owned.[48]

Marx was nonetheless well aware of the need, as his Chartist friend Ernest Jones said in 1852, to 'nationalise' co-operation and to 'destroy profitmongering' and 'supplant competition by the genial influence of fraternity' (11:581).[49] This could not be accomplished by dividing profits amongst shareholders, however – even if all were workers – but only by continuing to buy land and machinery to extend associative 'community of interest'.

At this point we should consider what evidence Marx had from contemporary co-operative endeavours that such developments were actually viable. First instituted around 1799, small-scale consumer and producer co-operation had flourished in Britain from the mid-1820s.[50] With the exchange bazaars movement of the early 1830s, where craftsmen aimed to eliminate middlemen in selling their wares, the prospect existed of expanding the movement and buying land to farm collectively on Owen's plan. In 1844–5, however, despite the support of several hundred thousand members meeting weekly at some fifty locations, the great Owenite community experiment at Queenwood collapsed. At the same time, a group of Owenite and Chartist flannel weavers in Rochdale set up a co-operative shop in Toad Lane. They also aimed to provide work for the unemployed in manufacturing and by purchasing land for them to cultivate. A corn mill was founded here in 1850, and a 'Manufacturing Society' in 1855, which employed some forty-six persons on ninety-six looms, shortly followed by a second mill. But bad management, amongst other things, brought the experiments to a close in 1864, after profit-sharing with the workers had been curtailed.[51]

While often relying on the Rochdale example, Marx appears to have known little of these later developments. Nonetheless while retail or 'shopkeeping' co-operation, with profits divided amongst members, was highly successful, large-scale enterprises owned and managed by workers, with elected managers, were few and far between, partly because legal barriers to limited liability made fraud much easier.[52] Acts in 1852 and 1862 eased this burden. Between 1848 and 1854 a number of Christian Socialist associations were founded, but most failed quickly.[53] Besides profit-sharing, co-ops promoted an ethos of fair trade, workers' education, thrift and democratic self-management, and reduced hours of labour (they introduced giving a weekly half-day off to workers). Hundreds of societies were formed thereafter, including bakers, tailors, millers, miners, shipbuilders and publishers. Most had a salary differential between manager and worker of 5:1, with profits shared proportionately. The movement's first historian, the former Owenite G. J. Holyoake, claimed that 'Co-operative workshops are the great means by which hired labour can be superseded'.[54] Co-op wholesale societies brought together unions of co-operatives represented at meetings in proportion to their numbers.

By the time Marx turned again to their efforts in the early 1860s, co-ops thus offered a remarkably promising application to the workplace of democracy and the principle of reward for effort. And some still aimed to have them replace the existing system, with the Owenite lecturer John Watts insisting in 1869 that if retail co-operatives engaged in co-operative production, then 'producers and consumers shall be the same persons, exchanges taking place only between one federation and another'. This would convert 'the greater part of middlemen into producers', he thought, and allow all to retire from labour at the age of fifty.[55] By 1893 co-ops had a million members in a population of some 38 million, and the Co-operative Wholesale Society federated 900 stores modelled on the Rochdale dividend-on-purchase system.[56] Many later Marxists, however, ignored the emphasis Marx gave to co-operation, with Eduard Bernstein influentially arguing that the failures of the 1860s proved Marx's overconfidence, while neglecting the political dimensions of Marx's approach.[57]

CHAPTER 8

The International (1864–1872) and the Paris Commune (1871)

Marx did not, as myth would later have it, 'found' the International Working Men's Association.[1] When it was established in London on 28 September 1864 he was a mere bystander, invited at the last minute to represent German workers by a French music teacher, Victor Le Lubez (42:15). But he had much to do with making the IWMA what it became. At the outset Marx was confronted with a confused melange of rewarmed Owenism, 'insubstantial scraps of French socialism' and Mazzinian abstractions (42:17). Reducing such chaos to order was precisely the kind of challenge he relished. He wrote the inaugural address for the organization, published a month later, which proclaimed that 'every fresh development of the productive powers of labour must deepen social contrasts and point social antagonisms', and insisted that to 'conquer political power has…become the great duty of the working classes' (42:9, 12). Revising the group's rules, Marx reluctantly conceded a few sentences on 'duty', 'right' and 'TRUTH, MORALITY AND JUSTICE', placing them where they could 'do no harm', and declaring the IWMA's ultimate aim to be 'the abolition of all class rule' (42:18, 20:14).

Marx also offered a strategy designed to appeal broadly to the very different levels of development and trajectories of the various European workers' organizations. Throughout the history of the IWMA he worked tirelessly to co-ordinate movements across Europe and even further afield, and to bring round the movements it represented to his own perspective. He now viewed its trade union affiliates in particular, it has been argued, as 'schools of socialism' which provided 'the means of the formation and consolidation of class identity and activity'.[2] To co-operative movements he offered the prospect of eventual national co-ordination of producers' co-ops. For the time being the various national associations, which included republicans, socialists and anarchists, remained independent in strategy and outlook. But in the General Council, based in London, Marx as Secretary for Germany slowly moved to a position of pre-eminence. In 1866 only four countries were affiliated to the IWMA. By 1869 this had grown to nine. The rousing anthem it inspired, 'The Internationale' (composed in 1871), would come to stand, at least emotionally, for the best that communism could offer, and the best humanity could aspire to. To some it still provokes both tears and the memory of the anger of days gone by: 'Stand up, damned of the Earth / Stand up, prisoners of starvation / Reason thunders in its volcano / This is the eruption of the end'. (Listen to the music and read all the words.)

Throughout the life of the International, Marx's activity was mostly behind the scenes. Even friends admitted that he was not a particularly gifted public speaker. Much of his effort was devoted to peacefully improving workers' lives, notably by agitating to shorten the workday. For Marx this period was defined by his commitment to hastening a transition to the society of 'associated producers' on the basis of developing existing institutions, economically and through the ballot box.[3] Capitalism might thus be overthrown without revolution or bloodshed. In Britain the International was instrumental in founding the Reform League, which aimed at universal manhood suffrage. The 1867 Reform Act, which enfranchised some affluent workers, followed its agitation.[4] When the General Union of German Workers met in 1868, Marx encouraged its struggle for political liberty in the hope that this would help promote a wider co-operative ideal.

In the IWMA Marx usually avoided general theoretical questions as divisive. Compromise was the order of the day. Indeed, Engels explained, the rules of the organization were set up 'in such a way that *all* working-class socialists of the period could join it' (48:9). By 1868, however, Proudhonist members began to push for 'mutualist' plans centring on small proprietorship, rather than eliminating private property; the creation of a 'people's bank' to extend credit to working-class organizations; and the collectivization of the railways. They also sought what Marx in 1866 condemned as 'Proudhonized Stirnerism', namely reducing everything to 'small *"groupes"* or *"communes"*', which in turn form an "association", but not a state' (42:287); whereas Marx insisted that in most cases only states could promote social reform. In 1868 a motion for land nationalization, which Marx now supported, was passed, but it was deemed that machines and the instruments of production were best left the property of the workers themselves. The 1868 Brussels conference of the International upheld the principle of state control over communal property in mines, forests and railways, thereby tilting the organization in Marx's direction. The Basel conference a year later endorsed abolishing private property in land. But this was still far from *The Communist Manifesto*'s programme.

By 1870 Marx was – along with the indefatigable Russian anarchist Mikhail Bakunin (1814–76) – the IWMA's leading figure, drafting the General Council's resolutions and preparing most of its congress reports, as membership rose to some 150,000. When they met in 1864, for the first time since 1848, Marx found much to admire in Bakunin, and hoped he could assist the Italian section of the International in particular. Bakunin in turn called Marx 'my dearest friend', and even declared himself Marx's disciple. He was the first translator of the *Manifesto* into Russian in 1869, and considered taking on *Capital* as well. But the two men soon fell out, and Bakunin – '*one of the most ignorant men in the field of social theory*', as Marx described him in 1870 (21:113) – became his chief antagonist. The quarrel between them, explored further below, centred on the desirability of a highly centralized state to oversee the post-revolutionary process. It eventually broke the organization apart.[5] Anarchists regarded all politics, particularly those involving states, as suspect and corrupting. Bakunin loved destruction, too, and wanted the revolution to eliminate the entire old society, down to making a bonfire of all laws, mortgages and property deeds. He ran his own secret society, the Fraternité Internationale (the first of several such groups), alongside the IWMA from 1865, 'with the aim', as Engels later put it, 'of putting into the hands of the anarchists control over the whole International' (27:346). Ironically, perhaps, it included a rigid hierarchy, a proposal for revolutionary dictatorship and the expectation of complete loyalty to Bakunin personally.

Marx was by far the most active IWMA member at the London conference of 1871, taking the floor over a hundred times. He now argued that 'insurrection would be a folly' in England, where peaceful propaganda could secure working-class goals.[6] In 1886 Engels wrote that Marx believed that England was 'the only country where the inevitable social revolution might be effected entirely by peaceful and legal means' (35:36). Marx turned against his erstwhile trade union friends, too, remarking that 'The TRADES UNIONS can do nothing by themselves – they will remain a minority – they have no power over the mass of proletarians – whereas the International works directly on these men' (22:614). Now, however, Bakunin's supporters were sufficiently numerous, especially in Southern Europe, that a split loomed. In 1872 the final congress of sixty-five delegates of the International convened in a small café in The Hague. Both Marx and Engels attended. Marx insisted that economic emancipation could only be achieved by seizing political power. In the USA, England and possibly the Netherlands he thought the 'workers may attain their goal by peaceful means' (23:255). But elsewhere, he added, this would probably not be the case. So these were exceptions rather than the rule. Bakunin was expelled. But to forestall further crises Engels, though opposed by the Blanquists and others, orchestrated the removal of the General Council from London to New York, which killed the IWMA off.

In Germany the International had to engage with two new working-class organizations: the General Union of German Workers, founded in 1863 and led by Lassalle until he was killed in a duel in 1864; and the Social Democratic Workers' Party (SDAP), established in 1869 and headed by Liebknecht and Bebel. Neither association was 'Marxist', and both initially kept their distance from the IWMA. In 1869, however, the SDAP affiliated with the International at a congress in Eisenach. From then until 1917, notwithstanding various setbacks, the

German model of a mass political party moving towards socialism would provide the most captivating evidence of the eventual triumph of Marx's aims. In 1875 the SDAP and the General Union of German Workers united at Gotha as the German Social Democratic Party. The new group's programme was at first largely inspired by Lassalle, but after suffering savage repression under Bismarck from 1878–90 it had come much closer to Marx's views.

The IWMA also raised once again the issue as to what role intellectuals and bourgeois sympathizers might play in the workers' movement. Though some wanted only manual labourers to be members, Marx did not object to 'professional men' joining, so long as the majority were workers. In 1872 he insisted that no new section should enter the organization unless two-thirds of its members were wage labourers. The issue of the purity of class origins did not trump education, as it often would later in the communist movement; for after all, both he and Engels were obviously 'bourgeois'.

By early 1871 the spectre haunting Europe was now named Karl Marx. Defeated in the Franco-Prussian War of 1870–71, France was declared a republic. Viewing Napoleon III as having begun the conflict, Marx regarded it as a 'war of defence' (22:5). But he now regarded the German working class as 'superior to the French both in theory and organisation' (44:4–5), and hoped that Prussia's victory would assist its progress. The armistice signed with Prussia sparked an insurrection in Paris. Marx initially warned against revolutionary adventurism, particularly in the name of the International. When the Paris Commune was proclaimed in March 1871, however, he was forcibly linked to its fate. He hoped that the Commune would inspire the 'self-government of the producers' throughout France (22:332). But it lasted only two months, and was suppressed with astonishing brutality, with some 20,000 executions, often of un- or disarmed workers. Nonetheless it became a key model for Marxism.

From the outset Marx was certain that the Commune was doomed to fail given Prussia's victory and the French government's opposition to it. Many of its leaders were not socialists. Yet Marx valued the experiment immensely, terming it 'a new point of departure of world-historic significance' (44:137). He even defended its execution of hostages, including the Archbishop of Paris, in retaliation for the wholesale massacre of prisoners by the Versailles government (see 22:352). Soon the IWMA was being blamed for the bloodshed, producing the first major red scare amongst the European bourgeoisie. As the reputed leader of the Commune, Marx was suddenly famous. In a vicious propaganda campaign 'the red terror doctor' became 'THE BEST CALUMNIATED AND MOST MENACED MAN OF LONDON' (44:158), and the IWMA was outlawed in various countries. Marx was deluged by a host of journalists anxious to see the '"MONSTER" with their own eyes' (44:176).

The Paris Commune was composed of some ninety municipal councillors chosen from the city's wards and serving on ten commissions. Here was the final revenge on Hegel. These were servants acting in the public eye, not a 'state' or 'trained caste'. Most were workers 'responsible and revocable at short terms' (22:331). Now universal suffrage served its 'real purposes', 'to choose by the communes their own functionaries of administration and initiation' (22:488). The Commune's key principles were replacing the state's standing army by a militia of armed workers; electing councillors, magistrates and judges by universal suffrage and paying them a workman's wage;[7] and freeing educational institutions from clerical influence by separating church and state and making education free. Freedom of religious practice was permitted. Its form, 'self-government of the producers', was to be adopted down to the smallest village, with rural communes sending delegates to towns, who would return deputies to a national delegation in Paris, leaving few functions to the remaining national government.[8] Thus the 'whole initiative hitherto exercised by the State was laid into the hands of the Commune' (22:331).

The Commune's immediate economic aims were to appropriate abandoned factories and make them co-operatives; to prohibit fines on workers' wages by employers; to suspend sales of pawned articles in pawnshops; to halt evictions and rents; and to end night work for bakers. To Marx its overall aim was to bring the workers into 'united co-operative societies' which would 'regulate national production upon a common plan' (22:335). And if it was achieved 'upon a common plan, thus taking it under their own control, and putting an end to the constant anarchy and periodical convulsions which are the fatality of Capitalist production – what else, gentlemen, would it be but Communism, "possible" Communism?' In this case 'Communism' was co-operation combined with communal government, not some blissful state in the distant future. But Marx admitted that there was little that was socialist in the existing programme, or even could be, even if nearly half of its council (thirty-four out of seventy-nine remaining members, after some republicans resigned) belonged to the International. And there were too many Proudhonists amongst them for his taste.

Nevertheless these measures, wrote Marx in his best-selling response to the Commune, *The Civil War in France* (1871), made it 'the political form at last discovered under which to work out the economical emancipation of Labour'. With 'labour emancipated, every man becomes a working man, and productive labour ceases to be a class attribute' (22:334–5). Here no professional political or administrative class existed.[9] The Commune represented a crucial step towards workers' self-government and abolishing coercive states and vampiric bureaucracies. It also exhibited certain humanitarian features, for example by burning two guillotines on 6 April 1871. But Marx said nothing about the relation of any communist party to the immediate government of workers in such revolutionary circumstances, and particularly whether universal suffrage and accountability should apply. In fact Marx's opponents, the Blanquists and Proudhonists, were in the majority in the Commune. So if this was the 'dictatorship of the proletariat', as Engels proclaimed (27:191), it was hardly the dictatorship of a Marxist party. It simply represented the working classes at their present level of political understanding, and a broad, left-leaning coalition, rather than a communist monopoly.

At the same time, Marx asserted that 'The communal constitution has been mistaken for an attempt to break up into a federation of small States' (22:333). Yet his own description indicated a more decentralized scheme than any he proposed elsewhere. To critics like G. P. Maximoff the federalist ideas expressed in *The Civil War in France* were 'in full contradiction to his previous as well as subsequent writings' promoting centralization.[10] This is a reasonable point. In the first draft Marx described the Commune as 'a Revolution against the *State* itself…a resumption by the people for the people, of its own social life'. Here the state was 'the centralized and organized governmental power usurping to be the master instead of the servant of society' (22:486–7). 'All France' would be 'organized into self-working and self-governing communes…the state functions reduced to a few functions for general national purposes' (22:490). In the second draft Marx stated that 'all public functions, even the few ones that would belong to the Central Government, were to be executed by communal agents, and, therefore, under the control of the Commune' (22:537). What, then, becomes of the need for the utmost centralization, and of extensive national planning and administration, as proclaimed in 1848? There is no simple answer to this question. Yet in early 1872 Marx was again writing that '*National centralisation of the means of production* will become the national basis of a society composed of associations of free and equal producers, carrying on the social business on a common and rational plan. Such is the humanitarian goal to which the great economic movement of the nineteenth century is tending' (23:136). And he reiterated shortly afterwards that 'the general principles laid down in the *Manifesto* are, on the whole, as correct as ever' (23:174).

So we are left with an unresolved contradiction on this point. Clearly, however, Marx did not want federalist principles extended too far. Again he simply underestimated the degree to which economic centralization would require much more complex administration. Admittedly he did not perceive these as 'state' or 'political' functions.[11] Yet individual productive units could not see what society as a whole required, or co-ordinate their efforts with hundreds of similar units elsewhere. So how were social needs to be ranked – how should we know whether we should be producing more shoes or more cannon? Or for import or export? Or for present or deferred gratification? With a view to maximizing production or minimizing environmental damage? Or maximizing free time? These are not questions safely left to even the most broad- and public-minded of cooks. They are moral, strategic and political, as well as technical. They require great knowledge and entail great responsibility. Answering them without great centralization seems well nigh impossible. Yet Marx, blind to anything smacking of Hegelianism, here ignored the certainty that a large administrative bureaucracy was demanded by his theory.

In the 1860s and 1870s the greatest test of Marx's tolerance for diversity of opinion was Bakunin, whose supporters rallied around his International Alliance of Social Democracy, founded in 1868. The son of a landowner, Bakunin had moved through Young Hegelianism into revolutionary activity. He was arrested in 1849, but after a dozen years of imprisonment and exile to Siberia he escaped, participated in the Polish insurrection in 1863 and then turned his attention to the IWMA. Bakunin's influence was strongest in Spain, Italy and Switzerland. In 1869 he sought to bring his organization into the International, but Marx feared it would become a state within a state, and eventually its members were admitted only as individuals. Bakunin not only advocated a brand of collectivist anarchism which was anathema to Marx, but like Blanqui he also supported the idea of secret organizations fomenting revolution, which Marx rejected. Bakunin's supporters in turn accused Marx of introducing the authority principle into the International by making it a hierarchical organization led by a committee.

Many serious issues were at stake here. Bakunin insisted that preserving the state throughout the revolutionary process would defeat the very ends of revolution. 'State' to him always meant 'dominion', 'the subjugation of the masses and consequently their exploitation for the sake of some ruling minority'.[12] He rejected all forms of constituent assembly and revolutionary dictatorship, and contended that when power was 'concentrated into…a few ruling individuals it inevitably and immediately becomes reaction'. He considered Marx the head of a 'sort of little Communist Church', who as a 'very clever politician and an ardent patriot' sought to establish 'a great Germanic State for the glory of the German people'.[13] The new 'People's State of Marx', he prophesied, meant 'the reign of scientific intelligence, the most aristocratic, despotic, arrogant and contemptuous of regimes', a 'privileged minority, allegedly knowing the interests of the people better than the people themselves'. It would justify itself according to the principle of state morality: 'The State, being the supreme objective, everything that is favourable to the development of its power is good; all that is contrary to it, even if it were the most humane thing in the world, is bad.'[14]

By now Bakunin did not like Marx at all, and he was not above spreading the rumour that he was Bismarck's agent (44:33). In *Statism and Anarchy* (1873) he accused Marx of being 'ambitious and vain, quarrelsome, intolerant, and absolute'. 'There is no lie or calumny', he insisted, 'that he would not invent and disseminate against anyone who had the misfortune to arouse his jealousy...by education and by nature he is a Jacobin, and his favourite dream is of a political dictatorship'. Marxists in power, he continued, would leave the position of the workers untouched, and a 'peasant rabble' or 'another proletariat' would 'be subject to this new rule'. Divided into two great armies, industrial and agricultural, the people would be 'under the direct command of state engineers'. Even if the workers ruled in 'State communism', they would soon 'cease to be workers and will begin to look upon the whole workers' world from the height of the state. They will no longer represent the people but themselves and their own pretensions to govern the people'. As for the 'dictatorship of the proletariat', Bakunin warned that 'no dictatorship can have any other objective than to perpetuate itself...Liberty can be created only by liberty, by an insurrection of all the people and the voluntary organisation of the workers from below upward'.[15] In his notes to the book Marx conceded that the proletariat must first 'use *forcible* means, that is to say, governmental means; as long as it remains a class itself, and the economic conditions which give rise to the class struggle and the existence of classes have not vanished' (24:517). Today we might nonetheless agree with Noam Chomsky that Bakunin's was 'a pretty good prediction'.[16] He remained a major influence on European anarchism into the twentieth century.

CHAPTER 9

Marx's Mature System

Amongst Marx's later writings, the *Critique of the Gotha Programme* (1875) offers the clearest indication of how he envisioned communism unfolding.[1] In the first stage of moving towards communist society the principle of equal right would apply. Work would be paid on the principle of 'to each according to his contribution', such that 'The same amount of labour which he has given to society in one form he receives back in another' (24:86), using some form of certificate to record the work done. As we have seen, this principle was endorsed by many early socialists. But it was bound to generate inequalities. Eventually, however, in the 'higher phase of communist society, after the enslaving subordination of the individual to the division of labour, and thereby also the antithesis between mental and physical labour, has vanished', and when 'the all-round development of the individual' has sufficiently progressed and sufficient plenty existed, this would change to the Saint-Simonian and Blancian principle, 'From each according to his abilities, to each according to his needs!' (24:87).[2] This we can safely assume constitutes justice in communist society, where reward based on labour is no longer necessary. But this reward was not the 'whole product of labour', since deductions would still be required for replacing the means of production, investing in expansion, providing reserves, paying for public services, and so on, even if the 'general costs of administration' would be 'very considerably restricted in comparison with present-day society' (24:85).

*   *   *

Five other problems dominated Marx's mature political theory. The first was whether communism might be achieved peacefully. In 1846 Engels, who had earlier opposed violence, stressed that 'democratic revolution by force' was the new political viewpoint (38:82). Marx certainly agreed until, by the early 1870s, both men conceded the possibility of a peaceful path to communism in democracies.[3] The working class had as its primary aim forming a political party *'distinct from, and opposed to, all old parties formed by the propertied classes'*. This alone could eventually achieve the *'abolition of classes'* (44:414). Against despotism violence would probably be required, and might even be salutary. As early as March 1850, in an address to the Communist League printed in its monthly circular, Marx could be quoted as advocating that the proletariat engage in 'excesses' against 'hated individuals or public buildings', with the aim of destroying 'bourgeois democracy' (10:282) – a text Lenin read. But this document was not signed personally by Marx, who lacked the nihilist tendency to glorify destruction.[4] In a letter to H. M. Hyndman in 1880, however, he wrote that 'if the unavoidable evolution turn into a revolution, it would not only be the fault of the ruling classes, but also of the working class', implying a preference for peaceful evolution that would make 'an English revolution not *necessary*, but – according to historical precedents – *possible*', whereas in Germany 'you cannot get rid of a military despotism but by a Revolution' (46:49).[5] But this needs to be balanced against Marx's insistence that no progress was possible in England until Ireland achieved independence, and this would probably be a violent process led by the Fenians.

Respecting the second question, whether less industrialized societies might simply avoid having to undergo capitalist development and/ or base socialist transformation on pre-capitalist institutions, Marx speculated as early as 1870 on a possible revolution in Russia (22:261). In 1870–71 he plunged into learning Russian, and the country dominated his thought in the last decade of his life. But this engagement represented a fundamental challenge to the *Manifesto*'s model of communism emerging only when the highest stage of capitalist development had sown the seeds of its own downfall, and the model of 'all-round dependence' linked to this, where 'the real intellectual wealth of the individual depends entirely on the wealth of his real connections' (5:51). In European Russia some three-fifths of arable land was possessed by peasant or Cossack households, which only held a small plot of land unconditionally and often farmed the rest collectively, with many local services (welfare, education) also run by the commune.[6] Revolutionary populists thought this an obvious starting point for socialism on a national scale. In 1875 Marx still insisted (against Bakunin) that a radical social revolution was 'only possible...where alongside capitalist production the industrial proletariat accounts for at least a significant portion of the mass of the people' (24:518). In 1877, when Russia and Turkey were at war, Marx wrote to Sorge, 'This time the revolution will begin in the East.' Indeed, he thought, 'if Russia continues along the path it has followed since 1861' (when the serfs were emancipated), 'it will miss the finest chance that history has ever offered to a nation, only to undergo all the fatal vicissitudes of the capitalist system' (24:199). This seemed to offer more than a sop to those who idealized the peasant commune.[7]

A letter from the Russian Vera Zasulich in February 1881 asking whether the *obshchina* (peasant commune) might form the basis for a future socialist society concentrated Marx's thoughts on these questions. Marx's four draft responses over two weeks indicate how seriously he took the issue. He observed that the commune could be 'the fulcrum of social regeneration in Russia' if it survived the 'deleterious influences which are assailing it from all sides' (24:371).[8] The 'historical inevitability' of the expropriation of agricultural producers was thus '*expressly* limited to the *countries of Western Europe*' (46:71–2).[9] A Russian edition of *The Communist Manifesto* in 1881 added that 'If the Russian Revolution becomes the signal for a proletarian revolution in the West, so that the two complement each other, the present Russian common ownership of land may serve as the starting point for communist development' (24:426). But again this was a contingent relationship: modern communism could not emerge on its own in Russia.

This sympathy with the Russian commune raised other problems. Was India similar to Russia? Was China? What about the 'Oriental' despotism common to such societies? What about their belief systems? How dependent was the prospect of such a development upon revolution in Europe, which Marx seemed to insist was a precondition for successfully developing the Russian commune? Was history cyclical rather than linear? Why was 'barracks communism' no longer a problem here? Why had medieval European communalism not been able to produce socialism? And if the peasantry would now play such a prominent role, what about the proletariat? Was Marx indulging the populists just to appease their revolutionary ardour, without lending credence to such potential deviations from the programme of the *Manifesto*?

Zasulich's letter also raised the question as to how revolution might proceed. Both Marx and Engels sympathized with Russian terrorists in the early 1880s, for instance when Tsar Alexander II was assassinated in 1881. Engels wrote to Zasulich in 1885 that a few dedicated revolutionaries might well tip the balance in Russia, and that 'if ever Blanquism, the fantasy of subverting the whole of a society through action by a small group of conspirators, had any rational foundation, it would assuredly be in St. Petersburg' (47:280). This observation, as we will see, tilts interpretations of Marxism towards Lenin significantly, particularly respecting Russia. In late 1848 Marx had written that 'there is only *one means* by which the murderous death agonies of the old society and the bloody birth throes of the new society can be *shortened*, simplified and concentrated – and that is by *revolutionary terror*' (7:506). But he generally regarded 'terror' as indicating that conditions were not ripe for revolution. There is little reason to believe that he did not agree with Engels' assertion in 1870 that 'Terror implies useless cruelties perpetrated by frightened people in order to reassure themselves' (44:63).

The prospect that revolution might commence from non-capitalist foundations nonetheless proved that Marx's analysis moved with the times and the circumstances.[10] It implied that communism might be introduced in nations with very limited educational levels, a low standard of living, little or no experience of democratic institutions or liberal values and little industry. Invariably, where no substantial educated and mature workforce existed, this implied a greater role for an educated minority of revolutionaries. These might well face the further problem of building democracy in countries untrained in its exercise, and indeed degraded by despotism as well as habituated to conspiracy and perhaps terror too. They also faced the prospect of having to modernize swiftly, thus entailing an even heavier than average burden of labour on the population. Then there was the issue of multiple classes, such as the bourgeoisie, petty bourgeoisie, peasantry, lumpenproletariat (miscreants at the margins of the working class) and intellectuals, who collectively might comprise a majority opposed to a weak proletariat and thus require suppression – exactly the scenario the Bolsheviks and most other later communists faced, as we will see.

Returning to other unresolved issues, thirdly, Marx never theorized clearly how nationally federated state- or worker-managed co-operatives would interact with the political leadership of any revolution and the dictatorship of the proletariat, the Communist Party in the organized sense. To balance democratic control over centralized and municipal as well as productive institutions with a Party that might not be subject to the constraints of election and recall would become one of the most pressing political issues of the coming century. The issue was further complicated if trade unions or other bodies retained substantial power in the future.

There was also, fourthly, the question of tolerating differing opinions within the broader movement. In the International, Marx aimed to suppress the 'sectarian' Proudhonists and Bakuninists, particularly in the General Council. He explained that

> The *International* was founded in order to replace the socialist or semi-socialist sects by a real organisation of the working class for struggle...The development of socialist sectarianism and that of the real labour movement always stand in indirect proportion to each other. So long as the sects are justified (historically), the working class is not yet ripe for an independent historical movement. (44:252)

One of Marxism's greatest traditional weaknesses has been its intolerance of minority – and particularly dissenting – rights, as we will see. Marx himself did not offer any later general defence of such rights, despite his early support for press freedom. Once the hollow pretensions of 'bourgeois' rights had been swept away, and with them 'bourgeois individuality, bourgeois independence, and bourgeois freedom' (6:499), he seemingly assumed, no socialist 'rights' would be needed, since society would unite around a common interest without class divisions. 'Rights' were thus understood as fundamentally aligned with property rather than persons.

The possibility of a non-communist opposition surviving any transitional arrangements does not seem to have occurred to Marx. The Paris Commune model of the dictatorship of the proletariat implied that 'bourgeois' parties would vanish. Yet divisions of opinion might persist. How could universal participation be reconciled with a potential deadlock between economic and supervisory organizations that were not class based but still potentially 'political'? This remained unresolved in Marx's thought. Related to it is his attitude to the idea of separation of powers in any government. Here it is generally agreed that while Marx supported subordinating executive to legislative power (as is normal today), he also upheld the idea of an independent, presumably elected, judiciary.[11] But if all these bodies were drawn from the same monolithic group, their independence would obviously be limited. This would be even more the case if they were all enjoined to share the same 'party line'.

These omissions now seem a grave oversight, given the centrality of the idea of freedom to Marx's moral, political and economic goals. Yet Engels also asserted that 'the workers can never win their emancipation' without 'freedom of the press, freedom of association and assembly, universal suffrage, local self-government' (20:69). Did he, or Marx, really intend that these freedoms would simply disappear in the future, once 'emancipation' had been achieved? This seems highly unlikely.[12] In 1889 Engels wrote in relation to the expulsion of some Danish Social Democrats that

> The labour movement depends on mercilessly criticising existing society, criticism is the breath of life to it, so how can it itself avoid being criticised or try to forbid discussion? Are we then asking that others concede to us the right of free speech merely so that we may abolish it again within our own ranks? (48:425)

Again this seems consistent with Marx's views, and his persistent opposition to police states generally, whether Prussian, Russian or French. Even Karl Popper, later one of Marx's sternest critics, conceded that in his love for freedom Marx was 'certainly not a collectivist, for he hoped that the state would "wither away"', and insisted that Marx's faith 'was fundamentally a faith in the open society'.[13]

Last, but not least, there was the problem of how far the new society could emancipate the working class from industrialism as such. Engels' essay 'On Authority' (1873) defined authority as 'the imposition of the will of another upon ours', and hinted that this was intrinsic to all large-scale industry. Even where 'if possible, by a majority vote', decisions over production were taken democratically, nonetheless 'the will of the single individual will still have to subordinate itself, which means that questions are settled in an authoritarian way'. While hours of work and so on might be chosen freely, 'the authority of the steam...cares nothing for individual autonomy'. The result was 'a veritable despotism independent of all social organisation'. Wanting to end it was 'tantamount to wanting to abolish industry itself, to destroy the power loom in order to return to the spinning wheel' (23:422–4). Here technological rationality seemingly defines the limits of political will, and challenges Marx's theory of consent. In volume three of *Capital*, however, Marx wrote that capitalist discipline would 'become superfluous under a social system in which the labourers work for their own account' (37:87). These positions are not necessarily contradictory. A system of unfair fines and reductions and excessive labour could be abolished while keeping production 'efficient'. The final goal remained ending the 'enslaving subordination of the individual to the division of labour' (24:87). Yet readers today may no longer feel, as we might in relation to Marx's 1844 manuscripts, that the complete liberation of humanity from all forms of alienation will be achieved. This is a compromise position, albeit a vast improvement for most over the present.

By the late 1870s it was increasingly obvious that capitalism was not facing imminent collapse. Crises were plentiful, but none threatened the epic confrontation heralded in the *Manifesto*. As well contingencies now appeared which had seemed unlikely or unattractive in 1848, including the possibility of communism being achieved through the ballot box. A much wider spectrum of opportunities and of legitimate interpretations of Marx's writings was now possible. Amongst these challenges was the expansion of imperialism in the second half of the nineteenth century.

Marx regarded the 'proper task of bourgeois society' as being 'the creation of the world market, at least in outline, and of the production based on that market' (40:347). Capitalism's extension during his lifetime lived up to this expectation, as the world was ceaselessly revolutionized to create just such a market. Marx's writings on British India in the early 1850s reveal a view of imperialism as progressive, if painful. He regarded India's conquest as inevitable, and saw her history as 'but the history of successive intruders who founded their empires on the passive basis of that unresisting and unchanging society'. Britain's 'double mission in India' was thus 'one destructive, the other regenerating – the annihilation of the old Asiatic society, and the laying of the material foundations of Western society in Asia'. Industry and the railways would destroy the caste system as well as 'all that was great and elevated in the native society' (12:217–18). 'Asiatic despotism and stagnation' thus had to give way to 'Europeanisation' (39:347). This implies that capitalism would similarly ride roughshod over other less developed societies, destroying each in turn. Capitalism could never be satisfied with anything less than world conquest: globalization was its very essence.

Although other opponents of imperialism in this period were less fatalistic about seeing these conquests as inevitable or 'progressive',[14] Marx's Germanocentric theory of history was clearly at work here. At any rate he became increasingly interested in earlier societies. From 1853 onwards he periodically speculated about an 'Asiatic Mode of Production' as a specific pre-capitalist stage characterized by the absence of private ownership in land, the persistence of village communities, the linkage of agriculture to vast irrigation works and the state's appropriation of most surplus value to maintain its despotism.[15] In the early 1880s Marx studied several writers who focused on primitive communalism, notably the American ethnographer Lewis Morgan, author of the influential *Ancient Society* (1877). Just what value there was in proving that most early societies were more collectivist or had little or no private property was not entirely clear, however. Was this the lure of Rousseau, or the ghost of Ferguson, hinting that this condition was more virtuous? Engels thought early societies were more co-operative and less competitive (45:109). But primitive community, whether in land, wives or other things, gradually dissolved throughout history (46:451–2). Engels had written in 1847 that 'Communism has only arisen since machinery and other inventions made it possible to hold out the prospect of an all-sided development, a happy existence, for all members of society' (6:101), and thought it obvious that the emancipation of women (half of humanity) could only occur with large-scale industry (26:262). Marx reiterated in the International that 'machinery creates the material conditions necessary for the superseding of the wages-system by a truly social system of production' (21:9). Primitive societies were just that, primitive. How could they resemble what would succeed capitalism? In some respects, indeed, they represented the very opposite – barbarism rather than civilization – and at best the prospect of that 'barracks communism' for which Marx had nothing but contempt.

Yet in the 1980s the sociologist Teodor Shanin dramatically claimed that Marx came to believe that 'The man of capitalism...was not the ultimate man of human history up-to-date. The Iroquois "red skin hunter" was, in some ways, more essentially human and liberated than a clerk in the City and in that sense closer to the man of the socialist future.'[16] This implied that the 'all-round' sociability created by large-scale co-operation under capitalism now paled beside the natural sociability of tribal society in terms of the collectivist outcome which would define the future. In conflating primitivism and virtue Marx had effectively moved much closer to Rousseau and Ferguson, and away from his own beliefs in 1844 or 1867. Such a conclusion however, envisioning one 'red' man as the forefather to another, now seems like an exaggerated, Karl May or Fenimore Cooper caricature of Marx.[17] Writing on 'the blockhead' Henry Maine, Marx described the 'satisfying and agreeable bonds of the group, of the primitive community', in contrast to those of civilization. Certainly the time and effort Marx devoted to this subject indicate a fascination with these developments, and the need to confront the 'one-sided elaboration of the individuality' that followed them. But Marx's chief concern was to study primitive communism and how private property emerged from it, not to idealize or romanticize it. No evidence exists that he saw the 'individuality of the person' which was often supposed to have arisen with the patriarchal family as anything other than progressive, and needing to be realized at a higher stage after the antagonism between individual and collective had ceased.[18] Morgan had suggested that future progress would witness 'a revival, in a higher form, of the liberty, equality and fraternity of the ancient gentes' (family group). Marx noted this, but did not elaborate on it.[19] Engels quoted it approvingly (26:276). Other passages suggest that Marx did not envision any return to primitive communalism: 'Man becomes individualised only through the process of history. Originally he is a species being, a tribal being, a herd animal...Exchange itself is a major agent of this individuation. It makes herd-like existence superfluous and dissolves it' (28:420). The communalism of the future would have to retain this individuation.[20] So the Russian commune could only ever be a starting point, and never anything approaching an end-state.

CHAPTER 10

The Problem of Engels

Thus far Friedrich Engels has appeared here as Marx's junior partner. Yet his contribution was at times a distinguished, even decisive one.[1] Born in Barmen, 'the Manchester of Germany', Engels was the eldest son of a pious factory owner. He too was somewhat rebellious; 'not even the fear of punishment seems to teach him unconditional obedience', complained his father in 1835 (2:582). As a youth he often 'gave all his little savings to the poor', records his first biographer, Gustav Mayer.[2] He early witnessed drunkenness and degradation amongst the workers, and already in 1839 blamed these excesses on factory work 'in low rooms where people breathe in more coal fumes and dust than oxygen' (2:9). Destined, he hoped, for literature, he dabbled first in the rationalist, progressive Young Germany movement. In 1841, while doing military service for a year in Berlin, he joined the group amongst the 'Hegelings' (as he called them) known as 'the Free'. Here he did battle with the reactionary Schelling, attacking the romantic theory of the state as a bald defence of the landed aristocracy. Next he embraced atheism, and then communism in October 1842. In England he studied the social problem while earning a living as a clerk in the Manchester cotton factory belonging to his father's firm. Here, as he later put it, he became 'the first whose eyes were opened' to what the new system implied (48:97). Immediately he lent his support to Chartism's campaign for universal male suffrage. Condemning the House of Commons as 'a corporation alien to the people, elected by means of wholesale bribery', he prophesied an inevitable violent revolution (2:371–4).

In Manchester, Engels encountered Robert Owen's numerous and well-organized followers, who already had a well worked-out theory of capitalist crisis. But they decried the more revolutionary tactics of their political opponents, the Chartists, some of whom had mounted an abortive uprising in 1842, which evidently made Engels overoptimistic about their later revolutionary potential.[3] Engels became an ardent admirer of Owen, and benefited greatly from the weekly talks of the local Owenite John Watts, published as *The Facts and Fictions of Political Economists* (1842).[4] Building on Watts, whose standpoint was vital to his 'Outlines of a Critique of Political Economy' (1843), Engels began before Marx to confront political economy, the 'science of enrichment born of the merchants' mutual envy and greed' (3:418). The 'critique of political economy' thus had Owenite origins, and became Marx's starting point soon after.

Like Marx, Engels was outraged at the selfishness, jealousy, cunning and violence which surrounded commerce and industry, and the 'hypocrisy, inconsistency and immorality' and 'legalised fraud' and 'vile avarice' which defined 'free trade' ideals (3:420, 422–3). As with Marx, a concept of enhanced sociability lurks behind Engels' early writings: 'private property isolates everyone in his own crude solitariness', and 'universal fragmentation, the concentration of each individual upon himself, isolation, the transformation of mankind into a collection of mutually repelling atoms' resulted (3:432, 475–6). Abolishing it by communism would ensure 'a world worthy of mankind' where production was planned rationally, 'a condition where everyone can freely develop his own human nature and live in a human relationship with his neighbours' (3:435, 4:263). This is a somewhat more communal starting-point than Marx's emphasis on self-realization. We get the sense of communism as realized humanity. 'If the producers as such knew how much the consumers required, if they were to organise production, if they were to share it out amongst themselves', Engels wrote, 'then the fluctuations of competition and its tendency to crisis would be impossible. Carry on production consciously as human beings – not as dispersed atoms without consciousness of your species' (3:434). Here too we already find taken up the Owenite theory of crisis, the concentration of wealth and the disappearance of small capitalists, themes which would loom large in *The Communist Manifesto*.

Engels thought existing experiments had abundantly proven 'the greatest success' of the communist principle (4:214). Amongst the North American Christian sect of Shakers 'no one is obliged to work against his will, and no one seeks work in vain'. Here were no police or poorhouses; 'all their needs are met and they fear no want' (4:216). So community of goods was 'by no means an impossibility' (4:227). What was required was to extend this principle universally. In the hands of 'the community and its administrative bodies' it would be but 'a trifling matter to regulate production according to needs' (4:246). Engels even thought that, 'strange though it may sound – precisely because the administrative body in this society would have to manage not merely individual aspects of social life, but the whole of social life, in all its various activities', the 'administrative and judicial bodies' would be 'vastly simplified' (4:248), though this was partly because crimes against property would disappear rather than a lack of economic complexity. Even here, however, Engels thought Owen's plans for communities of 500–1,500 people offered the 'greatest saving of labour power' through the economies of large-scale dwellings (4:252). But this was precisely the model he and Marx apparently would abandon in 1848.

Engels' second initial contribution to Marx came from *The Condition of the Working Class in England in 1844* (1845). This gave a powerfully emotional, detailed exposition and critique of the squalid, filthy, sickly and uncertain life in the factory districts and great towns for the modern proletariat and the 'brutal indifference, the unfeeling isolation of each in his private interest' of the entire society (4:329). Engels' initial share in the partnership with Marx was thus, in the first instance, a clear embrace of communism; and in the second, a command of British socialist and radical democratic theories as well as actual working-class conditions. Marx had no comparable experience to draw on. Clearly Marx was able to accept Engels as a partner not only because of the similarity of their ideas, but because, during Marx's life, Engels gladly 'played second fiddle' to him. After Marx's death Engels became first fiddle and was well aware that there would 'inevitably be blunders' as a result, even that he would become 'overrated' (47:202, 50:163). And so it has been. But as Carver and others argue, we can hardly ignore

Engels' contribution to Marxism.[5] We must indeed use him on occasion to fill in holes in Marx's narratives, and thus to speak for Marx. We cannot assume, however, particularly respecting the works published after Marx's death, that their views were identical.

It is here that the Engels 'problem' chiefly lies. It has long been alleged that Marxism – the term was probably first used by either Bakunin or Paul Brousse around 1882 – 'was conceived in the mind of Friedrich Engels' in a form that Marx neither intended nor indeed even wanted.[6] Though it had been suggested much earlier, by the 1970s the theory was broached that Engels was 'the first revisionist' in modelling Marx's ideas on the natural sciences.[7] (Whether these possible philosophical differences translated into political ones is another matter.) Since 1991 in particular Engels has borne much of the brunt of the criticism that Marxism degenerated so quickly into staid, scientistic, positivistic dogmatism.[8] There has been a pronounced tendency to see 'Engels as the scapegoat for all that they dislike in Soviet Marxism',[9] and to assume that, in Russell Jacoby's words, 'A reliance on Engels marked orthodox, especially Soviet, Marxism'.[10] The reading and citation history of Soviet leaders and readers alike bears this interpretation out.

The chief reason for this is Engels' association of the materialist conception of history with the natural sciences, with the implication that each rested on an equally exact, empirically based foundation. Engels' *Anti-Dühring* (1878), a polemic against the German socialist Eugen Dühring, was the first book to publicize Marxism to the German working classes; converts included the leading revisionist Eduard Bernstein (discussed later). This synthesized Marx's accomplishments into 'two great discoveries': the materialist conception of history and the theory of surplus value (25:27). In *Dialectics of Nature* (mostly written in 1878–82, but published in 1927) Engels was less Marx's popularizer and editor than an interpreter bent on proving his 'scientific' credentials.[11] This Marxism, in turn, is usually regarded as the interpretation favoured by Stalin, whose philosophy rested on the idea of a dialectic existing in nature.[12] It thus served as the philosophical basis *'behind the science of history'* (in Althusser's formulation) in 'dialectical materialism'.[13]

But many critics have asserted that Engels' 'mechanistic material-ism' 'differs sharply from' Marx's own formulations. There is good ev-idence for this view. Marx said in 1870 that F. A. Lange 'has not the slightest idea that this "free movement in matter" is nothing but a pa-raphrase for the *method* of dealing with matter – that is, the *dialectical method*' (43:528). This indicates that Marx did not see the dialectic as occurring in nature itself. He wrote of his 'dialectical method' in *Capi-tal* as the 'direct opposite' of Hegel's, meaning that 'the ideal is nothing else than the material world reflected by the human mind, and trans-lated into forms of thought' (35:19).[14] But he meant to describe it as a mode of exposition and explanation. By the 1860s he had in fact lost in-terest in much of philosophy as such. Engels, however, was much more insistent than Marx that 'in nature…the same dialectical laws of mo-tion force their way through as those which in history govern the ap-parent fortuitousness of events' (25:11). But whether this means much more than that 'struggle' and 'evolution' broadly mark both, or that 'the history of mankind' is 'the process of evolution of man himself' (25:24), is debatable. To accord the theory of class struggle the same status as that of evolution will not occur to most readers today. And Engels himself indeed later insisted that 'the production and repro-duction of actual life' was 'the determining factor in history' only in '*the final analysis*', and indeed apologized for stressing it unduly and for not doing 'justice to the other factors that interacted upon each other' (49:35–6).

Engels thus became Marx's first and greatest popularizer and sys-tematizer. His extremely successful *Socialism: Utopian and Scientific* (1880) and *Ludwig Feuerbach and the Outcome of German Philosophy* (1886) pounded home the theme that philosophy reached its apogee in 'scientific socialism'. In his studies of the early Germans, then in *The Origin of the Family, Private Property, and the State* (1884), Engels also extended Marx's ideas on Morgan's *Ancient Society* into uncharted territory, widening the system. The broad conclusion that communal property, a 'communistic household' and various forms of group mar-riage had defined most early societies, and declined as private prop-erty arose, was of course grist to the modern communist mill. So was the deduction that women had enjoyed greater social status and power under more communal conditions – even voting, for example amongst the Iroquois – having been downgraded only by the progressive division of labour outside the household (26:176, 191, 261).

At the very least, then, we need to acknowledge that Marx and Engels had different starting points in embarking upon careers as communist revolutionaries, and that they followed different trajectories to some degree. Yet both were enamoured of the scientific spirit of the period, with the sense that technology could alleviate most of humanity's woes, and that the chaos of human affairs could be rendered more orderly and rational by applying scientific principles. Both shared the zeitgeist which, particularly after Darwin, understood history as strongly evolutionary, inevitable and determined, and indeed saw all evolution in terms of a growing self-command in humanity and control over nature, and in terms of humanity's movement from necessity towards freedom. All this looked much less ominous or fatuous than it does to us today.

What defined these themes more than anything else was the appearance of Charles Darwin's *On the Origin of Species by Means of Natural Selection* in 1859. Darwin's unseating of man from the pedestal upon which God had perched him appealed greatly to secularists. So too did the apparent general drift of evolutionary theory. 'This is the book', wrote Marx in 1860, 'which, in the field of natural history, provides the basis for our views', meaning that 'historical class struggle' found its parallel in Darwin's 'survival of the fittest' (41:232, 246). Liebknecht later recalled that the German workers in London 'spoke for months of nothing else but Darwin and the revolutionizing power of his scientific conquests'.[15] 'As Darwin discovered the law of evolution of organic nature, so Marx discovered the law of evolution of human history', proclaimed Engels at Marx's graveside (24:467). 'That which Darwin did for Biology, Marx has done for Economics', echoed Marx's son-in-law Edward Aveling.[16]

But these oft-quoted remarks are misleading. The analogy turned out to be not perilously but tragically inexact. On a second reading Marx concluded that Darwin had found 'among the beasts and the plants' only 'the society of England with its division of labour, competition opening up of new markets, "inventions", and Malthusian "struggle for existence"' (41:381).[17] He later lamented that some Darwinians viewed his ideas as a 'conclusive reason for human society never to emancipate itself from its bestiality' (43:217). So Marx clearly did not think that Darwin had found a dialectic in nature analogous to one he himself had discovered in history. He never claimed explicitly that dialectical laws existed in matter, though he occasionally implied they did.[18] He meant merely that 'struggle' was crucial to both nature and history. Engels too insisted that Darwin's principle was none other than 'Hobbes's theory of the *bellum omnium contra omnes* [war of all against all] and of the bourgeois-economic theory of competition together with the Malthusian theory of population' as applied to nature. He also wrote that 'the mere consideration of previous history as a series of class struggles is enough to reveal the utter shallowness of the view of that same history as a slightly modified representation of the "struggle for existence"' (45:108–9). 'The conception of history as a series of class struggles', Engels thus conceded, 'is already much richer in content and deeper than merely reducing it to weakly distinguished phases of the struggle for existence' (25:585).

Yet the Italian socialist Enrico Ferri stated that as Darwinism showed that all animal evolution involved a struggle for existence between individuals and species, so Marx proved that 'all the mechanism of social evolution' was reduced to 'the law of the *struggle of the classes*'. Marx had thus 'finally completed in *Capital* in the social domain the scientific revolution commenced by Darwin and Spencer'.[19] While Marx was still alive, Engels wrote that 'Nature is the proof of dialectics', meaning by it not much more than it 'goes through a real historical evolution' (24:301). He also asserted that 'the Darwinian struggle of the individual for existence transferred from nature to society with intensified violence' characterized the latter stages of class struggle (25:260). For both Darwin and Marx, at any rate, the idea of 'struggle', whether of class or species, in fact originated in Malthus, who was Ricardo's (thus Marx's) as well as Darwin's key source. Marx nowhere envisioned applying to history what Engels regularly described as the three laws of dialectics (the transformation of quantity into quality and vice versa; the interpenetration of opposites; the negation of the negation; 25:356). Yet the broad influence of an 'evolutionary' viewpoint on Marxism is undisputed. Whether this actually promoted reformism during the Second International in particular, especially because of its influence on Karl Kautsky, as Lukács and others alleged, however, is a moot point.

CHAPTER 11

Utopia

If we must be wary about terming Marx's theories 'scientific', portraying him as 'utopian' will defy many readers' expectations.[1] Utopianism entails a process of imagining much better or ideal (but not 'perfect') societies, which serve as models to judge the inadequacies of the present, as well as the actual experiments which result from them. Marx's rejection of this approach seems well-established since at least 1845, when Karl Grün first juxtaposed 'utopianism' with 'scientific socialism'. Marx dismissed many early socialists as 'utopian' for not acknowledging that history showed that the proletariat would inevitably transform society through class struggle and revolution. Instead 'utopians' sought by example and philanthropy to raise the working classes' standard of living. From 1845, as we have seen, Marx felt compelled to avoid any charge of idealism by insisting that communism simply grew out of existing developments. So he repeated in 1871 that the Communards had 'no ready-made utopias to introduce *par décret du people*...They have no ideals to realize, but to set free elements of the new society with which old collapsing bourgeois society itself is pregnant' (22:335).

This said, Marx's insistence that, as the workers' movement developed, its theoreticians needed 'only to take note of what is happening before their eyes and become its mouthpiece' (6:177) is doubtless positivistic, not to say overoptimistic. Decrying the need, as *Capital* did, to write recipes 'for the cook-shops of the future' is one thing (35:17). But few cooks titillate or satiate without recipes, and it has been suggested that Marx's euphemism was only intended to disguise his embarrassment at remaining a utopian.[2] This approach was nonetheless repeated ad infinitum for a century. Lenin, invoking Marx on the Commune, agreed that 'There is no trace of Utopianism in Marx, in the sense of inventing or imagining a "new" society. No, he studies, as a process of natural history, the *birth* of the new society *from* the old, the forms of transition from the latter to the former.'[3] Some later Marxists, notably Ernst Bloch, came closer to finding in utopia a category of wider value, mainly by transforming it into a philosophy of hope and an act of will of a quasi-eschatological type, though without delineating what the future object was.[4] But most have contended that what distinguishes Marx's socialism from utopianism is its historical foundation and theory of proletarian revolution, and then the 'scientific' nature of Marx's account of surplus value.

These claims are, however, exceedingly disingenuous, even bordering on the intellectually dishonest. As we have seen, Marx had 'ideals to realize' (22:335), notably solidarity, co-operation, the society of consenting 'free producers', self-actualization and all-roundedness. He also admired and adapted aspects of the theories of Owen, Fourier, Saint-Simon and others. Owen is the outstanding figure here, both as the leading communist amongst the 'utopians', and because of his views on integrating labour and education, reducing working hours, and co-operation in particular. These key components in Marx's ultimate vision were ideals as well as practices. As late as 1851 Engels was still urging Marx to write down 'the much coveted secret', 'the much-vaunted "positive", being what you "really" want' (38:492). This never occurred, some infer, because both wished 'to conceal the core of utopia at the heart of their doctrine'.[5]

We have seen that by the 1860s what Marx meant by denying that he was utopian was that co-operative production was emerging within capitalism as the model of the future economy. This resulted from the naturally increasing socialized nature of production. True, he never explained just why this form of group was ethically superior (or how it nurtured the qualities he had earlier associated with species-being) and avoided becoming a mere primitive mass: the proletariat as 'crowd', as Bauer had warned, enslaved to 'puzzlement, indolence, fear and restriction' and 'hardly accessible to a Universal Idea'.[6] But the *normative* idea of producer co-operation was an ideal nonetheless, and indeed one quite at variance with that *natural* co-operation which the division of labour fostered, as well as with various forms of consumer co-operation.[7] And even producer co-operation did not inevitably achieve the ends Marx sought: they had to be created. So Marx's remark here does not accurately describe his own method of proceeding. 'Bourgeois' society carried many tendencies forwards, some progressive, some reactionary, some heralding higher social ideals, others relentlessly destructive of the best in human life. The Commune itself was also just such an incarnation of an ideal, and not merely something that emerged naturally out of capitalism.

Marx thus certainly wanted history to move in a particular direction, the outlines of which were clear by 1848.[8] The idea of the 'universal individual' – 'at the centre' of Marx's 'vision of utopia' for McLellan – was maintained as vehemently as ever.[9] Its halfway house was ensuring 'the communal satisfaction of needs' in the new society, such as 'schools, health services, etc.' (24:85). Marx was admittedly unwilling to put much flesh on the bones of his vision of communist society, and describe in detail what it envisioned, leaving this to the course of history and the discretion of its makers. Hence he left many key questions about the future unanswered. But the fact that his entire system was based on the principle of planning makes his reluctance to discuss the future doubly annoying. 'Planning' by definition involves imagining future needs and improving on past deficiencies. The 'ruthless criticism of all that exists' (3:142) is simply not enough: we need alternatives. Can't or shouldn't we plan how best the future should unfold? Indeed, don't we need to plan how to plan?

There is also a second, negative sense in which Marx's critics have portrayed him as utopian. 'We can admit that Marx's project is utopian, that it is based on the perfectibility of man – ideas which tell against it – without thereby agreeing that it is doomed to produce authoritarian regimes', writes David Lovell, noting Kolakowski's earlier charge 'that Marx's project is utopian because it is based on competing values of freedom and social unity'.[10] As sharply, Eric Voegelin, amongst others, sees Marx's vision in the early 1840s as quasi-religious and specifically chiliastic.[11] So does John Maguire, who describes Marx's 'early version of communism' as 'wildly utopian' (for example in seeing an end to all conflict between man and nature and man and man), but views it as already 'less millenarian' by *The Communist Manifesto*, where the idea of abolishing all distinctions has been replaced by ending private property in the means of production.[12] David Leopold, too, speaks of the 'perfectionist thread' in Marx's early writings, using this term to denote the desire to develop certain capacities rather than to describe the ideal end point which results.[13] The 1844 writings can certainly be read in this way. The 'complete *emancipation* of all human senses and qualities', which now become 'subjectively and objectively, *human*' (3:296–7, 300), was clearly a response to Hegel's theological resolution of alienation and, as such, remained on theological ground. But this perspective was surpassed in the writings of the late 1850s and after.

We cannot unpack here all the differences between utopian ideas and secular millenarian ones.[14] There are, however, at least seven ways in which Marx can be described as 'utopian' in a neutral or positive sense, that is, with a view to illuminating his ideas rather than merely belittling their 'scientific' pretensions.

The first and most obvious is that Marx's communism was associated with the tradition defined by Thomas More's *Utopia*. In 1845 Marx, Engels and Hess projected a 'library of the best foreign socialist writers', which was to include Thomas More and Tommaso Campanella (4:667). Here 'utopian' means 'advocating communism', thus giving priority to sociability over property ownership and to the public over the private; it also means overcoming the division between country and city (for More, by rotating labour). This enhanced sociability was broadly based upon an ideal of reciprocity, and solidarity or friendship.

Second comes Marx's persistent hostility to specialization. Jon Elster regards it as 'one of Marx's more utopian ideas that under communism there will be no more specialized occupations', for instance 'no more painters, only people who among other things also paint'.[15] A crucial question here is how far the later Marx still contemplated abolishing the division of labour, and what this implies. The *Critique of the Gotha Programme* described communism as ending 'the enslaving subordination of individuals under division of labour, and therewith also the antithesis between mental and physical labour' (24:87). Here, as in 1844, all-roundedness remained the ideal. But the concept is not unproblematic. If it implies a hostility to specialization and expertise, we must ask the question: in what field is amateurism a virtue? As the scalpel is poised do we want a heart surgeon whose heart is in poetry? As the plane lands do we want a pilot whose true love is gardening? And who does not want to be proficient at least at something, and to be recognized for it? Here the ideal of all-roundedness and the necessity for expertise – and possibly also personal fulfilment – are clearly at log-gerheads. This concept was simply not thought through carefully. Yet the 'all-round individual' remains utopia incarnate for Marx.

Marx's third utopian assumption is that social behaviour would im-prove dramatically once private property ended. Iring Fetscher claims that 'one of Marx's central ideas was that men are changed so greatly by the socialist revolution that they spontaneously behave in a spirit of solidarity and out of concern for the community'.[16] Like most socialists and anarchists Marx assumed private property was the chief source of social evil, particularly theft, personal violence and prostitution. His ideal of a future stage of peace and plenty, and the hint of gaining 'ul-timate unity here on this earth', has quasi-millenarian overtones, and seems at points like a secular version of Providential development. (Many forms of Marxism would be suffused with similar sentiments.) There are also hints here of an essentialist theory of human nature, particularly as linked to an ideal of working-class behaviour. Marx was reluctant, however, to describe this vision of *Gemeinschaft* (commu-nity) in detail. Closeness, trust and mutual support seem to be the op-posites of coercion, exploitation and fear. Marx's idea of community was clearly inspired by Feuerbach's theory of human unity, and relies centrally on utopian conceptions of 'trust'. But after Stirner's attack on communism, Marx fought shy of talking about 'the state founded on love' or a new religion of 'society' (5:211).[17] Something like resolv-ing 'the whole of society into voluntary groups' (5:416), an idea Marx attributed to Fourier, seems sometimes closer to his own inclinations, if uncomfortably Proudhonian. But the need for centralized produc-tion remained.[18] It might be added that the entire theory of 'Oriental' or 'Asiatic' despotism, where an absence of private property coincided with extreme political autocracy, indicated some pitfalls of these assumptions. With hindsight, the fact that later communist societies too exhibited just such a combination, as we will see, undermines such arguments.

The fourth utopian assumption lies in linking the earliest phases of society with the last stage. E. H. Carr saw Marx as sharing with the utopians 'their conception of the primitive state from which man had proceeded and of the future state to which man would eventually attain. On these essential points, Marx himself contributed nothing original, and was content to be the faithful disciple of the Utopian socialists.'[19] Primitive communism lacked class struggle: so would the future stage. But while most primitive groups have a much stronger sense of collective responsibility than modern ones, the future society would need to mitigate, if not abolish, that egoism which had been fostered by capitalism. Marx's late interest in Russian communes evinces his sense that some earlier societies might offer a clue as to how future communist organizations could avoid this problem. Maximilien Rubel called this a 'last tribute to Robert Owen'.[20] But there was similar evidence elsewhere. In 1868 Marx wrote, in reference to Georg Ludwig von Maurer's work on early German land tenure, that the 'primitive age of every people' 'corresponds to the socialist tendency' (42:557), egalitarianism being the leading quality. Communal property, he eventually concluded, was 'of *Indian* origin', and existed 'among all European peoples at the beginning of their development' (43:434). Yet the sociability they exhibited, where there was no need for the counterbalancing of some form of individuality, clearly threatened the perspective of *The Communist Manifesto*.

Fifth, we need to consider Marx's assumption that society had one future goal, communism, which could not be surpassed. Lukes describes 'Communist society' as 'Marx's and Engels' own utopia'.[21] Utopian visions give a form to change and a goal, concentrating the desire for improvement and resistance to oppression into an ideal to be attained. Even if successful, a revolution which merely aims to overthrow can scarce long survive. Ultimately the accusation that Marx was intellectually dishonest in refusing to detail how the future might (or ought to) unfold is mitigated by the fact that he did describe what organizations under capitalism would serve as the basis for socialism, namely co-operative production. But this remains a final end, at least prior to communism, unless we presume that a historical method dictates otherwise, which seems unlikely.

Marx's sixth utopian presumption is his own unwillingness to confront the full reality of the very principles he himself supported. Fritz Raddatz relates that Marx was once told by a house guest, 'I cannot picture you in an egalitarian period since your inclinations and habits are thoroughly aristocratic'. Marx replied: 'Neither can I; those times must come but we must be gone by then'.[22] This indicates his adherence to an ideal vastly at odds with his entire life's experience, and indeed his own outlook and preferences.

Seventh, we should recall Marx's expectation that advances in socialization, notably mitigating coercion and oppression, which were doubtless achievable in small-scale communities, could be emulated at the level of the nation-state. The problem of scale is here enormously important: much that can and has worked amongst a few thousand people, or only at the commune level, may be impossible with millions, or with a different organizational structure. Marx may however have assumed that the basic co-operative units would fulfil some of the functions previously associated with small-scale 'voluntary' or 'intentional' communities, as we would call them today.

None of these utopian qualities as such discounts the value of Marx's vision. Delineating them merely helps to clarify how we should understand him, and judge his ideas and proposals as realistic or otherwise. Alfred Schmidt called him 'the greatest utopian in the history of philosophy.'[23] Rubel termed him the 'greatest of social utopians', even 'the most utopian of the utopians', precisely because he 'gave socialist utopia a rational basis by linking the ethical postulate of socialism's realization to the scientific law of capitalism's destruction and the immanent consequences of this for human behavior'.[24] Others, however, would see just these attributes as perhaps the least utopian aspect of Marx's legacy. At times Marx himself acknowledged the value of some of his socialist predecessors, writing to Ludwig Kugelmann in 1866, for instance, that 'the Utopias of such as Fourier, Owen, etc., contain the presentiment and visionary expression of a new world' (42:326). We have seen here, however, that Marx in combining an ideal of all-roundedness with economic co-operation and democratic communal control offered a clear vision of the emancipated working class. Ironically it is precisely what is most utopian in Marx – and not what is most 'scientific' – that remains valuable. By conceiving a vastly improved society and overleaping all the prejudices of the day respecting the improvability of the masses, he became a visionary of the first order. The claim Marx makes about humanity's capacity for all-round development is an enduring one whose value remains untarnished. It may be fiendishly difficult to attain. But utopianism is nothing to be embarrassed about: it is a necessary guide to conduct.

CHAPTER 12

Concluding Marx

At three in the afternoon on 14 March 1883 Marx died quickly and quietly in his favourite armchair in his study, finally relieved of his many ailments at the age of sixty-four. A mere eleven mourners attended his funeral at Highgate cemetery three days afterwards.

A year later, however, some 6,000 marched to the gravesite. Marx soon achieved legendary status. His name and writings, Engels proclaimed, would 'endure through the ages' (24:469). To him fell the immediate task of editing the mountain of remaining manuscripts and crafting this legend. Marx's achievement lay chiefly, Georg Lukács once noted, in his singular ability to develop a theory of capitalism as a whole from specifically British conditions, and that too chiefly from books.[1] He was less a philosopher, economist, political theorist or leader of men than a prophet who, in E. H. Carr's words, 'imposed himself on history, with all the sheer force of a unique and dominant idea'. By heralding the possibility of an entirely new epoch in history he marked a 'turning-point in human thought'.[2] Kugelmann called him 'the thinker who deserves to be called the consciousness of the nineteenth century', a 'scholar compared to whom all the scholars since Aristotle are mere pygmies'.[3] Others have been less charitable. John Maynard Keynes declared *Capital* to be 'without interest or application for the modern world'. But this was clearly wrong. The 'best hated and best slandered man in Europe' Marx was (in Engels' words; 24:464). A slayer of monsters he was. But was he St George or Don Quixote? He was an immensely clever, erudite man. He regarded himself as, and (eventually) was, indisputably well ahead of most contemporary socialists in his analysis of capitalism. Yet he was also almost totally unwilling to see anyone else's viewpoint. The essence of democracy – compromise and the acceptance of opposition – was often beyond his capacity. Marx the man had many weaknesses that Marx the legend lacked.

Let us then briefly summarize Marx's accomplishments. What did he achieve and what do his theories not account for?

Most importantly, Marx offers us a cogent account of capitalist industrialization which stresses its destructiveness, waste and oppression. His alternative to this system maximizes self-actualization and minimizes necessary labour, to provide 'time for the full development of the individual' (29:97). Marx however failed to prove that the latter scheme inevitably emerges out of the former. (It hasn't.) He insists that no systems are permanent and all are constantly changing. (They are.) He posits a higher form of co-operative, social, communal existence where exploitation has ended, which he assures us we will find not only more rewarding, both collectively and individually, but also in large measure more just in the linkage of the two, than a life defined by the competitive ethos of capitalism. (The jury is still out on this one, but the argument remains compelling: supportive societies are easier on the psyche.)

At the broader historical level, Marx explains the chief developments in modernity with great acuity. Prioritizing property ownership in understanding social relations clearly cuts through a maze of other interpretations as to how societies operate, and how religion, law and government normally serve dominant classes. But Marx does not explain how, for lengthy periods of time, there may be great variations between the economic base and movements in the superstructure.[4] He is persuasive in viewing class as the chief determinant of most people's fate. Most have their lot in life assigned to them, and have little choice over what they do or even what they think. Most have been bound historically to the land as slaves or serfs. In an age supposedly defined by freedom, many have gained little of it. One of Marx's greatest and most enduring charges is against the mystifying ideology of the bourgeoisie.

Freedom of trade is not the basis of every other form of freedom. Freedom for the pike brings death to the minnow. And universal suffrage does not solve class conflict so much as reflect it. The liberal system is thus one of fraud and deception insofar as it promises 'liberty' but delivers plutocracy and wage-slavery for the majority. When it produces wider prosperity Marx has a case to answer.

Economically, then, Marx provides an impressive account as to how exploitation occurs, and why capitalism is prone to crisis. He does not ultimately allow sufficiently for the possibility that immiseration might not proceed as predicted, nor how or why the standard of living of workers might improve. The greatest theme in Marx's social theory is loss of control, or the predominance of coercion over consent, and for us this is more topical than ever. All the language of mystification, alienation, objectification and ideology, and the disguise of real relations by ideas, points to the need to guide society consciously towards ends which satisfy everyone's needs. Few today, however, see Marx's achievement as resting on the theory of surplus value. We now acknowledge that moral critique and economic assessment went hand in hand in the mature works. And Marx provides too little detail respecting the alternative economic model (mostly co-operation) which is intended to supplant capitalism, and how economic bodies might interact with states or other administrative institutions.

As crucially, the idea that an entire economy can be centrally planned has rarely been realized. If the co-operative decides we will work eight hours a day and the planners decree twelve, who triumphs? And if the planners triumph, doesn't the work cease to be unalienated? And still more if they are unelected? Marx fails to explain how priorities under communism might be adjusted to do more than merely give workers greater free time, and to give substance to the idea of 'attractive labour'. The hint that work itself needs to be altered, central to the 'Paris Manuscripts', seems later to have been put on the back burner. Moreover, even taken together, the critique of the division of labour and the account of surplus value do not give us an adequate theory of exploitation and oppression in the workplace, much less outside it. Many aspects of both individual and collective domination involving coercion – through racism, sexism and many other forms of prejudice – are not clearly addressed by Marx. Moreover, what he regards as the central contradiction that will trigger the downfall of capitalism – between the anarchy of exchange and individual concentration of wealth and the socialized nature of production, as evident in factory organization – has not materialized in this form.

The shift towards a greater stress on emancipation occurring in free time also left Marx with various problems. Increasing free time suggests that needs remain relatively constant, so that we do not choose to work more in order to consume more. But even under communism, Marx conceded, 'natural needs' might be 'constantly changing' (6:117). The constraints of the need for economy of time, 'the first economic law if communal production is taken as the basis', which would alone permit maximizing pleasures and 'other production, material or spiritual' (28:109) also remained. Marx clearly hoped that avarice and the quest for enrichment could be decoupled from 'the abstract quest for pleasure' as 'realised by money' in the future (28:155). But he does not explain how. *Capital* suggests that 'the notion of "means of existence" would considerably expand, and the labourer would lay claim to an altogether different standard of life' (35:530). This suggests that the workday might not be reduced much, unless machinery compensated.

Marx's later writings indeed seem to imply that owning the commodities they made, at least household goods and the like, was a component in workers' future happiness, as Hegel had insisted. The 'new needs arising from society itself; cultivating all the qualities of social man and producing him in a form as rich as possible in needs because rich in qualities and relations' might well be less spiritual than material (28:336).[5] Rather than assisting human fulfilment and creativity, 'free time' might be swallowed up by vacuous, deadening amusements guided by commodified delusions. Communists might acquire a taste for luxury and a passion for display and even become enslaved by these needs, ignoring the warnings of Babeuf, Weitling and others and encouraging inequality again. The assumption that consuming without private property would be more social, less possessive and less likely to generate jealousy and rivalry thus remains unproven. In fact conspicuous consumption might well increase if accumulation was discouraged. John Dewey noticed in Leningrad in 1928 that 'the chief reason why people spend money so freely, and on amusements as well as necessities, is because the entire political control is directed against personal accumulation, so that money counts as a means of direct and present enjoyment, not a tool of future action'.[6]

The single most important controversy around Marx consists of two aspects: what his original goals were for humanity, and how consistently he maintained them. McLellan and others rightly see alienation as the chief theme linking Marx's early and mature writings.[7] Yet this tells us less than we might expect. It indicates that the charge of a 'break' between the young Marx and a later 'scientific' viewpoint is implausible. Contrasted to the 'crippled', 'fragmented' person, *Capital* juxtaposes 'the fully developed individual, fit for a variety of labours, ready to face any change of production, and to whom the different social functions are but so many modes of giving free scope to his natural and acquired powers' (35:490–91). This idea consistently unites Marx's writings: his cause remains that of 'the free human being'. But Marx's later theory of alienation crucially was not Hegel's. The Hegelian legacy in the later Marx did not extend much beyond the scheme of categorical arrangements in the later economic works. Marx's dialectic was not Hegel's. Nor were the theory of communism, the ideal of all-roundedness, the account of sociability described as immanent in capitalism through co-operation, nor Marx's theories of revolution, politics, ideology and the state. Moreover, Marx's later treatment of alienation shifted from a philosophical to a political framework. What was initially a psychological and philosophical problem (the loss of control in the workplace) was now seen as a political problem in both economic management and the state, and as soluble through democracy and co-operation in the workplace rather than altering the process of work as such.

This implies that, if anything, Marx became more of a democrat in later life. To John Plamenatz, 'Marx conceived of proletarian government as being, from the very beginning, more truly democratic and liberal than anything known to bourgeois Europe.'[8] Two of Marx's key political concepts, however, now seem particularly suspect. First, he broadly accepted the Saint-Simonian principle of a progression from the 'government of persons' to the technocratic 'administration of things'. This optimism now seems very misplaced. Second, the 'dictatorship of the proletariat' was perhaps the worst thought-out major concept in the history of political thought. Marx's account of a fully class-conscious revolution led by a democratically organized majority was both unrealistic and romantic (in Plamenatz's charge).⁹ Bertram Wolfe wrote of the 'gap between what Marx meant and what Lenin meant by "dictatorship of the proletariat"'.¹⁰ To many, Lenin was a Blanquist rather than a Marxist, as we will see. But some also regard Marx's politics as haunted by a quest for social and intellectual unity which was realizable only 'in the cruel form of despotism', as Kolakowski insists.¹¹ For Marx not to have at least anticipated this possibility seems a grievous deficiency. Many have also seen the germs of later despotism in *The Communist Manifesto*'s proclamation of extreme centralization of power in the state, and of the formation of 'industrial armies' governed by a regimented plan.

Marx thus did not adequately explain how the transitional period, the dictatorship of the proletariat, would retain those democratic procedures and promote those very freedoms which formed part of the self-actualization ideal. Unwilling to reconsider Hegel, he nowhere demonstrated why even a relatively neutral and non-coercive state embodying a bureaucratic caste rather than an alien ruling class would disappear under communism, or on the road towards it, or why 'politics' would differ markedly from such processes in class society. Just why the proletariat should act in the way Marx assumed it ought to is also unclear. Here a 'fundamental weakness in Marx's thought', for Eugene Kamenka, is the lack of 'a theory of classes and organizations, and of freedom and servility, in *positive* terms, in terms of the *character* of the processes and movements involved'.¹² Describing the proletariat as a 'universal' class leaves much to be desired. Its suffering offered no particular advantage from a revolutionary viewpoint. Nor has it been especially inclined to communism, though we can see why Marx thought equality at a higher standard of living would clearly appear superior to desperate poverty. Marx's view of the peasantry has also proven very problematic.

It is difficult, too, not to see Marx's vision of communist society as a secular version of the Christian millennium or the Golden Age of the

Greeks, with the final titanic struggle between the forces of good and evil giving way to a new epoch of harmony, equality and plenty for all. We are rightly much more sceptical of such visions today. Marxism produced an age of steel rather than gold, but too much of it was used for making barbed wire. Yet, at another level, the peaceful transformation of opulent societies capable of providing a high standard of living for all and the democratic management of the productive process are all Marx ever contended for. Opulence, in this view – but defined by public rather than private luxury, and greater equality – was Marx's goal.

Several other weaknesses in Marx's system are also evident to readers today. The idea that the revolution somehow would permanently rather than temporarily 'forge' new forms of devotion to the common good – or enable release from earlier ones – seems unfounded. The tacit assumption that if 'exploiters' were the most amoral people, the exploited were the most virtuous, seems suspect at many levels. Nor did capitalism create a new type of worker capable of leadership.[13] Assuming that internationalism or cosmopolitanism would supersede nationalist loyalties also appears misconceived. Marx never theorized equality adequately either, or explained how differences in ability, ambition and so on, could avoid becoming ensconced, and even hereditary. He never considered whether 'barracks communism' might be worse than capitalism. Nor did he worry that the masses would not kill the privileged and intellectuals in particular. For people like Marx are usually the first victims of communist revolution.

Marx is weak on explaining how ideas function, and how ideologies are sometimes true and sometimes false. The relationship between leaders and followers, theoreticians and foot soldiers, is also poorly thought out. Most Marxist revolutions, we will see, were made by peasants acting with middle-class leaders, and not in advanced industrial countries. Leaders were central to these upheavals. Marx's theory of revolution does not explain why and when Carlylean heroes might lead, Rousseaus might inspire, Robespierres might engineer coups or, indeed, Marxes might theorize the revolution. Benedetto Croce would later term Marx the 'Machiavelli of the proletariat'.[14] But the account of how Louis-Napoléon Bonaparte actually emerged (in 1852) as a popular dictator, backed of course by the peasantry, goes some distance in exploring the role of leadership.

Here Marx exhibits an understandable confusion as to how to answer the third of the 'Theses on Feuerbach', as to who will educate the educators – the Owen question, for which Owen's answer was a paternalistic philanthropist. From the outset it was clear that the preconditions for a successful revolution included inundating the working classes with communist propaganda. This could only be produced by large numbers of theoretically astute participant-observers, that is, bourgeois intellectuals. They would of course react to the movement as it transmuted itself. But their role could obviously never be simply that of a passive mouthpiece, even if Marx did not want them to direct the movement. Some of them would invariably become leaders, and perhaps much more. Marx's psychology, both group and individual, is however very little developed. Not to foresee that hero worship of an extraordinary kind would emerge in these circumstances is puzzling. Indeed his acquaintance Karl Heinzen had already portrayed Marx himself satirically as a 'hero' of German communism in 1848.[15]

Many of these weaknesses and omissions can be synthesized in the charge that Marx never thought through adequately what he meant by 'freedom'. 'All-round development' remained an ideal linking the early and later Marx. It had to be aspired to, Marx's comments on utopia notwithstanding. The new system promised workers 'time for education, for intellectual development, for the fulfilling of social functions and for social intercourse, for the free play of his bodily and mental activity', as *Capital* put it (35:270). This to Marx was the most meaningful form of liberty, besides which all others were secondary, a point the hungry and oppressed might readily concede. At one time Marx (like Hegel) had been nostalgic about the ancient Greek *polis*, where, he thought, freedom had last 'vanished from the world' (3:137). 'Free development' was the central ideal of the 'Paris Manuscripts', *The Communist Manifesto* and *Capital*. It epitomized communism's superiority. Marx never abandoned the concept. It was the logical conclusion of his theory of alienation. Without freedom from exploitation other forms of liberty were for Marx essentially meaningless – this of course marks his distance from most forms of liberalism. The 'freedom' of 'equal' agents to buy and sell the produce of labour in particular was merely a farce, and a fiction. In reality only capital is free, and those without property are gravely constrained, for political and personal freedom can be bought by the possessing classes.

More than anyone else Marx brought home the contradiction between 'democracy' – the notional goal, we now imagine, of 1776 and 1789 – and 'civil society', commerce, the economy and economic power. But if Marx remained a radical democrat, he is consistently weak in exploring how democratic institutions actually work, and what makes some better than others. Marx's tragic failure to describe more fully the value of individuality, or at least to theorize how communism could promote it, needs little comment here. Without doubt, however, Marx thought that when the proletariat gained its freedom, it could not lose it again. Had Hegel not written that it was only because 'Orientals' lacked 'the consciousness of freedom' that 'they allow themselves to fall into despotism in religion and the political sphere'?[16] The case was analogous here. For the spirit of the times to go into reverse seemed unthinkable. All history seemed to indicate the opposite. And so the later moderns were caught off-balance, as we will now see.

PART TWO

Marxism

Conversion

It is paradoxical that much of Marx*ism* has relatively little to do with the Marx we know today, or with the revolutionary paradigms of 1848 or 1871.[1] Many of Marx's key texts remained unpublished until the 1940s, and even then most went unread. Half a dozen works, often by Engels, constituted what most people knew of Marx until Lenin appeared. The system they presented appealed primarily because of its mesmerizing combination of simplicity with complexity. The educated were alternatively challenged, delighted and perplexed by a new language brimming with concepts that flattered students by hinting at a secret wisdom whose possession would crown them as the chosen few. Marxism offered the allure and certainty of being 'scientific', of being the most insightful respecting modernity, most clearly on the side of history, and even the most ethical, because the most universal. It portrayed itself as the culmination of both history and philosophy. As a 'total' worldview it seemingly answered every question.

The appeal of totality cannot be underestimated. Here are no compromising, polluting half-measures or 'reforms' of capitalism or traditional, corrupt parties. In its completeness Marxism possesses an elegant, compelling purity. Change will be profound and all-encompassing: evil will be vanquished, and after the revolution everything will be rosy. This was immensely satisfying, both emotionally and intellectually. To the millions, a few brief formulae, duly memorized, became what most associated with Marx: capitalism is bad because it exploits the masses; the economic base generates the superstructure; the revolutionary party grows out of the class struggle; the state would wither away after a successful revolution; communist society would eliminate humanity's chief woes; the omnipotent and omniscient Party is always right. But the basic ideas were even simpler. To poor, often illiterate peasants, Marxism meant chiefly one thing: seizing land from landlords. To workers it meant ending wage-slavery.

Marx thus appeared a uniquely gifted prophet whose promise of justice often assumed a religious quality. His self-confidence was also key to his success. Even today what astonishes many readers about Marx is his audacity. He sweeps like a scythe through fields of previous thinkers, mowing down all before him. He *must* be right, we feel, for he crows so triumphantly, and is so contemptuous of his opponents. This self-confidence is highly contagious. It facilitated for many the process of conversion to communism, which was often a deeply emotional experience that transcended even falling in love. In an epoch of profound disruption, when vast numbers found themselves dislocated by war, industrialization and imperialism, Marxism provided an imaginary respite, a focus of identity and the repository of a higher ethical ideal. The sense of joining one universal human family was palpable. The prospect of secular salvation seemed – or claimed – to surpass every other intellectual system on offer for a century. Asked what communism was, Ho Chi Minh once replied, 'No one will be exploited any more, we will love each other and we will all be equal.'[2] These claims were unbeatable in this life: this was heaven on earth.

Followers came to Marxism from many directions. Most of the accounts we have come of course from the more educated. But the disenchanted and disoriented, the rebellious and angry, also often found meaning in Marx's ideals in an intense and lasting way. Embracing these was akin to religious conversion. Trotsky's onetime secretary, Bertrand Wolfe, first accepted Marxism as a 'faith', noting that 'its appeal derived in part because it was an untried ideal and that it was learnedly propounded', and that it 'cured everything at once by a simple change in property relations'. He added that some psychoanalysts 'see in it a cure for doubt, the provision of a purpose for living where life has seemed purposeless, an assurance of a kind of anonymous immortality, and a sublimating outlet for aggression'.[3] Marx's theory of history often provided the initial appeal. Angelica Balabanoff, who became secretary of the Third International in 1919, wrote that 'In Marx's materialist conception of history I found a light which illuminated every corner of my intellectual life.'[4]

In the 1930s the deepest capitalist crisis in history drove many to embrace the cause. Marx seemed finally to have been vindicated. The American Whittaker Chambers, who was for a time a Soviet spy before becoming religious and conservative, remembered that 'a man does not, as a rule, become a Communist because he is attracted to Communism, but because he is driven to despair by the crisis of history through which the world is passing'.[5] The 'strength of communism', the Briton Douglas Hyde recalled, 'is in its ability to take hatred, desire for retribution by those who have been ill-used, youthful idealism and the desire for a cleaner world, and then to harness all these powerful horses to its chariot'. 'A faith is not acquired by reasoning', recalled the Hungarian Arthur Koestler, adding that 'I became converted because I was ripe for it and lived in a disintegrating society thirsting for faith.'[6]

To some Marxism represented a higher form of radical humanism. The black American communist Richard Wright wrote that 'Of all the developments in the Soviet Union, the way scores of backward peoples had been led to unity on a national scale was what had enthralled me.' To others religion paved the way. 'What leads me to communism is not Marx, it is the Gospel', said the great French writer André Gide, having worked his way through *Capital* and *Anti-Dühring*. Concluding that 'happiness consists in making others happy', he recalled embracing Marxism 'like a faith': 'the plan of the Soviet Union seems to me to point to salvation', the USSR being a land 'where Utopia was in the process of becoming reality'.[7] To others, like the Pole Czeslaw Milosz, rationalism came to the fore, and Marxism was 'the inevitable outcome of a nineteenth-century scientific world view carried to its logical conclusion'.[8] Many saw Marxism as solving the isolation of nationalism. The American journalist Louis Fischer recalled that the 'unique appeal of the Bolshevik revolution was its universality': 'It envisaged the worldwide abolition of war, poverty, and suffering.'[9] Many early witnesses to the revolution were indeed ecstatic about what they saw. The American reporter Lincoln Steffens famously proclaimed after a

1919 visit that 'I have been over into the future, and it works.' So too the dancer Isadora Duncan wrote in 1921 that she was 'convinced that here in Russia is the greatest miracle that has happened to humanity for two thousand years'.[10] Jews flocked to the standard in disproportionate numbers, viewing the new cosmopolitanism as a respite from age-old anti-Semitism. Non-whites similarly perceived the revolution as colour-blind, and profoundly committed to racial equality. All saw Marx as unlocking the secrets of the complexity and uniqueness of the modern.

What sacrifices might not then be justified to achieve such an end? Whether they joined the Party or flirted on the sidelines as fellow travellers, believers often became fiercely loyal to the cause. The need for subterfuge was constant. Czeslaw Milosz had to flee to the bushes of islands in rivers in order to read the classics of Marxism.[11] Once converted, most risked their jobs by associating with the Party. Many infiltrated or 'captured' positions in non-communist organizations, where their affiliations had to remain hidden. Whenever possible they promoted only like-minded 'comrades'. Loyalty was the test of belief. A close-knit coterie resulted which gave meaning to the unity of humanity. Outwardly, 'bourgeois' convention was often flouted, as communists 'gloried in being "outrageous"'. Sexual freedom was common, 'bourgeois marriage' being regarded as 'legalised prostitution', though the Party claimed the right to discipline every aspect of personal life.[12] So new freedoms and new restrictions marched forwards hand in hand. Yet in one key area, German Social Democracy, Marxism became wedded to liberal democratic ideals in a manner destined to produce a grand collision with its more authoritarian interpreters at the time of the Russian Revolution.

CHAPTER 1

Marxism and Social Democracy, 1883–1918: The Revisionist Debate

Western Marxism dates from the 1870s, when it began to spread rapidly throughout Europe and then beyond.[1] Even anarchists and non-Marxian socialists like the British Fabians, who favoured gradual, peaceful change, were compelled to reckon with it. Besides Germany and Russia, movements appeared in Belgium, the Netherlands, Italy, France and Britain in particular. All brought unique historical trajectories to the debate about Marx's meaning and legacy and applied him to their own peculiar problems. In this period Marxism came widely to be seen as the most persuasive – indeed the only – alternative to capitalist industrialization and exploitation.[2] The epoch of the Second International (1889–1914) witnessed the first great triumph of the working-class movement, most notably in Germany.[3] At nine congresses, including Paris (1900), Amsterdam (1904), Stuttgart (1907) and Copenhagen (1910), working-class parties sought to forge global solidarity around the new ideals. At Stuttgart in 1907 a thousand delegates attended, a hundred of whom were members of parliaments. A key question now was avoiding war in Europe. The leading figure here was August Bebel (1840–1913), who had been imprisoned for voting against war credits during the Franco-Prussian War. He regarded a general strike as premature, but was opposed by Rosa Luxemburg, Karl Liebknecht and others. When world war finally erupted in 1914, internationalism dissipated rapidly in face of national chauvinism. Many Marxists were imprisoned. The French socialist leader Jean Jaurès was assassinated by a rabid nationalist. The German Social Democratic Party split into pro- and anti-war factions in 1916. But ironically the war, having proven the failure of internationalism, hastened the collapse of Tsarism in 1917.

By the First World War considerable disagreements had emerged as to what Marxism's end was and how it might be achieved. This was inevitable given the very varied circumstances the theory had to address. With the growing extension of the suffrage and of industrialization, one question came to supersede most others in Western Europe: could communism emerge gradually and peacefully out of capitalism? As we have seen, both Marx and Engels had suggested that in the West, at least, it might.

This scenario seemed most likely in Germany, which by the 1890s possessed a large Social Democratic party. Here, and wherever industrialization expanded and facilitated the political maturity of the proletariat, the insurrectionary models of 1792 and 1848 seemed obsolete. The early Social Democrats were mainly prosperous artisans who aspired to social integration rather than revolution. Most joined the party 'more from a vague feeling of injustice' than from any precise theoretical orientation.[4] Founded in 1875, the German Social Democratic Party (SPD) made Marxism its official doctrine in 1891, following the repeal of Bismarck's Anti-Socialist Laws in 1890. It was influenced by the flamboyant Ferdinand Lassalle (1825–64), who hoped (Marx thought unrealistically) to use the state to develop large-scale worker-dominated co-operative production. Since 'inciting one class against another' was still illegal, the SPD faced a long uphill battle politically. Seizures of publications and police disruption of meetings were common. Cultural agitation was easier. The SPD eventually published some seventy newspapers. It promoted insurance schemes, sports, theatrical, choral and educational societies, even cycling, smoking and stamp-collecting organizations, all under the party rubric, especially in the urban north of Germany. Festivals in restaurants, halls and parks also became common. Here, in the fusion of concept and activity, free time and all-roundedness, was socialist sociability in practice.[5] A counterculture was created awaiting the day of transition, and a sense of the distinctiveness of 'proletarian' as opposed to 'bourgeois' culture emerged, as expressed in celebrations like May Day.

This movement was very successful. Social Democracy's share of the vote rose from 10.1 per cent in 1887 to 31.7 per cent in 1903, when it gained eighty-one seats in the Reichstag. By 1912, with 34.8 per cent of voters, it was the nation's largest party, with 110 deputies, though it had no ministers before 1918. Besides helping to create a comprehensive welfare state, measures like the secret ballot and payment of MPs were passed. The eight-hour workday was achieved in 1918. Such a pattern clearly supported the idea of the inevitability of a final Social Democratic regime. Since at least its 1907 conference the party also became more mainstream, bureaucratic, trade unionist and imperialist in orientation. It moved towards greater collaboration with other parties in the 1912 election. Its members drew ever closer to a trade union perspective, embracing *embourgeoisement*, or the values and lifestyle of the middle class, and deepening ties with the existing system. A career as a party administrator became perfectly legitimate, and much that was once done voluntarily, out of enthusiasm, was now paid for out of party coffers.

This convivial easing into the new socialist world nonetheless betrayed deep-seated doctrinal divisions. A 'revisionist' debate erupted which eventually resulted, after 1917, in a breach between Social Democracy and communism.[6] Although the SPD had declared itself a revolutionary party at its 1883 Copenhagen congress in reaction to Bismarck's Anti-Socialist Laws, this viewpoint quickly dissipated once legal means of attaining power again became possible. The strategy of peaceful transformation was outlined most clearly in the Erfurt Programme of 1891. While Marxism became the official doctrine of the party, the dictatorship of the proletariat was formally renounced. Evolution was regarded as inevitable, the party's aim being, as its leading theorist Karl Kautsky put it, to transform the State into a 'co-operative commonwealth'.[7] Its programme also called for universal suffrage, proportional representation, and a graduated income tax.

The revisionist debate centred on Eduard Bernstein (1850–1932), who with August Bebel was Engels' executor.[8] The son of a Jewish locomotive driver, he was a banker's clerk before becoming interested in politics in the early 1870s. Exiled in Britain from 1888 to 1901, Bernstein was influenced by the Fabian Society (founded in 1884); he defended its gradualism even against Eleanor Marx and Edward Aveling, though he also consorted with the revolutionary H. M. Hyndman.[9] By 1891 Bernstein began suggesting that 'scientific socialism' was impossible.

In a series of articles between 1896 and 1898, published as *Problems of Socialism*, Bernstein queried Marx's accounts of catastrophic crisis and the immiseration of the proletariat in the face of increasing prosperity. He saw no evidence that some strata of the middle classes were disappearing, and some appeared to be growing. Nor was bourgeois capital becoming wholly concentrated in the hands of a few. Indeed Bernstein insisted that Social Democracy could raise the proletariat to the social position of the bourgeoisie.[10] Trade unions had now achieved an appreciable position in society. Workers' rights had advanced much further than Marx had predicted. Large-scale trusts and cartels regulated production and prices to a much greater degree than Marx had anticipated. To Bernstein, Marx's theory of value was a 'purely abstract entity' which ignored utility, subjective preference and supply and demand.[11] He felt that the dialectic, as a method, neglected empirical facts. He also thought that ethics had a much larger role to play in progress than Marx had conceded, and brought Kant in to shore up the case. Economic instability might persist, but a catastrophic crisis resulting in capitalism's downfall was unlikely. (Bernstein claimed Engels agreed.) Indeed a more equal division of wealth might develop. Evolution, particularly through gradually democratizing economic and political organizations, was thus the path forwards. Revolution was no longer necessary or desirable. So the state was not something to be abolished, but in the hands of the victorious proletariat was potentially a vehicle of social transformation.

These themes became Bernstein's trademark. In *The Preconditions of Socialism* (also entitled *Evolutionary Socialism*, 1899) he defended the idea that socialism was solely a proletarian doctrine or the inevitable outcome of capitalist development. The movement, he stressed, was much more important than the 'final goal'. 'Unable to believe in finalities at all', he declared, 'I cannot believe in a final aim of social-ism'.[12] Marx's perspective in 1848 he rejected as basically Blanquist. This made *The Communist Manifesto* a utopian tract insofar as it hinted at minority dictatorship rather than a revolution of the entire proletar-iat, a view taken up by Jean Jaurès and the French philosopher Georges Sorel – who tried to combine syndicalism and Marxism – amongst others. The 'dictatorship of the proletariat' was hence a harmful and 'atavistic', primitive concept insofar as it ignored the need for coali-tions with other classes or was anti-democratic. Nor would the state 'wither away', in Engels' term; here Bernstein thought Marx too close to Proudhon, and suggested instead that key bureaucratic functions might persist in the future. Moreover, the language of rights was cen-tral to Bernstein's theories, including an ideal of universal citizenship, the protection of minority rights and the 'security of civil freedom'. This Bernstein acknowledged was explicitly a liberal ideal. He even de-scribed socialism as 'organising liberalism' and liberalism's 'legitimate heir', statements Marx could not ever conceivably have made. This did not involve creating a 'proletarian society' but rather 'a socialist order of society instead of a capitalist one', and 'the evolution of civilisation' towards 'a higher view of morals and of legal rights'. Socialism would 'create no new bondage of any kind whatever', but would make each 'free from every economic compulsion in his action and choice of a calling'.[13] So, Bernstein wrote in 1900, he saw 'neither the possibility nor the necessity for giving socialist theory a purely materialistic foun-dation'. 'Marx's method', he insisted in 1903, 'was not without errors; his conclusions were not always accurate, and some of his presupposi-tions have been disproven by subsequent historical developments.' A radically new approach would make socialism simply 'the rational con-trol of economic life'.[14]

Thus was one interpretation of Marxism renounced in favour of a more contingent and sceptical form of democratic socialism. Yet Bern-stein also opposed workers electing their own factory managers, claim-ing this gave them too much power and encouraged inefficiency. Small wonder that some claim that he had 'overthrown every tenet of the Marxist philosophy'.[15] But the greatest breach was yet to come. In 1921 Bernstein condemned Bolshevism as essentially 'scholastic' insofar as it was 'directed at furnishing "proofs" for existing axioms or theories in a forced, deductive fashion', and he decried 'the unbridled terror of suppressing and silencing dissent' of Lenin's regime.[16]

Before 1914 Bernstein's main Social Democratic opponent was the most prominent Marxist writer of the period, Karl Kautsky (1854–1938), though they had much in common and together drew up the Erfurt Programme.[17] Born in Prague, the son of a stage designer and an actress, Kautsky studied at the University of Vienna before becoming a socialist in 1874. As editor from 1883 to 1917 of the chief Marxist journal of the age, *Die Neue Zeit*, he played an enormously influential role in shaping left-wing opinion. Kautsky's chief contribution was to insist that when a proletarian political party entered parliament it altered the latter's nature. A working-class majority might introduce a socialist system of production, especially through the slow transfer of private enterprises into public ownership.

But Kautsky was unwilling to accept Bernstein's proposed alliances with the bourgeoisie to facilitate this process. Even in Germany the proletariat was not yet the largest class. It also needed 'socialist consciousness' brought in from the outside, for instance by bourgeois intellectuals. Their 'social science' Kautsky saw – following Engels and Darwin in particular – as a branch of the natural sciences, and possessed of an analogous degree of certainty in inexorable (economic) laws. Kautsky maintained a more traditional view of recurrent and increasingly serious capitalist crises, and a more pessimistic outlook on capitalism's capacity to adapt to underconsumption and overproduction. He was amongst the first to link the search for new markets overseas to the growing imperialism of the epoch, and to condemn the plunder of natives under the pretext of colonial expansion.[18] Revolution he considered the unavoidable result of capitalism. Kautsky's best-selling tract, *The Economic Doctrines of Karl Marx* (1887), stressed the inevitability of class struggle between labour and capital, and thus the persistent relevance of the theory of surplus value. In *Ethics and the Materialist Conception of History* (1906) Kautsky contended that the ideal of a harmonious society might also derive from Darwin's description of social instincts and a materialist anthropology.[19] In *The*

Materialist Conception of History (1927) he offered a broad synthesis of Marx's system.[20] Marxian socialism, he insisted, was scientific and required no moral supplement. His own life, he wrote to Bernstein in 1897, would indeed 'have no meaning' if he abandoned the materialist conception of history and revolutionary role of the proletariat.[21] At the 1903 party conference Kautsky succeeded in defeating Bernstein's revisionism.

Much of this controversy thus focused on the consequences of socialist political parties participating in bourgeois parliaments or governments. Before 1914 Kautsky continued to stress the possibility of a peaceful transition to socialism in democracies, rightly claiming Marx had made the same point, and of the centrality of class consciousness to this transformation. *The Class Struggle* (1892) denied that 'violence and bloodshed' were ever necessary.[22] *The Social Revolution* (1902) emphasized that the proletariat could only attain its aims through political supremacy.[23] *The Road to Power* (1909) foresaw the proletariat achieving ascendancy through mass action of trade unions as well as the party, and disdained the use of force in favour of 'economic, legislative, and moral pressure'.[24] Kautsky rejected the strategy of a mass or general strike as inappropriate to the present, and likely to backfire. Even in his final days he rejected armed resistance to Hitler.

To Kautsky the key question of the epoch was to 'discover under which political constitution the political rule of the workers is possible'.[25] The answer was the democratic republic. But here, he indicated, Marx and Engels had not thought through some issues which had subsequently become pressing, such as the implications of merging legislative and executive powers in a new government, as in France in 1792 or in the Commune. The circumstances which necessitated this, thought Kautsky, would not be repeated in the transition to socialism. There would thus not be 'the slightest reason for combining the executive with the legislative power, and there would be many cogent reasons against it'. Amongst these were the advantages of a division of labour; the need to 'tolerate opposition' in a divided government, which he thought 'absolutely necessary for an assembly which is to enact laws'; the ability of legislatures to control the executive; and the need to avoid individual dictatorship. Kautsky thought that Marx in

The Civil War in France had urged ending independent states. But he insisted that, in arguing for 'a national delegation in Paris' confronting 'a central government with few but very important functions', the latter 'implied the same separation of legislative and executive powers which Marx desired to see abolished so far as the Commune was concerned'. He concluded that 'it may well be doubted whether Marx desired the same institution for the State as for the Commune'. This highlights the ambiguity surrounding Marx's writings on the Commune. Kautsky was concerned here to guarantee democratic control during and after the transitional period, and to avoid dictatorship.[26] Yet his account too failed to define clear boundaries between the power and role of the party and the sphere, scope and authority of the state.

Respecting the peasantry, Kautsky was generally no more sympathetic than Marx had been.[27] In *The Agrarian Question* (1899) Kautsky assumed that, whereas large farms were generally more efficient than small, in some circumstances the latter were more viable. (Another German socialist, Eduard David, actually thought the family farm the ideal model.) Industrialization had made agriculture 'lose in significance relative to industry'. The proletariat, he insisted, was the pre-eminent class, 'the heir to present-day society'. But a conflict of interests existed here: peasants wanted higher food prices; urban workers, lower. Kautsky thus urged the nationalization not only of the land but also of mortgages, the grain trade, forests and water. He also dismissed the idea that 'the village communism handed down from the Middle Ages could become an element in modern socialism', seeing it, indeed, as generally 'an obstacle to agricultural progress'.[28]

The implications of revisionism emerged most clearly after 1917, when Kautsky began moving quickly away from Bolshevism and found himself labelled the great 'renegade' by Lenin.[29] Before this Kautsky had happily acknowledged that socialist consciousness did not arise spontaneously from the masses, but needed to be imported from the outside, especially from the Social Democratic bourgeois intelligentsia, a view normally associated with Lenin.[30] But as early as November 1917 Kautsky warned that the Bolshevik takeover threatened chaos in Russia. In his view it was Lenin who was the true 'renegade' in imposing a 'bureaucratic-militarist' state on Russia.[31]

The crucial issue here was democracy, which Kautsky regarded as inseparable from socialism, and not merely a disposable means to an end. In 1918–19 he rejected the German communist Spartacus League as contemptuous of democracy. In *The Dictatorship of the Proletariat* (1918) he described Lenin's regime as state slavery, and insisted it meant an end of democracy, as defined particularly by universal suffrage in a workers' state. Lenin he thought aimed to destroy 'not only all organs of self-administration, but also all other parties and social organizations, except his own'. Both the Terror and the Civil War resulted from this dictatorship.[32] (Lenin's response is examined below.) Kautsky's brief was straightforward: 'Socialism without democracy is unthinkable.' Marx, he asserted, did not 'support dictatorship in preference to democracy', but described 'a political *condition*, and not a *form of government*'.[33] A socialist organization of production could not be achieved without a mature democracy and a proletariat educated by democratic practices. State organization by a bureaucracy was no substitute. When no European revolutions occurred to support them, the Bolsheviks were forced to promote a dictatorship that was not based on democracy. Nor would Kautsky concede that the 'Soviets', the workers' councils first formed in 1905, were a 'higher form' of democracy, since they disenfranchised all 'exploiters' (those who hired the labour of others) and non-workers. Lenin, Kautsky now implied, had paved the way for 'the exercise of dictatorial power by a single person' through his unwillingness to compromise. Kautsky insisted that the Bolsheviks relied on an ideal of revolutionary will which ignored actual economic developments. Their crucial failure came, he thought, in rejecting a 'united front of all Socialist parties' and allowing their 'insatiable yearning for power' to triumph. Bolshevik terror then followed the dissolution of the Constituent Assembly and the abolition of democracy.[34] With Bakunin's predictions, this proved a chillingly accurate forecast.

To Kautsky these developments also reinforced the view that socialism could only be built on capitalism's achievements, and especially 'large-scale industry', which rendered schemes like that projected in Thomas More's *Utopia* largely irrelevant.[35] 'The coming system of socialist production', Kautsky wrote in 1892, 'will not be the sequel to ancient communism; it will be the sequel to the capitalist system of production.'[36] In 1922 he condemned the ideal that 'the whole productive activity in the State would form a single factory, under one central control, which would assign its tasks to each single business, collect all the products of the entire population, and assign to each business its means of production and to each consumer the means of his consumption in kind', seeing this as akin to 'the prison or the barracks'. Again emphasizing that 'Socialism must connote an advance upon, and not a retreat from, Capitalism', he derided the early modern Jesuit regime in Paraguay as well as the primitive communism of the sixteenth-century Anabaptists, who sought 'the complete abolition of freedom of personality', with 'elders' assigning each person work, food rations and even their spouse. Soviet Russia, he thought, 'was the first and will doubtless be the last attempt of this kind' in the modern period.[37] Kautsky also thought that in socializing production the state and municipalities would be far more important than co-operatives. Yet he conceded that 'nobody manages industrial undertakings worse than the State', and opted with Otto Bauer for management by representatives of trade unions, workers and consumers.[38] By 1924, however, these proposals were largely unknown in Russia, where his works were now banned. In Germany, too, Kautsky found himself marginalized, and the butt of vehement communist opposition.

These controversies exposed the vast distance between Kautsky's – and Marx's – assumption that 'democracy' involved universal suffrage and popular assemblies, and Lenin's, that it meant securing the ultimate interests of the exploited by any means necessary. Kautsky's *Terrorism and Communism* (1919) asserted that Marxism demanded universal suffrage, even in a revolution. A class dictatorship was 'pure nonsense': all dictatorship became personal and 'Class-rule without laws and regulations is unthinkable'. Marx, he insisted, had changed his views on the subject between 1848 and 1871. Terrorism had not advanced the first French Revolution, nor in its Jacobin and Blanquist forms had it assisted the Commune, and it would not aid Bolshevism. At one level this represented a complete break from Marx's conception; at another it revealed its direct implications, with unerring historical accuracy. Kautsky thought Bolshevism would never become democratic: 'The fact alone that Bolshevism feels itself to be in a minority among the people makes it clear why it so obstinately rejects democracy'. He also warned of a thirst for vengeance against the bourgeoisie, and a branding of the latter as 'a special human species, whose characteristics are ineradicable'. This, again, proved chillingly accurate as a forecast of the bloodshed of the coming decades, as did the warning, echoing Bakunin, that the Bolsheviks represented a 'new class of governors'.[39] One of Kautsky's last works, *Bolshevism at a Deadlock* (1930), lamented the apparent imminent bankruptcy of the regime, the prohibition of all opposition within its electoral system, and the 'absolute arbitrary rule of the Communist Party'. It also claimed that Mussolini was 'merely aping Lenin' in his policies of repression.[40] The same would soon be said of Hitler. Despotism was contagious, it seemed.

The Bolshevik Revolution facilitated the split of the SPD in 1918. A new Communist Party (the KPD) emerging following the failed German revolution (1918–19), which resulted in the abdication of the emperor, Wilhelm II, and the creation of a republic, but in which a communist uprising in early 1919 was forcibly suppressed. From now on communism and Social Democracy were distinct and usually antagonistic trends on the left. The KPD's opposition to the SPD as 'social fascists' clearly assisted Hitler's rise to power, since Social Democracy now became the communists' main enemy.[41] After 1945 it was Bernstein's doctrines which formed the basis of the newly established SPD, which remains one of the main parties in contemporary Germany.

Besides Kautsky, Bernstein's most immediate early opponents were Karl Liebknecht (1871–1919) and Rosa Luxemburg (1871–1919), both of whom died in an abortive putsch. The Leipzig-born lawyer Liebknecht – whose father, Marx's friend, had been in the Frankfurt parliament in 1848 – in particular insisted on capitalism's necessary breakdown through a final crisis and an equally necessary ensuing revolution. The Polish Jewish daughter of a timber merchant, Luxemburg spoke Russian and German, and entered left-wing politics in 1886. She attacked

Bernstein's support for political democracy, trade unions and co-operatives, and his analysis of middle-class growth.[42]

In *Social Reform or Revolution?* (1899) Luxemburg stressed the scientific nature of Marxism and the inevitability of capitalism's catastrophic downfall. Social Democracy was incapable, she insisted, of moving beyond a trade union viewpoint. Parliamentary institutions were emanations of class society which could not be used for socialist ends. Denying the 'objective necessity' for socialism seemed akin to Luxemburg to renouncing belief in heaven for the good Christian. But she also contended, against Marx, that objecting to the 'premature' conquest of political power constituted a refusal to contemplate a proletarian seizure of power. Reformism, she thought, could never be a substitute for, but only a prelude to, revolution. 'Scientific socialism' predicted the inevitable demise of capitalism, whereby 'the progressive socialization of the process of production...creates the germs of the future social order'. The 'increased organization and consciousness of the proletarian class' was 'the active factor in the coming revolution'. The formation of great cartels would 'accelerate the coming of a general decline of capitalism', as marked by increasingly violent crises. Trade unions would not lay the ground for socialism, but would regularize relations under capitalism, and maintain the law of wages without changing 'the dimensions of production [or] the technical progress of production'. Nor would the class basis of capitalist states be altered by having working-class parties in parliament. Nonetheless capitalism would end, 'the inevitability of its collapse, leading...to socialism'. Neither trade unions nor co-operatives could tame the system by reducing profits.[43] Against the standpoint of the German trade unions, Luxemburg upheld the idea of a mass strike, which came to demarcate her strategy in general from the SPD's. She also rejected the need for Polish independence, contending that this would undermine proletarian class consciousness, whose internationalism she hoped would supersede narrower loyalties.

While still predicting capitalism's inevitable demise, Luxemburg's *The Accumulation of Capital* (1913) also stressed the role played by imperialism in prolonging it and in fostering militarism. Like J. A. Hobson's seminal account in *Imperialism: A Study* (1902), it explained how capitalism's incessant search for markets led to overseas expansion, and predicted that once the entire globe had been opened up, crisis would become unavoidable and terminal. Like Marx and Engels, Luxemburg was greatly interested in parallels between primitive communism and the future socialist society, even drawing analogies between the 'unconscious planning' based on 'collective instinct' of early groupings with the 'fully conscious, rational planning' of the future.

In 1917 Luxemburg insisted that Trotsky and Lenin sought the 'elimination of democracy as such', and famously said that 'Freedom only for the supporters of the government, only for the members of one party – however numerous they may be – is not freedom at all. Freedom is always and exclusively for the one who thinks differently.' In *The Russian Revolution* (1918) she accused Lenin and Trotsky of creating a regime 'worse than the evil it is supposed to cure'.[44] She also attacked Lenin's attempt (in his *One Step Forward, Two Steps Back*) to concentrate greater power in conspiratorial groups, and to encourage blind obedience to a small cohort of cadres, as heralding the dictatorship of 'a handful of politicians'. She was thus highly critical of the lack of elections, a free press and liberty of discussion and assembly after the revolution, insisting it was 'entirely unthinkable' that the masses could play any role without them.[45]

Outside Germany the fin-de-siècle epoch also produced a number of notable Marxist thinkers. (The Russians are considered below.) In Britain William Morris (1834–96) combined the romantic and aesthetic radicalism of John Ruskin with Marxian revolutionism. His philo-medievalism notwithstanding, Morris is often regarded today as amongst the most sympathetic thinkers to flirt with Marxism. Ruskin's insistence on the primacy of beauty in life made him a more popular figure in the early twentieth-century British labour movement than Marx himself. Morris adapted these aesthetic concerns into a new vision of work, in which individuals engaged in creative and decorative handicraft labour with a view to making life more beautiful and to maximizing capacities for personal expression. Machinery would still help to ease necessary labour.[46] Though this parallels Marx's interests in 1844, the centrality given to beauty is missing from Marx. Morris's vision represents an alternative worldview which surpasses technological rationality, rather than one which merely supplements it.

Austro-Hungary produced a powerful Social Democratic leader, Victor Adler, and several economists, notably Rudolf Hilferding (1877–1941), whose *Finance Capital* (1909) emphasized the increasing prominence of bankers over industrialists, and their efforts to create a strong state to secure their ends.[47] Other leading Austro-Marxist theorists included Max Adler, who wedded Marxism to neo-Kantianism, thus giving historical materialism a new ethical foundation. They also devoted considerable attention to the national question, as befitted a great empire embracing many disparate groups. Now regarded as a founder of multiculturalism, Otto Bauer (1881–1938) tried to mediate between communism and Social Democracy, and urged a federalist solution to the empire's competing nationalisms. Seeing the state as a higher form of 'personality', which many groups could identify with, rather than only the domain of one dominant group, he produced the most sophisticated study of nationality in relation to Social Democracy. Socialism, he contended, had to extend national sentiments to the masses in order to strengthen their sense of community, and even to sharpen national differentiation, rather than seek to eradicate it – an approach strikingly at odds with Marx's.[48]

Elsewhere, several notable thinkers emerged in Italy. Antonio Labriola (1843–1904) is best known for his *Essays on the Materialistic Conception of History* (1896), much of which eulogized *The Communist Manifesto* as heralding the progress of 'societies in the countries most advanced…into communism by the laws inherent in its own future'.[49] One of his main critics was Benedetto Croce (1866–1952), later a key source for Antonio Gramsci (discussed below).[50] In France the leading revisionist was Jean Jaurès (1859–1914), who developed humanist and democratic principles into a potent critique of orthodox Marxism, decried the spirit of hatred and urged conciliation and the avoidance of violence.[51] Another important leader was Jules Guesde (1845–1922), whose Parti Ouvrier Français was close to German Social Democracy. In Belgium, Émile Vandervelde (1866–1938) played a leading role, though he rejected the more determinist aspects of the materialist conception of history.

Many of these writers were gradualists who resisted claims that revolution was inevitable or desirable. Capitalism, they claimed, could be conquered peacefully and democratically. Those who lived to witness the rise of Bolshevism, however, soon discovered that a very different interpretation of Marx was now brought to the fore.

CHAPTER 2

Lenin and the Russian Revolution: 'Bread, Peace, Land'

As Marx is the leading social thinker of modern times, so the definitive event of the Marxian epoch was the greatest experiment in social engineering ever attempted to this time: the Bolshevik Revolution of 1917. So it must be considered here in proportion to its importance.[1]

In the 1870s Marxism began spreading in Russia, where *Capital* was first translated (in 1872; it appeared in English in 1887). Most Russian readers, however, thought Marx's framework irrelevant because capitalism was so little developed. Giving priority to economic factors over juridical or political ones in any historical analysis was applicable anywhere, though. This viewpoint was shared with Bakunin, and attracted the attention of numerous intellectuals. Many of these affiliated themselves with the largely middle-class populist or Narodnik movement, which began to arise in the 1860s and 1870s and which concentrated on protecting peasant communes, a view for which we have seen Marx had some sympathy. Some of these, especially the Narodnaya Volya (People's Will) group, formed in 1879, turned to terrorism.

Marxism's appeal in Russia also lay in its scientific, enlightened outlook. Western European ideas and technology were looked upon, as American ones would be a century later, as vastly superior to anything Russian. They epitomized modernity, as the revolution of 1917 would in turn. The leading Russian Marxist at home, and later in exile, was Georgi Plekhanov (1856–1918).[2] From a noble family whose father had possessed some fifty serfs, he was a striking figure and brilliant speaker. Plekhanov founded the Russian Social Democratic Party in Minsk in 1898 with just nine members, including Iurii (or Julius) Martov, later a leading Menshevik critic of Chekist excesses and an advocate of democracy. Plekhanov was evidently the first Russian to use the phrase 'dialectical materialism', in an 1891 essay. Amongst his many works, *On the Monist Conception of History* (1895) helped to 'educate a whole generation of Russian Marxists', Lenin recalled.[3] Here Marx's thought was seen as the culmination of Enlightenment materialism, Hegelianism and socialism. Drawing largely on Engels, Plekhanov described how dialectical materialism could overcome mere fatalistic submission to the iron laws of historical necessity. If for Hegel progress was the consciousness of freedom, for Marx it was recognizing necessity as the basis of freedom. This entailed mastering economic laws, which socialism promised.

In the late 1890s and early twentieth century the so-called Legal Marxists, including Peter Struve, M. Tugan-Baranovsky, Nikolai Berdyaev and Sergei Bulgakov, engaged with these issues. Viewing capitalism's development in Russia as progressive, they opposed populist arguments that peasant communes were a sufficient basis for a socialist future, and touted 'intellectual Europeanization' (in Bulgakov's phrase) as Russia's sole salvation. This implied, as *The Communist Manifesto* had urged, a revolutionary partnership with the bourgeoisie in order to overthrow Tsarism. Many members of this group wished to maintain a moral outlook that was independent of class struggle, and a concept of free will. By 1900 Lenin was criticizing their perspective as bourgeois and 'Bernsteinian' revisionist, while still seeing them as allies in the struggle against autocracy. Struve indeed did move towards liberalism, and a defence of natural law as a means of resisting the state's encroachments.[4] This was but one of many roads the revolution would not take.

Converted to Bakuninist revolutionary populism early on, Plekhanov came to reject both Bernstein's revisionism and Lenin's Bolshevism, as well as Pyotr Tkachev and the Russian Blanquists, and then Bakunin too. Though Plekhanov occasionally acknowledged terrorism's utility, he usually dismissed it in favour of mass revolution. In the late 1870s he thought the existing system of peasant communes might provide a collectivist basis for the future socialist society. A free federation of self-governing communes could be created without needing to pass through capitalism or build a strong centralized state. He hoped the intelligentsia could guide the peasantry in this direction. Factory workers might assist the peasants, but did not have to lead the revolution. 'No executive, administrative or any other committee', he thought, 'is entitled to represent the working class in history.'[5] All this Plekhanov regarded as commensurate with Marx's teachings, which did not in his view dictate a single path of development. Why indeed should Russia or any other country have to endure capitalism to reach socialism? This would become one of the great questions of the coming century.

During his long years of exile from 1880 to 1917, Plekhanov moved closer to Western Marxism. He began to appreciate Engels' and others' pessimism concerning the decay of Russia's communes, though a preface by Marx to Plekhanov's translation of *The Communist Manifesto* in 1882 still suggested they might form 'a starting point for a communist course of development'.[6] Increasingly Plekhanov anticipated a bourgeois-constitutional stage as the next to emerge in Russia, though he hoped revolutionary socialist demands could be made soon after the fall of absolutism. In the interim some coalition with the bourgeoisie in the political struggle was implied. Plekhanov's *Our Differences* (1885) established his distance from the Narodniks, who wished to avoid capitalism entirely. He now saw destroying the peasant communes and introducing capitalist agriculture and land concentration amongst wealthier peasants as inevitable, along with industrialization. But what to do then? It seemed that socialism could only arise after capitalism had matured, after a lengthy period of political training in democratic procedures, and after a class-conscious revolutionary proletariat had emerged. Here a socialist intelligentsia clearly had a major role to play in educating the proletariat, if not in leading the revolution. The peasantry were now clearly relegated to a lesser role. Industrial development would dictate the course of the revolution. In 1898 Plekhanov recoiled from Bernstein's first statements of revisionist Marxism, complaining that he understood '*nothing at all*' of socialism.[7] But then, in 1902, he fell out with Lenin over the latter's proposal to nationalize land as an immediate step against absolutism, amongst other issues.

Russian Social Democracy's great crisis occurred at its 1903 party congress in Brussels, and resulted in a split into Menshevik (minority) and Bolshevik (majority, from *bolshinstvo*) factions. The pretext was a dispute as to how broadly based the party should be. Though Lenin had hinted in 1902 that 'we could get on very well without a dictatorship' if the petty bourgeoisie and proletariat joined forces, he now supported a tighter, more restricted and more centralist, authoritarian grouping, with more power residing in the Central Committee, especially to control local organizations.[8] Lenin's *Letter to a Comrade on Our Organization Tasks* (1902) posited authoritarian centralism as the basis of conspiratorial activity. In his view 'class political consciousness' could not emerge spontaneously from the working classes, which could at most attain 'a trade-union consciousness' or bourgeois outlook. 'Social-Democratic consciousness' could only be 'brought to them from without', namely from a socialist party.[9] Fewer workers needed to be admitted to the party as a result. A plea for a broader party was supported by Iurii Martov, amongst others, for whom this evident mistrust of the masses was anathema. Other Russian Marxists, like V. P. Akimov, opposed both centralization and the inevitability of the dictatorship of the proletariat, and warned against the party's disdain for workers. Here Lenin was thus closer to Marx's views in the Communist League period, rather than the Marx of the mass movement of the First International.

From now on the Mensheviks assumed that the coming revolution would be political, and would supplant Tsarist rule with middle-class power. Some compromises would be required to make this government succeed – and locally in many places, for example in 1906, the Mensheviks actually supported moderate Kadet (Constitutional Democratic Party) candidates, and warned that demands for an eight-hour day would frighten Kadet voters off.[10] By contrast the Bolsheviks insisted that the revolution would be social in nature, and would eventuate in working-class rule. The Mensheviks also contended that Russia was too undeveloped to introduce socialism before it emerged elsewhere, while the Bolsheviks argued that not only might such a strategy permit enslavement to the nascent bourgeoisie, Russia could also use its pre-capitalist forms of organization to hasten socialism. Both however shared a strong faith in historical inevitability, and opposed acts of individual terrorism by the peasant-based Social-Revolutionaries and others. Lenin pointed to France in 1792 as indicating the path Russia should pursue in 1917.

Lenin's became the majority Bolshevik view, with Plekhanov supporting him. Democracy as such, it was even suggested, might be subordinated to achieving revolutionary success. As the split with the Mensheviks widened, however, Plekhanov became increasingly uncomfortable with Lenin's authoritarian centralism. Lenin's position, he warned, pointed towards Bonapartism, and the Bolsheviks 'evidently confuse the dictatorship of the proletariat with a dictatorship over the proletariat'.[11] Yet, on the principle that 'The success of the revolution is the highest law', Plekhanov also was willing to aver that 'the revolutionary proletariat might limit the political rights of the upper classes, just as the upper classes at one time have limited its rights'. Parliaments which failed to bring the desired results might be dissolved. Thus democracy was again chiefly a means to a socialist end, never an end in itself.[12] And Plekhanov implied as early as 1893 that, when the revolution was completed, freedom would be confined to the working class, 'led by comrades who correctly understand the teaching of Marx and draw from it the correct conclusion'.[13]

During these years few Russian Marxists portrayed the shape of the future communist society in any detail. One such illustration from around 1870, by the revolutionary Sergei Nechaev, hardly represented a majority view, but it is noteworthy. It proposed all property be made public, with all having common kitchens and identical bedrooms. Children would be educated in the same schools. Leaders would ensure that all workers joined unions, and those who did not would not be fed. Unions would regulate work and production, overseen by a committee which all would gladly obey 'because they have seen in practice its foresight, its vigilance, its energy and the usefulness of its orders and be convinced of the necessity of that discipline'.[14] Nechaev's simplistic portrait of a dictatorship seemingly caricatures what Marx derided as 'barracks communism'. But it would prove strikingly prescient. After 1917 Nechaev would be rehabilitated by the Bolsheviks as foreshadowing their efforts.

Then came the revolutions so long anticipated. In 1904–5 a general strike in St Petersburg, naval mutinies at Kronstadt and Sebastopol, and the creation of the first Duma (assembly) apparently sounded the death knell of the old regime. Despite its inadequacies, having no legislative powers and being based on a small electorate, the Duma demanded an eight-hour day, freedom of assembly for workers, a free press, and separation of church and state. Reaction triumphed, however, and it took the First World War and massive Russian losses finally to undermine the Tsar. Following revolution in March 1917 – which took the Bolsheviks by surprise – Nicholas II abdicated on the 15th, bringing the 300-year-old Romanov dynasty to an end.[15] For a time the country was led by a Provisional Government representing mostly landlords, industrialists and the professional classes, headed by a moderate Social-Revolutionary, Alexander Kerensky (1881–1970). It was confronted by Soviets of workers, soldiers and peasants, amongst whom the Mensheviks and some radical Social-Revolutionaries were most influential.[16] Here the Mensheviks saw themselves as a kind of 'legal opposition' during a supposed transitional 'dual power' phase of bourgeois revolution.

Exiled in Western Europe since 1900, and now in Switzerland, Lenin negotiated with the Germans to return to Russia. He famously reached the Finland Station in Petrograd (as St Petersburg had been renamed in 1914) by sealed train on 16 April. The 'Marseillaise' thundered out on the platform as it finally arrived, hours late. A vast throng mobbed the square as Lenin emerged, awkwardly carrying a large bouquet of flowers given to him by Alexandra Kollontai, later People's Commissar for Social Welfare. Slowly Lenin made his way by armoured car, preceded by a searchlight and constantly surrounded by surging, impatient and by no means entirely sympathetic crowds, to the palace of the ballerina Kshesinskaya, who had been Nicholas II's mistress. When he had moved out to the square, he announced, to the surprise of many, the collapse of capitalism and the beginning of worldwide socialist revolution. His first, two-hour speech in Russia, demanding the seizure of power, flabbergasted Marxists for its departure from every rule of materialist analysis. Lenin ignored the Constituent Assembly entirely, speaking only of the need for government by Soviets of workers, soldiers and farm labourers. The dogmas of necessary capitalist development were seemingly thrown to the winds. One Bolshevik despaired that Lenin had revived 'the old discarded primitive anarchist notions' of Bakunin.[17] As far away as Italy the country's leading socialist journalist Antonio Gramsci declared it to be 'a revolution against Marx's *Capital*...The Bolsheviks have denied Karl Marx, and they have affirmed by their actions, by their conquests, that the laws of historical materialism are less inflexible than was hitherto believed.'[18]

The politics of will now seemed triumphant, economics a distant second. Indeed Lenin presented no economic programme at all. Nor did he explain how the Soviets, representing a tiny minority, could construct socialism. The following day he sketched out his 'April Theses' concerning immediate progress towards socialist revolution, and supplanting a parliamentary republic with Soviet control.[19] The Paris Commune was a key model here: land was to be nationalized and bureaucracy abolished, replaced by elected officials receiving a worker's wage. The Marxist philosopher Alexander Bogdanov declaimed against 'the delirium of a madman'. Most thought Lenin had simply no idea what was happening in Russia. Caution, the rulebook, Marxism – all seemed thrown to the winds. Or so the Mensheviks and many others thought. But Trotsky was doubtless correct in writing later that 'If neither Lenin nor I had been present in Petersburg, there would have been no October Revolution'.[20] So much for inevitable 'historical necessity'. How could Marx's theory account for this?

Lenin's return to Russia thus opened up the possibility of an entirely new strategy. Other Bolsheviks, like Lev Kamenev (1886–1936), wondered aloud whether the bourgeois revolution could be completed if the bourgeoisie itself was hardly up to the task. Joseph Stalin and Grigory Zinoviev (1883–1936) rallied to Lenin's view ten days later, when a party conference resolved the rapid transfer of state power to the Soviets, which Lenin now proclaimed to be a 'power *of the same type* as the Paris Commune of 1871', that is, Marx's dictatorship of the proletariat.[21] To Lenin, Russia was now 'the nation which gave Karl Marx to the world'.[22] And indeed this was not inconsistent with one reading of some of Marx's writings, as Trotsky alleged. Yet it has been claimed that as early as 1905 Lenin regarded 'non-Party organisations like the Soviets' as 'superfluous' once communist 'work among the masses is properly and widely organised'.[23]

History had thrust the unfortunate Kerensky onto centre stage before he had learned his lines or knew the drama was to be a tragedy. Squeezed between Russia's collapsing western front and revolutionary upheaval, the Provisional Government now foundered. It did little to meet demands for peace, land and workers' control, and instead repressed those seeking to push the revolution further. Following an attempted uprising on 16–17 July, Kerensky struck back. Hundreds of Bolsheviks were imprisoned, including Trotsky and Kamenev. Lenin fled into hiding. When General Kornilov marched on Petrograd in September to make himself military dictator he too was arrested. His efforts, however, drove many waverers and Menshevik sympathizers towards the Bolsheviks. Kerensky lost much sympathy by continuing to support the Kadets, who backed Kornilov. Further military setbacks and general war-weariness pushed others in the same direction. Cries of 'All Power to the Soviets!' increasingly drowned out Kerensky's feeble protests.

At the first All-Russian Congress of Soviets in June 1917, the Bolsheviks had only 105 out of 800 delegates. By autumn, at the Second Congress, they had a majority (390 out of 649 delegates). A new coalition government was formed by Kerensky. But the Mensheviks and moderate Social-Revolutionaries were now tainted by association with the propertied classes and prevarication on ending the war. To the Bolsheviks this too was simply a bourgeois government. Plekhanov thought it rightly aimed at compromise, moderation and alleviating class hostilities. Lenin, he warned, was completely ignoring Russia's actual economic conditions in favour of a putschist attitude. A premature 'utopian' Bolshevik coup d'état was thus to be avoided at all costs.

Under the slogan 'All Power to the Soviets!' Lenin orchestrated just such a coup on 6–7 November. Many of the Soviets were still led by moderate socialists. For the workers, indisputably, the Soviets meant democracy in industry, 'labour control over production', the end of landlord tyranny in the countryside and the rejection alike of Tsarist autocracy and capitalist despotism. On the evening of 7 November Red Guards seized the Winter Palace in Petrograd, the seat of the Provisional Government. They were led by the Military Revolutionary Committee of the Petrograd Soviet, whose first minister of finance was a bank clerk, and the minister of commerce a historian. A crowd of unshaven, sleepless men, and a few women, shrouded in tobacco smoke, the Bolshevik leaders met continuously at the former aristocratic women's finishing school, the Smolny Institute. Kerensky was forced to flee, but most of his ministers were arrested in the Winter Palace. 'Bread, Peace, Land' was the slogan of the Bolshevik papers of 7 November, as Trotsky promised 'an experiment unique in history': 'to found a power which will have no other aim but to satisfy the needs of the soldiers, workers and peasants'.[24]

On Thursday 8 November hundreds of thousands went to work as usual, hoping to scrape out a subsistence in the midst of epochal turmoil. At its centre this day was Lenin. The Harvard-educated American journalist John Reed saw 'A short, stocky figure, with a big head set down in his shoulders, bald and bulging. Little eyes, a snubbish nose, wide, generous mouth, and heavy chin', shabbily dressed but clean-shaven, 'colourless, humourless, uncompromising and detached', but with 'the greatest intellectual audacity'. Lenin now heralded 'the era of the Social Revolution', and prophesied worldwide revolution, with 'a thousand simple faces looking up in intent adoration'.[25] Late that evening 'The Internationale' was sung. Shortly afterwards private property in land belonging to estate owners (not peasants) was abolished, along with hired labour. The programme was largely appropriated from the Social-Revolutionaries, who sought 'socialization of the land', meaning common ownership, with use-rights being granted both individually and collectively, until eventually the peasants voluntarily joined collective enterprises 'through the intrinsic attractiveness of a collectivist society'. But Lenin's plan was 'joint cultivation on large model farms', which after the interruption of the New Economic Policy (1921–8) was eventually Stalin's too.[26]

Meanwhile the revolutionary coalition began to dissolve. After the Bolsheviks received fewer votes than the Social-Revolutionaries in the December election (24 per cent to 38 per cent) Lenin dissolved the Constituent Assembly in January 1918 by force in yet another coup. The new Council of People's Commissars, the Sovnarkom, with Lenin as president, presided. His December 1917 'Theses on the Constituent Assembly' proclaimed that 'a republic of Soviets is a higher form of democracy than the usual bourgeois republic with a Constituent Assembly'.[27] The nation began to divide, many military units siding with the Bolsheviks while their officers supported Kerensky. Besides heading the new government, Lenin chaired the Party's Politburo and Central Committee. Now the dreaded winter crept on, the war continued to go badly, and hunger stalked the streets. Soviets now began to spring up everywhere. The new government quickly vested all local power in their hands, including the right to levy taxes.

Already, however, the cry was heard, 'The power of the Soviets is not a democratic power, but a dictatorship…*against* the proletariat'.[28] To Vera Zasulich, now a Menshevik, the Bolshevik coup perverted Marxism in not permitting sufficient time between the bourgeois and proletarian revolutions for an adequate political consciousness to emerge.[29] Yet there were also grounds for optimism. Amongst the early reforms introduced by the Bolsheviks was an eight-hour workday, the first in the world. Initially there was relatively little nationalization of enterprises, and Lenin spoke of 'a sort of state capitalism' operating. Nationalization was then extended to most major enterprises in June 1918. A month later the Tsar and his family were shot, with their doctor, nurse, several servants and two dogs (another dog, 'Joy', was the sole survivor of the massacre). Shortages of fuel, food and raw materials made the militarization of labour – 'proletarian compulsion', Bukharin called it[30] – almost inevitable. So workers' control in the factories gave way to strict discipline and compulsory labour, often overseen by soldiers.[31] But during the Civil War (1917–22) Lenin was forced to concede that

'War Communism' (1918–21), as it came to be called, with its mandatory grain requisitions from the peasants, bore little relation to previous plans for the transition to socialism, especially after hundreds of peasant uprisings broke out.

In the nation at large, at first, the intoxicating new revolutionary spirit of equality caught on quickly, though. Overseers were expelled in some factories. Engineers were forced down into the pits in some mines to see how they enjoyed swinging a pick while a few miners sat for a while at the bosses' desks. Workers rapidly set up factory committees elected by universal suffrage to oversee everyday management. Many demanded shorter working hours and substantial wage rises. Signs went up in restaurants saying 'Just because a man must make his living being a waiter do not insult him by offering him a tip.'[32] Hotel staff told guests to shine their own shoes.[33] Expensive corsets, dog collars and false hair – luxurious symbols of the old regime – suddenly became superfluous, even dangerous to flaunt. Upper-class manners, such as hand kissing, rapidly became passé. (They reappeared at the end of the 1920s.) Educated young women recoiled in shock when tram conductors called them 'comrade'. But as the German communist Rosa Leviné-Meyer recalled, 'to be called "lady" was nearly an insult'.[34] Looters were barely held in check, and violent theft became extremely common; bourgeois citizens – 'former people', in the menacing phrase – were relieved of their fur coats, shoes, wallets and much else.

An insatiable thirst for knowledge also produced a flood of pamphlets and newspapers which often sold out immediately. Tsarism had imposed a near-monastic political silence on the population. Now millions yearned to talk – and most of all, an American observer noted, about one thing: freedom, *Svoboda*, for peasants, workers, soldiers, Jews, women.[35] Every street corner was a public tribune, and Russia became 'the Kingdom of Speech', where at the slightest pretext workers would down tools to discuss Lenin's or the Soviets' latest policies.[36] But this freedom was short-lived. By late November 1917 most non-Bolshevik presses and journals were closed. Lenin ordered stocks of paper seized, and though he promised all parties could use printing plants in proportion to their numbers, this never happened. The pretext that these measures were 'temporary' and 'extraordinary' was used. But all 'bourgeois' periodicals were now prohibited in principle, and only the Bolsheviks had paper.

After the Winter Palace was seized, there was a veritable orgy of drunkenness in Petrograd for several days. Unit after unit succumbed to conquest by the Tsar's wine cellars, until it was necessary to destroy thousands of bottles with machine-gun fire and to prohibit the production and sale of alcohol. For at least half of the 'ten days that shook the world', wrote their most famous chronicler, John Reed, a large number of the shakers were utterly intoxicated.[37] Yet they prevailed.

Petrograd might have been carried, but what about the rest of the country? In many respects a European enclave, Petrograd was not Mother Russia. That vast nation did not in the least resemble Marx's vision of a highly developed capitalism, where concentrated wealth and a socialized labour process were to herald the final explosion. Indeed the serfs had only been emancipated from near-slavery in 1861, within living memory of some. In European Russia the condition of the peasants had actually deteriorated since then, with much formerly common land being privatized. Many remained oppressed by and indebted to their landlords, who exported large amounts of grain even in districts where starvation occurred. Over a third of the land was owned by the Tsar, his family, cabinet ministers or the church. About the same percentage belonged to peasant communes, some 80 per cent of the population. The Bolsheviks could thus easily exploit the great wartime slogan of 'Bread, Peace, Land'. By November 1917 an agrarian revolution was well underway in the provinces, the new Soviets often simply taking over buildings formerly occupied by the old commune or *mir*.[38]

Most of the Russian empire had been formed only in the last two centuries, and it embraced hundreds of nationalities and ethnic groups. In 1913, respecting the national question, Lenin had opposed secession, proclaiming that 'Marxists are, of course, hostile to federation and decentralization' because 'capitalism for its development demands as large and as highly centralized states as possible'.[39] Now he upheld in principle the potentially contradictory right of nations to self-determination, and opposed the 'Great-Russian nationalist poison'. Frontiers were to be determined 'by the will of the people'.[40]

In December 1917 Finland became independent. Ukraine followed in early 1918, and here the anarchist movement led by Nestor Makhno attempted to establish a republic and to guarantee a free press and self-government, fighting alternately against Red and anti-Bolshevik White alike. Lenin even considered allowing Makhno to retain part of Ukraine for a social experiment.

In Russia the pace of reform in other areas was swift. Religious freedom was granted. Most importantly, perhaps, peace was agreed with Germany and the other Central Powers in March 1918. Land was distributed as inalienable public property, without the right of hiring labour. Finally a decree on labour control abolished commercial secrecy and established an all-Russian Soviet to co-ordinate industry, the quantity of production to be dictated by the community's needs, and the price of goods by production costs. Government salaries were capped at an average skilled worker's wage of 500 roubles monthly (about $50, or around $1,000 in 2018 terms), with 100 roubles more for each dependent child. (Lenin reprimanded a colleague for raising his own salary as head of state to 800 roubles.) Night work for women and children was prohibited, and hours of labour limited to forty-eight per week, with the eventual aim of reducing work to six hours daily and equalizing wages. Social insurance for illness and unemployment was introduced. All titles of address were abolished, and replaced by one: 'comrade' (*tovarishch*). All this was in keeping with *The Communist Manifesto*'s proposals of 1848 and the Commune of 1871. This was, truly, Social Democracy as most nineteenth-century socialists had usually understood it. Or so it seemed.

The political course of the revolution flowed partly from Lenin's principles and partly from circumstances. How did these develop? The key issue, naturally, was power. Some believe Lenin never intended the Soviets to produce a workers' parliament, or to serve as a balancing weight against any government, as some Social-Revolutionaries, Mensheviks and anarchists presumed. On arriving in Petrograd in April 1917 Lenin said bluntly that 'Two powers *cannot exist* in a state', meaning, at that point, the Soviets and the Provisional Government.[41] But the same principle applied after the revolution too. Lenin's early tendencies towards Blanquism have often been noted. His 1902 pamphlet, *What Is to Be Done?* debated the need for a new Marxist party in Russia, and also glorified Tkachev's praise for mass terror. Now came the first inklings of a conspiratorial strategy which seemed markedly at odds with orthodox Marxism. (As we have seen, Marx distinguished between strategies appropriate to democratic societies and those which suited despotisms.) Yet it has been contended that Lenin was not a Blanquist insofar as he believed that revolutions emerged from historical conditions and could not be provoked by conspiracies at any time, and that the party should be closely integrated with proletarian mass movements.[42] These views were developed in the journal *Iskra* (Spark), which Lenin helped to edit in London.

At the 1903 conference of the Russian Social Democratic Labour Party in Brussels, Lenin insisted that the party embrace 'as much centralism as possible', including the right of the Central Committee to veto local decisions. Martov criticized the 'hypertrophy of centralism' this implied, but most of Lenin's colleagues were not unduly worried.[43] After breaking from the Mensheviks in 1903, Lenin portrayed his opponents as opportunists in *One Step Forward, Two Steps Back* (1904). 'Democratic centralism' – Lenin's chief contribution to Marxist theory – backed by 'discipline' now became the Party's organizational principle in the struggle against autocracy. Thus in 1921 Lenin insisted that while 'higher cells' must always be elected by 'lower cells', the directives of the former always had an 'absolute binding force' over the latter. Some later thought it was 'Lenin's centralization' that led to 'the concentration camp state', or carcerotopia.[44]

In 1905 Lenin portrayed himself as a radical Marxist democrat. 'Democracy', however, meant a stage before socialism, an inevitable 'democratic, not a socialist dictatorship' in the first (bourgeois) phase of the revolution. Elsewhere Lenin identified the quest for a 'democratic republic' with the petty bourgeoisie, and contrasted it with the 'revolutionary-democratic dictatorship of the proletariat and the peasantry'. Now Lenin distinguished between personal dictatorship, which he insisted Marx always opposed, and class dictatorship, which did not involve 'the annulment of all liberties and guarantees of democracy, arbitrariness of every kind, and every sort of abuse of power in a dictator's personal interest'. But he also bluntly said that placing 'the bayonet on the agenda' was 'the meaning of the slogan: dictatorship', namely 'iron rule' (or steel, anyway). From 1907 he insisted that the Bolsheviks must be professional revolutionaries, manifesting what some saw as a distrust of the masses in principle. After the idea of 'democratic centralism', this 'vanguard' idea was his most distinctive contribution to Marxism. Here Trotsky, who like the Mensheviks wanted a broader party, disagreed. And to critics like Vera Zasulich, Lenin confused 'party' with 'organization', the latter implying a rigid hierarchy which excluded those of different opinions, a concept in her view supported by Lenin because it enabled him to control its members.[45]

Lenin had other priorities at this time. Besides promoting the need for a bourgeois revolution in Russia as '*absolutely* necessary in the interests of the proletariat', *Two Tactics of Social Democracy in the Democratic Revolution* (1905) proposed an alliance between workers and peasants, which Lenin hoped would turn poorer peasants against the richer. Fellow Marxists however thought Lenin's admiration for Tkachev and endorsement of agrarian reform made him a renegade. Respecting the peasantry, all land was to be nationalized, and large estates transformed into model farms. Private tillage would continue, but Lenin thought small-scale farming inefficient. In 1913 he assured the poor peasants (quoting Engels) that the Bolsheviks in power would 'not even think of forcibly expropriating' them. In 1918, he denounced 'land nationalization' as a bourgeois slogan, claiming Marx had agreed.[46] Eventually, in August 1918, the Party changed its slogan to 'land socialization', giving the peasants freedom to dispose of land. But whatever Lenin said, his goal was to establish collective farms. When it came to workers' control in the factories, which now began in Petrograd, Lenin was nervous about the lack of Party supervision, but nonetheless anxious to garner support here too. He also hinted that revolution would be carried to Europe, giving Russia a breathing space, and implied that success was unlikely otherwise. Trotsky agreed.

In spring 1917 Lenin urged the Party to exploit the 'relative freedom of the new order', terming Russia 'the freest of all the belligerent countries in the world'. He deployed the slogan, 'power to the Soviets', where direct democracy meant 'a radical re-fashioning of the whole old state apparatus'. In circumstances of 'dual power' – the Soviets paralleling Kerensky's bourgeois 'dictatorship' – Lenin thought a revolutionary dictatorship could be created modelled on the Paris Commune, with an elected bureaucracy subject to recall and paid at ordinary workers' rates, and the standing army and police replaced by armed workers. Lenin was very self-conscious about his relationship to Marx. The Bolsheviks, he insisted, were 'not Blanquists, we do not stand for the seizure of power by a minority'.[47] He described his eventual goal as lying beyond democracy, stating in April that the regime was already ceasing to be a 'democracy' insofar as 'democracy means the domination of the people, and the armed people cannot dominate themselves.' Hence 'the term democracy', he added, was 'scientifically incorrect when applied to a Communist Party'.[48] In July 1917 Lenin still called his bid for power an 'insurrection'. The 'new type of state' would oversee the transition from capitalism to socialism. In November 1917 he emphasized that proletarian dictatorship would prepare the way for communism. Only then would 'truly complete democracy become possible and be realised', and 'only then would democracy begin to *wither away*'. Democracy thus was 'only one of the stages' on the road to communism. It meant '*formal* equality', but would be surpassed in the 'higher phase of communism' by 'actual equality' and 'equality of labour and pay'.[49]

Lenin's chief commentary on these themes was *The State and Revolution* (1918).[50] Engels is the chief source for the tract, which provided a simple blueprint for future generations of Marxists. Where 'the *irreconcilability* of class antagonisms' existed, Lenin wrote, state power was merely 'an organisation of violence for the suppression of some class'. He denigrated universal suffrage as 'an instrument of bourgeois rule' which did not necessarily reflect 'the will of the majority of the working people'. But through proletarian dictatorship it might also be used to suppress capitalists. A 'bourgeois state without the bourgeoisie' might survive even into communism. Lenin stressed that democracy was '*not* identical with the subordination of the minority to the majority', but was rather 'a *state* which recognises the subordination of the minority to the majority', which left open the question of the franchise and how the Party was chosen. His ambiguous use of the phrase the 'overcoming of democracy' in the 'democratic-republican state' seemingly weakened the case for voting and recall. But it also meant 'suppression by force, i.e., exclusion from democracy, of the oppressors and exploiters of the people'. Again Lenin's chief model was notionally the Paris Commune, but in conjunction with centralism, not federalism. Ultimately, however, the interim proletarian state 'or semi-state' would 'wither away' or 'die out', in Engels' famous phrase (25:268), and 'people will *become accustomed* to observing the elementary conditions of social life *without violence* and *without subordination*'. Without coercion, states as such would cease. A 'parasitic' bureaucracy would be replaced by a 'more and more simple' system of control and accounting accessible to all, 'so that *all* may become "bureaucrats" for a time and that, therefore, *nobody* may be able to become a "bureaucrat".'[51] Lenin still thought 'technicians of all sorts, types and degrees' would exist, and insisted with Engels that 'a certain amount of subordination...authority or power' would remain. Yet he was confident that such 'gentlemen are working today in obedience to the wishes of the capitalists, and will work even better tomorrow in obedience to the wishes of the armed workers'. (Kautsky retorted that 'the point of the bayonet is not the best incentive to labour'.[52]) In May 1918 Lenin acknowledged that some experts required high salaries as a 'compromise', if only temporarily. Clearly improvisation was necessary, and Lenin observed that Marx had never committed himself 'to ways and means of bringing about the revolution'.[53] Others, however, conclude that by now 'Lenin was not a Marxist' at all.[54] And we can certainly concede that a central absence here was a theory of political institutions.[55]

In *The Proletarian Revolution and the Renegade Kautsky* (1918) Lenin insisted that the proletarian dictatorship and 'the strictest observance of democracy' were utterly compatible. All forms of bourgeois state, monarchical or republican, were now seen as merely variants on 'the dictatorship of the bourgeoisie'. Lenin accused Kautsky of making Marx a 'common liberal' in denying the 'very *essence* of Marx's doctrine', the need for proletarian dictatorship. This dictatorship meant 'rule based directly upon force and unrestricted by any laws'. Infringements of 'pure democracy' related only to the equality and freedom of the exploiting classes, landlords and capitalists. All this was necessary to achieve 'the abolition of classes', 'that which permits one section of society to appropriate the labour of another section'.[56]

What Lenin meant by 'democracy' thus had little to do with governmental forms, or the numbers voting, much less checks and balances on executive power. Primarily it meant that workers were actually involved in administration, and that the government *represented* their class interest. For this no other political parties were necessary. By early 1918, after suppressing the 'bourgeois' parties and Mensheviks, only two remained, the Bolsheviks and the left or more radical Social-Revolutionaries. The collapse of the latter that summer after a failed revolt against the Bolsheviks ended the possibility of independent peasant representation. One observer called what remained 'a dictatorship of the Bolshevik Party or – better said – of the Central Committee of the Party over the proletariat and the entire nation'.[57] Now there were occasional justifications of personal dictatorship too. In March 1918 Lenin saw 'absolutely no contradiction' 'between Soviet democratism and the use of dictatorial power by single individuals...How can the strictest unity of will be ensured? By the subordination of the will of thousands to the will of one.'[58]

In principle, however, workers' control, introduced in 1917, persisted throughout this period. When Russia became a Republic of Soviets in January 1918 all power was notionally 'vested in these Soviets' without mention being made of the Party.[59] This fiction could not last. All other organs of power had also to be suppressed. In 1917 the trade unions were regarded as the basis of workers' control. In January 1918 it was decided that they could not be independent but must 'inevitably be transformed into organs of the socialist state'. In June 1918 workers' control in the factories was abandoned in favour of one-man management. 'Iron discipline' was imposed on the workplace, though not without resistance.[60] This was the death knell of union autonomy. The process of 'governmentalizing' the unions proceeded under Trotsky's leadership in January 1919, and the unions became primarily responsible for militarizing the labour force. During 'War Communism' (1918–21), however, it became evident that urban workers were still far from satisfied with the Bolsheviks. Accordingly Lenin imposed Party dictatorship over the Soviets. The Ninth Congress of the Russian Party

(1920) finally eradicated trade union autonomy and workers' control. Resistance to these moves was led in 1920–21 by the redoubtable feminist Alexandra Kollontai (1872–1952), who was savagely attacked by Lenin and doubtless spared only by being sent abroad on a diplomatic mission in 1923. The 'Workers' Opposition' claimed to be heir to the ideals of 1917. It railed against the growing power of the Party and state, and insisted on free elections of trade union leaders and Party officials and union control over the economy.[61]

Lenin however made it clear that, in relation to the trade unions, 'the dictatorship is exercised by the proletariat organised in the Soviets', and that he had no intention of sharing power. The consolidation of the Party's position continued apace. The bureaucracy – 'all that Soviet riff-raff', Lenin called it – began to proliferate, even if its wages were supposedly no more than the 'communist maximum' of a skilled worker. Though Lenin was widely associated with the suggestion that cooks might staff it, he wrote that 'We are not Utopians. We know that an unskilled labourer or a cook cannot immediately get on with the job of state administration'. Instead he insisted that training begin immediately of 'all the working people, all the poor, for this work'.[62] But by 1921 Lenin conceded that it was a 'fairy tale' to suggest that any worker could do the job.[63]

As the Civil War began to wind down in late 1920 there was hope that repression of the Bolsheviks' opponents would ease. When the Union of Soviet Socialist Republics was formed in 1922, the Party's power was concentrated in a Politburo of five members, later expanded to seven and then nine. Within the Party, Lenin resolutely rejected the right of criticism. In *What Is to Be Done?* he had denounced 'freedom of criticism' in the Party as 'freedom to introduce bourgeois ideas and bourgeois elements into socialism'. His contempt for 'the individualism of the intellectual, with its platonic acceptance of organisational relations' – or 'autonomism' (aimed at Plekhanov) – was contrasted to 'centralism'.[64] These views did not alter. In March 1920 Lenin proclaimed the need to 'wipe off the face of the earth all traces…of the policy of the Mensheviks and Social-Revolutionaries who speak about individual rights'. He repeatedly denounced the Mensheviks as a key threat to Bolshevik rule, and Trotsky condemned all opposition as 'Menshevism'.[65]

In February 1921 the Menshevik government in Georgia, which had declared independence in May 1918, was expelled when the country was invaded by the Red Army. Shortly after, the party – which had urged the abolition of the Cheka, the new political police – was outlawed. Lenin allowed a few prominent Mensheviks and anarchists to go into exile. But he now clearly established the limits of 'opposition'. 'To form ourselves into different groups (especially before a congress) is of course permissible (and so is to canvass for votes)', he declared; but, he added, 'it must be done within the limits of communism'. Party members were told that 'whatever luxury of discussion we permitted ourselves, rightly or wrongly, in the past, we now recognize the need for greater harmony and unity than ever before'. Press freedom was only 'freedom for the political organization of the bourgeoisie and its most trusted servants – the Mensheviks and Social-Revolutionists…it means to help the class enemy'.[66] Lenin's attitude towards opposition has been described as 'uppermost' amongst the factors producing Soviet authoritarianism. If only he, and the Party, represented the working-class interest, then anything opposed to them, or even outside them, was hostile, wrong, incorrect or 'bourgeois', and had to be eradicated.[67] Against Kautsky, in 1918, Lenin insisted that '"opposition" is a concept that belongs to the peaceful and only to the parliamentary struggle'.[68] In 1922–3 he briefly considered giving the state greater freedom from the Party, only to abandon the idea because it might fatally undermine the Bolsheviks' fragile grasp on power.[69] All the while Lenin proclaimed that the USSR was the freest society in the world because the Party represented much more of the population than governments elsewhere. Yet the broader message was clear: all 'opposition' was unacceptable in principle.

Hostility to dissent applied equally to the different branches of the state. Judicial independence was unthinkable in such circumstances. The old courts were replaced by a Military Revolutionary Tribunal on 5 December 1917. Its first case concerned the Countess Panina, who had withheld from the government some 93,000 roubles entrusted to her as a member of Kerensky's cabinet. The court, consisting of two peasants, two workers, two soldiers and a president – all but one Bolsheviks – insisted she return the funds, and sentenced her 'to the reprehension of society'.[70]

Such mercy was quickly exhausted. Though the death penalty, abolished in March 1917 but reinstated in July, was notionally repealed again in 1920, after perhaps 30,000 executions in 1919, the second respite was brief indeed – from 15 January to 24 May. In a curious tribute to legality, large numbers were shot in the days after the decree was passed but before it came into effect – 400 in Petrograd alone the night before. The principle of collective responsibility was also early established, whereby relatives of those detained might be arrested, shot or deported. By 1920 children were already being encouraged to report on their parents. Determined efforts now began to purge libraries of 'counter-revolutionary' works, including those 'on the Constituent Assembly, universal suffrage, democratic republic, etc.', anything on religion, and 'Agitational literature on questions which are now being approached by the Soviet power in a manner differing from that of the first period of the revolution'.[71] Librarians secreting 'books of a pernicious character' were liable to arrest. Lenin's wife, Nadezhda Krupskaya, led the campaign here, banning Kant, Schopenhauer, Descartes, Plato, Carlyle, Nietzsche, Spencer and others. Even lists of banned books were banned. In a few years many works by Marx too would be prohibited, partly because of his hostility to Russian foreign policy.

One of the greatest tragedies of this epoch was the Kronstadt uprising of 1921. The Kronstadt naval base near St Petersburg had been a hotbed of discontent as early as 1904. Kronstadt's sailors played an extraordinary and much-fêted role in the 1917 revolution – hence the pathos of their resistance in March 1921. Now, under the slogan 'all power to the local Soviets' – with the vital addition 'but not to the parties' – the original fervour of 1917 was reawakened. Events were sparked by a sharp reduction in the already meagre bread ration. Strikes by Petrograd workers protesting against starvation wages were transformed by the sailors into a more programmatic, Menshevik-inspired demand to end persecution and terror, restore freedom of speech and the press (including for anarchists and socialists) and provide free elections to the Soviets. 'From a slave of the capitalist the worker was transformed into a slave of state enterprises', the Kronstadt rebels proclaimed. In sum: 'Overthrow of Party dictatorship and return to Soviet Democracy.'[72] Political pluralism – at least of the left – was thus at the centre of this agenda. The Kronstadt rebels also supported peasant initiatives which did not involve hiring labour, and small-scale production elsewhere, on the same condition.[73] Social-Revolutionaries assisted the struggle, hoping to restore the Constituent Assembly, where they had had a majority. But the Kronstadt Committee rejected this demand in favour of a free Soviet model, and denounced the government as 'commissarocracy plus firing squads'. It also attacked the 'moral servitude' created by the new regime, and the fact that 'they laid their hands even on the inner life of the toilers and compelled them to think only in the Communist way'.[74] The sailors' Provisional Revolutionary Committee was the very type of free, elected Soviet that Lenin so distrusted, and which the Menshevik Martov now compared to the Paris Commune. The rebels even called themselves 'Communards'. In a moment of candour Lenin confessed that 'they do not want the White Guards, and they do not want our power either'.[75]

The experiment lasted sixteen days. On 7 March the naval base was stormed. For the task Lenin brought in Central Asian troops, Bashkirs and Kirghiz, as likely to be more reliable, having fewer sympathies with the rebels. Trotsky, who had previously saluted the Kronstadt sailors as 'the pride and the glory of the revolution', directed the suppression, and later condemned the 'deeply reactionary' ideas of the 'counter-revolutionary' uprising as 'a mortal danger to the dictatorship of the proletariat'.[76] He was (mistakenly) reported to have ordered his men 'to shoot them like partridges'. The Kronstadt sailors themselves abolished the death penalty and left the Bolsheviks in their midst untouched. But hundreds of the rebels' relatives were seized as hostages, and thousands of their supporters were arrested in Petrograd and elsewhere, including around 5,000 Mensheviks. Overwhelmed by some 50,000 troops, the fortress fell on 18 March. Many of its 18,000 defenders were shot or shipped off to the camps. At this moment many diehard believers lost their faith in the movement. For some, like the anarchist Alexander Berkman, 'the last thread' was now broken.[77]

Kronstadt spelt the demise of any concept of legitimate opposition in the Bolshevik state. At the Tenth Party Congress, held in Moscow during the uprising, Lenin proposed 'the complete abolition of all fractionalism'.[78] In elections to the Moscow Soviet, opposition candidates were arrested or insulted, and derided in the press. When they succeeded in getting onto the ballot, public elections meant their supporters were easily targeted by government agents. Declaring 'We need no opposition, comrades, now is not the time', Lenin insisted that 'it is a great deal better to "discuss with rifles" than with the theses of the opposition'.[79] Trotsky and Bukharin supported integrating trade unions into the state, while the Workers' Opposition urged transferring the organization of production to the workers themselves: a 'quasi-syndicalist view', in E. H. Carr's estimation. But the Congress then declared the 'syndicalist and anarchist deviation in our Party' incompatible with Party membership.[80] It ordered all groups dissolved forthwith 'in order to realize strict discipline within the party and attain the greatest unity through the elimination of any factionalism'. Some see this as 'a turning point in the organizational history of the party'.[81]

Other institutions soon met a similar fate. The autonomy of universities also ended in 1921. The co-operatives followed. In 1919 many leaders of the Russian co-operative movement had been arrested and its structures integrated into Bolshevik councils. Lenin insisted in 1923 that since 'political power is in the hands of the working class…the only task…that remains for us is to organise the population in co-operative societies' where 'the means of production are owned by the state'.[82] Initially the co-operatives responded by formally voting to approve measures forced on them by the government, thus preserving the fiction of autonomy. But this pretence could not last. Organization by organization, the vitality of difference and alternative was squeezed from the nation, until a single model of the hegemonic party-state virtually devoid of a civil society remained. And in 1923 Lenin again rejected the need for a free press as likely to aid the bourgeoisie.

The year 1921 thus proved decisive for the revolution. It witnessed the crushing of multiple workers' strikes in February and the Kronstadt uprising in March; the annexation of independent Georgia; and the Makhno movement's suppression in Ukraine. Widespread famine also occurred, as failure to collect the much-despised grain tax (despite usually being enforced at gunpoint) resulted in less food reaching the cities, and coincided with drought. Peasants were reduced to eating acorns and grass, and cannibalism occurred. Military cordons prevented people from leaving famine areas. Over 5 million died.

Five key turning points mark the tragic degeneration of the Russian Revolution. The first was the Bolshevik coup in November 1917, which ended the Provisional Government and the prospect of multiparty democracy. Then Lenin crushed opposition within his own party and from other parties, trade unions and co-operatives. Then came the insistence that the Party, rather than the proletariat, could alone represent progress within the revolution. Then followed Lenin's personal dictatorship. Finally, a brutal police state emerged, ruling outside and even above the Party.

This last step the veteran revolutionary Victor Serge thought was one of 'the gravest and most impermissible errors that the Bolshevik leaders committed in 1918'.[83] Many Bolsheviks regarded any means as justified to attain and preserve power. Lenin had not condemned banditry, including bank robbery, to support the cause, though the Mensheviks strongly opposed such methods. 'Our morality', Lenin said, 'is completely subordinated to the interests of the class struggle of the proletariat...Morality is that which serves to destroy the old exploiting society.'[84] The foundation of the secret police was foreshadowed in a speech by Trotsky threatening that 'the terror will assume very violent forms after the example of the great French revolutionaries' and that 'The guillotine will be ready for our enemies'.[85] The Cheka, or 'Commissariat for Social Annihilation', as Lenin jokingly thought it should be named, was established on 20 December 1917.[86] 'Find some truly hard people', Lenin instructed in August 1918, respecting his desire to execute *kulaks* by public hanging.[87] They were forthcoming. The Cheka was led by the incorruptible Felix Dzerzhinsky, 'tall forehead, bony nose, untidy goatee, and an expression of weariness and austerity'.[88] Its successor, the GPU, the reporter William Reswick noted with heavy irony, was the only ministry adorned with a bust of Karl Marx in the early 1920s: it stood in the infamous Lubianka prison in Moscow, where Dzerzhinsky had it placed over the main door.[89] We can but wonder what Marx would have thought.

Consumed by threats of conspiracy, the Cheka began mass arrests and executions of hostages in 1918. Killing was one of the few things it did liberally. Lenin even urged shooting proletarians who bunked off work because they were celebrating religious holidays, *pour encourager les autres*. The Cheka was deployed against the Bolsheviks' left-wing critics shortly after the Treaty of Brest-Litovsk (March 1918), which ended the war with Germany. On 11 April the anarchists became a key target. Dozens died in an attack on the House of Anarchy in Moscow, which was accused of 'harbouring bandits', and hundreds were arrested. Similar onslaughts occurred in many other cities. Other potential sources of opposition were also targeted. When the Russian-born Italian socialist leader Angelica Balabanoff objected to some Mensheviks being executed, Lenin insisted that 'if we do not shoot these few leaders we may be placed in a position where we would need to shoot ten thousand workers'.[90] Lenin hated religion, and denounced 'even flirting with the idea of God' as 'unutterable vileness'. He supposedly approved personally the executions of many priests.[91] In 1923 large numbers of Catholics were charged with supporting 'the international *bourgeoisie* in its struggle against the Soviet power', in other words, the papacy. A typical sentence was ten years.[92]

This process was hastened by foreign efforts to crush the revolution in 1918–20, when Russia was invaded by over 130,000 troops from Britain, the USA, Japan, Korea, France, Czechoslovakia and other countries. White armies fought fiercely against the Bolsheviks, at one point coming within a few miles of Petrograd. Red and White terror vied to outdo each other. Great brutality was the norm, not the exception. The Bolsheviks saw terror as 'a revolutionary necessity' instigated by foreign intervention and White reaction. The loss of a third of the population of Russia by the Treaty of Brest-Litovsk cost great anxiety. (Much of this territory was regained after 1945.) Whatever the cause, the trend towards suppressing all opposition was difficult to stem. Eventually even sympathizers came to see terror as 'implicit in the development of the Bolshevik method' after 1920.[93] As an early boss, Genrikh Yagoda, put it, 'We are a minority in a vast country. Abolish the GPU and we are through.'[94]

The new regime was also threatened by the crucial issue of the right of peasants to sell surplus grain at a profit, which Lenin regarded as exploitation. Indeed it became the reef upon which the revolution foundered. Echoing pre-revolutionary radical agrarian demands, the Bolsheviks divided the land in 1917–18 into more than 20 million family-run smallholdings. Soon requisitions of produce provoked widespread resistance from this vast new proprietor class. Proposals to extend the few recently established large state farms also aroused suspicions of a new mode of exploitation, even a new serfdom. Extreme centralization, introduced under 'War Communism' in March–April 1920, involved the compulsory seizure of grain, including the seed required for future crops, and abolished all private trade. This eventually produced a black market larger than the state distribution network, which necessitated in turn much-hated roadblocks outside the cities and arbitrary confiscation of anything worthwhile. Communists used the black market like everyone else.

But discipline was reinforced everywhere. Lenin presumed that it was in the Russian character 'to leave tasks undone and to relax when not tightened up by outside efforts'. He vowed 'in the most ruthless manner' to see that 'at any cost discipline and submission to orders are carried out with ruthless rigor'.[95] He was true to his word. The language of work became militarized. The 'bloodless front' of the workplace became a battlefield as significant as any military theatre, and part of an endless 'struggle' for 'victories'. In June 1918 most industries were nationalized. But this did little to halt the chaos. In the towns bread prices skyrocketed – by more than tenfold in 1920 alone. Inflation was rampant and the value of urban wages dropped dramatically. Rations available through the workplace shrank to almost nothing. Universal adult labour was mandated in 1920, and many former Red Army soldiers were enrolled directly into labour armies rather than being discharged. The 'militarization of labour' had begun. In 1921 Lenin introduced the idea of preferential treatment in remunerating labour and the idea of 'shock work' to accompany it. He told workers to 'govern with greater firmness than the capitalists did'. He admitted that in using shooting as punishment in the Red Army the Bolsheviks had deployed 'measures which even the old government did not visualize'.[96] Now he introduced the same methods into the labour process. Some Mensheviks compared all this to slavery under the Pharaohs.

In its brutality Lenin's economic policy often surpassed the most exploitative and oppressive forms of capitalism. *The Immediate Tasks of the Soviet Government* (1918) urged large-scale mechanization as the basis of socialism, iron discipline at work, wage differentials for specialists, one-man management (the opposite of workers' control), piecework and the use of the 'Taylor system' – which Lenin had once described as 'the enslavement of the man to the machine' – to speed up production.[97] Some of the Left opposition, including the trade union leader David Riazanov, objected to this, and to imposing piece rates, calling it a 'terrible mistake'.[98]

Economic chaos prevailed throughout 1920. Industrial output now fell to a fifth of the 1913 level. In the towns, tram fares were abolished, but then the carriages and rails deteriorated. Bank notes became worthless, though some rejoiced that this heralded the abolition of money. Paper and ink for printing postage stamps were unavailable, so postal charges ended. Horses and wagons – the main form of transport – were confiscated by the Red Army without payment. Food production fell dramatically, to as little as half pre-war levels. Perhaps a third of the 1920 harvest was hidden from government collection teams. The urban population decreased swiftly, with Moscow losing 44 per cent of its inhabitants, and Petrograd 57 per cent. Factory workers returned to their native villages in search of food. They took with them carpets, tapestries, linen, crockery, and the like: shoes could be made from sofas; clothing from curtains. Civil order was stretched to the breaking point; even Lenin was held up by bandits near a sanatorium outside Moscow where his wife was staying.

With some now turning to armed resistance, the peasants' pleas found little sympathy from the regime. The peasants were 'not socialists', Lenin lamented in 1920, but instead, it seemed, championed capitalism. The scene was now set for a collision between Russia's largest class and the Bolsheviks. Yet Lenin permitted peasants to trade in surplus agricultural produce – once their tax in kind, fixed in advance, had been paid to the state – even as terrible famine stalked the land in 1921–2. He restricted food distribution to those 'who are actually needed under conditions of maximum productivity of labour', thus 'making the whole matter an *instrumentality of politics*...with the view of cutting down on the number of those who are not absolutely necessary and to spur on those who are really needed'.[99] And so the number of those receiving such aid was reduced from 38 million to 8 million.

The Terror did not recede in the last two years of Lenin's life. In February 1922 the Cheka was renamed the GPU, or State Political Administration. But the change of title – which implied that 'politics' as such was now defined by terror – had no effect on policy, beyond greater secrecy surrounding executions. Campaigns against the Social-Revolutionaries and Mensheviks proceeded with great ferocity. The death toll mounted relentlessly. The Civil War claimed 7–12 million lives. In total perhaps 13–20 million died between 1917 and 1924.[100] Famine in 1924 killed another million. By 1924, therefore, the revolution had cost as much as 20 per cent of the population (which was about 110 million then). Contemporary estimates reckoned on another 9.5 million deaths from 1924 to 1934, bringing the total dead between 1917 and 1934 to as many as 30 million. The Soviet regime had resulted in the shedding of far more blood in two decades than Tsarism had done in as many centuries.

If political repression was one response to the threat of cataclysm, economic liberalism, in the form of the New Economic Policy (NEP), which lasted from 1921 to 1928, was another. Russia was exhausted after four years of war and revolution, shortages and overwork, hunger and constant queuing. A temporary reversion to the market seemed the only panacea. Lenin called the programme 'state capitalism': 'The best Communist is he who can drive the best bargain', he reportedly said. Elsewhere, though, he termed the NEP 'a retreat – for a new attack'. But he lamented that communists seemed to lack what every capitalist salesman possessed: knowledge of how trade, or *biznes*, worked.[101] The NEP chiefly aimed at bringing food back into the towns by allowing peasants to trade their grain surplus instead of trying to appropriate it directly from them. Industrial goods would be provided for them to buy to stimulate them to do this. Grain requisition was now replaced by a tax in kind, later paid in money. Partly under Trotsky's impetus, industrial production was shifted to consumer-oriented goods in order to spur farmers to produce more food. Big capital was now seen as having a progressive role to play in developing the Russian economy, while Lenin hoped that agricultural co-operatives might help build socialism in the countryside. Individual ownership was never an option: Lenin wrote earlier that 'If the peasants do not accept socialism when the dictatorship comes, we shall say to them: "It's no use wasting words when you have got to use force."'[102] Factories, raw materials and other resources were made available to capitalists in exchange for part of their profits. Large numbers of external experts were now invited to the USSR. Foreign factory owners enjoyed ideal conditions, for the state brutally suppressed all strikes, and free movement of labour was usually prohibited, often with the penalty of shooting. The state, however, attempted to maintain a monopoly on external trade, forcing foreign firms to negotiate with it. In 1922 Lenin and Stalin were on opposite sides of this question, with Lenin favouring monopoly.

A long-term partnership between the 'socialist' cities and the 'private' countryside never materialized on a viable scale. But genuine prosperity appeared for the first time since the revolution. In 1925 the hiring of labour and renting of land was legalized, as Bukharin told peasants to 'get rich' even if socialism grew only at 'a snail's pace'. Trotsky warned that a new capitalist class was emerging. Indeed 'red managers' were hired in increasing numbers from the old bourgeoisie, and paid more than formerly. Sometimes they treated their workers no better than they had before 1917. With rising prices, growing unemployment and falling wages, urban workers felt increasingly aggrieved. Some joked that NEP stood for 'new exploitation of the proletariat'. (A later saying ran, 'Capitalism is the exploitation of man by man. Socialism is just the opposite.') But finally there was at least food on the table for many. By 1922 even the Terror was in retreat, and non-communist writers were being published. In 1926–7 production supposedly reached pre-war levels, which even considering likely exaggeration was an astonishing achievement in the circumstances. It appeared that the Bolsheviks could compromise, could do *biznes* and could moderate their ambitions. This communism was worldly wise.

Yet the NEP also had the effect of making capitalism more attractive to the peasants, and alienating them still further from Bolshevism. The USSR might have survived, even prospered, by retaining it, but socialism would have receded further into the distance. More produce was transferred to the black market, and less was sold to the state at artificially low prices. Flashy upstart *nepmany* (NEP-men) now swarmed in the big cities, driving fancy foreign cars, patronizing fine restaurants, wearing furs, luxury watches and jewels. 'Debauchery, wild orgies, drunken all-night parties with nudity as a feature became the vogue among the *nouveau riche*', reported one onlooker. Government officials soon became corrupted.[103] For the less fortunate this was all a slap in the face, and indicated that everything the revolution had attempted, and at such cost, had failed. Drunkenness became rife after the state resumed the alcohol monopoly. Waiters assumed a subservient demeanour and began expecting tips again. Shoe-blacks went back to shining shoes. The peasants ate well, but the pace of industrialization slowed because less grain was available for export.

To the Right opposition, chiefly Mikhail Tomsky and Nikolai Bukharin, this was a price worth paying: industrialization could proceed slowly, with surplus agricultural produce gradually being used to acquire new machinery. Keen to export 'permanent revolution' to the world, Trotsky, on the left, disagreed. He proposed instead gradual collectivization by extending state credits and supplying machinery as incentives to join collective farms, combined with heavier taxation of the richer *kulaks* or 'rural bourgeoisie'. This would produce an agricultural surplus for use in developing heavy industry. Here he was supported by, amongst others, the economist Evgenii Preobrazhensky, who in 1923 protested against the ban on factions within the Party. Preobrazhensky made clear what many were thinking: that socialist accumulation, like capitalism, would require widespread exploitation of the workforce in both town and country.[104] And when the focus came increasingly on rapid heavy industrialization, as it did under Stalin, it became evident that such exploitation would have to intensify.

How far was the course of these events indebted to the character and outlook of one man, the revolution's leader? Lenin shared with Marx the supreme self-confidence of being right all of the time. A doctrine of will suited him: he aspired to instruct the ignorant and discipline the impudent. 'The Marxist doctrine is omnipotent because it is true', he avowed. 'It is comprehensive and harmonious, and provides men with an integral world outlook irreconcilable with any form of superstition, reaction, or defence of bourgeois oppression.'[105] His Commissar of Education, Anatoly Lunacharsky, commented that 'Lenin's love of power stems from his immense certainty about the rightness of his principles, and, probably, from his inability...to put himself in the position of an opponent.'[106] And it is indisputably the case that 'the will-power and the conceptions of the single individual Lenin dominated the whole course of events in Russia'.[107]

Who was this singular individual? Lenin was born as Vladimir Ilyich Ulyanov in 1870 in Simbirsk to a well-to-do thoroughly Russianized noble family of German, Jewish and, probably, 'Tatar' or Central Asian origin (more than a few noted his almond-shaped 'Mongolian' eyes). Radicalized by his brother's execution in 1887 for plotting against the Tsar, and thereafter obsessed by his hatred of the autocrat, Lenin became a leading agitator in St Petersburg, and was banished to Siberia for three years after 1897. Famine in the 1890s did much to drive him, with many others, towards Marxism. In 1894 he assailed the Narodniks' willingness to accommodate themselves to Tsarism in *What the 'Friends of the People' Are and How They Fight against the Social Democrats*. He was converted to Marxism through Plekhanov, whom he met in 1895 in Switzerland (Lenin said that he was 'in love with' Plekhanov as well as Karl Marx). Nevertheless Lenin continued to admire the Russian Blanquists. Chief amongst these was the agrarian radical Pyotr Tkachev, sometimes called the 'first Bolshevik', who stressed the power of the will, conspiracy and violence.[108] Tkachev epitomized the idea that a small revolutionary vanguard would introduce dictatorship by a coup d'état and maintain it by terror. Lenin further admired Sergei Nechaev, who vowed to liquidate the whole house of Romanovs, an idea Lenin, whose hatreds ran well ahead of his mercies, termed a stroke of genius.[109]

Lenin was immensely studious, publishing *The Development of Capitalism in Russia* (1899) as the fruit of his exile. His *Imperialism, the Highest Stage of Capitalism* (1916) – which built particularly on the British critic John Hobson – went on to explain how imperial and colonial rivalry was provoked by the export of capital in pursuit of higher profit rates in less developed countries, coupled with an intensified need for raw materials. Up to about 1900 Lenin assumed that bourgeois intellectuals like himself were mere appendages to any proletarian movement. Yet he also believed that he had been 'called', as he once confided to Zinoviev, and was a natural leader.[110] Lunacharsky said Lenin was defined by 'an extremely firm, extremely forceful will capable of concentrating itself on the most immediate task but which never strayed beyond the radius traced out by his powerful intellect'.[111] Privately Lenin was always meticulous and loved order. In exile he disparaged the chaos of the 'commune' his fellow *Iskra* editors lived in. (Curiously, Marx had had a similar reaction to his brief personal exposure to communal life in Paris in 1843.) These were the private limits of the appeal of collectivism.

In the end Lenin fell victim to the system he had helped design. Extreme centralization of power invariably meant that many decisions could only be taken at the very top. Just what a logjam this created is revealed by observing an ordinary day's activity for Lenin: 2 February 1921. Besides attending many meetings, receiving visitors, writing notes and sending telegrams, he deliberated personally on such matters as sending two trains to bring food supplies to Petrograd, giving bonuses to shipbuilding workers, securing labourers for ship repairs, and taking action against bureaucracy in the Commissariat of Transport.[112] People telephoned him just to obtain a railway ticket or hotel room.[113] Even though the USSR had 6 million administrators by 1920, much of this business apparently could not be completed without Lenin's intervention. Often indifferent to his diet and health, Lenin suffered greatly from the resulting workload.

So much concentrated attention upon his person naturally invited adulation and a cult of personality. Lenin resisted this to a degree. He avoided luxury, living initially in a single servant's room, then in a simply furnished four-room flat in the Kremlin, his small iron bedstead bedecked with a favourite plaid blanket, his mother's last gift. He too went without heat in the terrible winter of 1919–20. He took his turn at the barber's like everyone else. But as head of state he could indulge some desires legitimately. Lenin's rooms housed some 8,000 books on a vast range of subjects and in many languages (he could read or speak nine), which he constantly consulted. A section of the library was devoted to 'electrification': Lenin famously defined communism as *'Soviet power plus the electrification of the whole country'*.[114] He could wax lyrically on the theme, as he did when the British novelist H. G. Wells visited in 1920. More menacingly, perhaps, Lenin noted to the author of a book on the subject that 'this is how one should teach the Russian savage *from the ABC onwards'*.[115] Here were more than a few analogies about Soviet power.

Lenin's character was described by many in this period. Some who knew him well saw him as a master strategist who assessed 'every individual and every social event' from 'the viewpoint of the revolutionary struggle'.[116] Victor Serge thought him 'neither a great orator nor a first-rate lecturer', but equally 'never boring, on account of his mimic's liveliness and the reasoned conviction which drove him'. He was 'a man of basic simplicity, talking to you honestly with the sole purpose of convincing you, appealing exclusively to your judgement, to facts and sheer necessity'.[117] Bertrand Russell said he had 'never met a personage so destitute of self-importance', and found him 'dictatorial, calm, incapable of fear, extraordinarily devoid of self-seeking'; but he also noted that 'I got the impression that he despises a great many people and is an intellectual aristocrat' – surely a case of the pot and kettle.[118] The American journalist Louise Bryant was impressed by his 'sheer intellect – he is absorbed, cold, unattractive, impatient at interruption'.[119] The British suffragette Sylvia Pankhurst noted that his 'brown eyes often twinkle with amusement, but change suddenly to a cold, hard stare, as though he would pierce one's innermost thoughts'.[120] H. G. Wells encountered a pleasant, quick-changing, brownish face, with a lively smile and a habit (due perhaps to some defect in focussing) of screwing up one eye as he pauses in his talk; he is not very like the photographs you see of him because he is one of those people whose change of expression is more important than their features; he gesticulated a little with his hands over the heaped papers as he talked, and he talked quickly, very keen on his subject, without any posing or pretences or reservations, as a good type of scientific man will talk.[121]

The most familiar account of him was his wife Nadezhda Krupskaya's *Memories of Lenin* (1930). There are, needless to say, no warts or wrinkles here. Yet we do get a sense of Lenin's genuine sympathy for the working classes, as well as his capacities as a conspirator, able to write in invisible ink, elude police spies, smuggle secret literature in false-bottomed trunks and adopt all manner of aliases. So too his single-minded determination to subordinate everything to the revolution, giving up in turn chess-playing, skating and Latin when they hindered his studies, which were extremely methodical and painstaking. He was forceful, decisive, impatient with lesser mortals, and possessed of 'a most profound faith in the class instinct of the proletariat, in its creative forces, in its historic mission...the only really consistent revolutionary class'. He 'read and re-read' his beloved Marx and Engels 'at every new stage of our Revolution'.[122]

Lenin was, without doubt, absolutely single-minded, and single-mindedly absolute; Tugan-Baranovsky noted the 'coldness, contempt and cruelty' with which 'he marched, firm and unflinching', driven by an 'indomitable love of power'.[123] Ruthlessness came easily to him. Famously he once said he could not 'listen to music too often' because it made him 'want to say kind, stupid things, and pat the heads of people. But now you have to beat them on the head, beat them without mercy.'[124] And beat them he did.

Although Trotsky, Bukharin, Kamenev, Zinoviev and others played key roles in the struggle, Lenin became its indisputable symbol. Nonetheless he became increasingly aware that events were not going his way. In the final days of December 1922, Lenin drafted his famous 'testament' denouncing Stalin as too rude, coarse, capricious and intolerant to run the Party. 'He lacks the most elementary human honesty', complained Lenin.[125] Stalin, he warned, had 'unlimited authority in his hands' and might not 'be capable of using that authority with sufficient caution.' (He also had reservations about Trotsky's surfeit of 'self-confidence'.)[126] Early in 1923 Lenin proposed Stalin's demotion, and Krupskaya indeed reported to Kamenev that he intended to crush Stalin politically. But the Twelfth Party Congress in April that year saw a triumvirate emerge of Zinoviev, Kamenev and Stalin, while Trotsky and his allies were marginalized. 'The machine has got out of control', Lenin reputedly said as he lay dying. The mechanical metaphor was highly appropriate.

Lenin's death on 21 January 1924 left an immense void at the heart of the revolution. His life, a close observer noted, showed 'that a man's will, even when guided by uncommon intelligence, firmness of purpose, and exceptional courage cannot triumph in defiance of the basic laws of social development'. Despite his 'complete unselfishness and abnegation', he created a dictatorship from which the USSR, and eventually large parts of the rest of the world, never escaped.[127] Entombed in Red Square, his embalmed corpse – commencing a tradition which would be continued with Stalin, Ho Chi Minh and Mao Zedong – remains the principal icon of the revolution.

CHAPTER 3

Bolshevik Leaders: Bukharin, Trotsky, Stalin

The 'favourite of the whole party', 'the party's greatest and most valuable theoretician', as Lenin called him, Nikolai Bukharin (1888–1938) occupied a central position from Lenin's death in 1924 until Stalin ousted him in 1928.[1] Using language which would not be heard again for decades, he advocated Soviet development based on 'socialist humanism', meaning both giving priority to consumers, and permitting (even encouraging) competition in cultural and intellectual life rather than 'squeezing everybody into one fist'. In 1928–9, as Stalin moved towards forcible collectivization, Bukharin warned that 'a police state' would be needed to 'drown the revolts in blood'.[2] Yet Bukharin was also well aware that such a state already existed, and is often quoted for contending that 'proletarian compulsion in all its forms...beginning with summary execution and ending with compulsory labour is, however paradoxical it may sound, a method of reworking the human material of the capitalistic epoch into Communist humanity'.[3] He became the most famous victim of the 1938 show trials. He lives on as the face of what some suppose Bolshevism might have become had Stalin not triumphed. Yet he was no democrat, and never challenged the principle of a one-party state or the banning of factions within it.[4]

Bukharin's early writings included a 1915 essay on imperialism; applying the ideas of Rudolf Hilferding's *Finance Capital*, it described imperial states as a 'new Leviathan' in which capitalists collaborated to divide up profits worldwide. Here he envisioned the future society as one 'without a state organization', but also contended – in contrast to anarchism – that 'the socialists see a social economy resulting from the tendencies of concentration and centralization, the inevitable companions of development of the productive forces, whereas the economic utopia of the decentralist-anarchists carries us back to precapitalist forms'. His best-selling *The ABC of Communism* (1919) remained, until the mid-1930s, the main exposition of Bolshevism. It justified both terror and 'the need to deprive the bourgeoisie of freedom', but promised that 'the workers' State will gradually die out'.[5] He did not explain how 'the disappearance of proletarian dictatorship' would occur, or how to judge its progress. In *The Economics of the Transition Period* (1920) he reiterated that

> As state power withers away and all compulsory norms vanish from human relationships, communist humanity will create the most advanced type of 'management of things'. Then the very problem of collegiality or one-man management will disappear altogether, for in the future people will do voluntarily what is required by the dry columns of statistical calculations.

In communist society, he added, 'there will be complete "personal" freedom, with no external norms whatever governing the relations between people – in other words, self-regulated activity without constraint.'[6]

Before this a very different regime was required. Bukharin alarmed Lenin by hinting that a militaristic state capitalism might emerge in Russia, with state compulsion substituting for free exchange between city and country in particular. Lenin accused Bukharin of 'semi-anarchist' views, though in 1917 Krupskaya wrote that 'he no longer has any disagreements with you on the question of the state'. When Lenin introduced the NEP in 1921, Bukharin became an immediate convert, and played a major role in implementing it. As the leader of the Right opposition he favoured a slower revolutionary pace than the Left led by Trotsky. He also differed from the latter in estimating that world capitalism might well stabilize itself, rather than heading towards revolution. After the collapse of the German revolution, this seemed plausible, if heretical. By the late 1920s, however, Bukharin warned that a market mechanism was necessary in the USSR to compensate for shortcomings in the planning process, which threatened crises akin to capitalist ones. Now even Trotsky conceded the case for not abolishing the market prematurely.

Bukharin's *Historical Materialism* (1921) became a textbook for Party members. Its proclamation of the superiority of 'proletarian science' and of seeing reality through 'red glasses' rather than 'white ones' captured the essence of the new worldview. The social sciences were placed on as secure a footing as the natural. 'Psychical phenomena' were 'a property of matter organized in a certain manner', meaning chiefly that *'The mental life of society is a function of the forces of production.'* Causation was uniform, and if the time of social events could not be predicted, their direction and certainty could. 'Socialism will come inevitably', Bukharin predicted, 'because it is inevitable that men, definite classes of men, will stand for its realization, and they will do so under circumstances which make their victory certain.' But, anticipating the struggles of the next decade, he lamented that the 'peasant is not much inclined to feel any solidarity with the worker'.[7]

Though already famed as a writer and polemicist, Leon Trotsky (born Lev Bronstein, 1879–1940) was a latecomer to the Bolshevik cause, joining the Party only around July 1917 following a period of exile and internment abroad.[8] Trotsky's character was marked by intellectual brilliance but also immense arrogance. He was supremely ambitious; Angelica Balabanoff thought his 'habit of looking down on everybody and everything' 'created a wall of ice around him even when he meant to be kind'.[9] As the revolution's foremost military leader he was unsurpassed in energy and ability. Racing from front to front in his armoured train he appeared to be everywhere at once. Lunacharsky said he was 'prickly and overbearing', but possessed an 'impressive appearance' with his 'handsome, sweeping gestures, the powerful rhythm of his speech, his loud but never fatiguing voice, the remarkable coherence and literary skill of his phrasing, his richness of imagery, scalding irony, his soaring pathos, his rigid logic, clear as polished steel'.[10] Another account described his metallic voice, his regular gestures, his grave but deliberately martial bearing, the concentrated, self-assured, imperturbable energy that emanates from his whole person…the creases in his brow, the spectacles in front of those dark, lively eyes, the small moustache, the dark goatee of a beard, he is recognizable at first glance.[11]

Despite his later reputation as Bolshevism's greatest heretic, Trotsky asserted that the 'dictatorship of the Soviets became possible only by means of the dictatorship of the party'. This was not problematic because the Party embodied the interests of the working class.[12] And so Trotsky would later claim that 'one cannot be right against the party…for history has not created other ways for the realization of what is right'.[13] Yet, echoing Saint-Simon and Marx, he implied in 1920 that the time would come when the Communist Party would itself disappear, being replaced by a Supreme Council of Public Economy where only industrial groups, not political parties, would organize development. He also aspired to see a Federated Republic of Europe created in which 'economic evolution demands the abolition of national frontiers'.[14] When, in October 1923, he wrote a letter condemning bureaucratism and 'dictatorship within the party', he was attacked by other members of the Central Committee. In December Stalin led the assault on him, and in early 1924 Trotsky gave way. But the fight was not yet over, and Trotsky was pilloried constantly by the other leaders.

One important issue separating Stalin from Trotsky was the former's support (assisted by Bukharin) from 1924 for 'socialism in one country', or the idea that the USSR could move towards communism without revolutions elsewhere. To this Trotsky juxtaposed his idea – adopted as early as 1905 – of 'permanent revolution', which suggested that revolution could only succeed in Russia if uprisings occurred elsewhere; this had been Marx's view too. In 1925 Stalin used his disagreement over permanent revolution as a means of further isolating Trotsky, whom he forced into exile and finally had murdered in Mexico in 1940. A Fourth International was founded by Trotsky in 1936 to rival the Third International (1919–43) run from Moscow, but numbers of its few members were also murdered by the GPU. Trotskyism nonetheless lives on in sectarian Marxism even in the present day.

*   *   *

The key figure to emerge after Lenin's death was the 'Red Tsar', Joseph Stalin.[15] With great prescience, Plekhanov had warned as early as 1907 that at the 'final end...everything would revolve around one man who will *ex providentia*, unite all power in himself.'[16] That man was Stalin. In him were united the worst features of Leninism, and the myth of Lenin's infallibility. From him would emerge one of the most destructive totalitarian states created in the twentieth century, which would claim the lives of many millions, poor and rich alike. But under him the USSR would also rise to greatness, pushed and pulled into modernity, erratically and unevenly, at breakneck speed.

The great dictator sprang from inauspicious beginnings. Stalin was born Joseph Dzhugashvili in the small Georgian town of Gori on 18 December 1878 to a poor family descended from serfs.[17] Beaten by his drunken shoemaker father, he remained devoted to his mother, who hoped he would become a priest. He endured nearly five years in the theological seminary in Tiflis, where he read voraciously everything but theology. Curiously he later condemned its 'humiliating regime' of 'surveillance, spying, invasion of the inner life'. Small in stature (like Lenin: five feet four inches, or 162.5 centimetres), his ego grew to compensate.[18] Bent on success, he excelled as a schoolboy, but he was already vindictive: childhood friends remembered that 'To gain a victory and be feared was triumph for him.' Later he said that his 'greatest delight is to mark one's enemy, prepare everything, avenge oneself thoroughly, and then go to sleep'.[19] In the seminary Stalin discovered socialism, and perhaps even dipped into *Capital*. By 1899 he had begun a long revolutionary apprenticeship. His life became a 'never-ending endeavour to prove himself a revolutionary hero'.[20] By 1904 he was devoted to Lenin, whom he idolized. He quoted Lenin's works frequently, and his Bolshevism remained insistently Leninist. By contrast his later library held only thirteen volumes by Marx and Engels, who probably seemed largely irrelevant to him.[21] Between 1902 and 1913 he was arrested eight times, exiled seven times and escaped six times.

Stalin, the 'man of steel', as he came to term himself – taking his pseudonym from the first part of his surname, which meant 'steel' in Georgian (*dzhuga*) – rose through the Bolshevik ranks to become 'the

Boss' (*Vozhd*) by cunning, ruthlessness and a real talent for using others. Some, like the shoemaker-commissar Lazar Kaganovich, thought he had been 'a soft individual' at first, but that after so many long struggles 'It was difficult to avoid getting cruel.'[22] Whether ego or alter-ego, 'Stalin' was the result: never mind electricity – the man himself said simply that 'Stalin is Soviet power.'[23] His friends called him 'Koba', after an outlaw in a Georgian novel, and throughout his life he spoke Russian with a strong Georgian accent. He often had many more enemies than friends, though he killed plenty of the latter too. Paranoia and a lust for supremacy soon dominated his life. He became a loner; Nikita Khrushchev remembered that later, isolated by the cocoon of power and fear, Stalin 'felt so alone he didn't know what to do with himself'.[24] At the height of his dictatorship he entertained his circle of intimates frequently – all desperate to please, and living in mortal fear of him – and drank copiously. Amongst his close associates he loved to sing, play billiards and perform childish practical jokes on his guests; putting tomatoes on their seats was one, flicking breadballs another. Plying them with drink to see what they might divulge was a regular amusement. What they did not reveal he got from his spies, who monitored them all constantly.

Such sociability, always edgy and tinged with fear and jockeying for position, never inhibited his cruelty or fuelled his compassion. He found some solace in gardening at his dachas (he loved roses). His wife's suicide in 1932 disturbed him greatly, though his bullying was the cause, and provoked him to ever greater paranoia and terror. He disowned his son Yakov after he was captured by the Germans in 1941. His adored daughter Svetlana, often alienated by his prudish disapproval of her flirtatiousness, later defected to the USA. After meeting Stalin in 1934, H. G. Wells recalled a man of 'limited sociability' who was 'not easy to describe, and many descriptions exaggerate his darkness and stillness'. His first impression of a 'rather commonplace-looking man dressed in an embroidered white shirt, dark trousers and boots' gave way to the judgement that 'I have never met a man more candid, fair and honest, and to these qualities it is, and to nothing occult and sinister, that he owes his tremendous undisputed ascendancy in Russia.' 'Later on', he remembered, 'we discussed liberty of expression. He admitted the necessity and excellence of criticism, but preferred that it should be home-made by the party within the party organization. There, he declared, criticism was extraordinarily painstaking and free.'[25] When the Yugoslav communist partisan Milovan Djilas met Stalin near the end of the Second World War, this was his impression:

> Stalin was in a marshal's uniform and soft boots, without any medals except a golden star – the Order of Hero of the Soviet Union, on the left side of his breast…In his stance there was nothing artificial or posturing. This was not that majestic Stalin of the photographs or the newsreels – with the stiff, deliberate gait and posture. He was not quiet for a moment…I was also surprised at something else: he was of very small stature and ungainly build. His torso was short and narrow, while his legs and arms were too long. His left arm and shoulder seemed rather stiff. He had quite a large paunch, and his hair was sparse, though his scalp was not completely bald. His face was white, with ruddy cheeks.[26]

Stalin's ascent to dictatorship was marked by extraordinary political cunning. Possessed of a fine memory and superabundant ruthlessness, he was 'little known to the party, unknown to the masses, firm in character, Oriental in mind, limited, alert, and tricky'. He tirelessly used the General-Secretariat of the Party to place his own supporters in useful positions.[27] His first major theoretical work, *Marxism and the National Question* (1913), partly plagiarized from Otto Bauer and Karl Kautsky, decried most forms of nationalism, while acknowledging the value of regional autonomy in education and the use of local languages. By 1917 he was more opposed to secession, arguing that Russia could now make a 'union of nations' while preserving some devolved power. As early as August 1917 he was also amongst the first to contend that Russia might achieve socialism without revolution occurring in the West.

Stalin could be accommodating when it suited him. Early in 1917 he urged compromise with the Mensheviks, which Lenin rejected on his return in April. Lenin was crucial in getting Stalin appointed to the Central Committee on the strength of his revolutionary activities. Contrary to later official histories, Stalin played only a marginal role in the revolution itself. In April 1922 Stalin became General Secretary of the Party, and as Commissar for Nationalities proposed an 'auton-omization' programme which aimed to make 'autonomous republics' within the Russian Federation of the six national groupings existing in 1921–2, effectively reducing their independence. In September 1922 he accused Lenin of 'national liberalism' for supporting greater independ-ence for ethnic groupings, while Lenin in turn underscored his detes-tation of 'dominant-nation chauvinism' in October.

By 1923 Zinoviev was hinting at Stalin's ambitions of personal dicta-torship. Many heard these warnings, but few could do anything about them. After Lenin's death Stalin carefully constructed a highly cen-tralized political machine, staffed with men he trusted, and stretching spider-like downwards and outwards into the provinces. This gave him an unrivalled source of information and means of control which en-abled him to outflank the other two leaders, Zinoviev and Kamenev, with whom he shared power after Lenin's death. Kamenev asserted in 1925 that Stalin could not unify the Party, adding that 'We're against creating a theory of "the leader"; we're against making anyone into "the leader".'[28] But it was too late. Marginalized at the Fourteenth Party Congress in December 1925, Kamenev and Zinoviev joined with Trot-sky in 1926 to form a 'united opposition' or anti-Stalin faction within the Party. In 1927 diminishing food supplies to the cities brought wide-spread support for Trotsky's diatribes against the *kulaks*. Civil war be-tween town and country seemed a distinct possibility. Trotsky now loomed as Lenin's possible successor. Stalin responded by using the Right opposition led by Bukharin to isolate Trotsky. The Right little conceived that Stalin intended to seize absolute power at the earliest opportunity, and then to squash them as well. The bureaucracy was prepared to back him in order to retain its privileges, which a return to greater workers' control would have undermined.

In 1927 Trotsky, Kamenev and Zinoviev were expelled from the Party. The Fifteenth Party Congress in December completed the crushing of the opposition. Those ousted faced pitiless repression. Many were immediately sentenced 'by administrative measure' to three years' imprisonment, then were given another five years, with no reason assigned. The death penalty for opposition within the Party seems to have been introduced in 1932.[29] 'The iron curtain of History was falling', said Bukharin, anticipating Churchill's use of the phrase twenty years later. 'The regime had become "totalitarian"' *avant la lettre*, several years before the term arrived from Germany, Trotsky later wrote.[30] But the Party itself also connived at this to some degree. After Lenin's death the Party had expanded rapidly from 351,000 to 591,000 members, many of whom were workers-turned-functionaries. Many of them had sat on the sidelines in 1917. After 1928 they rudely shoved aside the generation who had made the revolution.

Having disposed of the Left opposition Stalin turned to the Right bloc around Bukharin. The murder on 1 December 1934 of the popular Leningrad Bolshevik Sergey Kirov, if not orchestrated by Stalin himself, was immediately exploited by him as he blamed the deed on the Zinoviev–Kamenev group.[31] A panicked search for disloyalty commenced. A law was quickly passed allowing the trial within ten days of accused terrorists and their immediate execution without appeal. Within a month over 6,500 had met this fate.

Stalin now proclaimed himself Lenin's sole legitimate heir. His ascent after Lenin's death owed much to the transformation of the Party from an elite group to a mass organization united by its privileges, discipline and intolerance of dissent. Stalin defined Leninism as 'the theory and tactic of the proletarian revolution', and insisted, against Zinoviev, that an alliance with the peasantry was possible only so far as 'the proletariat takes the lead'. He also declared that 'the dictatorship of the proletariat is, *substantially*, the "dictatorship" of its vanguard, the "dictatorship" of the Party, as the force which guides the proletariat'. This meant that 'no important political or organisational problem is ever decided by our soviets and other mass organisations without directives from the Party'. Stalin denied that the Party could 'impose its leadership on the class by force', adding that 'if such a thing were done, the leadership would not last long'. But he still asserted that the majority could 'force the minority' to comply with its views, even though it was 'by *persuading* the majority that the leadership is safeguarded.' Thus for Stalin, citing Lenin, 'dictatorship of one party' was a defensible slogan, since it meant not 'power based directly on force' but 'nothing more than Party leadership'. In practice the line between the two was slender indeed. And a denial that 'Party dictatorship…really means dictatorship of the leaders' could not but have sounded very hollow by 1928.[32]

As supreme leader, Stalin pressed ahead with collectivizing the peasantry and liquidating the *kulaks*. This was the real revolution in Russia, the ending of centuries-old traditions and the way of life of the vast majority. Under Lenin the Party's policy had been to ally with the rural poor and neutralize the 'middle' peasants. In 1925 Stalin thought this included 'firm alliance with the middle peasants'.[33] The rich peasants were never courted. By 1926 some 6 per cent of the peasants were selling about 60 per cent of Soviet wheat. The withholding of grain produced shortages in the cities, which urban workers blamed on the *kulaks*, and then the government for supporting them. From December 1927 the *kulaks* thus became the focus of Stalin's rapid collectivization programme, though in July 1928 he still supported the development of individual farms.[34] In 1928 there were only 45,000 households in collective farms. By 1929 there were a million, followed by 6 million in 1930. It was claimed that some 60 million people were collectivized in the first two months of 1930 alone. The pace of collectivization slowed dramatically following widespread resistance, and the proportion of collectivized households dropped from 56 per cent to 24 per cent in only a few months. Then the number rose again to over 15 million by 1933.

This campaign was conducted with great and often wanton brutality. Wholesale looting by 'dekulakization' brigades was common. Between 1929 and 1933 some 7 million people were deported to camps or dumped in the far eastern tundra to shift for themselves, without food, shelter or tools. Between 1931 and 1933 some 6 million – possibly 9 million – people, mostly Ukrainians, died of famine directly as a result of collectivization and industrialization policies. Peasants often refused to hand over grain or livestock, stubbornly preferring to destroy both rather than be robbed of them. They were as merciless to their animals as the commissars were to them. By 1933 the number of horses, sheep and pigs was half of the 1916 level. Beggars swarmed throughout the countryside and towns. Cannibalism occurred. Epidemics proliferated throughout the country.

To Stalin the chief aim of industrialization was to secure the USSR's independence from the capitalist powers. No price was too high to achieve this. Military necessity drove it. National pride demanded it. 'The history of old Russia', he insisted in a speech, 'consisted, among other things, in her being ceaselessly beaten for her backwardness.'[35] Without collectivization, he thought, neither the cities nor the army could be fed, and agricultural production itself would degenerate. What was necessary, he told Gorky, was the 'total breaking up of the old society and feverish building of the new'.[36] The *kulaks* became the chief obstacle to attaining socialism, which had to be based on heavy industry. So, to acquire foreign machinery and accelerate the rate of industrialization, the USSR sold vast amounts of produce abroad, including food, even when it was scarce at home. At the same time, salary differentials between ordinary and skilled workers, and between workers and managers, were widened. Stalin claimed that it was 'unbearable' to see 'the locomotive driver receiving the same wages as a copyist', even that it was virtually 'slandering Marxism' to assume that 'all humans had to wear the same clothes and to eat the same foodstuffs in the same quantities', either under socialism or communism.[37] Even so, having lost much of their expertise, and now led by Party loyalists, the collective farms were never a success, and Soviet agriculture was never very efficient or productive. Private plots, though scarcely 4 per cent of the land, consistently produced up to a third of total produce.

Stalin's personality cult began in earnest in the early 1930s. By 1936 every article in the press or reviews began with a quote from 'the Leader'. Stalin became 'the Great Locomotive Engineer of the Revolution', 'the greatest man of all times', the 'Father of Nations'. Minions vied to fawn excessively, and no absurdity was too great to be floated. At the Writers' Congress in 1936 a speech ended by announcing that the speaker's wife was expecting a baby, and the hope that 'the first word that our child shall pronounce will be the name of Stalin'.[38] Sadly for the parents, who cannot have resisted prompting the infant, apparently it did not. Few would have been surprised if it had: such a miracle would have been quite in keeping with the cult.

To many, Stalin's rule is synonymous with the great Terror of 1936–9, which peaked in 1937, when some 1.6 million were arrested and 780,000 were shot.[39] This arose partly from his paranoia respecting both rivalry from the so-called Old Bolsheviks who had made the Revolution, most of whom now perished, and also a possible coup by the military, which resulted in a purge of most higher commanders, and partly from the need to obscure the innumerable systematic failures in the Soviet economy by scapegoating 'wreckers', 'saboteurs' and 'Trotskyists'. A mere suspicion from Stalin, or many others, justified execution. Behind the scenes he was the Terror's 'director general', signing death warrants many pages long and constantly demanding increased zeal and ever more arrests.[40] A culture of denunciation swept the country. In the provinces and great cities alike hundreds of thousands of innocent victims died. In 1935 the death penalty was applied for theft by minors aged twelve. Yet if 10 per cent or even 20 per cent were innocent, Stalin reasoned, it was worth the price. Such were the moral mathematics of communism. And the sums added up. When the Eighteenth Party Congress was held in 1939, after a gap of five years, there was no criticism or debate. Dissent was well-nigh unthinkable. Yet Khrushchev reported in his famous 1956 speech on Stalin's 'errors' that, after January 1928, Stalin never visited another village in the country again. Perhaps the reality of what he had created was really too oppressive.

Stalin could now sleep soundly, in any case, because most of his opponents were dead or imprisoned. The penal-camp system – or 'Gulag' for short – had originated in 1918, and expanded massively and swiftly.[41] The immensity of its horrors became evident only after archives began to open up after 1991; they revealed murder on a scale previously only associated with Nazism, and possibly even worse, depending on how the numbers are counted.[42] Besides political prisoners, numerous ordinary criminals were held in circumstances hardly conducive to rehabilitation. Millions of lives were wasted digging useless canals and felling millions of trees in Siberia in extraordinarily harsh conditions. Worst of all were the mines of the frozen north. As many as 8 million, or 9 per cent of the population, were in camps by 1939. Repression throughout Stalin's rule affected perhaps 60 million and, depending on how it is measured, killed some 20 million. By contrast 7 million Soviet soldiers died in the Second World War (plus perhaps 18–20 million civilians), and 1.7 million Russian soldiers in the First.

From early on the Gulag functioned as a vast slave-labour system. The NKVD, as the GPU was called after 1934, controlled some 18 per cent of the national budget, and provided about 20 per cent of all labour. Slave labour was regarded as a justifiable use of national resources given the urgent need to develop immense sections of hitherto largely uninhabitable territory. During the Second World War vast numbers of those unfortunate enough to live in regions of the USSR conquered by Germany were sentenced to the camps when the Russians reoccupied their lands. Equally cruelly, many Soviet POWs lucky enough to survive wartime captivity, as well as civilians who had been transported to Germany to serve as forced labourers, were then shipped off to the Gulag at the war's end – either as traitors because they had not died in battle; or merely because, having seen life outside Russia, they were deemed dangerous to the regime. Millions more soldiers were sacrificed through Stalin's military ineptitude and disdain for life.[43] Nor were foreigners spared: some 26,000 Polish officers and members of Poland's elite were killed in early 1940 at Katyn; and similar massacres and deportations occurred soon after the annexation of Lithuania, Latvia and Estonia, followed by a strategy of Russian emigration and cultural Russification designed to ensure Soviet dominance.

Stalin's rule also rendered fear omnipresent in everyday life. Ordinary civilians were constantly paranoid through much of this period. To utter the slightest criticism, even in one's sleep, invited arrest. 'Speculation' in the black market was severely penalized. The joke ran that a visiting schoolteacher asked a mathematics class, 'If I buy a case of apples for 25 roubles and sell it for 50, what do I get?' The answer: 'Three years in jail'.[44] Another joke involved the questions on application forms for employment: 'Have you ever been in prison – if not, why?'[45] So many were hauled away that, in the early 1930s, hundreds of thousands of hungry orphaned children filled city railway stations begging. Stalin ordered all caught plundering food to be shot, as well as any who had contracted venereal diseases.[46]

nonetheless or because of?

* * *

Throughout this period the USSR nonetheless took great strides forwards in industrialization and modernization. Real wages rose slowly if steadily. In health care and many other areas Russia radically improved itself and generated both greater prosperity and greater equality. Its efforts in education, with the aim of creating the prototype of a classless society, were noteworthy. Literacy, estimated at 37.9 per cent of the male and 12.5 per cent of the female population in 1917, reached 87 per cent by 1939. In 1918 school uniforms, punishments and examinations were abolished, along with marks, medals and distinguishing insignia (these measures, however, were overturned in 1936). Children were educated in the new ideals; a game from around 1930 featured cut-out figures of American capitalists, British imperialists, Mexican priests and other exploiters; when knocked down by a ball they revealed on the reverse representatives of the main groups – blacks, Javanese, Chinese and so on – affected by them.[47] In the universities academic degrees were abolished.

The formal abolition of social classes and distinctions in November 1917 also saw the elimination of all insignia of office in government service and of all military ranks, titles, decorations and privileges. The word 'officer' was replaced by 'commander', and those up to regimental level were elected. The majority of personal ranks were reinstated in 1935, and the most senior general officer and admiral ranks in 1940. Stalin would later counsel his East German minions that 'the genuine Marxist approach' was to pay specialists more to avoid 'peasant-leveling', and to rely on a professional army rather than an armed militia.[48]

For women the new equality was a mixed bag. Their rights were broadly extended shortly after the revolution, and rapidly became more widespread than almost any other country. 'Bourgeois' morality, it was said, made women unfree. So marriage was now devalued. Divorce became easy, and the rate was soon the highest in the world. Illegitimacy was far less tainted, though some thought this disadvantaged women. Sex education and birth control were introduced. Abortion became easily accessible, and initially it was very frequent. A bohemian libertinism, at least in some cities, characterized the early years after 1917, with Alexandra Kollontai famously condoning promiscuity. But by 1935 divorce had become much more difficult. In 1936 abortion again became illegal, and the 'holy instinct of motherhood' was reinforced. One Professor Zalkind of Sverdlov University advised that flirting, courting and coquetry should be discouraged, physical attraction should give way to eugenic and class selection, and the sex act itself minimized even within marriage.[49] Even public displays of affection became punishable. Orwell was not far off the mark in his satire of all this in *Nineteen Eighty-Four.*

Economically the new system aimed to uphold Engels' dictum that the 'emancipation of women becomes possible only when women are enabled to take part in production on a large, social scale, and when domestic duties require their attention only to a minor degree' (26:262). In practice this often meant that women began doing heavy labour, driving tractors and trams, and cleaning streets. Their wages remained less than men's, and old age pensions were extremely low. The 'bourgeois' family did not disappear, however, as many had anticipated. Women certainly gained much more independence. But there is little evidence that men took on a greater portion of housework or childcare in the cramped new communal flats, where shared kitchens and toilets were introduced to enforce a group mentality, and whose close proximity and thin walls made private life virtually impossible.

The chief practical development in Soviet Marxism after 1917 lay in creating a centralized planning apparatus to replace the chaos and waste of the market with production according to human needs. Its conception, however, was deficient in many areas. The fact that planning required a vast bureaucracy staffed by officials who inevitably promoted their own sectional and personal interests, and the fact that planning in principle often contradicted workers' control, were not thought through. Lenin insisted by 1918 that '*Unqualified submission* to a single will is unconditionally necessary for the success of the process of labour organized on the pattern of large-scale industry'.[50] So it was not capitalism which dictated the nature of the labour process: it was machinery – as Engels had suggested in 'On Authority'. And so Taylor's revolution got the better of Marx's.

The chief mechanism of the new planning system, the State General Planning Commission (Gosplan), was established in 1921. Expanded in the late 1920s, its focus shifted to heavy industry under the First Five Year Plan (1928/9–1932/3). In 1926–7 the private sector still accounted for about half of the USSR's national income. This declined to almost nothing by 1933. The Soviet Union continued to endure chronic shortages of consumer goods, sporadic food supplies, low real wages, insufficient foreign exchange and poor quality products throughout its entire history. Agriculture suffered in particular as a result of using excessive force to solve the *kulak* problem and secure grain, and from lengthy incentive crises, resistance to collectivization, and poor storage facilities and transportation. Some huge prestige projects, like the White Sea–Baltic Canal – built in 1931–3 at the cost of perhaps 25,000 convict lives – were near-complete failures (the canal was too shallow to take most sea-going vessels). Fear of the repercussions of failure meant that accurate statistics were rarely available.

In certain areas – military hardware, and later the nuclear and space programmes – planning enjoyed much greater success. Here the ability to concentrate vast resources quickly was manifest. During the Second World War the USSR exceeded Germany in munitions manufacture by nearly double; and from 1950 to 1965 the Soviet Union's growth rate was some 3.4 per cent annually, compared to the USA's 2.3 per cent. But the strain of rapid industrialization eventually produced the worst ecological record of any major country, at least until China reached a similar level of development in the 1990s. By the 1960s too some Soviet economists estimated that, at current trends, the entire population of the country would need to be integrated into the planning bureaucracy. If this universalized the privileges of the new administrative order, sometimes called the *nomenklatura* or *apparatchiki*, it would have been no bad thing. But who would shine shoes?

So the state did not 'wither away', as Marx, Engels and Lenin prophesied. It became more coercive, more obsessed with its own power, and less capable of entertaining the possibility of meaningful opposition. It became what Trotsky called 'a dictatorship over the proletariat...the political rule of the class by organizational rule over the class'. 'We advance toward the abolition of the state by way of strengthening the state', Stalin said in 1930, calling this 'dialectics'.[51] Official Marxism, parroted as a state religion, degenerated into systematic lying on a vast scale, from production statistics to the Party's history. An omnipresent bureaucracy usurped the workers' powers. Ethnically, Russia predominated over the many minorities in the Soviet empire, and often trampled mercilessly over them – including, in the west, Ukrainians, Poles and the peoples of the Baltic states. After 1934 a nationalist and patriotic narrative was revived, which remains extremely powerful even today.

Under Bolshevism Soviet man and woman were not reborn as higher ethical, social types – nor cloned as higher biological types, as some scientists hoped. Instead, circumstances shaped a cowed, submissive, subservient and fearful population drained of most of its idealism. We should not forget, however, that the Party aspired to create a new type of person. We can glean what this ideal of humanity was meant to be from the discipline notionally imposed on members of the Party and on the Komsomol (Communist Youth League), the best and brightest of the rising generation. This future philosopher-elite was expected to set an example in personal conduct by refraining from excesses of all sorts. They were to be guided by the maxim that 'Morality is that which helps the destruction of the old exploiters' society and the unity of the workers who are building a new communist society.'[52] Outworn 'bourgeois' attitudes were condemned. Yet the Party also represented the triumph of other bourgeois virtues. Members were encouraged to be faithful to their spouses, to abstain from scandal and excessive drinking, and to despise hooliganism, swearing and the like. In general, private pleasure was to be subordinated to public sacrifice. Cleanliness, moderation and, above all, hard work were prized.

For a while – and to a degree throughout Soviet history, where cynicism and systematic lethargy did not set in – more than lip service was paid to these ideals. In the 'golden era' of the early years after the revolution, as Kirov's assassin later recalled while being interrogated by Stalin, 'The party membership was infused with a passion for self-sacrifice' and 'There were loyal friendships, a desire to help one another, a spirit of comradeship'. But then everything 'became bureaucratized'.[53] The new elite was a bourgeoisie in all but name, and indeed the word *sovbour* – 'Soviet bourgeois' – entered the vocabulary. Besides the furs, jewellery and perfumes, the *nomenklatura*'s privileges included special apartments, dachas, holidays, sports and educational facilities, dedicated traffic lanes for official limousines, their own shops stocked with goods unavailable to most, the right to travel abroad and more. The thorough purge of the old bourgeoisie, aristocracy and intelligentsia, whose children were denied any possibility not only of advancement but sometimes even of employment, meant that thousands of positions fell open to new Party members with a working-class background. These became Stalin's firmest supporters. To the austere, selfless image of the Young Pioneers and Komsomols was now juxtaposed the self-serving, nest-feathering Diamat bureaucrat. They conquered the state and Party until finally, in Trotsky's words, 'the leaden rump of the bureaucracy outweighed the head of the revolution'.[54] Far from being more virtuous simply on account of having been exploited, the proletariat in power – having never known the temptation – succumbed to the lure of luxury as quickly as any other group.

At its apex the 'new class', the holders of the precious Party card, comprised at most about 12–15 per cent of the population by the mid-1930s.[55] At the very top many in this group ran semi-independent fiefdoms, particularly after the Terror, when Stalin's appointees predominated. The paperwork associated with this vast new bureaucracy was mind-numbingly complex. Efficiency was rare, and shoddiness, haste and waste were widespread. Amongst Stalin's entourage sexual excess, rape and drunkenness were common. Terror indeed encouraged bizarre risk-taking: who knew who would be alive tomorrow?

In the workplace circumstances remained very difficult for decades. Throughout the 1930s wages were often at poverty level. So people worked after hours and at second or third jobs. Elite employees who greatly exceeded work norms, like the Stakhanovites, might share in some of this largesse. (They were named after the miner Alexey Stakhanov, who cut 100 tons of coal in one six-hour shift on 31 August 1935; he received a small furnished flat and a horse-drawn cart, as well as the enmity of many of his co-workers, for his efforts.) Wage differentials now grew considerably, and perhaps enormously.[56] At work pilfering and absenteeism were common. Wastage was the norm from the 1920s onwards. Labour discipline was extremely harsh, as bad as anything Victorian England had seen and often worse. Ten per cent of salary was customarily deducted as a 'voluntary' state loan. Managers were appointed and promoted on the basis of Party loyalty. Planning in general was extremely chaotic, with attempts to match the supply of raw materials and power to industrial construction often failing. Labour turnover was great as workers sought better conditions, though the Tsarist system of internal passports, abolished in 1917 and reintroduced in 1932, hindered movement.[57] The falsification of statistics was normal, fulfilment of the paper 'plan' becoming the only end. Nonfulfilment was often as severely penalized as sabotage and 'wrecking'. 'Voluntary' days of work were frequently demanded, and those who refused might find their passports stamped 'discharged for the sabotage of the production plan' – which could mean a ticket to the Gulag.[58]

The Soviet economy thus never achieved a high level of efficiency outside military production and a few other spheres. Shoddiness was common, and shortages of consumer goods, even necessities, persisted right up to 1991. Queues became a common sight from the outset: much of the free time socialism generated was spent in them, but they were a poor place to acquire all-roundedness. Low wages were the greatest problem. For decades workers were so ill fed that they often had little capacity for exertion. In the mid-1930s people were 'unanimous in confirming' that conditions were worse than before the revolution.[59] *Blat*, a service-for-service or favours system which would have been recognizable to the early socialist theorists of equal exchange, prevailed everywhere. The housing shortage meant that entire families often lived in a single room, with divorced husbands or wives sometimes relegated to a corner, separated from their successors by a curtain. In such irritatingly close proximity, theft and quarrelling were common; particularly in Moscow so were prostitution and suicide. In the early years workers sometimes lived in vast dormitories of 500 or more – the scheme was sometimes colloquially called 'barracks socialism'.

In principle, of course, all these failings were widely supposed to be temporary. With a communist education, it was assumed, a new generation untainted by pre-revolutionary habits and prejudices would grow up marked by its enthusiasm for the common good. In the meantime the Party and state made immense efforts to disguise the system's shortcomings. The much-touted 1936 Constitution guaranteed many rights, including freedom of religion, speech, press, assembly and demonstration, none of which existed in practice. Imitated in most communist states, this became the sham, hypocritical compliment which the 'people's democracies' paid to liberalism for half a century and more. But some observers, most famously the British Fabian leaders Beatrice and Sidney Webb, even declared the USSR 'the most inclusive and equalised democracy in the world'.[60]

At the same time, a real effort was made in the cultural sphere to maximize a sense of the worth and dignity of labour by creating a genuine workers' culture. Millions more film viewers and radio listeners were created by the 1930s. Much of the content of what they saw and heard was dictated by the new ideology. In Soviet films, typically, 'the girl was won by a tractor-driver who had fulfilled his schedule by 200 per cent'.[61] Here, as with literature, the Party exerted a stranglehold by the mid-1930s. Where once, as in the avant-garde posters of the immediate post-revolutionary period, creativity and innovation had brought colour and a delirious, adventurous sense of novelty and vivacity to the new ideals, a cold, clammy grey mist now enveloped the arts. Censors intervened at every stage of the progress of a work. Socialist realism, glorifying ordinary workers, was the only accepted style. Approved authors, directors and artists enjoyed large incomes, dachas in the country, privileged positions in organizations like the Writers' Union and the adulation of large audiences. But the price of deviation was high, like the suicide rate amongst writers. Even in the natural sciences rigid conformism to the Party line was demanded. Geologists, bacteriologists, agronomists and physiologists, amongst many others, who produced 'erroneous' research suffered the consequences – including execution.

The official ideology of the Stalinist epoch was a crude version of Leninism. Its continuity with Marx is debatable. There was, Kautsky wrote, 'nothing that Marx feared so much as the degeneration of his school into a rigid sect'. To Marx, he insisted, 'there was no ultimate knowledge, only an infinite process of learning'.[62] These warnings were ignored. Under Stalin, Marxism meant whatever the Party said on any given day. Marx of course never had to grapple with the realities of political power. Industrialization, centralization and collectivization were the main planks in his economic platform. But concentrating all revolutionary power in a party not subject to democratic control, and then in the hands of one individual, are not suggested anywhere in his writings. Nor was creating a vast empire of slave labourers, though labour armies were proposed in *The Communist Manifesto*. Marx's system sanctioned some of these developments, at least partially. But Marx himself was not a Blanquist, and never favoured prolonged mass coercion. In this era Marx ultimately would probably have found himself much closer to the revisionists, and later to the Workers' Opposition, than to Stalin.

Yet Stalinism was also, in the leading Polish philosopher Leszek Kolakowski's view, a 'legitimate' interpretation of Marx's philosophy of history. Its successful achievement might well retrospectively have justified some if not most of the means employed. Even persecuted and imprisoned Party members agonized over whether, if communist society actually was attained, with peace, plenty and universal content, everything Stalin did would have to be exonerated. But this blissful day never arrived. Whether Marx's anticipation of the complete unity of mankind and the superseding of alienated labour resulted in totalitarianism, as Kolakowski alleged – because these 'basic values could hardly be materialized otherwise – is another matter. This hinges partly on how far we suppose Marx imagined both that disagreements would continue even in communist society and also that no party could claim an infallible grasp of the truth. William Morris, for instance, certainly assumed this. A Marxist thus might plausibly presume that 'unity' could be limited rather than total. And not all utopias are 'visions of a perfectly unified society', as Kolakowski suggests.[63] But this one essentially was.

Much of the official brand of Soviet Marxism formed at this time was more indebted to Engels than Marx, and especially to *Anti-Dühring*, then *Dialectics of Nature* and *Socialism: Utopian and Scientific*.[64] These works collectively advanced the view that, Moses-like, Marx had 'discovered' 'laws of history' which were immutable, inevitable and ir-resistible, and that Bolshevism's opponents were in effect flat-earthers or Canute-imitating sea-defiers, who merited pity at best, but who at worst were mad heretics who deserved extermination. The creation of a dogmatic Marxian orthodoxy, already well underway, was hastened by the Russian Revolution. Bertrand Russell likened it to a religion in which 'those who accept Bolshevism become impervious to scientific evidence and commit intellectual suicide'.[65] Its principles were applied to every science and every form of study, from agronomy to physics, chemistry, philology, genetics and cosmology – even cookery – in all of which idealism was defeated as surely as the dragon by St George.

As in politics, factions were quickly outlawed, so in ideas deviant trends soon became punishable heresies. Stalin must assume primary responsibility for this process. Philosophical contention was formally abolished by decree of the Central Committee on 25 January 1931. A set of 'classic' texts was laid down, of Marx, Engels, Lenin and Sta-lin, which defined systematic dialectical materialism. This was gener-ally regarded as a conception governing both the natural and human worlds, with the law of the dialectic, and particularly the universality of contradiction, being inscribed in matter itself. Debate was limited to citing chapter and verse in support of the Party line, and competing to claim greater orthodoxy according to holy writ. Dialectics became the science of the mystic and charlatan, designed to bewitch and obscure, and to avoid empirical truths wherever possible. Stalin was elevated to world-historical philosophical stature for his writings on the national question, Leninism and linguistics in particular. These trends pro-duced an atmosphere of dishonesty, hypocrisy and self-delusion from which Marxism never recovered.

The rewriting of Soviet history and creation of Stalin's personality cult were centrally associated with the *Short Course of the History of the All-Union Communist Party*, some 50 million copies of which appeared between 1938 and 1953. Its narrative, written in barbarous Diamat prose, was 'edited' by Stalin (at one point the newspaper *Pravda* claimed he wrote it).[66] In keeping with Stalin's view that Marxism was first and foremost 'an entire world-view' whose singular focus was class war, the book emphasized (or invented) his central role in the revolution and his position as Lenin's heir. Party members were often examined on its contents during episodes of *chistka*, or 'cleansing'. The text portrayed socialism as the 'inevitable outcome of the development of modern capitalist society', achievable 'only by revolutionary violence against the bourgeoisie'. Here all the opponents of Lenin and then Stalin are neatly lined up like bowling pins, then knocked over, and the necessity for their disposal justified, the arch-traitor of course being 'Judas Trotsky' (supposedly Lenin's term). Stalin is presented as Lenin's natural successor. Taking a theoretical leaf from Stalin's *Foundations of Leninism* (1924), 'dialectical materialism' is defined as 'the world outlook of the Marxist-Leninist party', 'dialectical' being the method of study, 'materialism' the 'interpretation of the phenomena of nature', considered as interdependent and constantly in flux (the source here being chiefly Engels' *Dialectics of Nature* and *Anti-Dühring*).[67]

In any case Stalin's dedication to Marxism and socialism has been described as only 'skin deep'. He was contemptuous of the masses, keen to impose his own dogmas by force wherever he deemed it necessary and little concerned with the other possible ends of communist society, like increasing liberty and equality for the majority. His commitment was to industrialization as a path to restoring and increasing Russia's prestige. He had long since renounced, if he had ever held them, any beliefs in Marx's idea of a 'free association of producers'.[68] Instead, as one Moscow student put it in 1945, 'Marxism is the history of the party'.[69] This 'Marxism', and a history of it that was constantly being rewritten, could never have been embraced by Marx, to whom the workers' movement broadly conceived was always central.

CHAPTER 4

After Stalin, 1953–1968

Stalin bore a considerable responsibility for the colossal tragedies of the early years of the Second World War, having schemed with Hitler to divide Poland ånd seize the Baltic states for himself, as well as decimating his officer corps just before the war. But though his hair turned grey and his health was shaken, Stalin retrieved much of his reputation by being identified with the USSR's victory in 1945. The Marshal of the Soviet Union, as he crowned himself after the victory at Stalingrad in 1943, was now more than ever a national hero, despite devastating destruction and the immense loss of life. The USSR then acquired nuclear weapons in 1949, and a mere thirty-two years after the revolution was looked upon as America's equal. Setting the human suffering involved to one side, it was a stupendous achievement. Together with Mao's victory in China in the same year, it seemed to herald the final, worldwide triumph of communism.

Hundreds of thousands wept openly at Stalin's passing on 5 March 1953. Hundreds were trampled in the crowds which gathered to view his corpse before it was placed, embalmed, next to Lenin's, in Red Square. (It was removed in 1961 during the Khrushchev thaw.) Nonetheless the legacy of the Terror was hard to shake. Death and devastation had followed everywhere in Stalin's wake. In 1953 grain output per capita was still below the 1913 level. The Soviet premier Nikita Khrushchev's famous secret speech at the 1956 Party Congress denouncing Stalin's 'mass repressions' and 'cult of personality' was the first official reckoning with Stalinism, and assisted a brief ideological lull (1953–9).

Emphasis was now given to the need for 'socialist humanism' to form the basis of communist morality, rather than merely anything that served the class struggle.[1]

In the next decade some 7–8 million were freed from the Gulag, which had expanded to its greatest extent only in 1952. Material incentives were restored to agriculture, and collective farms given a greater degree of independence. Single-family flats were promised to the entire population and a vast building programme commenced. From 1928 onwards the USSR had an average growth rate estimated at 4.2 per cent a year, and by 1977 Soviet GDP was 57 per cent of the USA's.[2] But Soviet consumer goods were notoriously shoddy (TVs blew up from time to time). Liberalization, which had included attempts to curb the privileges of the *nomenklatura*, was reversed under Khrushchev's successor as premier in 1964, Leonid Brezhnev, and Stalin was partially rehabilitated, as he has been again under Vladimir Putin.[3] By the mid-1950s, however, and especially after Stalin's most powerful police chief, Lavrentiy Beria's, execution in 1953, the secret police ceased to be a state within a state and came under the Party's control. But the state as a whole showed no inclination to 'wither away', and as late as 1970 was still described as 'totalitarian' by Western experts.[4] Still later the KGB would be succeeded by the FSB, but the regime's opponents continue to be murdered in the present day. Old habits die hard.

The Red Army's victory in 1945 gained the USSR vast tracts of territory in the west, and a sphere of influence in which Soviet governments were imposed by 1948. The Cold War quickly developed in response, triggering war in Korea (1950–53), fuelling that in Vietnam (1945–75) and assisting conflicts elsewhere. Dictators poured from the Stalin mould were put in place, notably Walter Ulbricht and Erich Honecker in East Germany (the GDR), the megalomaniac Nicolae Ceaușescu in Romania (who occasionally entertained diplomats seated on a large golden throne)[5] and Mátyás Rákosi and János Kádár in Hungary. Though their regimes were milder than Stalin's, all were brutal, and torture and show trials were plentiful. Death rates varied greatly, however, from perhaps a few hundred in Czechoslovakia to many hundreds of thousands in Romania. Even the pretence of independence was removed from the

Baltic nations, whose intelligentsia were ruthlessly decimated when they were incorporated into the USSR, though resistance by the 'Forest Brothers' continued into the 1950s. Under the Stasi (secret police), supervision of the population in East Germany actually surpassed that in Stalin's USSR, with at least 2.5 per cent of citizens eventually regularly serving as informers, rising to as many as 25 per cent if occasional assistance is counted. In Hungary one in ten were informers by 1956.

Throughout the post-war period an economic and cultural gap opened as the West grew wealthy while the East stagnated under centralized planning, incompetence and excessive bureaucracy. On a visit to the USA in 1959 Khrushchev blurted out, 'I have seen the slaves of capitalism and they live well' – which was jammed by Soviet censors when Western radio rebroadcast it to the USSR. To the younger generation, jeans, pop music, whatever of Hollywood leaked through (Tarzan was a favourite), and an intellectual diet free of the incessant water-torture drip of ideology increasingly symbolized the difference. Here a deficit of personal freedom was widely felt. Staged elections, where often only one party alone was permitted, and which resulted in near-unanimous victories, were widely regarded as fraudulent. Slowly, amidst economic stagnation, the legitimacy of these regimes eroded, and internal criticism grew more vocal. In a despondent USSR alcoholism became endemic. Spontaneous social life was stifled and deadened. Further repression only hastened the process of dissolution.

In the USSR post-war revisionists seeking to improve the system from within had a steep uphill battle. Lenin's polemics against 'the renegade Kautsky' had fixed the template. Defining 'revisionism', the Soviet *Political Dictionary* stated that mere 're-examination' of Marx implied the 'distortion and negation' of his tenets. Outside Western Social Democracy, little remained of alternative forms of socialism. Inside the USSR all traces of the former opposition had been eradicated by the 1950s. Then came a new wave of criticism. Anticipated by his novel *One Day in the Life of Ivan Denisovich* (1962), Alexander Solzhenitsyn's *The Gulag Archipelago, 1918–1956* (1973) brilliantly exposed the scale and devastating brutality of Stalin's oppression, and caused a furore on its appearance, building on the powerful literary critique of totalitarianism led a generation earlier by George Orwell's *Nineteen*

Eighty-Four (1949). The circulation of dissenting opinions, often via underground *samizdat* presses, was frequently severely repressed. Many dissidents, like the renowned physicist Andrei Sakharov, regarded the USSR as 'a society based on state capitalism', differing only from other forms of capitalism in having 'complete nationalization' and a Party-state monopoly over much of life.[6] But using Marx's writings to criticize the system was rare before the 1960s.

In the Soviet-dominated Eastern bloc, however, cracks began appearing everywhere immediately on its establishment in the late 1940s, as philosophers, playwrights, economists and literary critics sought various types of reform. Led by Josip Broz Tito (1892–1980), and spurred on by resentment of Soviet interference, Yugoslavia was the first nation in the Soviet sphere of influence to break from Stalinism. It was expelled in 1948 from the Cominform, which succeeded the International (abolished in 1943) in 1947, for resisting land collectivization and Soviet domination over Eastern Europe.[7] A Soviet attempt to overthrow Tito by coup d'état failed. The Yugoslav Milovan Djilas analysed the 'new class' of bureaucratic technocrats in nominally socialist societies whose exploitation of labour paralleled that in capitalist societies. (He had the temerity to demand an end to the Party's monopoly on power, and was expelled from it in 1954.) Marxist humanism was championed by writers like Gajo Petrović, an editor of the journal *Praxis*, which stressed the contemporary relevance of the young Marx's theory of alienation. Yugoslav economic experiments also emphasized decentralization and market socialism.

Uprisings occurred in the GDR (June 1953), Poznán and Warsaw (June and October 1956), Hungary (October–November 1956), Czechoslovakia (January–August 1968), Gdańsk (December 1970, August 1980) and Romania (August 1977). The most serious were crushed by Soviet troops, proving that Stalinism had survived Stalin. In the GDR the threat of increased work norms in 1953 triggered popular revolt, though there were also demands for free unions and free elections. Unrest in Poland in 1956 was spurred on by Khrushchev's secret speech in February, and later food prices played a major role. Inspired by Yugoslav developments, calls were made in Hungary in 1956 for elected independent workers' councils. Here too free elections of Party members 'from top to bottom' and for a new national assembly were demanded. On the streets of Budapest symbols of Soviet occupation were targeted. Crowds demolished a colossal statue of Stalin which overlooked the city like an Olympian god, leaving only a six-foot high pair of boots. Its head rolled down the street, and was subject to all manner of abuse. The short-lived Nagy government withdrew from the Warsaw Pact, seeking neutrality, and began dissolving the Communist Party and introducing a multiparty system. But there were some 2,500 deaths following Soviet intervention, and 200,000 fled the country. Nagy was secretly executed for treason in 1958.

In all these cases some blamed the disasters of Soviet rule on Stalin personally, or even Lenin, and more generally the 'cult of personality'. Others sought flaws in the communist system, particularly in the idea of the 'dictatorship of the proletariat', and in orthodox (mis) interpretation of the Marxist classics. The rigidity of central planning frequently came under fire, and the predominance of the USSR over other socialist regimes was questioned. These developments pointed to the possibility of multiple roads to socialism and of differing interpretations of Marx, and to a general insistence on much more popular involvement in and free debate over decision-making and goals. But all equally indicated that there was something wrong with the leading trends of modern communism. Coercion was not the essence of what Marx had projected, but rather its antithesis. Yet it epitomized the system which bore his name.

In the West the literature on disillusionment spread rapidly by the early 1940s as converts to communism like Arthur Koestler, Ignazio Silone and Richard Wright fled the fold and the exhilaration of true belief was displaced by the cold sobriety of disappointment.[8] In the USSR visiting dignitaries, such as foreign communists, were often fêted and shown model factories and houses. Banquets were laid on and filmed for propaganda purposes. Some soon realized that 'everything had been staged for our benefit' and was 'humbug and lies'. Potemkin-like villages had false fronts to disguise their poverty, and 'real workers' turned out to be secret policemen. But some voluntarily censored what they learned for fear of aiding the regime's enemies. The most idealistic, who stayed to work, were soon as destitute as their Soviet peers.[9] The

Molotov–Ribbentrop pact of August 1939 was an early turning-point in this loss of faith. It provoked the American Marxist Max Eastman to conclude not only that 'there is not a hope left for the classless society in present-day Russia', but that 'Stalinism is worse than fascism – more ruthless, barbarous, unjust, immoral, anti-democratic, unredeemed by any hope or scruple.'[10] Some who drifted away slowly sought other solutions to world problems, as Douglas Hyde did in Catholicism and 'a new God'. Many began to believe that the doctrine that 'the end justified the means' was no longer acceptable.[11] Still more were driven away by the USSR's suppression of the Hungarian uprising in 1956 and then its invasion of Czechoslovakia in 1968, which lost it the goodwill and sympathy of millions in the West. Arrogance, heavy-handedness, and brutality prevailed where milder regimes might have prevailed.

CHAPTER 5

Western European Marxism, 1920–1968, and Beyond

For about a century Marxism exerted considerable influence on the intellectual life of Western Europe. National Marxist variations depended in part on pre-existing political milieux. Marxism was more likely to be blended into or tinged with liberalism where the latter had been influential politically, as in Britain. Sometimes spontaneous developments co-existed with the USSR's direct influence. Born in Moscow out of the pressing need to garner support everywhere for the nascent regime, the Third International (1919–43) was firmly under Soviet control from the outset. All but one of the delegates present at its first meeting were chosen by Moscow, as Russia now proclaimed itself to be the fatherland of the international proletariat. As an agit-prop (agitation and propaganda) organization and master puppeteer, the International's efforts were unsurpassed. Local communist leaders constantly jockeyed for the apparently unlimited resources Moscow provided the compliant. Fortunes were made and lives lost by acceding to or failing to anticipate changes in the Party line, to which loyalty was the chief virtue prized.

With the Italian fascist Benito Mussolini's ascent to power in 1922 the battle lines formed which would dominate world politics until 1945. After the Wall Street Crash of 1929 the stark political choice seemed to be between Bolshevism and capitalism/fascism. 'One had to choose between fascism and fellow-travelling', remembered Richard Cobb, a British historian resident in Paris.[1] Hitler's rise to power in 1933, and the viciousness of his anti-Semitism and anti-Bolshevism, did much to augment the Soviet Union's influence. So did the USSR's huge, prestigious building and other projects, and the endless dazzling lists of statistics of expanding production, employment, education and consumption, which impressed naïve visitors who often saw what they wanted to see and blithely ignored anything that contradicted official propaganda. In the depths of the Great Depression such apparent successes, endlessly repeated, made the USSR seem to be advancing rapidly just as the dole queues in the West were lengthening. The USA had been the great nation of the future of the late nineteenth and early twentieth centuries; now, for many, the USSR took its place as the beacon of progressive modernity. The mood of the epoch expressed an explosive resentment of the poverty, cruelty and injustice of a system that now spread worldwide chaos. So writers like the American John Dos Passos predicted the fall of American capitalism, while Upton Sinclair thought 'Soviet Russia is coming up, the capitalist nations are going down.'[2] To many, communism became the obvious choice for the future. 'Writers in uniform', as Max Eastman called them, proliferated rapidly, as did fellow travellers who sympathized but fell short of full-scale conversion. Dos Passos, Ernest Hemingway, John Steinbeck, Charlie Chaplin, Romain Rolland, Upton Sinclair, Arnold Zweig and a host of others echoed such sentiments.

These sentiments crystallized in one year, 1936. Triggered by Francisco Franco's fascist coup against the Republic, the Spanish Civil War (1936–9) symbolized the colossal altercation of the epoch like no other event. Here Soviet intervention often harmed the Republic's cause. Stalin's elimination of all but his most loyal followers as 'rivals' did much to undermine the struggle against Franco. In Germany the communist line that Social Democrats were 'social fascists' alienated millions more potential supporters and weakened opposition to Hitler. Well-trained Marxists indeed sometimes asserted that 'all non-Soviet believers were Fascists'.[3] The Molotov–Ribbentrop non-aggression pact (1939–41) between the USSR and Germany shocked and alienated many sympathizers: 'It's dialectics, comrade', no longer cut the mustard. Yet when Stalin became Britain's and America's ally during the Second World War, Marxism once again was acceptable in liberal circles. Many in this period also saw communism as a worthy option for Russia and other backward nations, but did not want it adopted in advanced Western countries: thus Beatrice Webb, for example, thought 'Russian communism is the only hope for China' in 1932.[4]

Lukács and Gramsci

The most important Marxist writers to emerge in the 1920s and 1930s were György (Georg) Lukács, in Hungary, and Antonio Gramsci, in Italy. The son of a wealthy banker and student of Georg Simmel and Max Weber, Lukács (1885–1971) became Commissar for Culture in the ill-fated Hungarian People's Republic of 1919, then moved to Vienna and, in 1929, to Moscow.[5] In 1918 he still embraced ethical idealism, demanding 'the creation of institutions that are congruent with its ideal'. He worried, too, that Bolshevism presented 'an insoluble moral dilemma' in positing that 'good can come from evil'. In an article entitled 'The Ethical Foundation of Communism' (1918–19) he portrayed the aim of the class struggle as 'mutual love and solidarity'.[6]

When the 1919 Republic collapsed, Lukács barely escaped with his life. In Vienna he rewrote the essays which make up his chief work, *History and Class Consciousness: Studies in Marxist Dialectics* (1923).[7] A main concern here was to undermine the scientific basis of official Marxism. Lukács rejected Engels' application of dialectics to nature. Anticipating the rediscovery of the young Marx's humanism – the Hungarian claimed that 'the problem of alienation was raised for the first time there' – Lukács stressed the subjective aspects of class consciousness.[8] His revolutionary idealism, even 'Platonism', was thus at odds with Bolshevism. His secular eschatology was more indebted to Hegel, rather than the mechanistic materialism of Bukharin and other Bolsheviks.[9] But his ideal of communism was little different from Marx's or Lenin's, its ultimate objective being 'the construction of a society in which freedom of morality will take the place of legal compulsion in the regulation of all behaviour'.[10] Taking his cue from Marx's discussion of commodity fetishism, Lukács developed the concept of reification to explain distortions in our consciousness of reality, and particularly the idea that we are ruled by laws beyond our control and thus fail to understand the 'totality' of the world (implying this is actually possible). This process Lukács thought could be overcome through proletarian consciousness, which would enable the working class to become the subject of history.

In Moscow in 1921 for the third Comintern congress, Lukács succumbed to Lenin's charisma, and after his death produced a fawning account of him. Thereafter, though critical of Stalin in later years, he never renounced Leninism, insisting on the Party's leading role as embodying the dictatorship of the proletariat and proletarian consciousness.[11] Exiled in Moscow from 1930 to 1945, Lukács worked with David Riazanov, and miraculously survived the purges by remaining a resolute Stalinist in public. He disowned his key work three times as a 'mistaken book' riven with 'revolutionary messianism'. In 1956 he joined the cabinet of Imre Nagy's government, which abolished the one-party state in Hungary before being expelled by Soviet intervention. But Lukács wanted neither political pluralism nor withdrawal from the Warsaw Pact. He still insisted that only Marxists should teach philosophy at university, and thought books like Hitler's *Mein Kampf* (1925) should not freely circulate. Victor Serge accused Lukács of embracing totalitarianism, particularly in the belief that since history could not be divorced from politics it should be written by Communist Party functionaries.[12]

Even late in life Lukács denied that 'Marxism itself is in need of revision', in 1971 accusing Marcuse and Bloch of being 'utopians' while proclaiming 'I am a Marxist.' But he also asserted that 'the economic theories of Marx are not really correct', and that 'The core of Marx is really his view of history and his analysis of social consciousness.' One of Lukács's last works, *Democratization: Its Present and Future* (1968), rejected the idea of a multiparty state, and pleaded instead for a 'total transformation' of human nature, a view some associate with 'totalitarianism'.[13] After 1956 Stalinists attacked Lukács as a revisionist who introduced a Hegelian emphasis on consciousness into Marxism, and he did indeed do much to revive interest in the Hegelian roots of Marxism, notably through *The Young Hegel* (1948). He also became an influential aesthetic and literary critic, and wrote an important study of irrationalism as a source of National Socialism, as well as an unfinished work entitled 'The Ontology of Social Being'.[14]

Although his impact outside Italy only developed in the 1960s, the single most influential Western European Marxist theorist has been the Sardinian-born Antonio Gramsci (1891–1937).[15] Barely five feet tall, owing to a hunchback, here is Gramsci in Victor Serge's description of him: 'His head was heavy, his brow high and broad, his lips thin; the whole was carried on a puny, square-shouldered, weak-chested, hump-backed body. There was grace in the movement of his fine, lanky hands.'[16] A socialist by 1914, Gramsci believed the future would bring 'the maximum of liberty with the minimum of constraint'.[17] Active in organizing industrial workers in Turin, he viewed factory councils as anticipating a new form of elected socialist management, albeit with the Party still playing a leading role. He attended the second Comintern congress in Moscow in 1920, and on his return set about founding the Italian Communist Party. When Mussolini's fascists came to power, Gramsci viewed them as a petty-bourgeois mass movement animated by hatred of the working class. In November 1926 he was arrested and sentenced to twenty years' imprisonment. Plentifully supplied with books, he read and wrote widely on subjects as diverse as folklore, linguistics and the Italian intelligentsia, filling some thirty-two notebooks. He was never freed, and died eleven years later of maltreatment and ill health.

Gramsci's most enduring theme lay in the judgement that capitalism's success involved its hegemonic control over the worldview of the majority through the manufacturing and ordering of consent. Another central issue emerging from his studies was the need for a new class of intellectuals who could woo the peasantry while detaching themselves from a bourgeois worldview. His great influence was Benedetto Croce, who had emphasized the role of human activity, or willpower, in making history. Notwithstanding the obvious danger of relativism which it implied, the reduction of all history to praxis for Gramsci became a counterweight to the prevailing economism and determinism of mainstream Marxism, and especially Engels' later writings. The agency of this will was to be, following Machiavelli, the 'Modern Prince': not a 'concrete individual' or particular ruler, but the intellectual organism of the revolutionary political party representing the collective will of the proletariat.[18] This however undermined the possibility of any independent intellectual outlook. 'Traditional' intellectuals, as Gramsci termed them, saw themselves as autonomous from other classes, while 'organic' intellectuals embodied the class outlook of the group from which they emerged. What the proletariat needed, he thought, was its own organic intellectuals. (Stalin of course thought the same thing, but wanted them to be utterly submissive and thoroughly indoctrinated in proletarian culture.) Gramsci also insisted that any successful political movement would have to reflect its indigenous origins, that is, often, its national character. Like Lukács, Gramsci thought Engels' version of materialism vulgarized Marx's more subtle Hegelian formulations. He rejected any hard interpretation of historical inevitability, insisting that the revolutionary contest would be protracted. He also adhered to the idea of unitary party rule, dismissing liberal ideas of the separation of powers as permitting coercive rule by bureaucracies and reflecting a class-divided society.[19]

Gramsci's *Prison Letters* and *Prison Notebooks* (written 1929–35) thus established him as first and foremost a theorist of cultural hegemony within capitalism, and of the means of overcoming it. 'False consciousness' explained why the working classes could not grasp capitalism's true nature. Gramsci thought politics central to both attaining and constructing socialism, and as not wholly determined by economic factors. More than most Marxists, he assigned intellectuals a central role in this struggle, particularly in civil society. His theory of hegemony described how some intellectuals promoted and defended the position and power of the ruling class, and presented its outlook as inevitable and natural. This was particularly true of capitalism, where attaining proletarian counter-hegemony was clearly extremely difficult. At the centre of the class struggle was a contest of intellectuals versus intellectuals, a concept which of course flattered intellectuals then and now. This theory remains Gramsci's main legacy, whose relevance today in an era of even greater media concentration is obvious.[20]

A few other early twentieth-century Marxists merit mention here. After the Second World War the leading Italian Marxist of note was Galvano Della Volpe (1895–1968). Initially he became known for asserting that Hegel often confused abstract and real in historical movement, was essentially a religious mystic and was little help in reading or extending Marx. Rejecting Social Democracy's evolutionary strategies, Della Volpe was keen to move beyond Engels' reading of Marx. He produced an important study of Marx and Rousseau – 'the spiritual father of modern democracy' – which insisted on the former's superiority over the latter's republican egalitarianism and idea of the 'abstract man'.[21] He also rejected Kant's liberalism as unduly wedded to egoism, and attempted to exonerate Lenin from the charge of authoritarianism.[22]

A leading German Marxist in this period was Karl Korsch (1886–1961). His *Marxism and Philosophy* (1923) was, like Lukács, critical of Engels' identification of materialism with natural science, and concerned with returning to Hegel. Yet Korsch still maintained that Marxism implied 'the abolition of' philosophy as such, including ethics, and that Marxist politics was a sufficiently 'scientific system' and 'account of the laws of motion of society' to be 'free of value judgments', positions which are obviously untenable today.[23] Korsch centrally defined socialism as 'a struggle to realise freedom'.[24] Critical of both Leninist and Stalinist authoritarianism (which he linked), the Fabian-influenced Korsch also supported industrial democracy, in the form of workers' councils, as a means of fomenting class consciousness and avoiding bureaucratization and as an alternative to both state socialism and syndicalism. Consequently he was expelled from the KPD in 1926, and criticized by Stalin in 1931. Korsch also particularly stressed the necessity for psychological preparation to precede any attempted revolution. He was, with Lukács, amongst the first writers to use Marx's early works against Stalinism.

In the inter- and post-war period Marxism was increasingly combined with extraneous ideas and movements, with varying degrees of success. These included Surrealism, which promoted radical forms of liberty and sought to unify personal and sexual liberation with social transformation. The *Surrealist Manifesto* (1924) of André Breton famously proclaimed that 'freedom is the only cause worth serving'. It remains a starting point for libertarian Marxists keen to challenge the commodification of consciousness by reanimating the world through the imagination. Here anarchism and Marxism were united in the demand that every revolution must 'assure an anarchist ideal of individual freedom for cultural creation'.[25]

Feminism also remained a theme ambiguously wedded to Marxism throughout this period. Following *The Communist Manifesto*'s suggestions, Engels' *Origin of the Family, Private Property, and the State* hinted that the traditional sexual division of labour would eventually disappear, along with the bourgeois family. Though women as a source of cheap labour were exploited by capitalism, their struggle – like those of race, nation and ethnicity – had been subordinated by Marxists, from the outset of the movement, to that of the revolution generally. Soviet propaganda, for example, emphasized that integrating women into the workplace meant that communal dining, for example, would relieve them of the burden of cooking at home. Few women rose to positions of power in communist parties anywhere. Nonetheless August Bebel's *Women and Socialism* (1879) early on integrated feminist demands into the socialist agenda, and became one of the most influential tracts to reach SPD readers in Germany before 1914.[26] Other feminist Marxists in this period included two other Germans, the journalist Lily Braun and the teacher Clara Zetkin, the latter being a particularly vehement opponent of 'bourgeois' feminism.[27]

The Frankfurt School

The shift in Marxism towards analysing bourgeois ideology and cultural hegemony is nowhere more evident than amongst the writers of the Frankfurt School. A sense of the failure of Marxism's revolutionary vision, already evident by 1933, helps account for the pessimistic outlook of many of its theorists.[28] The weaknesses in Marx's economics, too, invited a return to a less empirical, more philosophical stance, which could not be 'disproven' as such. Some indeed argued that after the proletariat failed Marxism, it was necessary to abandon both, move beyond real-world politics and revolutionism and revert to theoretical criticism in order to maintain vitality in the tradition and to confront the ideological and psychological bastions of capitalism more fully.

Founded as the Institut für Sozialforschung (Institute for Social Research) in 1923, the Frankfurt School consisted chiefly at first of Walter Benjamin (1892–1940), Max Horkheimer (1895–1973), who became its director in 1930, and Theodor Adorno (1903–69); then, in a later generation, of Herbert Marcuse (1898–1979) and Jürgen Habermas (1929–). All were influenced by Marx to varying degrees, but also by other thinkers, notably Freud and Weber. After 1930 most were hostile to Stalinism as well as to reformist Social Democracy. The school was responsible for making Marxism respectable, particularly in Western universities, under the rubric of critical theory – or what Adorno termed 'negative dialectics' – whose starting point for Horkheimer was Marx's critique of political economy.[29] Exiled in America from 1933 to 1950, the school's later impact on the American New Left through Marcuse in particular was notable.

Just how 'Marxist' these writers were has been much debated. Adorno has been described as attempting to 'prove immanently that dialectical materialism was the only valid structure of cognitive experience'.[30] Horkheimer paralleled Lukács in viewing all knowledge as embedded in the society around it, but did not accept that proletarian class consciousness represented the realized unity of theory and practice. Benjamin, perhaps thinking of the 'ensemble of social relations', wrote that 'Not man or men but the struggling oppressed class is the depository of historical knowledge.'[31] But Adorno's *Negative Dialectics* (1966) also resoundingly rejected the idea that history had a rational telos as such. Benjamin evidently became disillusioned as early as a visit to Russia in 1927, when he concluded that 'to be a Communist in a state where the proletariat rules means completely giving up your private independence'.[32]

A critique without an alternative can seem a sterile position. In their constant focus on 'criticism' most of these writers nonetheless clearly echo Marx's critique of capitalism, if not the means for overthrowing it or the end which might result. Freud's writings on the unconscious helped to shed light on the techniques of capitalist persuasion and manipulation in particular, as well as underpinning various studies of authoritarianism (especially Adorno et al., *The Authoritarian Personality*, 1950) by revealing how the patriarchal family helped reinforce ideological stereotypes. Probing into the role played by irrationality in capitalism, especially in the manipulation of consumer behaviour, also proved a fertile means of extending Marx's theory of commodity fetishism.

The leading Frankfurt School thinkers also contextualized Marx. Horkheimer's *Dialectic of Enlightenment* (1944) conceived Marx's aims as extending the 'Enlightenment project' (as it is now often called) – though perhaps more in the negative sense of 'enlightenment as mass deception' by the 'culture industry', than in a positive one.[33] Nonetheless, as a paradigm of progress, albeit one thwarted by the tragedy of Nazi anti-Semitism in particular, the Enlightenment's aims of 'liberating mankind from fear and establishing their sovereignty', dispelling myth and conquering illusion clearly anticipated Marx's intentions.[34] Horkheimer's discussion of a purely 'instrumental reason', which underpinned ideas of the domination of nature, anticipated the proto-ecological consciousness of the 1960s.

Central to the Frankfurt School's perspective was the allegation that capitalism produced what Horkheimer called a 'culture industry' of 'mass deception'.[35] Marx's theories of ideology and of commodity fetishism were obviously useful in unmasking processes of domination, for instance through luxury branding or the seamless intertwining of amusement and advertising. To Horkheimer critical theory also took up the essence of Marx's historical method in remaining permanently antagonistic to positivism, and especially rooting philosophy in the natural sciences, by contrast to a dialectical theory based on the totality of reality, even if the standpoint and class consciousness of the proletariat were no longer the key frame of reference.

Yet there were also real differences between Horkheimer's starting position and Marx's. To the former in particular, 'To make labour into a transcendent category of human activity is an ascetic ideology... Because socialists hold to this general concept, they make themselves into carriers of capitalist propaganda.' Adorno, too, complained that

Marx 'wanted to turn the whole world into a giant workhouse'.[36] (It is worth recalling that in 1844 Marx caricatured the first phase of 'crude and thoughtless communism' as one in which 'The category of the *worker* is not done away with, but extended to all men'; 3:294.) This approach implies that Marxism can never criticize capitalism successfully because it too mirrors and even parodies to excess a work ethic.[37] A truly critical viewpoint by contrast must commence by positing a human end not defined by labour.

We have seen that Marx by 1867 had already partly reached this position: human wealth lay in free time, not in fulfilment within labour, though political control over the conditions of work remained central. Briefly restating *The Communist Manifesto*'s aims in 1956, Horkheimer and Adorno again denied that work should be 'regarded as an absolute'. Horkheimer even rejected the idea 'that human beings naturally enjoy working, whether their work has a purpose or not', and concluded pessimistically that 'we can expect nothing more from mankind than a more or less worn-out version of the American system'. Adorno too noted that while 'Marx imagined liberation from work' entirely, many seemed satisfied merely with 'the possibility of choosing one's work'.[38] The false consciousness of ideological domination in capitalism, and within this the centrality of philosophies of consumerist hedonism and 'freedom of choice', was palpably evident, even if no 'true consciousness' could now be juxtaposed with this immanent reality. And so too Marx's insistence that the realm of free time would be defined by self-development was now colonized by the 'unfreedom', as Adorno expressed it, which followed conscription into the leisure patterns or hobbies approved by the majority.[39] Here we get a powerful sense of the degree to which degraded amusements squander and corrode our creative capacities.

The coincidence of rediscovering the young Marx's theory of alienation and the emergence in the 1960s of a counterculture sceptical about 'bourgeois materialism' and keen on 'personal liberation' 'from the affluent society' made Herbert Marcuse the most influential of all post-war Western Marxists.[40] The problem for him was not servitude in work (though it might be *to* work), or to the boss. It was imprisonment within the restrictions of bourgeois conventionalism, defined both by an attachment to things – which was where Marx and some Asian philosophies like Buddhism seemed to converge – and sexual repression. Marcuse united Marx and Freud in a potent critique of the 'false needs' of capitalism, which was contrasted to a supposedly non-manipulative and self-consciously utopian ideal of autonomy and independence. A theory of sexual liberation rooted in Freudian ideas of repression was central in this case.[41]

But the broader problem was the emergence of consumer society as such. As early as a 1938 essay 'On Hedonism', Marcuse recognized that the key problem lay not in pursuing pleasure but in believing that it could be realized only through competitive individualism.[42] 'Consumer society', he argued, now served 'to sustain capitalist productive relations, to ensure popular support, and to discredit the rationale of socialism.' To offer an alternative to this enticing worldview, socialism not only had to abolish poverty but equally had to 'change the quality of existence – change the needs and satisfactions themselves'.[43]

Marcuse found Marx's theory of alienation a potent weapon, exploring some of its sources in *Reason and Revolution* (1941). His *Eros and Civilization* (1955) described capitalism as inhibiting mankind's desires for happiness, particularly by sexual repression. Here the idea of a life not centred in work but in free time came to the fore. The problem was no longer the proletariat, which was ignored here, but rather human liberation as such. The demand for sexual liberation generated by recognizing the pleasure principle was easily integrated into the hedonistic ethos of capitalist culture, becoming a countercultural utopian radical variant on capitalism rather than an alternative to it.

These reflections also demanded a critique of existing communism. Marcuse's *Soviet Marxism* (1958) commenced with 'the failure of the proletariat to act as the revolutionary class', the *embourgeoisement* of Western workers and the shift to less developed regions for revolutionary potential, the 'immaturity' of which dictated the need for concentrating power in the Party. Lenin, however, was described as establishing 'the priority of industrialization over socialist liberation', as ensconced in the Soviet goal *'to outstrip the economic level of the chief capitalist countries'*. This resulted in Soviet and Western systems converging, with both exhibiting not only centralization and rationalization which superseded individual enterprise and autonomy, but also the 'joint rule of economic and political bureaucracies' and the prevalence of mass media. Official Marxism, however, had become something worse than ideology: it was, rather, 'consciousness of falsehood, a falsehood which is "corrected" in the context of the "higher truth" represented by objective *historical* interest'; and the rendering of the dialectic from 'a mode of critical thought' into official ideology had merely destroyed it. Meanwhile the Soviet state also encouraged 'technological terror' by punishing inefficiency and poor performance.[44]

Repression, however, also characterized capitalism. Compared to his *Eros and Civilization*, Marcuse's *One-Dimensional Man* (1964) described modernity much more pessimistically. Advanced liberal capitalist regimes are portrayed as essentially totalitarian in their 'manipulation of needs by vested interests', and especially by their distortion through sales techniques and the language of advertising, which eventually engulf politics too. This implied only a faint hope of escaping the omnipresent dominant ideology, particularly in the face of the decline of any revolutionary agency, the proletariat being mesmerized by the system like every other group. The inevitability of both hierarchy and the triumph of scientific and mechanical rationality seemingly dictated the suppression of the individual under all regimes, as technology fundamentally shaped every aspect of human life. Any prospective 'liberation of inherent possibilities', in either capitalism or 'actually existing socialism', seemed increasingly remote. Yet Marcuse agreed with Marx that a 'new civilization' could emerge, with complete 'automation in the realm of necessity', when the 'dimension of free time' became the domain in which 'man's private *and* societal existence would constitute itself'.[45]

Marcuse thus embraced Marx's theory of alienation and explored Marx's early writings more thoroughly than Horkheimer or Adorno. But he remained sceptical as to whether Marx's ends could be realized, writing in 1968 that 'the Marxian image of the realm of freedom beyond the realm of necessity must appear "romantic". For it stipulates an individual subject of labour, an autonomy of creative activity and leisure, and a dimension of unspoiled nature that have long since been liquidated in the progress of domination and industrialization.'[46] The events of 1968, however, particularly the Prague Spring and the student revolt in Paris, inspired the hope that capitalism might yet erupt from within. In *An Essay on Liberation* (1969) Marcuse took 'liberation' to be the cause of Third World revolutionaries and of Western student and minority militants alike. Seeing the upheavals as 'a turning point', he hoped 'The temporary suppression of the rebellion will not reverse the trend.' There had arisen 'the spectre of a revolution which subordinates the development of productive forces and higher standards of living to the requirements of creating solidarity for the human species, for abolishing poverty and misery…for the attainment of peace'. 'Utopia' was no longer 'unreal', but represented 'a more rational and equitable use of resources, minimization of destructive conflicts, and enlargement of the realm of freedom'. Now the possibility existed of creating Marx's 'all-round individual', albeit one based on pleasure rather than creative work, and not brought about by the proletariat.[47]

This scenario of course did not pan out. By the late 1970s enthusiasm for Marcuse waned, as the counterculture became increasingly commodified, integrated into mainstream culture and shorn of most of its radicalism, and as affluent working classes in developed countries everywhere showed ever less inclination to revolution. Marxist-inspired urban guerrilla groups emerged in some European countries (the Red Brigades in Italy, the Baader-Meinhof group in West Germany). Some Third World independence movements occasionally spilled over into Europe. From the 1970s onwards the emphasis on ideological domination through systems of communication rather than through the labour process was also central to the work of Jürgen Habermas. His focus has been on the emergence of a bourgeois public sphere and problems arising from its attempts to produce a more rational, humane and democratic ethos, especially those occurring in epistemology and method.[48] A central concern has been the degeneration of reason from possessing an emancipatory potential to becoming a merely instrumental servant of technology. Habermas has distanced himself from Marx in various ways, not least by contending that religion might play a positive role in promoting equality and rights. His central aim has been to create a public sphere free of domination, where science and technology in particular can be subject to rational debate – an eminently Marxian aim, if one equally hampered by the limits of the 'Enlightenment project' as such.

The various amendments and additions to Marxism discussed so far implied that it might be liberalized and reformed, and made humane and relevant, especially to a new generation. In Western Europe by the 1970s various 'Eurocommunists' attempted to rescue Leninism from the clutches of Stalinism, and also perhaps Marxism from Leninism. France and Italy were the bastions of communist support. In Italy, where the largest Western European communist party existed, with 34.4 per cent of the vote in 1976, Palmiro Togliatti proclaimed the possibility of a multiparty socialist system. The French Communist Party had 5 million supporters in 1945, and over 20 per cent of the vote in 1968, but remained tainted by Stalinism; it renounced the goal of attaining the dictatorship of the proletariat in 1976.

In post-war French philosophy Marxism broke free from Stalinism by engaging with existentialism. This was chiefly due to Jean-Paul Sartre (1905–80), though his main works, especially the *Critique of Dialectical Reason* (1960), are marred by what Perry Anderson calls 'a hermetic and unrelenting maze of neologisms'.[49] Sartre was torn between believing that pursuing freedom was an overwhelmingly individual and mostly futile process, and sympathy for the proletariat and for Marxism's desire to liberate it, which required demolishing Marxism's determinist variants. But while faith in history was not possible, the universal truth contained in the proletariat's embodiment of humanity's essential alienation could still be maintained. Sartre's starting point was the conflict between need and desire – the necessary and the possible – and the role of scarcity in their relations. If these problems could be overcome, a true philosophy of liberty was possible – but this remained a big 'if'. Sartre broke with the French Communist Party over Hungary in 1956, but continued to view Marxism as the only valid philosophy, insisting that if truth existed 'it must be a truth that has *become*, and it must make itself a *totalization*'. He was also one of the few Marxists to explore group psychology as a means of understanding how sociability functioned, even positing that freedom was only possible within groups.[50]

Another French existentialist, Albert Camus, linked Marx with that extension of the powers of the state which seemingly followed modern revolutions and stymied rather than furthered the 'metaphysical revolt' of slave against master. In philosophy, Marxism was also linked with phenomenology by Maurice Merleau-Ponty and his disciple Claude Lefort, who was later critical of totalitarianism. Louis Althusser and Maurice Godelier, amongst others, wedded Marx to structuralism. In urban sociology Henri Lefebvre made a substantial contribution.[51] Several of these writers returned to Hegel as a means of scrutinizing Marx's philosophical first principles.

Many of these efforts now seem sterile and dated, and often stylistically driven, to the point of impenetrability. Efforts were made to reach out to the workers in other ways though. Pseudo-proletarian affectations (leather jackets, jeans, working-class accents) by middle-class intellectuals became all the rage again, as in the 1930s. This did little to diminish the distance between philosophical trends, Party organization and the masses, or between the universities and the working class. Language and appearance were poles apart. As it soared into the ethereal realms of neo-Hegelian, existentialist and structuralist speculation, Marxism grew increasingly alienated from the lives of the many. Challenges to Marx's dominance came via Nietzsche and Freud in particular; and new theories of power, notably as voiced by Michel Foucault, came to displace Marx's and, even more, Lenin's.

For a time in the 1960s, however, it seemed as if Marxist pluralism might break out everywhere, at least in Europe. *Les événements* – the student uprising in Paris in 1968 – in particular hinted at profound cultural and political crisis from which Marxism could easily profit. Young Westerners were tired of war (hot or cold), anxious about nuclear holocaust, guilty about imperialism and embarrassed by materialism. Neither the USA nor the USSR appealed to them as ideal models of society. Anti-colonial revolutions, which now reinvented Marxism once again, helped radicalize them. The rediscovery of the young Marx, and the evident relevance of the theory of alienation, greatly increased interest in Marxism. Few, however, turned to the staid tomes of Lenin or Stalin. Mao fared better, though accurate information about China was scarce, and the mass murder of intellectuals and the almost complete destruction of the country's cultural heritage were not reported widely in the West, where students and intellectuals celebrated what was seen as an anti-bureaucratic movement of mass democracy from below.[52]

In the USA and Britain in particular, where organized communism was weak, the New Left emerged in the late 1950s in the wake of the Hungarian uprising but also in response to independence movements erupting throughout the less developed world, as well as, in the US, to domestic racism. The New Left generally contended that a non-repressive democratic socialism without an exploitative bureaucracy was possible. It was not always communist, sometimes seeking to overturn the social system in the name of 'self-expression, self-realization, autonomy or community'. It also aimed to extend anti-racist movements and women's and gay liberation into a *totalistic redefinition of the content of liberation*.[53] To those seeking alternatives to capitalism the young Marx in particular became an appealing figure. Under the slogan 'the personal is political', Marxism again combined with feminism at a number of levels, challenging the patriarchal bias of the classics. Marxism was associated with sexual liberation, promiscuity, abolishing the bourgeois nuclear family and dropout hedonism. Revolutionary chic became fashionable as the young manifested their symbolic cultural solidarity with the dispossessed by wearing Che T-shirts and adorning their walls with Mao posters.

Twentieth-century Marxism also spawned a rich tradition of history writing, particularly in pioneering a 'history from below' of the working classes and popular culture. In Britain empirical historical studies were pursued by Christopher Hill, E. P. Thompson and Eric Hobsbawm in particular. In France prominent Marxist historians included Albert Soboul, Daniel Guérin and Georges Lefebvre. In India D. D. Kosambi and Romila Thapar amongst many others made key contributions. In sociology and economics, too, Marxism had a substantial impact in many countries, including Japan. Poverty, class and revolution have been recurring themes amongst Marxist authors. In literary criticism Raymond Williams was an important influence. The *New Left Review* remains to the present day a leading champion of Marxist criticism in many areas.

In Eastern Europe, though revisionism as such was denounced already in the trials of the 1956 Hungarian leaders, the critical trends of the 1956 generation were continued, despite constant repression, by thinkers like Adam Michnik in Poland and the Czech Václav Havel, who became his country's president after the Velvet Revolution of 1989. Leszek Kolakowski emerged as the leading philosopher of this epoch. The Prague Spring (1968) was regarded by the USSR as downright treason, and provoked brutal repression. Dissidents nonetheless formed pro-democracy, rights-oriented groups like KOR in Poland (Committee for the Defence of Workers, 1977) and Charter 77 in Czechoslovakia (1976–92).[54] But reformist Marxism had not one but two great enemies. For while the US usually encouraged anti-Soviet dissent in Eastern Europe, elsewhere, where more liberal communist regimes might have emerged (as in Salvador Allende's Chile, 1970–73), they were quickly crushed by American-aided intervention.

By the 1980s, however, communism in Eastern Europe seemed increasingly doomed. In Poland the Solidarity trade union, founded in 1980 and led by Lech Wałęsa, garnered massive popular support. 'For the Soviet system', Michnik has explained, it was 'the same thing the Reformation was for the Catholic Church – a challenge to all the dogmas of the institution'.[55] Eventually it broke the stranglehold of Party power, and precipitated the collapse of the Soviet empire when it won free parliamentary elections in 1989. Here the principle of independent trade unions was crucial. The relative decline in living standards compared to the West was certainly as important, however. Even Goulash Communism, as the Hungarian variant was called, and equivalent strategies elsewhere that provided consumer goods for the masses, fell far short of demand. Efficiency was poor: 'they pretend to pay us, we pretend to work' was a slogan of the period.

In the late 1980s President Mikhail Gorbachev made the last great effort to salvage the Soviet system in the USSR. His programme of *perestroika* (restructuring) in some respects attempted to return to the NEP agenda. The policy of *glasnost* (openness) invoked the freer atmosphere of political discussion of the mid-1920s. Yet the system could not be preserved. The USSR could not become an 'open society' because none of the prerequisites for this existed. Economically the arms race with the USA made the satisfaction of consumer demand difficult, and eventually bankrupted the country. In November 1989 the Berlin Wall collapsed after Hungary permitted large numbers of East Germans to emigrate across its border with Austria. The USSR's demise in 1991 effectively marked the end of Marxism's appeal as an ideal of freedom to millions. Communism, it now appeared, could not be given a human face. The Party was banned by the Russian president, Boris Yeltsin, in November. (It was later revived.) Marx's dream, which became the nightmare created by Lenin, came to an end. Yet under Putin, Stalin remains a surprisingly popular figure in Russia, the ideal of the strong man and military genius dwarfing the legacy of the Gulag.

By the early twenty-first century most of the main left-oriented parties in Europe – Labour in Britain, the SPD in Germany, the Socialists in France – had abandoned any pretence of wanting to alter capitalism fundamentally. As humane variants on the harsher forms of liberalism they retained some appeal, at least more than 'Eurocommunism', which portrayed itself as a reformist alternative to Stalinism. Traditional political divisions were, however, being redrawn. In the early 1970s Marxism combined with ecological movements in several countries, most notably West Germany, whose Green Party enjoyed considerable electoral success. The destructiveness of rapid industrialization in the USSR and China in particular now became increasingly evident. Both capitalism and Marxism, it appeared, were based on a model of expanding consumption and unimpeded commerce and industrialization. Meanwhile globalization and new technology were altering traditional economic arrangements. By the late 1980s writers heralded the 'end of the working class', and with it the potential irrelevance of classical Marxist analysis.[56] Out of the ashes of the collapse of 'real existing socialism' rose, amongst other things, the phoenix of political ecology. A movement prominently associated with André Gorz, it is characterized by the condemnation of crisis-ridden capitalism obsessed with 'growth', of ideology promoting inequality and of luxury-centred ideals of consumption.[57] Some, regarding full automation as a recipe for 'complete unemployment', portray this process as opening up a potential 'paradise' defined by 'liberation from work'.[58] Here the relevance of Marx's later discussions of free time have often been noted.

CHAPTER 6

Other Marxisms

We saw earlier that Marx's investigations into non-Western, less developed or 'primitive' societies never advanced far. Until the late 1870s too Marx's disdain for peasants made him disinclined to consider their possible centrality in future revolutionary movements. By the early twentieth century, however, these questions became increasingly crucial to his followers. After the Second World War, much of the globe was still under the thumb of one or other colonial masters. However, the war had bankrupted most of the great European empires – British, French, Dutch – and had facilitated a desire for independence in colonies throughout the world. As the colossal injustice of imperialism became clearer, its critique became central to the emergence of Third World Marxism in the early 1920s in the writings of the Indian M. N. Roy and others. Key problems here included collusion between the native bourgeoisie and the colonizers, and between Western workers and imperialism, as well as the absence of a native proletariat.

While Marxism faltered in Europe in the 1950s and 1960s, it leapt forward in Asia and Africa, commencing with China. Many of these movements were inspired by Marxism–Leninism in the first instance. Students, trade unionists, intellectuals and peasant leaders typically led the way. Most sought to align Marxism with nationalism in order to mobilize large numbers against colonial occupiers. The USSR's triumph against Hitler, then its Cold War resistance to American neo-imperialism and its status as a nuclear power and in the space race, lent great prestige to its ideology. Its spirit of sacrifice, justice and racial tolerance seemingly epitomized everything that a greedy consumerist capitalism was not and could not be. The focus of Marxists on Third World developments after 1945 invariably shifted the debate about Marx's legacy towards issues of race and of non-proletarian, usually peasant-based, revolts. The complicity of white European and North American working classes in imperialist exploitation, which Marx had noted vis-à-vis the English working class and Ireland, now defined a new stage in Marxism.

This shift effectively made much of Marx redundant, or mere window dressing. The world had moved on. Revolution would not occur in developed capitalist countries. Peasants led by intellectuals would do the job elsewhere. Hundreds of millions now understood Marx's legacy as liberation from colonialism. By the 1960s Marxist economists in more advanced nations began exploring theories of neo-imperialism and underdevelopment. The anti-colonial revolts of the 1950s onwards took place in overwhelmingly agricultural countries with a small urban bourgeoisie and large-scale exploitation of raw materials by local landowners and foreign investors and/or occupiers. Many of these struggles were nationalist in orientation, though colonial boundaries were often artificial markers of imperial sovereignty which were not coterminous with tribal or ethnic divisions. Some ninety new nations were created after 1945. Even after achieving independence, however, many countries found themselves in thrall both to lending bodies – cheap 'development' loans being easily accessible and often subject to corrupt misappropriation – and to an international market which provided cheaper manufactured goods than could be produced locally and which prized raw materials in exchange. This produced the phenomenon known as 'underdevelopment', where relative national economic independence is hampered by indebtedness and the international division of labour, as well as by endemic corruption.

In this period Paul Baran's *The Political Economy of Growth* (1957) helped popularize the concept of underdevelopment, along with works by Paul Sweezy, Samir Amin, Andre Gunder Frank, Immanuel Wallerstein and others, who assessed the degree to which formerly colonized or imperial territories could remain imprisoned within dependency relationships, especially through indebtedness and enforced monoculture.[1] What we now call globalization was linked with an increasing tendency towards the deliberate underdevelopment of peripheries by the capitalist core. This was cheaper than formal imperialism, for the political costs of securing the extraction of raw materials could be transferred to newly independent states. As multinational corporations grew vastly larger and richer the possibility of these states challenging their supremacy diminished. Indeed corporations began to grow so mighty, mimicking the great trading companies of earlier periods, that they began to usurp the sovereign functions of nations, to exempt themselves from profit controls and to disguise their revenue and reduce taxation on it. Through lobbying, corruption and simple economic clout they became able to dictate state policy very widely.

China and Mao Zedong

The Chinese Revolution was the greatest Marxist-inspired event of the post-war period. By 1949 China had suffered more than a century of foreign invasions, humiliation, civil war and famine. During the Opium Wars (1839–42, 1856–60) Britain had forced on an unwilling China a deadly but highly profitable crop, producing millions of addicts but making British India financially viable. In China foreign concessions were established which enhanced resource exploitation. Native rebellions were suppressed with great brutality. The Chinese Communist Party was founded in 1921, but from the mid-1920s faced incessant competition from the Nationalists, led first by Sun Yat-sen and then Chiang Kai-shek. The Third International forced the Chinese communists to ally with Chiang in 1927, resulting in their near annihilation. Then, commencing in 1931, came Japanese invasion and a lengthy and brutal occupation. China remained divided amongst corrupt, fractious warlords until 1949.

The most talented of China's Marxists was Mao Zedong (1893–1976), a sometime librarian and schoolteacher. Converted to Marxism chiefly by The Communist Manifesto in 1920, he was the founding member of the Chinese Communist Party, rising to power between 1928 and 1935.[2]

The American journalist Edgar Snow famously described the forty-three-year-old Mao:

> a gaunt, rather Lincolnesque figure, above average height for a Chinese, somewhat stooped, with a head of thick black hair grown very long, and with large, searching eyes, a high-bridged nose and prominent cheekbones…Mao seemed to me a very interesting and complex man. He had the simplicity and naturalness of the Chinese peasant, with a lively sense of humor and love of rustic laughter…yet was an accomplished scholar of Classical Chinese, an omnivorous reader, a deep student of philosophy and history, a good speaker, a man with an unusual memory and extraordinary powers of concentration, an able writer, careless in his personal habits and appearance but astonishingly meticulous about details of duty, a man of tireless energy, and a military and political strategist of considerable genius.[3]

When Snow met him in 1936 Mao lived in a two-room hut whose chief luxury was a mosquito net. He owned only his blankets and a few personal belongings, including a pair of uniforms adorned with the two red bars of an ordinary soldier. This was not a party of privilege alienated from the masses.

Mao triumphed against enormous odds indeed, chiefly by winning over the peasants during decades of arduous struggle. By a 6,000-mile strategic retreat, later called the Long March (1934–5), he evaded Chiang Kai-shek's armies, and slowly acquired power and territory in the struggle against the Japanese. Through 'Robin Hood' policies, such as land redistribution and abolishing or reducing taxation and ending usury, and by strict military discipline, Mao gained the peasants' confidence in communist-occupied areas. His victory in 1949 forced the Nationalists to flee to Taiwan. It also instantly shifted the balance of power in the post-war world. Until the Sino-Soviet split (1960) the world's most populous nation was linked with the USSR in enmity to capitalism and imperialism. Over half the world's population was now ruled by regimes inspired by Marx. China, however, was an overwhelmingly agricultural nation with a tiny proletariat, concentrated mainly in Shanghai. Most exploitation involved rich landlords and several hundred million poor peasants. Stalin's model before him, Mao had necessarily to adapt Marxism–Leninism to these circumstances. The issues of class struggle, the nature and pace of industrialization and the description of communism had to be addressed. The Party had to assume the role which a non-existent proletariat could not. Chiefly this meant conquering the countryside. As early as 1926 Mao proclaimed the peasantry to be more revolutionary than the urban proletariat. Thereafter his Marxism increasingly diverged from that of the Soviet Union. By 1969 he was condemning 'Soviet social imperialism' and calling the USSR a 'bourgeois dictatorship'.[4] But his antagonism towards the 'paper tiger' USA always remained constant.

Land reform was Mao's first priority. In the 1930s some 2.5 per cent of the population owned about 40 per cent of the land. While Mao allied with some rich peasants during the struggle for victory, confiscation of landlords' properties commenced in earnest as early as October 1947. By 1951 perhaps 40 per cent of the land was held by 60 per cent of the population, with the Party aiming 'to topple the entire landlord class'.[5] Initially poor peasants were granted small plots of land to farm as private property, and by the early 1950s rich peasants owned only 2 per cent of the land. Co-operatives were created which owned machinery while land was still held privately. Emulating Stalin, Mao then sought to collectivize agriculture. Ninety-one per cent of peasant households were enrolled in co-operatives by 1956, and by 1958 all belonged to collective farms, called communes. By 1971, 95 per cent of cultivated land was held by 70,000 communes; each averaged some 15,000 people, subdivided into production brigades of about 220 households, in turn subdivided into teams of about 30 households. Mao retained a greater sympathy for the peasantry than Stalin had done, and collectivization was not as harsh in China as in the USSR. In many communes food was free to members and private ownership of housing was permitted. Small-scale industry provided for most other needs. But movement from the commune was difficult. Most crops were sold to the state at mandatory but low prices, which sometimes produced rural unrest. As a cadre class formed some corruption appeared. At the same time, while rigid egalitarianism was not official policy, it appeared at some points; for example army officers were criticized for riding horses.[6]

Urban life also altered quickly. Here rationing even for basic food-stuffs was common right through the 1970s, and other consumer goods remained in short supply. Housing was always scarce, with shared and communal accommodation the norm. By the mid-1950s household registration restricted travel, especially from the country to the cities. City residents were subject to constant supervision as surveillance networks expanded rapidly. The state began assigning work. Soon the work unit became the source of housing, food rations, health care and pensions. It also conducted political campaigns, and approved applications for marriage and divorce, travel permits and much else. Employment was permanent – the 'iron rice bowl' – but changing jobs was difficult. Most industries were expropriated by 1956, but former owners could remain as managers, often assisted by Soviet technicians. Wage differentials to restore financial incentives were reintroduced, though Mao warned against making them too wide. Urban vice, notably prostitution, the drug trade, and organized crime, was quickly suppressed. Universities were subject to thought reform campaigns from 1951, a particular target being 'worship of the so-called "American way of life"'.

Repression in the early years was severe, with at least 710,000 executions by the early 1950s, many victims later found to be innocent, and about 2 million imprisoned. (Mao suggested a 'correct' execution rate of 0.01 per cent of the population, or 500,000.)[7] The Hundred Flowers campaign, instigated by Mao early in 1957, briefly encouraged open debate about social goals. An outpouring of complaints and agitation for change and better wages resulted. Strikes, boycotts, petitions and demonstrations proliferated. Collective-farm membership plummeted. A few weeks later Mao condemned the 'poisonous weeds' which grew amongst the flowers: 'criticism' of the Party was only meant to be positive. Student leaders and strike organizers were executed.

As Party chairman, Mao then decided to launch a mass industrialization programme, the Great Leap Forward (1958–61). Compared to the Soviet model of centralized planning and concentrated heavy industry – favoured by Liu Shaoqi, the head of state – this involved creating nationwide local steel-making capacity, turning millions of tons of metal into useable steel in backyard smelters, and decentralizing economic planning. One aim was making large numbers of new agricultural implements. But 'the most important thing' was 'self-reliance', meaning chiefly surviving without Soviet aid and expertise.[8] In 1958 Mao vowed that China might surpass Britain in industrial output within fifteen years, later shortening this to only three. The programme was a disaster. Some 600,000 small blast furnaces were created. But their output was meagre and of poor quality. Food cultivation suffered as some 60 million people were diverted into smelting and refining. Many useful items were melted down which were more costly to replace. Transportation of so much coal and iron had not been taken into account. Mao belatedly conceded that he was a 'complete outsider when it comes to economic construction', and confessed in 1959 that he 'understood nothing about industrial planning'.[9] Overestimating the harvest also led to excessive procurement of grain, some of which was exported or given away as foreign aid. The resulting famine claimed the lives of between 20 and 46 millions.[10] Per capita income dropped by over a third between 1959 and 1962. Afterwards Mao thought it might take a hundred years to build socialism in China.

By the mid-1960s, however, price stability returned, and basic goods like bicycles, radios, watches and clothing were available, plus communal welfare provisions for most. Much of China's population was now much better off. The position of women improved greatly. Birth control was universally available. Arranged marriages, dowries and concubinage were ended. Medical care was primitive but, for the majority, far better than anything beforehand. Many diseases disappeared, and 'barefoot doctors' penetrated far into the countryside. Opium addiction was virtually eliminated. Enthrallment to money-lenders, tax-collectors and rich landlords ended, especially for the two-thirds of the peasant population who owned virtually no land. Average life expectancy rose from forty years in 1953 to sixty-four in 1976. 'Barracks communism' this may have been, but for many millions it was vastly superior to their ancestors' lives. And psychologically, too, China recovered its sense of pride and national identity, and threw off the inferiority complex foisted upon it by foreign invaders. The explosion of the first Chinese nuclear bomb (in 1964) provided a significant status symbol.

At the core of Mao's China was the Communist Party, which had some 18.7 million members by 1965 (out of some 706 million people), and was gradated into twenty-six ranks. As in the USSR this hierarchy was marked by privileges rather than salary: in housing, transport, access to special shops, and the right of travel. There were no other centres of power. Every important decision required Party approval. Politically, reversion to a mandarinate, or rule by intellectuals, was an ever-present danger. Suspicion of the educated elite was marked after 1957. By the late 1950s Mao planned in principle for all higher cadres to be 'sent down' periodically 'as a kind of routine political therapy' to 'proletarianize Party thinking' (in Edgar Snow's words).[11] Mao insisted that while class struggle would continue throughout the transition period, contradictions between the bourgeoisie and other classes were essentially 'non-antagonistic', that is, not threatening to the new order. By 1957, however, he pointed towards contradictions between the new state and the people. Corruption of Party cadres, especially in the countryside, had become extremely common. Functionaries chosen and promoted solely on the basis of their class background and ideological enthusiasm proved no more resistant to temptation than any other group.

Mao was now convinced that China was in danger of following a Soviet 'revisionist' path of creating a new bureaucracy divorced from the people and exacerbating the gap between city and countryside. A personal struggle between Mao as Party leader and Liu Shaoqi was also ongoing. (Liu was removed in 1968.) Mao's response, the Chinese Cultural Revolution (1966–9), involved emphasizing greater egalitarianism. It commenced with a massive purge of Party members. Most were sent to the countryside for manual labour and re-education, with a view to making their mere 'book philosophy' real, or 'red', by contact with peasants and nature. The aim of reducing, simplifying and purifying the bureaucratic structure and overcoming the growing gulf between intellectual and manual labour had been central to Marx, as we have seen. But this was perhaps the moment when a future arrived that

Marx could not have imagined living in himself. We cannot really see him swilling the pigs any more than we can panning for Californian gold in 1849.

The enthusiasm these measures unleashed soon got out of hand. Anti-intellectualism rapidly reached fever pitch. Clutching the *Little Red Book* epitomizing Mao's teachings (first issued in 1964), young Red Guards zealously attacked teachers, professors and Party leaders as 'capitalist-roaders'. Mao had once confessed to being 'terrified' of 'bourgeois' professors whose 'piles of learning' made communists feel 'good for nothing'.[12] Now he got his revenge. 'Too much study' was 'exceedingly harmful', he said in 1964, even telling medical students that 'More study only makes them stupid'.[13] Mao's target was also the old Imperial examination system and rote memorization of the classics. 'Teachers should do manual work', he wrote in 1958. Less theory, more practice, he urged repeatedly in the 1960s. 'Books by Marx should be read, but not too many of them. A few dozen volumes will do', he urged in 1964; 'Too much reading will lead you to the opposite of what you expect to be, a bookworm, a dogmatist, a revisionist'.[14] So while a little learning was acceptable, a lot was dangerous: better 'red' than well-read. Expertise and bureaucracy were equated, and 'redness' or political zeal and ideological purity promoted by contrast. Mao tried to quell the unrest, but hundreds of thousands were paraded through the streets wearing dunces' hats. Beatings were common. Over a million died. The universities closed for ten years. Nonetheless Mao condemned the 'extreme anarchism' of the Shanghai People's Committee, which called for the abolition of all 'heads', insisting that 'there will still always be "heads".' And so he defended reverence for leaders, including 'the correct side of Stalin', though not 'blind obedience'.[15]

This reverence, indeed, was taken to new extremes. By 1965 'worship of the individual' (in Mao's own phrase) was used to reassert control over the Party, and Mao's cult of personality dwarfed even Stalin's.[16] In 1969 border clashes with Soviet troops and the Sino-Soviet split (which began in 1960) induced a return to something like normality. Ultra-leftists were suppressed and the Party in general rehabilitated. It would be mistaken to view the Cultural Revolution as an experiment in 'democracy' gone awry. In principle Mao had urged the

Party to consult the masses on important questions. In practice the Party was still the ruling body, though the state bureaucracy was (and remains) immensely privileged, at least at the top. By 1970 almost all of those who had been 'sent down' had been reinstated.

Chinese Marxism was dominated until the 1980s by what became known as 'Mao Zedong thought'.[17] In broad terms Mao accepted dialectical materialism as true without qualification. His contribution to Marxism came first in his widely emulated writings on guerrilla warfare. Mao's most famous sayings were that 'revolution is not a dinner party' but 'an act of violence', and that 'political power grows out of the barrel of a gun'. Both implied giving armed force a leading role in the new regime. Mao also insisted that all philosophy was rooted in class struggle, which in Chinese terms meant, as we have seen, that all students, and especially those in the humanities and social sciences, needed to work in the countryside.

Mao's style is direct, pithy, sometimes earthy and as oriented towards the Chinese as the Marxist classics. Philosophically he is best known for two 1937 lectures. 'On Practice' emphasized the centrality of labour to human activity. 'On Contradiction' stressed the universality of tension between opposites and the need to give priorities to different types of contradictions within different processes, and it defined dialectics (following Lenin) as 'the study of the contradiction within the very essence of things'.[18] Here Mao distinguished in particular between 'antagonistic' and 'non-antagonistic' contradictions, the former posing a more serious challenge to any order. In 'On New Democracy' (1940) he argued it was necessary for a bourgeois democratic revolution to precede a socialist one, but that the bourgeoisie might assist this process. In the mid-1950s he still maintained that the proletariat had the central role in the revolutionary struggle, but envisioned the Party leading in the absence of a large urban working class. 'Democracy' within the Party meant that decisions were in principle arrived at through collective discussion, but then had to be obeyed unconditionally. The Politburo of the Central Committee of the Party was the key body, even if its connection to the masses was supposedly dialectical. In all enterprises major decisions had to be taken by the Party.

Mao's relaxed approach to dialectics is often associated more with Chinese philosophy than Marxism. 'The most basic thing is the unity of opposites', he said in 1964, remarking also that 'There is no such thing as the negation of the negation'. 'Going to bed and getting up is also a unity of opposites', he wrote in 1958. So were production and consumption, sowing and reaping, birth and death, war and peace, and the seasons of the year. Every process was finite, and implied its opposite.[19] Mao was flexible about the classics of Marxism, averring that Marx too had made mistakes, in anticipating European revolution and in first opposing the Paris Commune. But equally Mao insisted that the Party have 'iron' rather than 'bean-curd' discipline.[20] No retreat was possible from 'democratic centralism', without which it was 'impossible to consolidate the proletarian dictatorship'. By this Mao also meant encouraging the masses to speak out occasionally, and orienting the Party towards the peasants first and foremost.[21]

Practically, Mao placed a greater emphasis upon changing consciousness, as the prelude to successful revolution, than altering material conditions. Bloodshed was perhaps limited by his principle that 'To exercise dictatorship over the reactionary classes does not mean that we should totally eliminate all reactionary elements, but rather that we should eliminate the classes to which they belong. We should use appropriate methods to remould them and transform them into new men.'[22] He reversed the assumption that industrial development was required to produce a revolutionary proletariat; poverty and the suffering it induced were alone necessary. As with Lenin, the vanguard role was associated with the Party rather than the working class, but the Party was defined by its ideological outlook rather than its objective class position.

It has been claimed that 'Mao Tse-tung thought is a return to pre-Marxist doctrines of socialism and to philosophical Idealism.'[23] As early as 1926 Mao stressed the revolutionary role to be played by the poor peasantry, whom he regarded as most responsive to Communist leadership. In general Mao valued human factors, especially revolutionary will and ideological zeal, over economic determinism. Mistakes and failure he thought probable, but self-criticism and reform could help overcome them. China's great population made many problems soluble through sheer numbers rather than technological innovation. But her weak proletariat meant that class consciousness had to reflect personal outlook rather than relationship to the means of production. This stress on reform and self-criticism implied that even the 'five bad categories' (landlords, rich peasants, counter-revolutionaries, bad elements and rightists) might 'correct' their outlook by resolving their inner contradictions in favour of the Party line. Mao also wanted to make Marxism more specifically Chinese. He rejected the idea that 'natural rights' or 'the theory of evolution' were useful to China, and asserted that 'We can only use Western technology.'[24]

'Democracy' to Mao meant Leninist 'democratic centralism', two concepts Mao juxtaposed rather than fused, as well as 'ideas coming from the masses'. It also implied constant criticism and self-criticism, the 'Marxist dialectical method' being '"splitting one into two", achievements and shortcomings, truth and mistakes'.[25] Mao insisted that, as First Secretary of the Party, he was bound by a majority view within the Standing Committee of the Politburo, 'Otherwise you have one-man tyranny.'[26] But there are few signs of liberalism here: 'freedom of speech for counter-revolutionary purposes' was never permissible, and 'dictatorial and totalitarian' methods were acceptable, even if this principally meant 'persuasion not suppression'. Mao thought that 'ideological and political struggles' would 'never cease', even under communism, though class conflict might be supplanted by 'struggles between advanced and backward techniques'. Nonetheless both the Communist Party and the dictatorship of the proletariat would 'disappear one day'.[27]

Maoism was exported for a time to several other countries, including Portugal, India, Nepal and Colombia, and was briefly fashionable in the late 1960s in some Western student movements. China assisted various guerrilla movements hostile to Soviet proxy groups, notably in Angola. For a time in the mid-1970s tiny Albania under Enver Hoxha rallied to Maoism. China's split from the USSR in 1960 for some implied a criticism of Stalinism by contrast to the mass-based populist outlook associated with Mao.

The China we know today only began to emerge in the 1980s. China's growth rate was very modest throughout the 1970s, and averaged about

2.9 per cent a year from 1950 to 1973. The economy actually stagnated in the mid-1970s. Housing shortages increased and some consumer goods remained scarce. Rural poverty was endemic. The changes introduced after Deng Xiaoping became leader in 1978 made China an economic, political and military world power by the early 2000s. Deng opened up the market to competition and private investment, in effect beginning a bourgeois revolution and enriching a substantial middle class, including many leading Party members. Collectivized agriculture was abandoned. Concentration of wealth has become extreme, with wages for some two-thirds of workers remaining low and stagnant. Retaining the state monopoly on land ownership made both investment in property and speculation in land simpler than under capitalism. Whether such a society should be termed 'Marxist' is a moot point. The monopolistic position of the Communist Party remains the main legacy of the Maoist period. There are few signs of political liberalization generally, and the suppression of dissent remains common.

Cuba: Castro and Guevara

In Latin and South America the impact of Marxism was most lasting in Cuba. Here, in 1959, Fidel Castro (1926–2016) overthrew the Batista regime backed by the US government and by American crime syndicates and corporations.[28] Batista, who seized power in a 1952 coup and cancelled scheduled elections, had depleted some 90 per cent of the country's treasury reserves.[29] At this time, Castro later estimated, some 600,000 people were unemployed in Cuba out of a population of 7.1 million, 37.5 per cent were illiterate and a cumulative trade deficit existed with the USA over the previous ten years of about $1 billion. The telephone and electricity suppliers and other key industries like mining were US monopolies. Sugarcane cultivation accounted for 80 per cent of exports. To please the Americans, black Cubans were banned from clubs and hotels, except to work. Castro held the view that armed resistance by a mostly middle-class minority commencing in the countryside could trigger a revolution. Beginning with only eighty-two men, his force of 3,000 defeated an army of some 37,000, in part because Batista terrorized his middle-class supporters, especially students, and thus fatally undermined support for the regime. Within a short time the tall, fatigue-capped, bearded, cigar-smoking figure became internationally recognizable as the David to America's Goliath.

The son of a well-to-do Spanish farmer, Castro did not commence his revolutionary career as a Marxist. On his own he reached a 'utopian Communist' position. But reading Marx, he later recalled, particularly *The Communist Manifesto*, 'made an enormous impact', and 'taught me what society was…and the history of its evolution'.[30] In his *Life* (2006) Castro claimed that he became 'a convinced Marxist-Leninist' by 1950 or so, while still deriving his ethics from the famed Cuban nationalist and Christian humanist José Martí. He thought Lenin had been 'the first to address the problem of colonies'.[31] Castro promised free elections as late as 1958, and argued for land reform with compensation for the expropriated owners, but no nationalization of industry. In May 1959 he proclaimed that 'Our revolution is neither capitalist nor communist!…Capitalism sacrifices the human being, communism with its totalitarian conceptions sacrifices human rights'.[32] After seizing power he began forming large-scale state farms, however, and no elections ever took place. While denying that he was a communist as late as March 1959, Castro started promoting Marxists in his 26th of July Movement later that year. He then found support in the USSR in the face of US antagonism, and a Soviet–Cuban agreement was signed in early 1960, swiftly followed by large-scale imports of Soviet arms and oil. Total rupture with the US finally came in mid-1960 after US-owned firms were expropriated, followed by a large number of Cuban enterprises.

Castro's stark choice now seems to have been communism or defeat. Pushed by the Marxist-leaning Che Guevara, he pronounced himself a communist in early 1961, and began referring to the Marxist classics. (Privately he condemned Stalin's 'serious errors', including 'his abuse of force, the repression'.[33]) An abortive invasion attempt was mounted by the CIA at the Bay of Pigs in April 1961. The day after, Castro proclaimed the 'Socialist nature of our Revolution'.[34] Then followed the Cuban Missile Crisis in 1962, when nuclear war nearly resulted after the USSR stationed nuclear missiles on Cuban soil. Thereafter Cuba relied on Soviet assistance, paid for chiefly by sugar exports, forcing it into a monoculture which made economic diversification difficult in the face of a US economic boycott. US subversion was constant, and included biological warfare against Cuban agriculture and over 600 attempts to assassinate Castro, including providing him with exploding cigars. Chronic shortages were exacerbated by poor planning and the difficulties of transport from the USSR and Eastern Europe, where 75 per cent of Cuba's exports now went. Economic hardship and political repression drove some 1.5 million Cubans from the island. A few hundred Batista officials were executed soon after the revolution, but many others were integrated into the new regime. Castro resisted a domestic cult of personality to a degree, refusing to allow streets to be named after leaders, or to have his portrait hung in public offices.

With slender resources, Cuba nonetheless made impressive advances in health care and education, and against race and gender discrimination, outstripping many wealthier countries in the region and elsewhere. Average life expectancy reached 79.1 years in 2015 (versus 78.74 in the US), a remarkable achievement. The Party eventually admitted religious believers to its ranks, as Castro himself became more receptive to the revolutionary appeal of liberation theology in Central and South America.[35] Throughout his long reign as prime minister (1959–76), then president (1976–2008), Castro's personality dominated the Party, of which he was also the First Secretary, utterly, and opposition was very limited. He assisted anti-imperialist movements elsewhere, including Bolivia, Venezuela, the Congo, Ethiopia, Angola and Mozambique. He also sent medical aid to many poorer countries: in 2005 there were 30,000 Cuban doctors overseas, more than from any single industrialized country, and only 40,000 in Cuba itself.

In Europe disillusionment with Castro came when he supported the Soviet suppression of the Prague Spring in 1968. But his regime also provided the single most important icon Marxism generated in the late twentieth century. In the 1960s the cult of the striking, bearded, beret-clad Argentinian doctor Ernesto Guevara (1928–67) made him a more recognizable figure than Marx himself.[36] Revolution now had a poster boy, known to all merely as 'Che' (meaning 'friend' in Argentine Spanish). Suddenly Marxism was sexy and cool, and youth and rebellion became synonymous. Before his iconic image became just another fashion symbol and merchandizing tool, Guevara was associated with attempts to forge a new communist morality of self-sacrifice and opposition to imperialism and exploitation. He had, Castro said, 'created a great aura, a great mystique'.[37] Dying young, while attempting to export revolution to Bolivia, helped leave this image untarnished. Cuba rarely prospered in the next decades, however, and nearly collapsed during the 'special period' following the end of Soviet aid in the mid-1990s. Early in the twenty-first century reforms permitted more private businesses, and tourism has helped balance the books.

African Marxism

In the aftermath of the Second World War, resistance movements sprang up throughout Africa to fight against colonialism. Many of these had a Marxist component and some were sponsored directly by the USSR or China. Independence was rapidly achieved everywhere, and in 1960 alone some seventeen new states emerged.

Amongst those advocating decolonization from a Marxist viewpoint, the best known is the Martinique-born psychiatrist Frantz Fanon (1925–61), who became involved in the Algerian independence struggle (1954–62). His advocacy of the liberating effects of violence in *The Wretched of the Earth* (1961) spawned an enduring debate about the nature and effects of this 'cleansing force' in freeing native peoples from their 'inferiority complex' during the revolutionary process, particularly amongst the peasantry of less developed regions.[38]

In sub-Saharan Africa various prominent politicians were inspired by Marxism. In the Gold Coast the independence leader Kwame Nkrumah (1909–72) became Ghana's first president in 1957. Nkrumah first encountered Marx through the Caribbean Trotskyite C. L. R. James.[39] Nkrumah regarded 'neo-colonialism' – the continuing domination of foreign capital in former colonies and elsewhere, especially by the USA – as 'the worst form of imperialism'.[40] Nkrumah advocated Pan-Africanism, which aimed at co-operation between eventually independent former colonies on a federal, socialist basis. Here, transcending tribal divisions, even having them 'broken down completely', was more important than class struggle, though anti-imperialism was the starting point.[41] A welfare state was another aim, as was promoting women in government. Reliance on a monoculture (cocoa) was to be succeeded by industrialization and centralized planning. Gradually Nkrumah wielded ever greater power in Ghana, and in 1964 he made his Convention People's Party the sole political party in the country, condemning multiparty systems in principle as perpetuating 'the inherent struggle between the "haves" and the "have-nots"'.[42] Two years later he was overthrown by a coup which the USA probably assisted. While Nkrumah identified himself as an African nationalist rather than a communist, he emphasized the notions of egalitarianism in African society and of socialism as a higher form of communalism.[43]

The first writer to articulate a consciously African socialism was Léopold Sédar Senghor (1906–2001), who led Senegal to independence in 1960, becoming the country's president. During his time as a student and teacher in France he helped develop the concept of *négritude* – a term coined by the Martinique-born poet Aimé Césaire to denote 'Negro-African cultural values' and expressing a blood-based idea of racial pride and even superiority rooted in emotional warmth. This was intended to serve as a unifying concept for Africans.[44] Nonetheless, even while working for Senegal independence, he supported a federalist ideal in which France, as the former colonial power, would continue to play a role.

Senghor's idea of a specifically African socialism was inspired initially by Marx's correspondence with Vera Zasulich respecting the Russian peasant commune. But his engagement with Marxism was often critical. He felt Marxism–Leninism was guilty of 'cultural imperialism' in insisting on one road to socialism. The dictatorship of the proletariat had produced 'an omnipotent, soulless monster', 'contrary to the teachings of Marx', leading him to conclude that Africans 'no longer accept Marx's vision of the future'. Marx had also failed in other key areas, such as in his assessment of the peasantry – which in developing countries had often become revolutionary – and in predicting capitalism's collapse. Senghor rejected both atheistic materialism and a wholly publicly owned, state-managed economy, preferring some private investment while not allowing free-market economics to dominate. He denounced the USSR for seeking a path which 'increasingly resembles capitalistic growth in the United States, the American way of life', and pleaded for 'a middle course, for a *democratic socialism*…which ties in with the old ethical current of the French socialists'. He praised Marx's theory of alienation, which (like Fanon) he extended towards the colonized. But he thought communism, and especially Stalinism, had paid too little heed to the 'anxiety for human dignity and the need for freedom', as well as to nationalism.[45]

Although Marxism influenced in varying degrees many other popular African leaders, including Nelson Mandela (1918–2013) in South Africa and Julius Nyerere (1922–99) in Tanzania, today its significance in African politics has waned substantially.[46]

Vietnam (Ho Chi Minh), Cambodia (Pol Pot) and North Korea

In Southeast and East Asia communist regimes emerged in the 1950s in Vietnam and Korea and the 1970s in Laos and Cambodia.[47] Vietnam's great leader, Ho Chi Minh ('Ho the Most Enlightened') (1890–1969), was born Nguyen Tat Thanh to a peasant family in French Indochina, in what is now central Vietnam. Aged nine, Ho was already aiding his father carrying messages for the anti-French resistance. He spent some years as a mess boy on board ships, and was even reputed to have been a pastry cook for Escoffier in London. (If so, finally Lenin's supposed dictum about cooks becoming statesmen would be fulfilled.)[48] At the Versailles peace conference (1919) he made an impassioned plea in a petition for Vietnamese self-determination, for which he could have been condemned to death at home, where socialists were sometimes executed without trial. A founding member of the French Communist Party in 1920, Ho retained a strong sense of national identity and resentment of the racism endemic in imperialism. During the 1920s and 1930s, as Nguyen Ai Quoc ('Nguyen the Patriot'), he worked for the Comintern in France, China, Thailand and then in Vietnam, where he returned in 1941 to lead resistance against Japan. After France's defeat at Dien Bien Phu in 1954 he led the northern half of the now-divided

Vietnam, and remained its leader throughout most of the American War (as Vietnamese term it). His image was one of personal austerity, of the kindly 'uncle', a gentle and witty man, yet also an 'intransigent and incorruptible revolutionary, à la Saint-Just', as a French acquaintance, Paul Mus, remembered him.[49]

Ho's Marxism began by embracing Lenin (whom he tried to meet in Moscow in 1923) as 'a great patriot who liberated his compatriots', 'the embodiment of universal brotherhood' and 'the first man determinedly to denounce all prejudices against colonial peoples'. Reading Lenin on colonialism, Ho recalled, 'roused me to great emotion, great enthusiasm, great faith, and helped me see the problems clearly. My joy was so great that at times I was reduced to tears.'[50] But he also wanted to 'revise Marxism…by strengthening it with Oriental ethnology' and wished to 'stir up nationalism'.[51] He protested at length not only at France's treatment of Indochina but at her cruelty in other colonies too. France, he complained, was a 'strange country. It is a breeding-ground of admirable ideas, but when it goes travelling it does not export them.'[52]

The original programme of the Communist Party of Indochina (1930) included redistributing plantations to poor peasants. But Ho also emphasized the need for a broad coalition to gain independence, and paid homage to the American Declaration of Independence and its language of rights; he long cherished Abraham Lincoln because of his emancipation of the slaves. In 1944 he stressed that Vietnam's independence, not communism, was his priority. In 1945 he hoped the USA could be persuaded to resist France's return to power in Indochina after Japan's defeat, an idea supported by Roosevelt but then abandoned by Truman. Soon, however, the US was funding the war against the Viet Minh, an independence coalition formed in 1941, who infiltrated the south with the aim of reuniting the country.

Once in power in independent North Vietnam there was never any question of Ho abandoning Leninism or democratic centralism. As elsewhere, land collectivization, urged by China (1953–61), proved bloody and protracted, and famine resulted. All businesses were collectivized between 1958 and 1960, but a focus on heavy industry as 'essential to socialist construction' produced difficulties too. In his foreign policy Ho used both China and the USSR as levers. Heavily reliant on Soviet aid, he praised the suppression of the Hungarian revolt of 1956. (Stalin nonetheless called him a 'communist troglodyte'.[53]) Yet despite Chinese pressure in 1950–51, Ho refused to allow his subordinates to be weeded out because their class background was 'incorrect'. By the mid-1950s Vietnam became increasingly Stalinist, and included substantial surveillance of its citizens and the growing ascendancy of a privileged Party elite. In 1956 journalists and writers who urged greater freedom of speech were silenced.[54] By the 1960s, however, during the latter stages of the American War, the frail old man with the benign if enigmatic smile who still wore sandals wrought from rubber tyres was an international symbol of resistance to imperialism. Simplicity, endurance, fairness and brotherhood were pitted against the brash, racist technocracy of the superpower. In the moral Cold War, Goliath grew measurably weaker by the contrast.

The American war also spilled over into neighbouring countries. The conquest of Cambodia in April 1975 by Khmer Rouge troops led by Pol Pot (born Saloth Sar, 1925–98) produced the greatest national catastrophe of any communist revolution.[55] In only four years, before the regime was overthrown by Vietnam in 1979, as much as a third of the population, some 2 million people, was killed or died of famine and neglect. Much of this 'autogenocide' resulted from classifying the urban population as corrupt 'new people' and forcibly emptying the war-swollen cities almost immediately. This was the most extreme example of the hatred caused by class struggle resulting in mass murder.

Theoretically the Khmer Rouge state was the most peasant oriented of all the Marxist–Leninist regimes, and the one which gave greatest priority to the virtue, innocence and ignorance of the least educated. But it was also the crudest of all communist tyrannies. Money was abolished, libraries and hospitals emptied, and the virtues of a pure life on the land were extolled. Personal decoration, wearing colourful clothes or glasses, expressing affection, speaking a foreign language or acting individualistically were all discouraged, and even punished by death. Extreme collectivism in all things became the norm, along with absolute subservience to the shadowy Party organization, known as 'Angkar'. Intense paranoia was directed at the educated and members of the former American-backed regime in particular, as well as Soviet, American and Vietnamese 'spies' and ethnic minorities.[56] Large numbers were executed or died in vast forced-labour projects. Pol Pot described these euphemistically as a 'Super Great Leap Forward', in imitation of China, and boasted that 'Compared to other countries, in terms of method, we are extremely fast.'[57] He also bragged that the training time for helicopter pilots had been greatly reduced, even though the pilots 'could not read a great deal', in order to prove that 'political consciousness is the decisive factor'.[58] Their safety record is unknown. The fact that Party cadres were reported studying the ideas of 'Max-Lenin' does not inspire confidence in a close reading of the classical sources.

The world's last surviving wholly Stalinist regime is the Democratic People's Republic of Korea, founded in 1945 after the Korean peninsula was divided. Led initially by Kim Il-sung (1912–94), then subsequently by dynastic succession, the regime has proven as merciless to internal opponents and incompetent economically as any other of its type. As late as the mid-1990s famine killed as many as 3.5 million people. The regime is known for its extravagant cult of personality, which is the focus of virtually all art and culture in the country; its intense ideology of self-reliance, or *Juche*, which began in 1955 and extends to complete cultural isolation; and its extreme militarization, with some 25 per cent of the population serving in the armed forces. Police surveillance is widespread and punishment for deviance is swift and severe. In the 1990s *Juche* succeeded Marxism–Leninism as the official state ideology.

Marxism for the Twenty-First Century

By the 1980s Marxism had fallen into a steep decline. This was an era 'hijacked by Solzhenitsyn, *nouveaux philosophes* and boat people', as the French revolutionary Régis Debray recalled. Brand Marx was tarnished chiefly by the revelations of the Gulag and the cumulative effects of 1956 and 1968. But its image also jarred with the spirit of the times. 'Marxian' discourse now became akin to 'a kind of obsolescent Sanskrit' which no longer resonated with the epoch.[1] Both the predictive and millenarian aspects of Marx's philosophy of history naturally lent themselves to dogmatism, and Leninism reinforced this by suppressing dissent. The world revolution began to sink into ossified self-caricature as its notional ends became detached, obscure and dystopian. The zest for 'liberation' died away, evidently for many generations. 'Revolution' lost its allure as political violence was denounced as 'terrorism'. Teetering Soviet gerontocrats symbolized the sclerosis which had long since invaded the philosophy and model they crudely imposed on their satellites. Their grey Party, wobbling in the aspic of dementia – not Che's glamorous zeal – now embodied the revolution. After 1978 China abruptly changed course and abandoned the command economy, followed by Vietnam in 1990. In the 1980s Afghanistan devoured the USSR's army. Making a revolution, governing justly, providing plenty and assisting human 'liberation' were evidently very different propositions. The golden age of Petrograd in 1917 now seemed but a dream.

With the USSR's collapse in 1991 Soviet aid to client states ended. Cuba and North Korea struggled to survive the transition while retaining a command economy. In Russia average male life expectancy plunged from sixty-three years in 1990 to fifty-eight in 2000 (it is now about sixty-five). The former states of the Eastern European Soviet bloc quickly reverted to capitalism, though many suffered as outdated subsidized state industries folded, or survived in new form only in low-wage zones dominated by foreign multinationals. In the early 2000s several of these countries embraced right-wing nationalist, even authoritarian and xenophobic principles. This was a reaction in part to Soviet occupation and decades of official Marxism–Leninism, to the losses of people and territory in the Second World War, and in part to the shock of globalization. Recent regimes in Hungary and Poland have occasionally expressed an overt hostility to liberalism redolent of the communist epoch. Acquiring a respect for democratic opposition has proven more difficult than many hoped in 1989.

The history of Marxism can be seen as dividing naturally into seven stages. The first witnessed Marx's and Engels' early efforts to form a 'Marx party' after 1848. The second was marked by the growth of German Social Democracy and reformism to 1914. Lenin, the Russian Revolution and the setting in concrete of dialectical materialism (1917 to around 1937) define the third. In the fourth the Chinese Revolution of 1949 dominates. In the fifth, after 1945, Marxism–Leninism proliferated throughout the Third World. A sixth stage (1950s–1980s) of official ossification and (at best) sluggish development through command economies runs parallel with a revival of interest in Marx, driven by the early writings. A seventh stage of degeneration and collapse (1989–91) then follows, excepting a few societies: most were utterly transformed (China, Vietnam), others fossilized in extreme Stalinism (North Korea) or more moderate variations thereon (Cuba, Belarus). Thus, like the seven ages of man in Shakespeare's As You Like It, a progression from infancy to decrepitude can be traced.

Until a return to humanist themes in the 1960s in the West, Marxism became ever more estranged from Marx himself at each of these stages. Within this chronology, the most crucial turning point came with Lenin and the Bolshevik Revolution. Marx saw two main paths as implied by his agenda, one peaceful and one revolutionary. He also insisted, however, that his theories had to adapt to change. As Eric Hobsbawm observes, there is no 'correct' or 'incorrect' Marxism as such: 'Kautsky and Bernstein were heirs of Marx as much...as Plekhanov and Lenin.'[2] But this holds only up to a point. Marx's consistent adherence to an ideal of mass democracy of 'freely associated men' which would achieve and maintain proletarian power, and his insistence on consent as a first principle, imply that he would probably not have followed Lenin's 'democratic centralism' past the Kronstadt uprising, or the securing of the revolution. But this judgement too remains contentious. Hobsbawm, for instance, infers that if Marx had lived into the twentieth century he would 'almost certainly have given the greatest initial priority to the maintenance of revolutionary proletarian power against the dangers of overthrow'.[3] The key question here, which is entirely counterfactual, is what Marx would have done about and after Kronstadt, in allowing or prohibiting competing sources of power in bodies besides the Party. For proletarian power – workers' control – is not Party power. But it is difficult to conceive that Marx, whose ultimate goal was a society defined by 'free individuality', would have found the intense collectivism of Marxism–Leninism attractive.

Beyond the economic issues, many problems which emerged in Marxist–Leninist regimes resulted from their systematic disregard of personal and public liberty. Marx proposed no schema similar to John Stuart Mill's extremely useful 'harm principle' to distinguish between what was permissible in state and public interference in individual conduct and what was not. Few of his followers have been inclined to draw such a line, or to recognize any limits to collectivism, which is not to say this cannot be done in principle. Intolerance of dissent became the norm. Marxism's hostility to a rights-centred approach to freedom has clearly been counterproductive and misconceived. The resulting repression is hard to associate with Marx himself. But it is true that *The German Ideology* left open the possibility of justifying any means to achieve successful revolution. To writers like Kolakowski, too, only despotism could bring about the romantic idea of social unity proposed by Marx.[4] A morality harnessed to the chariot of history rides as roughshod over human beings as one shackled to technology. Trotsky justified killing the Tsar's children on the grounds of political expediency. But the principle applied to anyone else's children too.

There were, however, many potential turning points at which Marxism might have been softened. The desire for complete unanimity was not an inevitable result of either utopianism or Marxism. Unfortunately, counterfactual speculation helps little here. We may imagine what might have happened if, for example, the Workers' Opposition had triumphed in 1921, or if Trotsky had succeeded Lenin rather than Stalin, or if the NEP had continued, or if Cuba or Vietnam had been further assisted in their independence struggles by the US, or if one or another of the Eastern European regimes had freed themselves from Stalinism while remaining Marxist in orientation. What if Gorbachev had wedded a reformed USSR to the market? Would this have resulted in a liberal Marxist system? Or would the USSR, or Russia, like China and Vietnam, have maintained stringent Party control, suppressing democratic rights and freedom of expression and only permitting economic liberty? We will never know. No viable socially and politically liberal regime has coexisted with a Leninist communist party regime. Mao said, 'There is no such thing as liberal Stalinism.'[5] But it was Leninism which prevented revisionism from becoming the dominant political philosophy of any ruling communist state. The moral of Marxism–Leninism, in part, has been that those who gain power never seek to relinquish it and will retain it at any cost, as Bakunin had warned and Orwell reiterated.

Since 1991, consequently, humanity's judgement on Marxism has more often been harsh than not. Some believe 'it was Marx and Engels whose ideas led to the perfection of slavery and inhumanity, from the Gulag archipelago to the extermination camps of Cambodia'.[6] To most the problem is Lenin and Leninism. Even Marxist critics, like Angelica Balabanoff, see Bolshevism as a 'perversion of Marxism' which 'appropriated the Socialist theory and made it into a hateful caricature' and 'falsified our terminology and defiled our principles'. This 'antithesis to socialism' was 'entirely Lenin's creation'.[7] The 'price mankind must pay to achieve communism by Bolshevik methods is too terrible', complained Bertrand Russell in 1920, and even afterwards he doubted whether 'the result would be what the Bolsheviks profess to desire'.[8] Yet many on the left remain unwilling to confront the more tragic aspects of Bolshevism's legacy.

Attempts to rescue Marxism from the most degenerate form of Leninism, philosophical and political Stalinism, have generally been of three types. The first involves reverting to the young Marx, and building a theory of freedom on his account of alienation. The second rejects Engels' account of materialism, often at the same time, and by going back to Hegel, and denies that Marxism was ever 'scientific' (in the Diamat sense). The third utilizes Marx's championing of workers' democracy and co-operation to criticize Leninism and Stalinism. By 1991 all of these efforts had seemingly failed. 'Today', wrote the French Marxist Roger Garaudy in 1964, 'Marx and his work polarize the hopes or the hostilities of all mankind.'[9] This is no longer the case. China aside, only a few decaying communist states remain. They offer humanity no beacon of hope, and no revolutionary proletariat aspires to imitate them. Marx's ideal, or at least Lenin's caricature of it, is tarnished beyond recognition. (Just as authoritarianism is again becoming respectable!) To many, communism stands for slavery rather than freedom, and Marxism–Leninism is an intellectual prison rather than a promise of liberation. The quest for quasi-religious historical certainty is now disreputable. Most writers for whom Leninism and the Party's or the proletariat's embodiment of 'truth' were starting points are consequently no longer readable. Attempts to wed liberalism to Marxism have moreover been seen as akin to mixing oil and water. So where a John Stuart Mill, for example, might serve to counterbalance bits of Marx's politics, or even more obviously Lenin's, the effort has rarely been made, though we might still point to Morris, Bernstein, the Fabians or some of Marcuse.[10] So Marxism–Leninism, at least, now appears obsolete, a Model-T of revolutionary aspiration in an age of electric cars. The 'greatest fantasy of our [twentieth] century', as Kolakowski termed it derogatorily, now seems fit only for embalming in what Georges Sorel called the 'necropolis of departed gods'.[11]

This is a sad ending (if it is this) to an ideal which has inspired millions to seek liberation from colonialism, imperialism and oppression, and which courageously challenges the very idea of the unjust, exploitative subordination of one human being to another. It indicates a substantial setback in the pursuit of that ideal of equality which underpinned the American and Bolshevik revolutions alike, and arguably modernity as such. Nonetheless, after 1991 triumphalist claims of the 'end of ideology' and 'end of history' marked the apparent American and capitalist conquest of Marxism. Capitalism can claim some significant victories (with considerable assistance from socialism, social democracy and trade unionism): in the 1950s an estimated two-thirds of the world's population was hungry. The figure today is one-ninth, and obesity is a greater problem than hunger. Nonetheless millions suffer food and water shortage, even in the richest nations, and the problem is growing and may rapidly become critical. Yet while capitalism's deficiencies are clear, few now embrace Marxism as a remedy. It is no longer the 'correct' alternative, in a black-and-white world, to 'bourgeois' philosophy. Few now entertain narratives which view 'philosophy' as the 'culmination' of the Enlightenment, and possibly also of the Reformation and the French Revolution. Still less do we construe revolutionary movements as the culmination of philosophy itself. We are rightly suspicious of governments which unify executive, legislative and judicial functions, usually in the executive: this promotes dictatorship. We are much less confident about 'progress', and the idea that history is governed by 'laws'. We are more doubtful of any ultimate success for humanity, of the primacy or sovereignty of any principle of 'reason', or of the prospect of abolishing exploitation. Whatever meaning history may have is opaque to us.

This is all dispiriting. But if we are less inclined to seek collective salvation today, that is no bad thing. For if Marxism represents humanity's last great secular millenarian attempt to attain paradise on earth, we may well gain more by settling for less. Nonetheless recent years have witnessed a revival of interest in Marx, as 1991 recedes and the more immediate problems resulting from the financial crisis of 2008 refuse to retreat. Globalization continues its relentless search for new markets. The transfer of manufacturing capacity to cheap labour regions, like Mexico, South, Southeast and East Asia, and Eastern Europe, in order to sustain profit rates, has depleted the industrial base of nations in Europe and the US, provoking a protectionist backlash by the un- and underemployed. Neoliberal economic policy, from the Reagan–Thatcher epoch in the 1980s onwards, has also weakened trade unions and eased the transition to minimalist states and (some fear) a dystopia of corporate dictatorship.[12] Indebtedness, low wages, long working hours, zero-hours contracts, reduced pensions, child poverty and similar effects are all increasing amongst the precariat.[13] Tax breaks for the rich and corporations commonly accompany 'austerity' cuts to social services, schools, health and welfare. For the unemployed, and increasingly even those in work, homelessness and soup kitchens are a bleak alternative. One result is a greater concentration of wealth than at any time in the past century.[14] In the US twenty people own as much as the bottom half of the entire population. There are now some 2,000 US$ billionaires in the world, with the wealthiest eight owning as much as half the human race. Some $21 trillion–$32 trillion of all assets (or up to 32 per cent of all global investments, and 25 per cent of the wealth of the ultra-rich) is hidden in tax havens.

This might appear to be an explosive scenario. But neither worsening poverty in developed countries nor the growth of proletariats elsewhere has fuelled revolutionary movements or sympathy for Marxist solutions. Following the USSR's collapse, a hegemonic ideal of liberty has instead enjoyed an ideological monopoly. Large-scale multinationals and right-wing billionaires have an enormous impact on both the media and politics. In a 'post-truth' epoch propaganda, disinformation or downright lies relentlessly distract us from examining our malaise.[15] In the UK two billionaires, both very right wing, control perhaps 80 per cent of papers sold. Even the multiplicity of internet sources can scarcely counterbalance the bland formulae of film and TV which promote narcissistic consumption, celebrity, hedonism, competition, personal success and devil take the hindmost. Targeted advertising on social media makes the 'echo chamber' effect of reinforcing opinion even stronger. The class war is going well, a joke of our times runs: the rich are winning.

In some places the 2008 crisis has nonetheless dented the reputation of neoliberalism to a degree, and brought Marxist-inspired parties like Syriza in Greece into power, albeit in the most straitened of circumstances. Elsewhere the traditional left vote has often weakened if not collapsed. A social democratic will to stabilize the system and return to the greater equality of the post–Second World War epoch has not yet returned, and some think will not.[16] Even the word 'radical' has been hijacked by being coupled with 'fundamentalism' and 'terrorism'. The poor, employed or not, do not identify themselves in a class-conscious manner. Their fears are often manipulated by politicians and the popular press to whip up a nationalist and xenophobic loathing of foreigners and immigrants in particular. In Eastern Europe memories of communism's collapse are increasingly displaced by new anxieties about Russia or the EU, foreigners, liberalism, and the dubious benefits of the new economic (dis)order and the new political elites.[17] Half a century ago it was his theory of alienation which made Marx seem strikingly relevant. Now millions scramble for crumbs falling from capitalism's banquet. Prosperity, it seems, is more likely to provoke revolt than 'austerity'. Alienation is a luxury.

Many nonetheless are dissatisfied with capitalism, and also deeply alarmed about the threat it poses to the planet. Fewer can imagine abolishing it. But it is useful to have a single figure like Marx to turn to in order to help us organize our thoughts, while recognizing that he was not infallible. Being a 'Marxist' now may actually appear more 'conservative' than embracing other forms of radicalism. Marx's own historical method might indeed suggest that being 'radical' today requires jettisoning a large part of Marxism. Before considering his relevance today, let us summarize Marx's failures and achievements. We can then consider the question of how far our world differs from that examined by classical Marxist theory, and so demands new strategies and ideas.

On the negative side of the ledger, the failings of Marxism include: an overly determinist idea of progress, especially respecting the 'inevitability' of socialist revolution; the belief in what Bertrand Russell termed a 'militant certainty',[18] which brought a pompous arrogance to both policy and outlook; adherence to the 'scientific' nature of the theory of surplus value, while excluding other theories of exploitation; an overly vague and optimistic conception of the end point, 'communist society'; a romanticized view of the proletariat which wrongly assumed that it was more virtuous than other groups, coupled with antagonism towards 'class enemies'; the simple-minded, cruel morality of 'the end justifies the means', which with an inflation of the description of the end has meant justifying mass murder repeatedly; an overoptimistic assumption that the state might disappear in a future democratic society; a lack of sympathy with the peasantry; a weak theory of social, civil and personal liberty and the inability to conceive of these as anything but 'bourgeois morality'; too little stress on the value of individuality; a tendency to reduce human motives to the economic, albeit excluding the pursuit of power in particular; extreme economic centralization and bureaucratization; a poorly conceived theory of the 'dictatorship of the proletariat' which has been used to excuse the excesses of arbitrary power; extreme quasi-religious cults of personality; an obsession with rapid modernization centred on heavy industry; a harsh work regimen with poor wages; the persecution of traditional religions and ethnic minorities; an inability to assess adequately the power of ideas; an overemphasis on the centrality of work to life; a mesmerizing language of critical analysis which nonetheless remains inaccessible to many; a fetishized concept of 'revolution' as a panacea for existing woes; and an incapacity to comprehend the recurrent power of nationalism and ethnic and religious identity.

This is quite a list: no wonder we approach Marx much less reverentially today, and can even portray Marxism as a conservative, even reactionary, brand of sectarian socialism. It is quite plausible, on this account, to see the Marxist paradigm as exhausted, and as no longer presenting a means of moving forwards. But on the positive side, what remains useable in Marx? Three features stand out.

First, Marx's vision of a fulfilling life after and beyond work is perhaps now more valuable than ever. More forcefully than most of his contemporaries, Marx raised the questions: How do we want to live? Must we assume the present system to be the 'best of all possible worlds'? Can we not do much better, both by envisioning a far better future (the utopian mode) and by planning how the present might lead to it? To Marx it *was* possible to imagine a world far better than the one we live in, and even to create it. Slavery and serfdom were once regarded as natural, then abolished: why should wage-slavery be any different? Can we really speak of human progress when such cruelty persists? Surely a more humane and equal society would be happier for all. The single great idea at the heart of socialism, ending human exploitation, remains as appealing as ever. Here the utopian rather than the scientific Marx can assist us.

Machines, Marx realized, made free time possible for the many. This could not occur in his time: it can in ours. Many medieval Europeans enjoyed as much as a third of the year off. Many today are scarcely so fortunate, and indeed have found their hours of labour increasing in recent years, and the age of retirement rising inexorably. Poverty can be abolished, and much additional misery besides. Utopians today continue to aspire to a 'post-capitalist' and 'post-work' society. Pleas for a universal basic income become increasingly plausible as we move towards both more skeletal welfare systems and a persistent shortage of well-paid jobs. A new surge of mechanization may make possible a 'post-work' society.[19] This may seem a pale shadow of the idea of abolishing all servitude and providing a humane environment in which our best qualities can flourish. But if utopia must be local as well as global, and must have some grounding in reality, it is certainly a step in the right direction.

Second, we have seen that Marx's image of the future rested on his theory of alienation and its counterpart, an ideal of all-round development. With some modifications, applying this to the twenty-first century is not difficult. There is no evidence that work has become more satisfying even for the middle class. Millions of workers slip further into the precariat and are increasingly anxious about their employment, health and futures. In the less developed world large numbers of factory workers endure Victorian conditions. Outside work, loneliness increases everywhere. In large cities we are ever more estranged from those around us, even from our own families; as the divorce rate increases, more people live alone; our sense of responsibility for the elderly declines. Egoism and competitiveness have a higher value than sociability, sympathy for the needy and altruism. Our feeling of community declines apace. People we encounter on the streets are for the most part strangers to us, and too often the objects of sullen disregard or even antagonism. Politically a sense of being dominated and of not controlling our lives is strong, and apathy is widespread. In leisure and culture, obsessions with consumption and luxury goods predominate as never before. As we incessantly destroy the natural world around us, and as we become increasingly urban, we are less a part of nature than ever.

Our sociability diminishes in other areas too. Servitude to machines reduces some forms of human contact. Ours is a century which maximizes excitement of the senses by constantly bombarding us with stimuli. In public spaces muzak and flashing images increasingly provide distraction from conversation and direct human interaction. (But we seem to like this.) In an era of Facebook 'friendship' and obsessive-compulsive smartphone use, personal interaction often takes second place to the addictive clicking of virtual engagement. (Ditto.) Here a fetishistic technophilia, or addiction to the machine, literally fuses us with the commodity, and disconnection from our devices brings disorientation and a feeling of losing power and meaning. If we take Marx to have prioritized direct personal communication – and that largely between equals – this indicates a massive increase in technologically induced alienation, though not all forms of illusion and alternative reality fall into this category. Culturally, too, mass manipulation – including, most recently, nationalist and xenophobic hate-mongering – forces us into further antagonisms. Though many of these forms derive not from capitalism but from our relationship to machinery, alienation remains a vital way of approaching our condition. Yet curiously we hardly speak of it today, when few yearn for 'liberation' or 'emancipation' from their 'one-dimensionality'.

Third, Marx's analysis of capitalism, suitably updated, remains extremely relevant. Marx emphasized the organic nature of modes of production, their constant propensity to change and the motivation of their key actors by relentless greed. The primacy of economic factors is his central assumption. Although toleration of differences in race, gender and other distinctions has grown, in the early twenty-first century the concentration of wealth continues unimpeded, and is fuelled by recurrent and severe crises. Here Marx still retains some emancipatory potential. We do not need a theory of surplus value to show us that more unequal societies are crueller and less happy, even for the wealthy.[20] Marx's theory of ideology, bolstered by the insights of Gramsci, the Frankfurt School and other theorists of hegemonic mass manipulation – as well as those of its satirists, like Aldous Huxley and George Orwell – is more useful than ever. But 'false consciousness' turns out in many ways to be the toughest of nuts to crack: misinformation, disinformation, spin and 'fake news' abound as never before.

We still have crisis then, and we still have critique: it is programme and agency which seem to be missing. Several attractive policies might form the basis of a left agenda. These include reinforcing ever more skeletal welfare provisions; national debt forgiveness; abolishing tax havens; moving towards financial transparency where, in a 'glass revolution', everyone's income and tax are made public; creating a worldwide register of financial wealth in stocks and bonds, as a prelude to taxing income on all forms of property;[21] abolishing corporate tax avoidance (at least $130 billion a year in the US, and far more globally), especially through harmonizing corporation tax worldwide; and providing universal free medical care and a universal basic income. The latter might supplant many current welfare arrangements. It would also alleviate unemployment, since increasing mechanization may soon render universal labour not only unnecessary but impossible. It is not at all clear that capitalism will be able to adjust to such policies without serious disruption. These developments moreover indicate the need for centralized and co-ordinated planning rather than 'free-market' solutions, lending credence once again to Marx's proposition that social control must be the basis of collective emancipation.

In one key area, the environment, Marx's obsolescence today is obvious. Humanity's increasingly rapid dystopian descent in the twenty-first century will more likely result from environmental devastation than capitalist crisis. Not only is progress, either revolutionary or evolutionary, not automatic: regression, degeneration and even civilizational collapse are possible. Our very survival is not inevitable. Here Marx cannot help us, beyond indicating the environmental destructiveness of capitalism. Marxism became an alternative vision of 'progress', 'growth' and 'development', aiming to distribute opulence more justly while notionally improving working conditions for the majority. But utopia does not consist in maximizing our productive powers and capacity to exploit nature. We cannot abolish poverty if the price is destroying the planet. Socialism cannot satisfy all human needs: resources are decreasing. Greater scarcity looms, and may become endemic. The progress of global warming, resource depletion and overpopulation mean that any critical standpoint today must commence not with dominating nature but with preserving it. To start, we can replace all fossil fuels with renewable sources of energy, wind, solar, tidal, water. Otherwise the coming world will have nothing left to hunt or fish, if plenty to criticize.

If Marx were alive today, he would doubtless observe that capitalism remains a system which prevents humanity from realizing much of its potential. Would he still imagine that exploitation might someday end? Undoubtedly. Would he still be a communist? He would have to concede that socialist bureaucracies can be as oppressive as rapacious aristocracies or a greedy bourgeoisie. He would probably still demand a democratically accountable system of property ownership and economic management. Would he still insist that the world needs to be changed for the better? More than ever. 'The merit of Marx', wrote Che Guevara, was 'in suddenly producing a qualitative change in the history of social thought', in going beyond interpretation and prediction to demand change.[22] To imagine a better, more humane future is the first stage in creating one. But history will not deliver it for us. We have to do the job ourselves. 'Work for humanity', Marx often said. That message has stood the test of time.

ACKNOWLEDGEMENTS

For comments on various aspects or parts of this book I am grateful to Sorin Antohi; Myriam Bienenstock; Artur Blaim; Zsolt Czigányik; Casiana Ionita; Christine Lattek; Michael Levin; Aladár Madarász; Rudolf Muhs; Kit Shepherd; Keith Tribe; Norbert Waszek; and to audiences at the Central European University, Budapest, Hungary; Southern Federal University, Rostov-on-Don, Russia; the Utopian Studies Society, Gdańsk, Poland; the University of Campinas, Brazil; Bucharest City Museum, Romania; and participants in the 2017 conference on 'Utopia and Revolution' in Sinaia, Romania. Thanks also go to the British Library, the London Library, and the Interlibrary Loan staff at Royal Holloway, University of London.

NOTES

The notes here are intended to provide a summary guide only to some of the English-language literature on Marx and Marxism.

ABBREVIATIONS

All English references in brackets (for example, '43:449') refer to Karl Marx and Frederick Engels. *Collected Works* (50 vols., Lawrence & Wishart, 1975–2005).
- *Karl Marx-Friedrich Engels Werke* (43 vols., Dietz Verlag, 1957–68) is cited as W.
- *Karl Marx Friedrich Engels Gesamtausgabe* (prospectively 120 vols., Dietz Verlag, 1975–98, then Akademie Verlag, 1998–) is cited as MEGA2.

MANY MARXES

1. William Hard. *Raymond Robins' Own Story* (Harper & Row, 1920), p. 226.
2. Quoted in Francis Wheen. *Karl Marx* (Fourth Estate, 1999), p. 298.
3. For a summary of their impact see Eric Hobsbawm. 'The Fortunes of Marx's and Engels's Writings', in Eric Hobsbawm, ed. *The History of Marxism, Volume One. Marxism in Marx's Day* (Harvester Press, 1982), pp. 327–44.
4. For example by Shlomo Avineri. *The Social and Political Thought of Karl Marx* (Cambridge University Press, 1968).

PART ONE: MARX
CHAPTER 1: THE YOUNG KARL

1. The chief later biographies of Marx are Edward Hallett Carr. *Karl Marx. A Study in Fanaticism* (2nd edn, J. M. Dent, 1938); Robert Payne. *Marx* (W. H. Allen, 1968); Jerrold Seigel. *Marx's Fate. The Shape of a Life* (Princeton University Press, 1978); Francis Wheen. *Karl Marx* (Fourth Estate, 1999); Mary Gabriel. *Love and Capital. Karl and Jenny Marx and the Birth of a Revolution* (Little, Brown, 2011); Jonathan Sperber. *Karl Marx. A Nineteenth-Century Life* (Liveright, 2013);

Gareth Stedman Jones. *Karl Marx. Greatness and Illusion* (Allen Lane, 2016). A good chronological summary of Marx's life is Maximilien Rubel. *Marx. Life and Works* (Macmillan, 1980). A good brief survey is Jon Elster. *An Introduction to Karl Marx* (Cambridge University Press, 1986). Still helpful is Isaiah Berlin. *Karl Marx. His Life and Environment* (4th edn, Oxford University Press, 1978). David McLellan has examined Marx in various works, including *The Young Hegelians and Karl Marx* (Macmillan, 1969), *Marx before Marxism* (Macmillan, 1970) and *Karl Marx. His Life and Thought* (Harper & Row, 1973).

2.   Here and throughout the text the original gendering of formulations such as 'man', 'mankind', 'humanity' and so on in earlier writers are retained. Obviously, gender-neutral formulations would be used today. *Man* in German signifies the universal, however.

3.   *Reminiscences of Marx and Engels* (Foreign Languages Publishing House, n.d.), p. 72.

4.   A recent study of Marx's early development is David Leopold. *The Young Karl Marx. German Philosophy, Modern Politics, and Human Flourishing* (Cambridge University Press, 2007).

5.   G. W. F. Hegel. *Lectures on the History of Philosophy, 1825–6* (3 vols., Clarendon Press, 2009), vol. 1, p. 53.

6.   Charles Taylor. *Hegel* (Cambridge University Press, 1975), p. 51.

7.   Shlomo Avineri. *Hegel's Theory of the Modern State* (Cambridge University Press, 1972), p. 84.

8.   Judith Shklar. *Freedom and Independence. A Study of the Political Ideas of Hegel's 'Phenomenology of Mind'* (Cambridge University Press, 1976), p. 13.

9.   Hegel. *Lectures on the History of Philosophy*, vol. 1, p. 195.

10. Herbert Marcuse. *Reason and Revolution. Hegel and the Rise of Social Theory* (2nd edn, Routledge & Kegan Paul, 1954), p. 5.

11. The main account here is Norbert Waszek. *The Scottish Enlightenment and Hegel's Account of 'Civil Society'* (Kluwer, 1988). A good introduction is Michael O. Hardimon. *Hegel's Social Philosophy. The Project of Reconciliation* (Cambridge University Press, 1994).

12. G. W. F. Hegel. *System of Ethical Life* (1802/3) *and First Philosophy of Spirit* (1803/4) (State University of New York Press, 1979), p. 248; Marcuse. *Reason and Revolution*, p. 79.

13. Waszek. *Scottish Enlightenment*, pp. 224–5.

14. G. W. F. Hegel. *Philosophy of Right* (1821), §51.

15. G. W. F. Hegel. *Lectures on Natural Right and Political Science* [1817–18] (Oxford University Press, 2012), p. 177.

16. On this group see Sidney Hook. *From Hegel to Marx. Studies in the Intellectual Development of Karl Marx* (Victor Gollancz, 1936); William Brazill. *The Young*

Hegelians (Yale University Press, 1970); John Toews. *Hegelianism. The Path towards Dialectical Humanism, 1805–1841* (Cambridge University Press, 1980); Robert Gascoigne. *Religion, Rationality and Community. Sacred and Secular in the Thought of Hegel and His Critics* (Martinus Nijhoff, 1985); Harold Mah. *The End of Philosophy, the Origin of 'Ideology'. Karl Marx and the Crisis of the Young Hegelians* (University of California Press, 1987); David Brudney. *Marx's Attempt to Leave Philosophy* (Harvard University Press, 1998); Warren Breckman. *Marx, the Young Hegelians, and the Origins of Radical Social Theory* (Cambridge University Press, 1999).

17. André Liebich, ed. *Selected Writings of August Cieszkowski* (Cambridge University Press, 1979), p. 77.

18. On Bauer see Zvi Rosen. *Bruno Bauer and Karl Marx* (Martinus Nijhoff, 1977); Douglas Moggach. *The Philosophy and Politics of Bruno Bauer* (Cambridge University Press, 2003).

19. Bruno Bauer. *The Trumpet of the Last Judgment against Hegel the Atheist and Antichrist* (1841).

20. In 'The Genus and the Crowd' (1844), in Lawrence S. Stepelevich, ed. *The Young Hegelians. An Anthology* (Cambridge University Press, 1983), p. 204. See Moggach. *Philosophy and Politics of Bruno Bauer*, p. 168; Brudney. *Marx's Attempt*, p. 118.

21. Ludwig Feuerbach. *The Essence of Christianity* [1841] (Harper & Row, 1957), p. xvi. On Feuerbach see: Eugene Kamenka. *The Philosophy of Ludwig Feuerbach* (Routledge & Kegan Paul, 1970); Marx W. Wartofsky. *Feuerbach* (Cambridge University Press, 1977).

22. Ludwig Feuerbach. *Lectures on the Essence of Religion* [1843] (Harper & Row, 1967), p. 17. Here an account based on group psychology is essential. See my *Dystopia. A Natural History* (Oxford University Press, 2016), Part 1. The divine could equally have been seen as an idealized image of humanity rather than its 'essence': 'man's God is nothing other than the deified essence of man' (Feuerbach, *Lectures*, p. 17). Or God could have been viewed as a cruel image of humanity, heaven as a perverted community, and species-life as herd-like identity rather than morally superior existence. Any 'need for community' can similarly be expressed in both ways.

23. Strauss explains Christianity: 'By faith in this Christ, especially in his death and resurrection, man is justified before God; that is, by the kindling within him of the idea of Humanity, the individual man participates in the divinely human life of the species' (*The Life of Jesus Critically Examined* [1835], SCM Press, 1975, p. 780).

24. Toews. *Hegelianism*, p. 353.

25. Antonio Labriola. *Essays on the Materialist Conception of History* (Charles H. Kerr, 1908), pp. 75–6.

26. Ludwig Feuerbach. *Principles of the Philosophy of the Future* [1843] (Bobbs-Merrill, 1966), p. 71.

27. Feuerbach. *Essence of Christianity*, p. 266.

28. Like Marx, Edgar Bauer pronounced that 'From now on history is a self-conscious history, because mankind knows the principles by which it moves forward, because mankind has history's goal – freedom – in sight' ('Critique's Quarrel with Church and State' (1844), in Stepelevich, ed. *Young Hegelians*, p. 273).

29. *The Doctrine of Saint-Simon: An Exposition. First Year, 1828–1829*, ed. George Iggers (Schocken Books, 1972), pp. 62–3, 84.

30. See H. G. Reissner. *Eduard Gans. Ein Leben im Vormärz* (Mohr, 1965), pp. 141–2; Norbert Waszek. 'Eduard Gans on Poverty. Between Hegel and Saint-Simon', *Owl of Minerva*, 18 (1987), 173–8; Michael H. Hoffheimer. *Eduard Gans and the Hegelian Philosophy of Law* (Kluwer, 1995); Reinhard Blänker, Gerhard Göhler and Norbert Waszek, eds. *Eduard Gans (1797–1839). Politischer Professor zwischen Restauration und Vormärz* (Leipziger Universitätsverlag, 2002); Myriam Bienenstock. 'Between Hegel and Marx. Eduard Gans on the "Social Question"', in Douglas Moggach, ed. *Politics, Religion, and Art. Hegelian Debates* (Northwestern University Press, 2011), p. 167.

31. See Albert Fried and Ronald Sanders, eds. *Socialist Thought. A Documentary History* (Edinburgh University Press, 1964), pp. 51–5.

32. See Noel Thompson. *The People's Science. The Popular Political Economy of Exploitation and Crisis, 1816–34* (Cambridge University Press, 1984) and my *Machinery, Money, and the Millennium. From Moral Economy to Socialism, 1815–1860* (Princeton University Press, 1987).

33. Adam Smith. *An Inquiry into the Nature and Causes of the Wealth of Nations* [1776] (2 vols., Clarendon Press, 1869), vol. 2, p. 365. See generally Ali Rattansi. *Marx and the Division of Labour* (Macmillan, 1982).

34. Wilhelm Liebknecht. *Karl Marx. Biographical Memoirs* [1901] (Journeyman Press, 1975), p. 82.

35. Friedrich Lessner. *Sixty Years in the Social-Democratic Movement* (Twentieth Century Press, 1907), p. 13.

36. Engels uses the phrase in *Anti-Dühring* (1878) (25:247).

37. *The Doctrine of Saint-Simon*, pp. 13, 89.

38. In Blanc's plan the government could assist setting up workshops for a year by providing funding, but thereafter leaders elected by the workers would control them, eventually under a system of collective ownership. Competition would be limited by a national system of workshops linking all industries, and eventually eliminated. Though Blanc did not want the state to become the 'proprietor' of industry, he 'never discussed the relation between the political and the economic

hierarchies', though he preferred ultimate control to rest with the legislature. In 1847 he supported equal salaries, but in 1848 abandoned the idea (Louis A. Loubère. *Louis Blanc. His Life and His Contribution to the Rise of French Jacobin-Socialism*, Northwestern University Press, 1961, pp. 38–40). Blanc complained, however, that the schemes which actually commenced were far from his own ideal and fell far short of socialism (Louis Blanc. *1848. Historical Revelations*, Chapman & Hall, 1858, pp. 111, 197).

39. Johann Gottlieb Fichte (1762–1814) is sometimes considered a precursor of this group, particularly through his essay on *The Closed Commercial State* (1800).

40. On Cieszkowski see André Liebich. *Between Ideology and Utopia. The Politics and Philosophy of August Cieszkowski* (D. Reidel, 1979).

41. Moses Hess. *Briefwechsel*, ed. Edmund Silberner (Mouton & Co., 1959), pp. 102–3.

42. Ibid., pp. 103, 80.

43. Quoted in John Weiss. *Moses Hess. Utopian Socialist* (Wayne State University Press, 1960), p. 55. In 1846 both Marx and Engels did their utmost to undermine Hess in the eyes of the workers, even insinuating that his common-law wife was a prostitute (W. O. Henderson. *The Life of Friedrich Engels*, 2 vols., Frank Cass, 1976, vol. 1, pp. 88–9).

44. Marx was equally dismissive of the 'universal Spartan frugality' he thought Robespierre commended (3:199), as well as any ascetic 'levelling down to a pre-conceived minimum' (3:295).

45. P. V. Annenkov. *The Extraordinary Decade. Literary Memoirs* [1880] (University of Michigan Press, 1968), pp. 169–70. Weitling later wrote to Hess that Marx was 'no more than a good encyclopaedia, but no genius' (Hess. *Briefwechsel*, p. 151).

46. On their relations see J. Hampden Jackson. *Marx, Proudhon and European Socialism* (Collier Books, 1957).

47. George Woodcock. *Pierre-Joseph Proudhon. A Biography* (Routledge & Kegan Paul, 1956), p. 91.

CHAPTER 2: MARX'S CONVERSION TO COMMUNISM

1. Compare this with Marx's account of freedom of the press in 1848 (7:250–52).

2. M. Cabet. *Voyage en Icarie* [1840] (Bureau du Populaire, 1848), p. 568. It was juxtaposed to the 'system of egoism'.

3. On Marx's treatment of the concept see R. N. Berki. *Insight and Vision. The Problem of Communism in Marx's Thought* (J. M. Dent, 1983).

4. On this theme generally see Michael Levin. *Marx, Engels and Liberal Democracy* (Macmillan, 1989).

5. The original is 'das Gemeinwesen, das kommunistische Wesen' (W1:283), the latter term being translated as 'communal being' in the English edition (3:79).

6. The text of Hegel's *Philosophy of Right* has 360 paragraphs; Marx's 'Critique' ends at §313.

7. Robert Payne. *Marx* (W. H. Allen, 1968), p. 185.

8. 'Enhanced sociability' here meaning 'artificial, conscious and hostile to overly competitive individualism', as opposed to the 'natural' sociability of any given society, which of course varies enormously. See my *Searching for Utopia. The History of an Idea* (Thames & Hudson, 2011).

9. Bauer's essay is partly translated in Lawrence S. Stepelevich, ed. *The Young Hegelians. An Anthology* (Cambridge University Press, 1983), pp. 187-97.

10. On Marx's use of 'class' see Hal Draper. *Karl Marx's Theory of Revolution, Volume Two. The Politics of Social Classes* (Monthly Review Press, 1978).

11. The German is 'völlige Wiedergewinnung des Menschen' (W1:390).

12. David McLellan. *Karl Marx. His Life and Thought* (Harper & Row, 1973), p. 96; Berki. *Insight and Vision*, p. 51.

13. Hess was moving in exactly this direction in his essay 'Über das Geldwesen', published in 1845. See Moses Hess. *Philosophische und Sozialistische Schriften, 1837-1850*, eds. Auguste Cornu and Wolfgang Mönke (Akademie-Verlag, 1961), pp. 329-47.

14. Marx's notes on Engels' essay are dated 'the first half of 1844' (3:375-6). See my 'Engels' *Outlines of a Critique of Political Economy* (1843) and the Origins of the Marxian Critique of Capitalism', *History of Political Economy*, 16 (1984), pp. 207-232.

15. See Moses Hess. 'Die eine und ganze Freiheit' [1843], in Moses Hess. *Ausgewählte Schriften*, ed. Horst Lademacher (Fourier Verlag, 1962), pp. 148-9.

16. Moses Hess. *The Holy History of Mankind* [1837], in Shlomo Avineri, ed. *The Holy History of Mankind and Other Writings* (Cambridge University Press, 2004), pp. 101-2, 104, 106, 117, 119, 122.

17. David McLellan describes this passage as 'eschatological' (*The Young Hegelians and Karl Marx*, Macmillan, 1969, p. 152). Others agree that Marx 'carries on one of the great eschatological myths of the Middle Eastern and Mediterranean world, namely: the redemptive part to be played by the Just...in our days the proletariat' (Mircea Eliade. *Myths, Dreams and Mysteries*, Harvill Press, 1960, p. 25).

CHAPTER 3: THE 'PARIS MANUSCRIPTS', ALIENATION AND HUMANISM

1. The main studies are Bertell Ollman. *Alienation. Marx's Conception of Man in Capitalist Society* (Cambridge University Press, 1971); John Maguire. *Marx's Paris Writings. An Analysis* (Gill and Macmillan, 1972); István Mészáros. *Marx's Theory of Alienation* (Merlin Press, 1972). See also Richard Schacht. *Alienation* (Doubleday, 1970). On the fragmented nature of the text itself see Keith Tribe.

The Economy of the Word. Language, History, and Economics (Oxford University Press, 2015), pp. 215–22. On its publication and interpretative history, see Marcello Musto. 'The "Young Marx" Myth in Interpretations of the Economic-Philosophic Manuscripts of 1844', *Critique*, 43 (2015), pp. 233–60.

2. For example, Franz Mehring. *Karl Marx. The Story of His Life* (George Allen & Unwin, 1936).

3. Henri Lefebvre. *Dialectical Materialism* (Jonathan Cape, 1968), p. 13.

4. See MEGA2, I (2), for the clearest version of the original texts.

5. Maguire. *Marx's Paris Writings*, p. 12.

6. The German term translated here as 'association' is the same: *Assoziation* (W40:508). In this period the concept was most commonly linked with Fourier. This is one of Marx's few rare moments of acknowledging the potential value of agricultural life.

7. See Shlomo Avineri. *The Social and Political Thought of Karl Marx* (Cambridge University Press, 1968), p. 97.

8. This approach is explored thoroughly in John Plamenatz. *Karl Marx's Philosophy of Man* (Clarendon Press, 1975).

9. The juxtaposition of 'free' and 'coerced' or 'forced' labour was also central to Hess (see *The Holy History of Mankind* [1837], in Shlomo Avineri, ed. *The Holy History of Mankind and Other Writings*, Cambridge University Press, 2004, pp. 116–17). But Hess also defined free activity as 'pleasure or virtue'. Marx's is a much more political definition.

10. Allen W. Wood. *Karl Marx* (Routledge & Kegan Paul, 1981), p. 8. On Marx as an existentialist see, for example, Erich Fromm. *Marx's Concept of Man* (Frederick Ungar, 1966).

11. 'From the character of this relationship', Marx continues, 'follows how much *man* as a *species-being*, as *man*, has come to be himself and to comprehend himself' (3:296).

12. 'Free labour and voluntary exchanges' was an Owenite slogan: William Thompson. *An Inquiry into the Principles of the Distribution of Wealth Most Conducive to Human Happiness* (Longman, Hurst, Rees, Orme, Brown, and Green, 1824), p. 26.

13. The original is 'Gattungsbewußtsein und Gattungsverhalten des Menschen' (W2:41).

14. Philip J. Kain. *Marx and Ethics* (Clarendon Press, 1988), p. 3.

15. Smith wrote that 'It is not from the benevolence of the butcher, the brewer, or the baker, that we expect our dinner, but from their regard to their own interest' (*An Inquiry into the Nature and Causes of the Wealth of Nations* [1776], 2 vols., Clarendon Press, 1869, vol. 1, p. 15).

16. See generally W. H. Bruford. *The German Tradition of Self-Cultivation. 'Bildung' from Humboldt to Thomas Mann* (Cambridge University Press, 1975).

17. Friedrich Schiller. *On the Aesthetic Education of Man, in a Series of Letters* [1795] (Clarendon Press, 1967), pp. 33, 41, 43. Hess wrote in 1845 that 'A Socialist establishes the proposal that we should become *real species-being*, and thereby proposes a society in which everyone can cultivate, exercise and perfect their human qualities' ('The Recent Philosophers', in Lawrence S. Stepelevich, ed. *The Young Hegelians. An Anthology*, Cambridge University Press, 1983, p. 373).

18. Iring Fetscher asserts (*Marx and Marxism*, Herder & Herder, 1971, p. 22) that *Capital* borrows the phrase 'association of free people' from Stirner (W23:92: 'einen Verein freier Menschen'; 35:89: 'community of free individuals'). But Stirner writes only of a 'Verein der Freien' (Hans G. Helms, ed. *Der Einzige und sein Eigentum und Andere Schriften*, Carl Hanser Verlag, 1969, p. 25).

19. As late as 1865 Marx still regarded Proudhon's *What Is Property?* (1840) as standing 'in approximately the same relation to Saint-Simon and Fourier as Feuerbach stands to Hegel' (20:26).

20. *New Moral World*, 6 (26 July 1845), p. 461. For details see my *Citizens and Saints. Politics and Anti-Politics in Early British Socialism* (Cambridge University Press, 1989), pp. 247–61.

CHAPTER 4: *THE GERMAN IDEOLOGY*, HISTORY AND PRODUCTION

1. See Terrell Carver and Daniel Blank. *A Political History of the Editions of Marx and Engels's 'German Ideology Manuscripts'* (Palgrave Macmillan, 2014); *Marx and Engels's 'German Ideology' Manuscripts. Presentation and Analysis of the Feuerbach Chapter* (Palgrave Macmillan, 2014).

2. Engels later said it was 'very tattered and fragmentary – and is still in need of re-arrangement' (49:136). Hess had gone over much of the same ground more concisely in 'The Recent Philosophers' (1845) (see Lawrence S. Stepelevich, ed. *The Young Hegelians. An Anthology*, Cambridge University Press, 1983, pp. 359–75), a fact he pointed out to Marx in January 1845 (MEGA2, III (1), pp. 450–52).

3. For a parallel juxtaposition of both texts, see Terrell Carver. *Marx and Engels. The Intellectual Relationship* (Wheatsheaf, 1983), pp. 72–6.

4. This echoed Hess's assertion that human nature was 'social, involving the co-operative activity of all individuals for the same ends and interests', which ended with the resounding claim that if 'theology is *anthropology*' for Feuerbach, to Hess himself '*anthropology is socialism*': Moses Hess. *Philosophische und Sozialistische Schriften, 1837–1850*, eds. Auguste Cornu and Wolfgang Mönke (Akademie-Verlag, 1961), p. 293.

5. On this point, see generally Norman Geras. *Marx and Human Nature. Refutation of a Legend* (NLB, 1983).

6. Marx uses 'ideologists' here to mean those adhering to a system of ideas without good reason.

7. See M. M. Bober. *Karl Marx's Interpretation of History* (2nd edn, Harvard University Press, 1950); Helmut Fleischer. *Marxism and History* (Harper Torchbooks, 1973); William H. Shaw. *Marx's Theory of History* (Hutchinson, 1978); and especially G. A. Cohen. *Karl Marx's Theory of History. A Defence* (Clarendon Press, 1978).

8. Cohen. *Karl Marx's Theory of History*, p. 151.

9. Hess's 'Philosophy of Action' (1843) insisted that 'In History, in the life of the spirit, results mean nothing; it is only the carrying out of legacies that is effective' (Albert Fried and Ronald Sanders, eds. *Socialist Thought. A Documentary History*, Edinburgh University Press, 1964, p. 268). ('In der Geschichte, im Leben des Geistes, handelt es sich nicht um Resultate, sondern um das Hervorbringen derselben. Das "Wirken, nicht das Werk" ist die Hauptsache': Moses Hess. *Ausgewählte Schriften*, ed. Horst Lademacher, Fourier Verlag, 1962, p. 144.) Hess also wrote in 1845 that 'All of these attempts to theoretically resolve the difference between the particular man and the human species must miscarry, for even if the singular man does indeed comprehend the world and mankind, nature and history, he yet in actuality remains only a sundered man [*Vereinzelung*] as long as the division of man is not *practically* overcome' (in Lawrence S. Stepelevich, ed. *The Young Hegelians. An Anthology*, Cambridge University Press, 1983, p. 360). He continued: 'this separation of man will only be practically resolved through Socialism – that is, if men unite themselves in community life and activity, and surrender private gain. So long as they are separated in actual life...the individual man will remain divided in his "consciousness"'.

10. Jerrold Seigel, for instance, claims that 'what replaced alienation theory as the keystone of Marx's historical vision in *The German Ideology* was...the division of labor': *Marx's Fate. The Shape of a Life* (Princeton University Press, 1978), p. 173.

11. The original is 'einer allseitigen Entwicklung der Individuen' (W3:424).

12. So concludes Terrell Carver: 'Communism for Critical Critics? A New Look at *The German Ideology*', *History of Political Thought*, 9 (1988), 129–36.

13. Engels stated that 'the basic thought belongs solely and exclusively to Marx', who 'had it already worked out' when they met in Brussels in spring 1845 (26:119). *Capital* said that Ricardo had taken 'the antagonism of class interests, of wages and profits, of profits and rent', as his 'starting-point' (35:14). Behind Ricardo stands Malthus, whose population doctrine introduced this idea of struggle into political economy.

14. Georgi Plekhanov. *Selected Philosophical Works* (3rd edn, 5 vols., Progress Publishers, 1977), vol. 2, p. 425.

15. The best introduction here is Istvan Hont. *Jealousy of Trade. International Competition and the Nation-State in Historical Perspective* (Harvard University Press,

2005). Eduard Bernstein would later claim that Harrington 'came very close to a materialist conception of history' (*Selected Writings of Eduard Bernstein, 1900–1921*, ed. Manfred Steger, Humanities Press, 1996, p. 47).

16. See Keith Tribe. 'Capitalism and Its Critics', in Gregory Claeys, ed. *The Cambridge Companion to Nineteenth-Century Thought* (Cambridge University Press, 2018).

17. Adam Smith. *An Inquiry into the Nature and Causes of the Wealth of Nations* [1776] (2 vols., Clarendon Press, 1869), vol. 2, p. 298.

18. 49:59; W37:490. In 1859 Engels termed the system 'the materialist conception of history' (16:469), and in 1886 'the Marxian conception of history' (26:396).

19. See generally Paul Thomas. *Marxism and Scientific Socialism. From Engels to Althusser* (Routledge, 2008).

20. See Bhikhu Parekh. *Marx's Theory of Ideology* (Croom Helm, 1982); J. Larrain. *Marxism and Ideology* (Macmillan, 1983); John Torrance. *Karl Marx's Theory of Ideas* (Cambridge University Press, 1995); Michael Rosen. *On Voluntary Servitude. False Consciousness and the Theory of Ideology* (Polity Press, 1996).

21. Allen W. Wood. *Karl Marx* (Routledge & Kegan Paul, 1981), pp. 117–19.

22. Leszek Kolakowski. *Main Currents of Marxism* (3 vols., Clarendon Press, 1978), vol. 1, pp. 155, 176.

23. A phrase Engels invented: 'einem falschen Bewußtsein' (W39:97).

24. See Leszek Kolakowski. 'Karl Marx and the Classical Definition of Truth', in Leopold Labedz, ed. *Revisionism. Essays on the History of Marxist Ideas* (George Allen & Unwin, 1962), pp. 179–87.

25. Louis Dupré. *The Philosophical Foundations of Marxism* (Harcourt, Brace & World, 1966), p. 208.

26. Steven Lukes. *Marxism and Morality* (Oxford University Press, 1985), p. 29.

27. Later Marx and Engels associated the phrase 'free development of all capacities' with Saint-Simon, and 'attractive labour' with Fourier (5:481).

28. Eugene Kamenka. *Marxism and Ethics* (Macmillan, 1969), p. 5.

29. Richard N. Hunt. *Marxism and Totalitarian Democracy, 1818–1850* (University of Pittsburgh Press, 1974), p. 131. See also Eugene Kamenka. *The Ethical Foundations of Marxism* (Routledge & Kegan Paul, 1962).

30. Philip J. Kain. *Marx and Ethics* (Clarendon Press, 1988), p. 1.

31. Bertell Ollman. *Alienation. Marx's Conception of Man in Capitalist Society* (Cambridge University Press, 1971), p. 47.

32. Kain. *Marx and Ethics*, p. 117. Peter Singer similarly dismisses the assumption that Marxism is a 'scientific system, free from any ethical judgments or postulates' as 'obviously nonsense' (*Marx*, Oxford University Press, 1980, p. 81). The best caricature of this is in George Orwell's *Nineteen Eighty-Four* (1949), when O'Brien explains the system by asserting that 'The Party seeks power entirely for its own sake.'

33. Robert Payne. *Marx* (W. H. Allen, 1968), p. 132.
34. V. I. Lenin. *Selected Works* (3 vols., Progress Publishers, 1977), vol. 3, p. 419. So what ordinary communists understood were 'Lenin's words, "morality is subordinate to the class struggle"' (Douglas Hyde. *I Believed. The Autobiography of a Former British Communist*, William Heinemann, 1950, p. 45).
35. Wood. *Karl Marx*, pp. 138–9.
36. Jon Elster. *An Introduction to Karl Marx* (Cambridge University Press, 1986), p. 92.
37. Jay Bergman. *Vera Zasulich. A Biography* (Stanford University Press, 1983), pp. 176–7.
38. Kolakowski nonetheless argues that 'Marx never adopts the ethical, normative point of view which first establishes an aim and then seeks the best means of achieving it' (*Main Currents of Marxism*, vol. 1, p. 222). This is taking Marx at his word.
39. Nicolas Berdyaev. *The Origins of Russian Communism* (The Centenary Press, 1937), p. 118.
40. 'The state is not abolished: it dies out': 'Der Staat wird nicht "abgeschafft", *er stirbt ab*' (W20:262).

CHAPTER 5: SOCIALISM, THE REVOLUTIONS OF 1848 AND *THE COMMUNIST MANIFESTO*

1. Alexander Herzen. *From the Other Shore* (Weidenfeld & Nicolson, 1956), p. 64.
2. But Marx added: 'Universal suffrage had fulfilled its mission. The majority of the people had passed through the school of development, which is all that universal suffrage can serve for in a revolutionary period. It had to be set aside by a revolution or by the reaction' (10:137, repeated at 517–18). This passage has considerable bearing on the question of Marx's proximity to Lenin. The original is: 'Die Majorität des Volkes hatte die Entwicklungsschule durchgemacht, zu der es allein in einer revolutionären Epoche dienen kann' (W7:100).
3. The essays in Gareth Stedman Jones and Douglas Moggach, eds. *The 1848 Revolutions and European Political Thought* (Cambridge University Press, 2018), offer a good context for understanding these developments.
4. Cited in Richard N. Hunt. *The Political Ideas of Marx and Engels* (2 vols., Macmillan, 1975–84), vol. 1, p. 157.
5. 'Superstitious belief in authority' is translated by Richard N. Hunt as 'authoritarian superstitions' (*Political Ideas of Marx and Engels*, vol. 1, p. 265). The original is 'Autoritätsaberglauben' (W34:308).
6. See Hess. 'A Communist *Credo*. Questions and Answers' [1844] and 'Consequences of a Revolution of the Proletariat' [1847], in Shlomo Avineri, ed. *The Holy History of Mankind and Other Writings* (Cambridge University Press, 2004),

pp. 116–35, especially p. 132. In the 'Draft' Engels describes the goal of communism as being 'To organise society in such a way that every member can develop and use all his capacities and powers in complete freedom and without thereby infringing the basic conditions of this society' (6:96).

7. Owen's plan involved sequential movement through all the major activities of life. The first 'class', from birth to the age of five, would attend school. Those aged between five and ten would assist with domestic labour, supervised in part by those aged between ten and fifteen, who would also learn agricultural and industrial skills. Between the ages of fifteen and twenty all would engage in production, and also help to supervise the next youngest age-group. Those aged between twenty and twenty-five would supervise all branches of production and education. All aged between twenty-five and thirty would preserve and distribute wealth, while those aged between thirty and forty would govern communities. The most mature (aged between forty and sixty) would conduct 'foreign affairs'. See G. Claeys, ed. *The Selected Works of Robert Owen* (4 vols., Pickering & Chatto, 1993), vol. 3, pp. 286–95. Fourier proposed that individuals, including children, have as many as eight different activities each day, so that although 'the division of labour be carried to the last degree…each sex and age may devote itself to duties that are suited to it' and be 'in full enjoyment of the right to labour or the right to engage in such branch of labour as they may please to select, provided they give proof of integrity and ability' (Charles Gide, ed. *Selections from the Works of Fourier*, Swan Sonnenschein, 1901, pp. 163–71, here p. 164). There is some evidence that Marx's ideal was taken up. The first Soviet Commissar of Education, Anatoly Lunacharsky, later wrote that 'The real, complete, Marxist school, such as Marx foresaw it, can only be realized in practice in an educational establishment which stands alongside the industrial establishment and shares in the latter's life' (*On Education*, Progress Publishers, 1981, p. 190). He termed this 'Marx's principle of the labour school' (ibid., p. 210).

8. The Penguin Books edition of *The Communist Manifesto* (ed. Gareth Stedman Jones, 2000) is the most useful for background and reception. Commentary is provided in Terrell Carver and James Farr, eds. *The Cambridge Companion to The Communist Manifesto* (Cambridge University Press, 2015). Engels' contribution should however not be downplayed: see Carver. *Marx and Engels. The Intellectual Relationship* (Wheatsheaf, 1983), pp. 78–95. The title was Engels' (38:149). But he described the work as 'substantially' Marx's (21:61).

9. Later Engels reinforced the divide, terming socialism by 1847 'a middle-class movement', compared with the 'working class movement' of communism (26:516).

10. Marx thought 'every child above the age of nine ought to be employed at productive labour a portion of its time', but not as at present (21:383). In 1875 he called 'an early combination of productive labour with education…one of the

most potent means for the transformation of present-day society', and stated that 'A general prohibition of child labour is incompatible with the existence of large-scale industry' (24:98).

11. See Jon Elster. *An Introduction to Karl Marx* (Cambridge University Press, 1986), p. 147.

12. Hunt. *Political Ideas of Marx and Engels*, vol. 1, p. 248. Engels later noted that it was 'edited by Marx and myself' (26:326).

13. Marx to P. G. Röser, July 1850, quoted in Hunt. *Political Ideas of Marx and Engels*, vol. 1, p. 238. For the argument that it may not have reflected Marx's and Engels' personal views see ibid., pp. 235–6. Here the phrase 'permanent revolution' is also used, which was not adopted in any other writings signed by either.

14. Isaiah Berlin. *Karl Marx. His Life and Development* (2nd edn, Oxford University Press, 1948), p. 188.

15. In 1848 Engels thought that, amongst the Slavic peoples, only the Poles and Russians had a future; others were doomed to disappear as 'entire reactionary peoples' (8:238). See Roman Rosdolsky. *Engels and the 'Nonhistoric Peoples'. The National Question in 1848* (Critique Books, 1987), especially p. 86. The German socialist Ferdinand Lassalle wrote that he was 'no advocate of nationalities on principle...I attribute the right of nationality only to the *great culture nations*' (quoted in Bertram D. Wolfe. *Marxism. One Hundred Years in the Life of a Doctrine*, Chapman & Hall, 1967, p. 30).

16. This too is a collective document, and we cannot be sure of Marx's authorship of any one part of it.

17. Further policies Marx recommended were an Irish agrarian revolution and the imposition of protective tariffs against England by an independent Ireland (42:487).

18. Quoted in Gustav Mayer. *Friedrich Engels. A Biography* (Chapman & Hall, 1936), p. 99. In 1848 Engels described the peasant of France and Germany as a 'barbarian living in the midst of civilisation' (7:519). See generally Athar Hussain and Keith Tribe. *Marxism and the Agrarian Question* (2 vols., Macmillan, 1981). Engels added in 1894 that 'We have no more use for the peasant as a Party member if he expects us to perpetuate his property in his smallholding than for the small handicraftsman who would fain be perpetuated as a boss' (27:495). But he also wrote: 'we shall not interfere in their property relations by force, against their will' (27:497). See also Hal Draper. *Karl Marx's Theory of Revolution, Volume Two. The Politics of Social Classes* (Monthly Review Press, 1978), pp. 317–452.

19. See, for example, David Mitrany. *Marx against the Peasant. A Study in Social Dogmatism* (George Weidenfeld & Nicolson, 1951).

20. The main treatment of the concept is Hal Draper. *Karl Marx's Theory of Revolution, Volume Three. The 'Dictatorship of the Proletariat'* (Monthly Review Press, 1986).

21. See ibid., pp. 175–8, for the initial usages.

22. In 1866 Marx also moved to abolish the office of president of the International Working Men's Association.

23. See Hunt. *Political Ideas of Marx and Engels*, vol. 1; J. L. Talmon. *The Origins of Totalitarian Democracy* (Secker & Warburg, 1952).

24. Hunt. *Political Ideas of Marx and Engels*, vol. 1, pp. 292–8.

25. Weydemeyer had emigrated to the USA, where he served in the Union army during the Civil War, rising to the rank of colonel. He became probably the only senior American officer ever to distribute copies of Marx's works (the Inaugural Address of the International Working Men's Association, 1864) to his troops.

26. But Karl Kautsky thought that in early 1850 Marx 'regarded the Blanquists as properly the workers' party of France. They, above all others, had his sympathy': *Social Democracy versus Communism* [1933–4] (Rand School Press, 1946), p. 32.

CHAPTER 6: EXILE, 1850s–1880s

1. Wilhelm Liebknecht. *Karl Marx. Biographical Memoirs* [1901] (Journeyman Press, 1975), p. 121.

2. On this period see Christine Lattek. *Revolutionary Refugees. German Socialism in Britain, 1840–1860* (Routledge, 2006).

3. Ibid., pp. 79, 113–15, 127, 158. Schapper was said to 'repudiate "leadership"' as such (MEGA2, III (1), p. 526).

4. Quoted in Jerrold Seigel. *Marx's Fate. The Shape of a Life* (Princeton University Press, 1978), p. 231.

5. Some biographers differ here, for example Saul Padover. *Karl Marx. An Intimate Biography* (McGraw-Hill, 1978), pp. 170–71. See Engels' comments against anti-Semitism (27:50–52). Marx called Lassalle a 'Jewish nigger' (41:389).

6. *Marx and Engels through the Eyes of Their Contemporaries* (Progress Publishers, 1972), pp. 127, 184.

7. Liebknecht. *Karl Marx*, pp. 11, 71.

8. Friedrich Lessner. *Sixty Years in the Social-Democratic Movement* (Twentieth Century Press, 1907), pp. 13–14, 58–9.

9. Robert Payne. *Marx* (W. H. Allen, 1968), pp. 154–6; Carl Schurz. *The Reminiscences of Carl Schurz* (The McClure Company, 1907), p. 139.

10. Payne. *Marx*, p. 321.

11. P. V. Annenkov. *The Extraordinary Decade. Literary Memoirs* [1880] (University of Michigan Press, 1968), pp. 167–8.

12. H. F. Peters. *Red Jenny. A Life with Karl Marx* (Allen & Unwin, 1986), p. xiii.

13. Ibid., p. 73.

14. Lessner. *Sixty Years*, p. 58.

15. Quoted in Francis Wheen. *Karl Marx* (Fourth Estate, 1999), p. 64.

16. Lenin stayed with Frederick Demuth during one of his visits to London. He lived until 1929, and was active in Hackney Labour Party. His own son Harry later remembered entering Engels' house in Regent's Park Road with his father through the tradesmen's entrance.

17. Quoted in Boris Nicolaievsky and Otto Maenchen-Helfen. *Karl Marx. Man and Fighter* (Allen Lane The Penguin Press, 1973), pp. 256–7.

18. Wheen. *Karl Marx*, p. 268.

19. Ibid., pp. 356–7.

20. H. M. Hyndman. *The Record of an Adventurous Life* (Macmillan & Co., 1911), p. 288.

21. An intimate portrait can be gleaned from Olga Meier, ed. *The Daughters of Karl Marx. Family Correspondence, 1866–1898* (André Deutsch, 1982).

22. Biographies include Chushichi Tsuzuki. *The Life of Eleanor Marx, 1855–1898. A Socialist Tragedy* (Clarendon Press, 1967); Yvonne Kapp. *Eleanor Marx* (2 vols., Lawrence & Wishart, 1972–6); Rachel Holmes. *Eleanor Marx. A Life* (Bloomsbury, 2014).

23. See Leslie Derfler. *Paul Lafargue and the Founding of French Marxism, 1842–1882* (Harvard University Press, 1991).

24. Lafargue later wrote *The Right to Be Lazy* (1907), a satirical defence of greater free time which derided the moderns' obsession with work.

CHAPTER 7: POLITICAL ECONOMY

1. On Marx's economic thought generally see Ernest Mandel. *The Formation of the Economic Thought of Karl Marx* (NLB, 1971); Allen Oakley. *Marx's Critique of Political Economy. Intellectual Sources and Evolution* (2 vols., Routledge & Kegan Paul, 1984–5). A critical account of his economic project as a whole is given in Keith Tribe. *The Economy of the Word. Language, History, and Economics* (Oxford University Press, 2015), pp. 171–254.

2. David McLellan, ed. *Marx's Grundrisse* (Macmillan, 1971), p. 15.

3. On the text, see Roman Rosdolsky. *The Making of Marx's 'Capital'* (Pluto Press, 1977); Geoffrey Pilling. *Marx's 'Capital'. Philosophy and Political Economy* (Routledge & Kegan Paul, 1980); Anthony Brewer. *A Guide to Marx's 'Capital'* (Cambridge University Press, 1984); David Harvey. *A Companion to Marx's 'Capital'* (Verso, 2010); Ben Fine and Alfredo Saad-Filho. *Marx's 'Capital'* (6th edn, Pluto Press, 2016).

4. William Morris et al. *How I Became A Socialist* (Twentieth Century Press, 1896), p. 18.

5. Other accounts have p. 270 (Andrés Suárez. *Cuba. Castroism and Communism, 1959–1966*, MIT Press, 1966, p. 16).

6. Pierre Brocheux. *Ho Chi Minh. A Biography* (Cambridge University Press, 2007), p. 14.

7. Compare Max Stirner: 'I do not demand any right, therefore I need not recognize any either. What I can get by force I get by force, and what I do not get by force I have no right to' (*The Ego and His Own* [1844], A. C. Fifield, 1913, p. 275).

8. The Factory Acts commenced in 1802, and were subsequently extended in scope and ambition throughout the nineteenth century.

9. Marx and Mill, however, were reported to be friends by Wilhelm Pieper, Marx's sometime secretary (Pieper to Engels, 27 January 1851; 38:269–70). This opens up the tantalizing possibility that Mill's shift towards socialism in this period may have owed something to Marx, though his embrace of co-operation preceded this. See my *Mill and Paternalism* (Cambridge University Press, 2013), pp. 153–72. This point has largely been overlooked by those who have compared them, for example Graeme Duncan. *Marx and Mill. Two Views of Social Conflict and Social Harmony* (Cambridge University Press, 1973). But Mill was of course keen to retain economic competition.

10. The radical physician Charles Hall had described all economic relations in terms of a desire for power over others in 1805. See my 'Republicanism, Commerce and the Origins of Modern Social Theory in Britain, 1796–1805', *Journal of Modern History*, 66 (1994), pp. 249–90.

11. Julius Braunthal. *History of the International, Volume One. 1864–1914* (Nelson, 1966), p. 265.

12. G. D. H. Cole, introduction to Karl Marx. *Capital* (J. M. Dent, 1933), p. xxi.

13. Louis Althusser. *The Future Lasts a Long Time and the Facts* (Chatto & Windus, 1993), p. 211.

14. J. Bonar, preface to Eugen v. Böhm-Bawerk. *Karl Marx and the Close of His System. A Criticism* (T. Fisher Unwin, 1898), p. 7.

15. J. F. Bray. *Labour's Wrongs and Labour's Remedy. Or, The Age of Might and the Age of Right* (David Green, 1839), p. 49.

16. William Thompson. *An Inquiry into the Principles of the Distribution of Wealth Most Conducive to Human Happiness* (Longman, Hurst, Rees, Orme, Brown, and Green, 1824), p. 224.

17. Beatrice Potter. *The Co-operative Movement in Great Britain* (Swan Sonnenschein, 1893), p. 47. The social theorist Anton Menger made a similar allegation in 1886 (26:609). His *The Right to the Whole Produce of Labour* (Macmillan & Co., 1899) says 'the whole theory of surplus value' was 'borrowed in all essentials from Thompson's writings' (p. 101).

18. See Paul Mason. *Postcapitalism. A Guide to Our Future* (Allen Lane, 2015), p. 137.

19. Marx had previously categorized Proudhon's calculation of value by labour time as 'the utopian interpretation of Ricardo's theory' (6:124). Marx's rejection of

the exchange of labour for labour theory focused on the fact that it did 'not change the reciprocal position of the producers', which might be very unequal both before the exchange and after it, and so leave their inequality, and indeed class antagonism, unchanged (6:126, 133). The scheme would only work, Marx insisted, if 'the number of hours to be spent on material production is agreed on beforehand', which 'negates individual exchange' (6:143).

20. As Marx acknowledged in 1848 (8:130) and Engels again in 1872 (23:329).

21. Robert C. Tucker. *The Marxian Revolutionary Idea* (Norton, 1970), p. 51.

22. Engels later wrote of the 'socialist application of the Ricardian theory', that its claim that 'the entire social product belongs to the workers as *their* product, because they are the sole real producers', was 'incorrect in formal economic terms, for it is simply an application of morality to economics'. Marx by contrast 'never based his communist demands upon this, but upon the inevitable collapse of the capitalist mode of production...he says only that surplus value consists of unpaid labour, which is a simple fact' (26:281–2). The economist Joan Robinson has been interpreted as seeing Marx as adopting this strategy as an ideal system of reward (Rosdolsky. *Making of Marx's 'Capital'*, p. 542).

23. The author of the pamphlet was Charles Wentworth Dilke, whose inspiration was William Godwin, one of Robert Owen's teachers.

24. Alfred Schmidt. *The Concept of Nature in Marx* (NLB, 1971), pp. 139, 142.

25. The phrase 'Wiedergewinnung des Menschen' (W1:390) apparently does not occur in Marx's later writings. 'Emancipation' is of course used in a variety of ways, including 'vollständige Emanzipation von der Lohnsklaverei' (W10:128); 'Emanzipation des Proletariers' (W12:3); and 'Emanzipation der Arbeiterklassen' (W16:13).

26. The sentiment was repeated in 1878 at 25:279. Engels wrote that 'The Utopians were already perfectly clear in their minds as to the effects of the division of labour, the stunting on the one hand of the labourer, and on the other of the labour function, which is restricted to the lifelong, uniform mechanical repetition of one and the same operation' (25:278).

27. Engels continued to use the language of 'universal emancipation' in *Socialism. Utopian and Scientific* (1880), linked to 'socialised production upon a predetermined plan' and the dying out of the authority of the state in proportion as 'anarchy in social production vanishes' (24:325). Marx elsewhere wrote of 'Free development of individualities, and hence not the reduction of necessary labour time in order to posit surplus labour, but in general the reduction of the necessary labour of society to a minimum, to which then corresponds the artistic, scientific, etc., development of individuals, made possible by the time thus set free and the means produced for all of them' (29:91).

28. See, for example, John Plamenatz. *Karl Marx's Philosophy of Man* (Clarendon Press, 1975), p. 144.

29. See Mandel. *The Formation of the Economic Thought of Karl Marx*, pp. 164–86; Leszek Kolakowski. *Main Currents of Marxism* (3 vols., Clarendon Press, 1978), vol. 1, pp. 262–7.

30. David McLellan, ed. *Karl Marx. Early Texts* (Barnes & Noble, 1972), pp. xxxvi, xxxix. So, from this perspective, McLellan insists, 'to take the "1844 Manuscripts" as his central work…is to exaggerate their significance': *Karl Marx. His Life and Thought* (Harper & Row, 1973), p. 296.

31. István Mészáros. *Marx's Theory of Alienation* (Merlin Press, 1972), p. 227.

32. Kolakowski. *Main Currents*, vol. 1, p. 173.

33. The editors of the *Collected Works*, for instance, suggest that the concept of alienation 'was superseded to a considerable degree by other, more concrete determinations revealing more completely and more clearly…the exploitation of wage-labour' (3:xviii).

34. Louis Althusser. *For Marx* (Allen Lane, 1969); *Essays in Self-Criticism* (NLB, 1976), p. 153. 'Anti-humanist' implies abandoning Feuerbach's 'man' and related 'moral-idealistic' concepts, including 'alienation' (Louis Althusser. *The Humanist Controversy and Other Writings* (1966–67), Verso, 2003, p. 186). Originally written at the time of a debate over Stalinism, 'anti-humanist' was, to say the least, an unfortunate choice of terms.

35. Althusser. *For Marx*, p. 227.

36. Hence Marx would later write of 'my *analytic* method, which does not proceed from *man* but from a given economic period of society' (24:547).

37. Sidney Hook. *From Hegel to Marx* (Victor Gollancz, 1936), pp. 5–6.

38. Daniel Bell. 'The Debate on Alienation', in Leopold Labedz, ed. *Revisionism. Essays on the History of Marxist Ideas* (George Allen & Unwin, 1962), p. 204.

39. John McMurtry. *The Structure of Marx's World-View* (Princeton University Press, 1978), p. 222.

40. See William Clare Roberts. *Marx's Inferno. The Political Theory of 'Capital'* (Princeton University Press, 2016).

41. It is ignored entirely, for example, in Mehring's *Karl Marx*, and in Jonathan Sperber. *Karl Marx. A Nineteenth-Century Life* (Liveright, 2013).

42. Terrell Carver. *The Postmodern Marx* (Manchester University Press, 1998), p. 126.

43. Plamenatz. *Karl Marx's Philosophy of Man*, p. 132.

44. The editors of the *Collected Works* refer readers to the Rochdale Pioneers' consumer co-operative commenced in 1844 (32:562n135 and 35:784n254). This was not a co-operatively owned factory of the sort Marx describes here.

45. Roberts. *Marx's Inferno*, pp. 254–5. Marx's preference is clearly for industrial co-operation rather than any sort of 'village' life.

46. On the overlap of republicanism and co-operation here, see Roberts. *Marx's Inferno*, pp. 246–57. Marx's language on this issue is often closer to William Thompson than to Owen.

47. The note in this edition refers to the Rochdale consumer co-operative founded in 1844.

48. Engels wrote in 1886: 'Nor have Marx and I ever doubted that, in the course of transition to a wholly communist economy, widespread use would have to be made of co-operative management as an intermediate stage. Only it will mean so organising things that society, i.e., initially the State, retains an ownership of the means of production and thus prevents the particular interests of the co-operatives from taking precedence over those of society as a whole' (47:389).

49. Ernest Jones defined 'co-operation' here as 'the abolition of profitmongering and wages-slavery, by the development of independent and associated labour' (11:587).

50. The chief contemporary sources are George Jacob Holyoake. *The History of Co-operation in England. Its Literature and Its Advocates* (2 vols., Trubner & Co., 1875–9); Beatrice Potter. *The Co-operative Movement in Great Britain* (Swan Sonnenschein, 1893); Benjamin Jones. *Co-operative Production* (2 vols., Clarendon Press, 1894).

51. George Jacob Holyoake. *Self-Help by the People. The History of the Rochdale Pioneers, 1844–1892* (10th edn, Swan Sonnenschein, 1900), pp. 12, 28, 38, 81. Holyoake commented that 'It was known as a rule that workmen made bad masters' who aimed at 'getting the utmost work out of those they employ, just as the worst master under which they have served did unto them' (ibid., pp. 106–7).

52. Holyoake wrote that the Rochdale Pioneers 'planned employment of their profits in productive manufactures' (*History of Co-operation*, vol. 2, p. 17). They established the Rochdale Co-operative Corn Mill Society, and for three years ran a large spinning-mill on co-operative principles until it was converted to joint-stock by outside investors (ibid., p. 52). This may be what Marx refers to. The two sixty-horsepower spinning machines, 'Co-operation' and 'Perseverance', were renamed 'Joint-Stock' and 'Greed'.

53. Amongst their advocates, E. V. Neale stressed that 'Co-operation desires to uphold the principle of individualism, while socialism sought to eradicate it' (quoted in Jones. *Co-operative Production*, vol. 2, p. 738).

54. George Jacob Holyoake. *The History of Co-operation* (revised edn, 2 vols., T. Fisher Unwin, 1906), vol. 2, p. 342.

55. Quoted in Jones. *Co-operative Production*, vol. 2, p. 755.

56. Potter. *Co-operative Movement*, p. 83.

57. Eduard Bernstein. *Evolutionary Socialism. A Criticism and Affirmation* [1899, revised 1909] (Schocken Books, 1967), pp. 109–27. Bernstein instead regarded the trades unions as 'the democratic element in industry' (ibid., p. 139).

CHAPTER 8: THE INTERNATIONAL (1864–1872) AND THE PARIS COMMUNE (1871)

1. 'When Marx founded the International…' wrote Engels (48:9) – meaning, 'when it became a fully formed organization'.
2. Gareth Stedman Jones. *Karl Marx. Greatness and Illusion* (Allen Lane, 2016), pp. 471–2.
3. Ibid., p. 467.
4. The electorate rose to about a third of adult males, doubling the male voters from around 1 million to roughly 2.5 million. At this point some 77 per cent of the adult population were classified as manual labourers.
5. For a contextual collection of contemporary writings by Marx and others see Marcello Musto, ed. *Workers Unite! The International 150 Years Later* (Bloomsbury Academic, 2014). A collection of essays assessing the organization is Fabrice Bensimon, Quentin Deluermoz and Jeanne Moisand, eds. *'Arise, Ye Wretched of the Earth'. The First International in a Global Perspective* (Brill, 2017). See also Paul Thomas. *Karl Marx and the Anarchists* (Routledge, 1980), pp. 249–340.
6. Quoted in *Woodhull & Claflin's Weekly*, 12 August 1871, as cited in Shlomo Avineri. *The Social and Political Thought of Karl Marx* (Cambridge University Press, 1968), p. 216.
7. The councillors' wage, 6,000 francs a year, was in fact perhaps four times the average French worker's wage in this period.
8. Engels in 1891 insisted that while religious communities were to be deprived of all state support and of all influence on public education, 'They cannot be prohibited from forming their *own* schools out of their *own* funds and from teaching their own nonsense in them' (27:229).
9. 'Democracy without professionals', in Richard N. Hunt's phrase: *The Political Ideas of Marx and Engels* (2 vols., Macmillan, 1975–84), vol. 2, p. xi.
10. G. P. Maximoff. *The Guillotine at Work. Twenty Years of Terror in Russia: Data and Documents* (The Chicago Section of the Alexander Berkman Fund, 1940), p. 21.
11. Engels, however, wrote to August Bebel in 1875 to 'suggest that *Gemeinwesen* be universally substituted for *state*; it is a good old German word that can very well do service for the French "Commune"' (45:64). See generally Joseph M. Schwartz. *The Permanence of the Political. A Democratic Critique of the Radical Impulse to Transcend Politics* (Princeton University Press, 1995).

12. Michael Bakunin. *Selected Writings*, ed. Arthur Lehning (Grove Press, 1973), pp. 236–7.

13. Michael Bakunin. *Marxism, Freedom and the State*, ed. K. J. Kenafick (Freedom Press, 1950), pp. 27–8.

14. Ibid., pp. 38, 30. In the early twentieth century such themes were extended by the Polish Marxist Wacław Machajski in particular, who warned that Marx's scheme would 'substitute for the capitalists a class of hereditary soft-handed intellectuals, who would perpetuate the slavery of the manual workers and their offspring' (quoted in Max Nomad. *Rebels and Renegades*, Macmillan, 1932, p. 208). The first to explore this 'new class' in detail, Machajski as early as 1905 anticipated much that would be popularized in Milovan Djilas's more famous 1957 work, *The New Class. An Analysis of the Communist System*. See Marshall S. Shatz. *Jan Wacław Machajski. A Radical Critic of the Russian Intelligentsia and Socialism* (University of Pittsburgh Press, 1989).

15. Michael Bakunin. *Statism and Anarchy* [1873] (Cambridge University Press, 1990), pp. 177, 136–40, 178, 181.

16. Noam Chomsky. *Power Systems. Conversations with David Barsamian on Global Democratic Uprisings and the New Challenges to U.S. Empire* (Hamish Hamilton, 2013), p. 173.

CHAPTER 9: MARX'S MATURE SYSTEM

1. On Marx's political theory see J. B. Sanderson. *An Interpretation of the Political Ideas of Marx and Engels* (Longman, 1969); Hal Draper. *Karl Marx's Theory of Revolution* (5 vols., Monthly Review Press, 1977–2005); John M. Maguire. *Marx's Theory of Politics* (Cambridge University Press, 1978); Alan Gilbert. *Marx's Politics. Communists and Citizens* (Martin Robertson, 1981).

2. The juxtaposition first appears in *The German Ideology* (5:537). The eighteenth-century utopian Étienne-Gabriel Morelly, author of *The Code of Nature* (1755), is the likely source for this motto for both Blanc and Marx (Louis A. Loubère. *Louis Blanc. His Life and His Contribution to the Rise of French Jacobin-Socialism*, Northwestern University Press, p. 42). The Saint-Simonian formulation was 'la justice divine qui veut que chacun soit classé selon sa capacité et rémunéré selon ses oeuvres' (*Œuvres de Claude-Henri de Saint-Simon*, 6 vols., Éditions Anthropos, 1966, vol. 4, pp. xxiv–xxv).

3. On vacillations in these positions see my 'The Political Ideas of the Young Engels, 1842–1845. Owenism, Chartism, and the Question of Violence in the Transition from "Utopian" to "Scientific" Socialism', *History of Political Thought*, 6 (1985), 455–78.

4. Richard N. Hunt argues that it does not represent Marx's views: *The Political Ideas of Marx and Engels* (2 vols., Macmillan, 1975–84), vol. 1, p. 247.

5. As late as 1893 Engels thought that if 'only revolutionary means will enable Germany to hold its own…there is every likelihood that we may be forced to take the helm and play at 1793' (49:266–7), in other words, to push the revolution in a more radical direction, following the Jacobins. In 1895 he wrote of 'peaceful and anti-violent tactics' that 'I preach those tactics only for the *Germany of to-day* and even then with many *reservations*. For France, Belgium, Italy, Austria, such tactics could not be followed as a whole and, for Germany, they could become inapplicable tomorrow' (50:490).

6. Teodor Shanin, ed. *Late Marx and the Russian Road. Marx and the 'Peripheries of Capitalism'* (Routledge & Kegan Paul, 1983), p. 11.

7. But, as Keith Tribe points out, Marx restricted the 'historical fatality' of capitalism's movement to the countries of Western Europe only in the French edition of *Capital* (*The Economy of the Word. Language, History, and Economics*, Oxford University Press, 2015, p. 174).

8. But by 1892 Engels was writing that 'I am afraid we shall have to treat the Obshchina as a dream of the past and reckon, in future, with a capitalist Russia' (49:384).

9. As early as 1852 Engels had dismissed 'the old pan-Slavic DODGE of transmogrifying the old Slav system of communal property into communism and depicting the Russian peasants as born communists' (39:67). In 1893 he thought 'that no more in Russia than anywhere else would it have been possible to develop a higher social form out of primitive agrarian communism unless that higher form was *already in existence* somewhere else' (50:214).

10. In 1894 Engels insisted that any transformation of the Russian commune into a higher form 'cannot come from the commune itself, but only from the industrial proletarians of the West…and, linked to this, the replacement of capitalist production by socially managed production' (27:425). So a 'shortened process of development' was possible in 'all countries in the pre-capitalist stage', but only after capitalism had been abolished in its heartlands (27:426).

11. See Hunt. *Political Ideas of Marx and Engels*, vol. 2, pp. 135–7.

12. See ibid., pp. 162–211.

13. Karl Popper. *The Open Society and Its Enemies* (2nd edn, 2 vols., Routledge & Kegan Paul, 1952), vol. 2, p. 200.

14. Notably the positivist philosopher Auguste Comte's British followers, one of whom, Edward Beesly, Marx knew well. See my *Imperial Sceptics. British Critics of Empire, 1850–1920* (Cambridge University Press, 2010), pp. 131–40.

15. See Lawrence Krader. *The Asiatic Mode of Production. Sources, Development and Critique in the Writings of Karl Marx* (Van Gorcum & Co., 1975); Kevin B.

Anderson. *Marx at the Margins. On Nationalism, Ethnicity, and Non-Western Societies* (University of Chicago Press, 2010).

16. Shanin, ed. *Late Marx*, p. 15.

17. May was the author of the 'Winnetou' stories glorifying Native American life, and beloved of every German schoolchild from the mid-1870s onwards. James Fenimore Cooper wrote *The Last of the Mohicans* (1826) and other tales of frontier life. Even where Marx apparently praises the Iroquois – for example when he wrote that being 'Eloquent in oratory, vindictive in war, and indomitable in perseverance, they have gained a place in history' (Lawrence Krader, ed. *The Ethnological Notebooks of Karl Marx. Studies of Morgan, Phear, Maine, Lubbock*, Van Gorcum & Co., 1972, p. 172) – we find that this is taken word for word from Lewis Morgan (*Ancient Society. Or, Researches in the Lines of Human Progress from Savagery, through Barbarism to Civilization*, Henry Holt, 1877, p. 149). Krader contends that Marx's position 'is a rejection of Rousseau in general' in viewing primitive mankind as essentially unfree (*Asiatic Mode of Production*, p. 259).

18. See Krader, ed. *Ethnological Notebooks*, pp. 39, 60, 119, 329.

19. Morgan. *Ancient Society*, p. 552; Krader, ed. *Ethnological Notebooks*, p. 139.

20. So implies Leszek Kolakowski. *Main Currents of Marxism* (3 vols., Clarendon Press, 1978), vol. 1, p. 162. An early Russian account of Marx insisted that 'socialism is nothing else but individualism carried to its utmost extent' (M. Tugan-Baranowsky. *Modern Socialism in Its Historical Development*, Swan Sonnenschein, 1910, p. 29).

CHAPTER 10: THE PROBLEM OF ENGELS

1. A recent biography is Tristram Hunt. *The Frock-Coated Communist. The Revolutionary Life of Friedrich Engels* (Allen Lane, 2009). A brief introduction is Terrell Carver. *Engels* (Oxford University Press, 1981).

2. Gustav Mayer. *Friedrich Engels. A Biography* (Chapman & Hall, 1936), p. 13.

3. In 1846 the Chartist George Julius Harney wrote to Engels that 'To organise, to propose a revolution in this country would be a vain and foolish project' (MEGA2, III (1), p. 524).

4. This text is mentioned as late as *The German Ideology* (5:212).

5. Terrell Carver. *Marx and Engels. The Intellectual Relationship* (Wheatsheaf, 1983), p. xiv.

6. Maximilien Rubel. *Rubel on Karl Marx. Five Essays*, ed. Joseph O'Malley and Keith Algozin (Cambridge University Press, 1981), p. 17. Bakunin uses the term 'Marxists' in 1873, in *Statism and Anarchy*. Engels apparently first used 'Marxist' disparagingly in June 1882 (46:289), and in November recalled Marx's comment that, to Lafargue, '*Ce qu'il y a de certain c'est que moi, je ne suis pas Marxiste*'

(46:356). In February 1887 he decried 'the usual intolerance of the Marxists' (again in France; 48:14). Then, in February 1888, he used the term more neutrally, referring to the Scottish socialist Robert Cunninghame Graham as 'a declared Marxist', meaning that he sought to 'confiscate *all the means of production*' (48:156–7). But he also said that Graham had stated publicly 'that he stood on the basis of Karl Marx "absolutely and entirely"' (48:159). By 1889 he was contrasting the 'so-called Marxists' with 'our Marxists' (48:246). He later condemned 'the people who make themselves out to be orthodox Marxists and have changed the concept of our movement into a rigid dogma to be learned by rote', who had made a '*mere sect*' out of it (49:197).

7. Norman Levine. *The Tragic Deception. Marx contra Engels* (Clio Press, 1975), p. xv.

8. This theme is treated in Manfred B. Steger and Terrell Carver, eds. *Engels after Marx* (Penn State University Press, 1999). See also Gareth Stedman Jones. 'Engels and the History of Marxism', in Eric Hobsbawm, ed. *The History of Marxism, Volume One. Marxism in Marx's Day* (Harvester Press, 1982), pp. 290–326.

9. J. D. Hunley. *The Life and Thought of Friedrich Engels. A Reinterpretation* (Yale University Press, 1991), p. x. The strongest statement of this view is Levine. *Tragic Deception*.

10. Russell Jacoby. *Dialectic of Defeat. Contours of Western Marxism* (Cambridge University Press, 1981), p. 53. See generally Marcel van der Linden. *Western Marxism and the Soviet Union. A Survey of Critical Theories and Debates since 1917* (Brill, 2007).

11. For a summary of the interpretations of Engels, see S. H. Rigby. *Engels and the Formation of Marxism. History, Dialectics and Revolution* (Manchester University Press, 1992).

12. Henri Lefebvre. *Dialectical Materialism* (Jonathan Cape, 1968), p. 16.

13. Louis Althusser. *Politics and History. Montesquieu, Rousseau, Hegel and Marx* (NLB, 1972), p. 167.

14. Elsewhere Marx insisted that his 'method of exposition is *not* Hegelian, since I am a materialist and Hegel an idealist' (42:544).

15. Wilhelm Liebknecht. *Karl Marx. Biographical Memoirs* [1901] (Journeyman Press, 1975), pp. 91–2.

16. Edward Aveling. *The Students' Marx. An Introduction to the Study of Karl Marx* (George Allen & Unwin, 1920), p. iv.

17. See my 'Social Darwinism. Power-Worship and the "Survival of the Fittest"', in Gregory Claeys, ed. *The Cambridge Companion to Nineteenth-Century Thought* (Cambridge University Press, 2018).

18. Carver. *Marx and Engels*, p. 133.

19. Enrico Ferri. *Socialism and Positive Science (Darwin–Spencer–Marx)* (Independent Labour Party, 1905), pp. 62, 81. Herbert Spencer (1820–1903) was a leading evolutionary sociologist.

CHAPTER 11: UTOPIA

1. The chief exception is Ernst Bloch, for example *The Principle of Hope* (3 vols., Basil Blackwell, 1986). See generally, Vincent Geoghegan. *Utopianism and Marxism* (Methuen, 1987); Darren Webb. *Marx, Marxism and Utopia* (Ashgate, 2000).
2. Benedetto Croce. *Essays on Marx and Russia* (Frederick Ungar, 1966), p. 34.
3. V. I. Lenin. *Selected Works* (3 vols., Progress Publishers, 1977), vol. 2, p. 272.
4. Notably in *The Principle of Hope*.
5. Bertram D. Wolfe. *Marxism. One Hundred Years in the Life of a Doctrine* (Chapman & Hall, 1967), p. 337.
6. Bruno Bauer. 'The Genus and the Crowd' (1844), in Lawrence S. Stepelevich, ed. *The Young Hegelians. An Anthology* (Cambridge University Press, 1983), pp. 198–9, 204. Ruge was similarly critical: Robert Gascoigne. *Religion, Rationality and Community. Sacred and Secular in the Thought of Hegel and His Critics* (Martinus Nijhoff, 1985), p. 122.
7. Herbert Spencer later described 'industrial solidarity' as resulting from the division of labour (*Principles of Sociology*, 1874–5). Émile Durkheim developed a distinction between mechanical and organic solidarity: see *The Division of Labor in Society* (Free Press, 1960), where 'positive or co-operative relations' are identified with the division of labour.
8. Karl Marx. *The Civil War in France* (1871), in Karl Marx and V. I. Lenin. *The Civil War in France. The Paris Commune* (International Publishers, 1968), p. 116.
9. David McLellan. *Karl Marx: His Life and Thought* (Harper & Row, 1973), p. 300.
10. David W. Lovell. *From Marx to Lenin. An Evaluation of Marx's Responsibility for Soviet Authoritarianism* (Cambridge University Press, 1984), p. 18.
11. For example Eric Voegelin. *Political Religions* (Edwin Mellen Press, 1986), p. 62. Karl Löwith discusses the role of 'Jewish messianism and prophetism' in *The Communist Manifesto*: see his *Meaning in History. The Theological Implications of the Philosophy of History* (University of Chicago Press, 1949), p. 45.
12. John M. Maguire. *Marx's Theory of Politics* (Cambridge University Press, 1978), p. 234.
13. David Leopold. *The Young Karl Marx. German Philosophy, Modern Politics, and Human Flourishing* (Cambridge University Press, 2007), pp. 185–6, 223.
14. See my *Dystopia. A Natural History* (Oxford University Press, 2016), pp. 236–68.
15. Jon Elster. *An Introduction to Karl Marx* (Cambridge University Press, 1986), p. 43.

16. Iring Fetscher. *Marx and Marxism* (Herder & Herder, 1971), p. 45.

17. Marx still insisted here that 'Private property alienates [*entfremdet*] the individuality not only of people but also of things' (5:230). See *The Communist Manifesto*, ed. Gareth Stedman Jones (Penguin Books, 2000), pp. 140–44, for an account of Stirner's impact on Marx. The thesis that Stirner assisted Marx in moving beyond Feuerbach is defended by Nicholas Lobkowicz. 'Karl Marx and Max Stirner', in Frederick J. Adelmann, ed. *Demythologizing Marxism. A Series of Studies on Marxism* (Martinus Nijhoff, 1969), pp. 64–95. Engels thought Stirner's ideas 'must immediately change into communism' because he had taken bourgeois egoism to its logically absurd conclusion (38:11).

18. This was a problem vis-à-vis Proudhon and later Bakunin.

19. Edward Hallett Carr. *Karl Marx. A Study in Fanaticism* (2nd edn, J. M. Dent, 1938), p. 81.

20. Maximilien Rubel. *Rubel on Karl Marx. Five Essays*, ed. Joseph O'Malley and Keith Algozin (Cambridge University Press, 1981), p. 18. This was later echoed in Engels' quotation in *The Origin of the Family, Private Property and the State* (1884) of Lewis Morgan's belief that future communism would involve reviving 'in a higher form…the liberty, equality and fraternity of the ancient gentes' (26:276). This theme would re-emerge in Russia in the Narodnaya Volya programme, which Georgi Plekhanov described as an 'idealisation of the primitive forms of national life': *Selected Philosophical Works* (5 vols., Lawrence & Wishart, 1977), vol. 1, p. 119.

21. Stephen Lukes. 'Marxism and Utopianism', in Peter Alexander and Roger Gill, eds. *Utopias* (Duckworth, 1984), p. 156.

22. Fritz J. Raddatz. *Karl Marx. A Political Biography* (Weidenfeld & Nicolson, 1979), p. 273.

23. Alfred Schmidt. *The Concept of Nature in Marx* (NLB, 1971), p. 127.

24. Rubel. *Rubel on Karl Marx*, pp. 26–8.

CHAPTER 12: CONCLUDING MARX

1. Georg Lukács. *Lenin. A Study on the Unity of His Thought* (MIT Press, 1971), p. 10.

2. Edward Hallett Carr. *Karl Marx. A Study in Fanaticism* (2nd edn, J. M. Dent, 1938), pp. 300–301.

3. Quoted in Robert Payne. *Marx* (W. H. Allen, 1968), p. 399.

4. A fairly orthodox approach to this question is Franz Jakubowski. *Ideology and Superstructure in Historical Materialism* (Allison & Busby, 1976).

5. Agnes Heller contends that Marx believed that in the future society 'Human needs and capacities will be of a qualitative nature: the qualitative can be "exchanged" only with the qualitative', thus avoiding this problem (*The Theory of*

Need in Marx, Allison & Busby, 1976, p. 56). An alternative view might be that the consumption of public goods (including experiences) would supplant much of the consumption of private goods under capitalism.

6. John Dewey. *The Later Works, 1925–1953, Volume Three. 1927–1928* (Southern Illinois University Press, 1984), p. 206.

7. David McLellan. *Marx before Marxism* (Macmillan, 1970), p. 216.

8. John Plamenatz. *German Marxism and Russian Communism* (Harper Torchbooks, 1965), p. 159.

9. John Plamenatz. *Karl Marx's Philosophy of Man* (Clarendon Press, 1975), pp. 173–201.

10. Bertram D. Wolfe. *A Life in Two Centuries. An Autobiography* (Stein and Day, 1981), p. 197.

11. Leszek Kolakowski, introduction to Leszek Kolakowski and Stuart Hampshire, eds. *The Socialist Idea. A Reappraisal* (Weidenfeld & Nicolson, 1974), p. 35.

12. Eugene Kamenka. *The Ethical Foundations of Marxism* (Routledge & Kegan Paul, 1962), p. 163. Nonetheless Kamenka wrongly asserts that Marx 'was not prepared to…see socialism as the extension and culmination of the freedom and enterprise already displayed by the worker' (ibid., p. 164). This is why he supported co-operation so centrally by the mid-1860s.

13. 'Wir wissen, daß die neuen Kräfte der Gesellschaft, um richtig zur Wirkung zu kommen, nur neuer Menschen bedürfen, die ihrer Meister werden – und das sind die Arbeiter' (W12:4). Translated as: 'We know that to work well the new-fangled forces of society, they only want to be mastered by new-fangled men – and such are the working men' (14:656).

14. Benedetto Croce. *Essays on Marx and Russia* (Frederick Ungar, 1966), p. 39.

15. Karl Heinzen. *Die Helden des teutschen Kommunismus* (1848). Marx called it a 'trashy piece' (38:181).

16. G. W. F. Hegel. *Lectures on the History of Philosophy, 1825–6* (3 vols., Clarendon Press, 2009), vol. 1, p. 243.

PART TWO: MARXISM
INTRODUCTION: CONVERSION

1. General accounts of the 'ism' include Alasdair C. Macintyre. *Marxism. An Interpretation* (SCM Press, 1953); Sidney Hook. *Marx and the Marxists. The Ambiguous Legacy* (Van Nostrand Co., 1955); George Lichtheim. *Marxism. A Critical and Historical Study* (Routledge & Kegan Paul, 1961); C. Wright Mills. *The Marxists* (Dell, 1962). Of the longer introductions, the clearest exposition is by the only major historian and philosopher to have experienced Marxism-Leninism from the inside, Leszek Kolakowski. See his *Main Currents of Marxism* (3 vols.,

Clarendon Press, 1978). A good account of the first phase is John Plamenatz. *German Marxism and Russian Communism* (Harper Torchbooks, 1965).

2. Quoted in Pierre Brocheux. *Ho Chi Minh. A Biography* (Cambridge University Press, 2007), p. 65.

3. Richard Kindersley. *The First Russian Revisionists. A Study of 'Legal Marxism' in Russia* (Clarendon Press, 1962), p. 218; Bertram D. Wolfe. *A Life in Two Centuries. An Autobiography* (Stein and Day, 1981), p. 175.

4. Angelica Balabanoff. *My Life as a Rebel* (Hamish Hamilton, 1938), p. 32.

5. Whittaker Chambers. *Witness* (André Deutsch, 1953), p. 146.

6. Douglas Hyde. *I Believed. The Autobiography of a Former British Communist* (William Heinemann, 1950), p. 61; Arthur Koestler et al. *The God That Failed. Six Studies in Communism* (Hamilton, 1950), p. 15.

7. Koestler et al. *The God That Failed*, pp. 130, 166; André Gide, *Journals* (4 vols., Secker & Warburg, 1949), vol. 3, p. 276; André Gide, *Back from the USSR* (Martin Secker & Warburg, 1937), p. 15.

8. Czeslaw Milosz. *Native Realm. A Search for Self-Definition* (Sidgwick & Jackson, 1981), p. 113. 'One often heard the remark, "if Marxism is rejected, then history has no meaning"', he recalled (ibid., pp. 114–15).

9. Koestler et al. *The God That Failed*, p. 202.

10. Quoted in David Caute. *The Fellow-Travellers. A Postscript to the Enlightenment* (Weidenfeld & Nicolson, 1973), pp. 24, 33.

11. Milosz. *Native Realm*, p. 119.

12. Hyde. *I Believed*, pp. 56, 80, 89, 111.

CHAPTER 1: MARXISM AND SOCIAL DEMOCRACY, 1883–1918: THE REVISIONIST DEBATE

1. Surveys of Marxism in this period include Perry Anderson. *Considerations on Western Marxism* (NLB, 1976); Eric J. Hobsbawm, ed. *The History of Marxism, Volume One. Marxism in Marx's Day* (Harvester Press, 1982); Martin Jay. *Marxism and Totality. The Adventures of a Concept from Lukács to Habermas* (Polity Press, 1984).

2. On the thought of this period see G. D. H. Cole. *A History of Socialist Thought, Volume Three. The Second International, 1889–1914* (2 parts, Macmillan, 1963). On revisionism as such see also H. Kendall Rogers. *Before the Revisionist Controversy. Kautsky, Bernstein, and the Meaning of Marxism, 1895–1898* (Garland, 1992).

3. See James Joll. *The Second International, 1889–1914* (revised edn, Routledge & Kegan Paul, 1974).

4. W. L. Guttsman. *The German Social Democratic Party, 1875–1933. From Ghetto to Government* (Allen & Unwin, 1981), p. 50.

5. Vernon L. Lidtke. *The Alternative Culture. Socialist Labor in Imperial Germany* (Oxford University Press, 1985), p. 195. Curiously, there were apparently no SPD festivals devoted to Marx, and few workers borrowed his works from its libraries.

6. See generally Carl E. Schorske. *German Social Democracy 1905–1917. The Development of the Great Schism* (Russell & Russell, 1970).

7   Karl Kautsky. *The Class Struggle* [1892] (W. W. Norton, 1971), p. 110.

8. On Bernstein see Peter Gay. *The Dilemma of Democratic Socialism. Eduard Bernstein's Challenge to Marx* (Collier Books, 1962); Manfred B. Steger. *The Quest for Evolutionary Socialism. Eduard Bernstein and Social Democracy* (Cambridge University Press, 1997). On the state of play in Marx criticism by 1905, see Louis B. Boudin. *The Theoretical System of Karl Marx in the Light of Recent Criticism* (Charles H. Kerr, 1907).

9. Eduard Bernstein. *My Years of Exile. Reminiscences of a Socialist* (Leonard Parsons, 1921), p. 237.

10. Engels wrote to Kautsky in 1891 that 'recent investigations…have rendered obsolete Marx's chapter on the historical trend of capitalist accumulation' (49:315).

11 Eduard Bernstein. *Evolutionary Socialism. A Criticism and Affirmation* [1899, revised 1909] (Schocken Books, 1967), p. 34.

12. Ibid., pp. xxii, xxix.

13. Ibid., pp. 148–9, 153–4, 222.

14. Eduard Bernstein. *Selected Writings of Eduard Bernstein, 1900–1921*, ed. Manfred Steger (Humanities Press, 1996), pp. 36, 45, 156.

15. Schorske. *German Social Democracy*, p. 19.

16. Bernstein. *Selected Writings*, pp. 181, 189.

17. On Kautsky see Gary P. Steenson. *Karl Kautsky, 1854–1938. Marxism in the Classical Years* (University of Pittsburgh Press, 1978); Massimo Salvadori. *Karl Kautsky and the Socialist Revolution, 1880–1938* (Verso, 1979); Dick Geary. *Karl Kautsky* (Manchester University Press, 1987); John H. Kautsky, ed. *Karl Kautsky and the Social Science of Classical Marxism* (E. J. Brill, 1989); John H. Kautsky. *Karl Kautsky. Marxism, Revolution and Democracy* (Transaction Publishers, 1994).

18. For the wider context see my *Imperial Sceptics. British Critics of Empire, 1850–1920* (Cambridge University Press, 2010). For Germany in particular, see Roger Fletcher. *Revisionism and Empire. Socialist Imperialism in Germany, 1897–1914* (Allen & Unwin, 1984).

19. Karl Kautsky. *Ethics and the Materialist Conception of History* (4th edn, Charles H. Kerr, 1918), pp. 56, 198.

20. Abridged as Karl Kautsky. *The Materialist Conception of History*, ed. John H. Kautsky (Yale University Press, 1988).

21. Quoted in Geary. *Karl Kautsky*, p. 44.

22. Kautsky. *Class Struggle*, p. 91.

23. Karl Kautsky. *The Social Revolution* [1902] (Charles H. Kerr, 1916), p. 3

24. Karl Kautsky. *The Road to Power* [1909] (Humanities Press, 1996), p. xlviii.

25. Karl Kautsky. *The Labour Revolution* (George Allen and Unwin, 1925), p. 63.

26. Ibid., pp. 77, 80–83.

27. David Mitrany. *Marx against the Peasant. A Study in Social Dogmatism* (George Weidenfeld & Nicolson, 1951), p. 38.

28. Karl Kautsky. *The Agrarian Question* [1899] (2 vols., Zwan Publications, 1988), vol. 1, pp. 147–8, vol. 2, pp. 311–13, 329–40.

29. On the evolution of Western Marxist views of Bolshevism see Marcel van der Linden. *Western Marxism and the Soviet Union. A Survey of Critical Theories and Debates since 1917* (Brill, 2007).

30. Moira Donald. *Marxism and Revolution. Karl Kautsky and the Russian Marxists, 1900–1924* (Yale University Press, 1993), p. 30.

31. A similar view is evident in the American Marxist John Spargo's *Bolshevism. The Enemy of Political and Industrial Democracy* (John Murray, 1919), which described the regime as a tyranny 'as infamous as anything in the annals of autocracy' (p. 261) and as 'the negation of Marxian Socialism' (p. 266).

32. Karl Kautsky. *Social Democracy versus Communism* [1933–4] (Rand School Press, 1946), p. 57; *Labour Revolution*, p. 86.

33. Karl Kautsky. *The Dictatorship of the Proletariat* [1918] (University of Michigan Press, 1971), pp. 6, 45, 140.

34. Kautsky. *Social Democracy versus Communism*, pp. 59, 65.

35. Karl Kautsky. *Thomas More and His Utopia* [1888] (A. & C. Black, 1927), p. 204.

36. Kautsky. *Class Struggle*, p. 98.

37. Kautsky. *Labour Revolution*, pp. 281–2.

38. Ibid., pp. 185, 207–8. But critics have found this scheme, too, liable to the same objection of creating a new ruling class (Max Nomad. *Aspects of Revolt*, Bookman Associates, 1959, p. 42).

39. Karl Kautsky. *Terrorism and Communism* (George Allen & Unwin, 1920), pp. 32, 171, 201, 220.

40. Karl Kautsky. *Bolshevism at a Deadlock* (George Allen & Unwin, 1931), pp. 118–19, 139.

41. In 1931, for example, the KPD supported the Nazis in Prussia against the SPD.

42. On Rosa Luxemburg see Peter Nettl. *Rosa Luxemburg* (2 vols., Oxford University Press, 1966); Paul Frölich. *Rosa Luxemburg. Her Life and Work* (Monthly Review Press, 1972); Stephen Eric Bronner. *Rosa Luxemburg. A Revolutionary for Our Times* (Columbia University Press, 1987); Richard Abraham. *Rosa Luxemburg. A Life for the International* (Berg, 1989).

43. Rosa Luxemburg. *Social Reform or Revolution?* [1899] (Young Socialist Publications, n.d.), pp. 13, 22, 37, 39, 58, 61, 63, 81–2.

44. Rosa Luxemburg. *The Russian Revolution and Leninism or Marxism?* (University of Michigan Press, 1970), pp. 69, 62.

45. Ibid., pp. 62, 72, 67.

46. William Morris. *News from Nowhere* [1890] (Longmans, Green & Co., 1899), pp. 104–5.

47. An introduction is Tom Bottomore and Patrick Goode, eds. *Austro-Marxism* (Clarendon Press, 1978).

48. See Otto Bauer. *The Question of Nationalities and Social Democracy* [1924] (University of Minnesota Press, 2000).

49. Antonio Labriola. *Essays on the Materialist Conception of History* [1896] (Charles H. Kerr, 1908), p. 17.

50. See Benedetto Croce. *Historical Materialism and the Economics of Karl Marx* (Howard Latimer, 1914); *Essays on Marx and Russia* (Frederick Ungar, 1966).

51. See Harvey Goldberg. *The Life of Jean Jaurès* (University of Wisconsin Press, 1968). Jaurès's *Studies in Socialism* (Independent Labour Party, 1909) describes 'respect for all life' as 'the very essence of Communism', as defined by *The Communist Manifesto* (p. 12).

CHAPTER 2: LENIN AND THE RUSSIAN REVOLUTION: 'BREAD, PEACE, LAND'

1. A recent overview in this series is Orlando Figes. *Revolutionary Russia, 1891–1991* (Pelican, 2014).

2. See Samuel H. Baron. *Plekhanov. The Father of Russian Marxism* (Routledge & Kegan Paul, 1963).

3. Georgi Plekhanov. *Selected Philosophical Works* (3rd edn, 5 vols., Progress Publishers, 1977), vol. 1, p. 16.

4. Richard Kindersley. *The First Russian Revisionists. A Study of 'Legal Marxism' in Russia* (Clarendon Press, 1962), p. 218.

5. Quoted in Andrzej Walicki. *Marxism and the Leap to the Kingdom of Freedom. The Rise and Fall of the Communist Utopia* (Stanford University Press, 1995), p. 230.

6. Plekhanov. *Selected Philosophical Works*, vol. 1, p. 69.

7. Ibid., vol. 3, p. 45.

8. V. I. Lenin. *Collected Works* (47 vols., Foreign Languages Publishing House, 1960–80), vol. 6, p. 51.

9. V. I. Lenin. *Selected Works* (3 vols., Progress Publishers, 1977), vol. 1, p. 114. This is often seen as Lenin's most innovative development, for example by Leszek

Kolakowski. *Main Currents of Marxism* (3 vols., Clarendon Press, 1978), vol. 2, p. 389.

10. O. Piatnitsky. *Memoirs of a Bolshevik* (Martin Lawrence, 1933), p. 146.

11. Quoted in Baron. *Plekhanov*, p. 248.

12. Theodore Dan. *The Origins of Bolshevism* (Secker & Warburg, 1964), p. 325. Lenin hurled this passage back at Plekhanov in January 1918, as he prepared to dissolve the elected Constituent Assembly.

13. Quoted in David W. Lovell. *From Marx to Lenin. An Evaluation of Marx's Responsibility for Soviet Authoritarianism* (Cambridge University Press, 1984), p. 161.

14. Michael Prawdin. *The Unmentionable Nechaev. A Key to Bolshevism* (George Allen & Unwin, 1961), pp. 48–9.

15. Nicholas II's abdication in fact occurred on 2 March under the Old Style (Julian calendar) dating system, which was replaced in Russia by the Gregorian calendar in February 1918, when the Julian dates 1–13 February were dropped. For ease of reference, New Style dates have been used for all events in Russia prior to the adoption of the new calendar.

16. One of the most accessible contemporary accounts is N. N. Sukhanov. *The Russian Revolution 1917. A Personal Record* (Oxford University Press, 1955).

17. Quoted in Edmund Wilson. *To the Finland Station. A Study in the Writing and Acting of History* (Penguin Books, 1972), p. 553.

18. Quoted in Giuseppe Fiori. *Antonio Gramsci. Life of a Revolutionary* (NLB, 1970), p. 112.

19. Published as *On the Tasks of the Proletariat in the Present Revolution* (1917).

20. E. H. Carr. *The Bolshevik Revolution, 1917–1923* (3 vols., Macmillan & Co., 1950–53), vol. 1, p. 79; Leon Trotsky. *Trotsky's Diary in Exile, 1935* (Faber and Faber, 1959), p. 146.

21. Quoted in Carr. *Bolshevik Revolution*, vol. 1, p. 86.

22. M. Philips Price. *My Reminiscences of the Russian Revolution* (George Allen & Unwin, 1921), p. 145.

23. Bertram D. Wolfe. *Three Who Made a Revolution. A Biographical History* (Beacon Press, 1948), p. 369.

24. John Reed. *Ten Days That Shook the World* [1919] (Lawrence & Wishart, 1961), p. 72.

25. Ibid., pp. 72, 103–5.

26. Oliver H. Radkey. *The Agrarian Foes of Bolshevism. Promise and Default of the Russian Socialist Revolutionaries, February to October 1917* (Columbia University Press, 1958), pp. 24–32.

27. Lenin. *Selected Works*, vol. 2, p. 456.

28. Reed. *Ten Days That Shook the World*, p. 125. Reed thought the Bolshevik view was 'democracy of the working class, and no democracy for anyone else' (quoted

in Granville Hicks. *John Reed. The Making of a Revolutionary* (Macmillan, 1936), p. 342).

29. Jay Bergman. *Vera Zasulich. A Biography* (Stanford University Press, 1983), p. 213.

30. N. I. Bukharin. *Selected Writings on the State and the Transition to Socialism*, ed. Richard B. Day (Spokesman Books, 1982), p. 61.

31. On this development see Maurice Brinton. *The Bolsheviks and Workers' Control, 1917 to 1921. The State and Counter-Revolution* (Black Rose Books, 1975).

32. Louise Bryant. *Six Red Months in Russia* (George H. Doran Co., 1918), p. 39.

33. Helen Rappaport. *Caught in the Revolution. Petrograd, 1917* (Hutchinson, 2016), p. 147.

34. Rosa Leviné-Meyer. *Inside German Communism. Memoirs of Party Life in the Weimar Republic* (Pluto Press, 1977), p. 99.

35. Bessie Beatty. *The Red Heart of Russia* (The Century Co., 1919), pp. 28–9.

36. Reed. *Ten Days That Shook the World*, pp. 10–12; Émile Vandervelde. *Three Aspects of the Russian Revolution* (George Allen & Unwin, 1918), pp. 53–4.

37. Reed himself died of typhoid in 1920 after eating a watermelon he bought in Daghestan, and is today buried next to Lenin in Red Square.

38. Price. *My Reminiscences of the Russian Revolution*, p. 265.

39. Quoted in Carr. *Bolshevik Revolution*, vol. 1, pp. 136–7.

40. Lenin. *Selected Works*, vol. 2, p. 108.

41. Ibid., p. 40.

42. Kolakowski. *Main Currents of Marxism*, vol. 2, p. 396; G. D. H. Cole. *A History of Socialist Thought, Volume Three. The Second International 1889–1914* (2 parts, Macmillan, 1963), part 1, p. 504.

43. Dan. *Origins of Bolshevism*, p. 239.

44. Nikolay Valentinov. *Encounters with Lenin* (Oxford University Press, 1968), p. 122.

45. Bergman. *Vera Zasulich*, p. 197.

46. Lenin. *Selected Works*, vol. 1, p. 39, vol. 3, p. 86.

47. Ibid., vol. 2, pp. 34–6. The point was reiterated in September, when Lenin stressed that the Bolsheviks now had a majority amongst the proletariat (ibid., pp. 331–5).

48. Ibid., pp. 60–61.

49. Ibid., pp. 302–3, 310–12.

50. For commentary see A. J. Polan. *Lenin and the End of Politics* (Methuen, 1984).

51. Lenin. *Selected Works*, vol. 2, pp. 238–327; Robert Service. *Lenin. A Biography* (Macmillan, 2000), p. 353.

52. Karl Kautsky. *The Labour Revolution* (George Allen & Unwin, 1925), p. 135.

53. Lenin. *Selected Works*, vol. 2, pp. 621, 638.

54. John H. Kautsky. *Karl Kautsky. Marxism, Revolution and Democracy* (Transaction Publishers, 1994), p. 4.

55. Polan. *Lenin and the End of Politics*, p. 129.

56. Lenin. *Selected Works*, vol. 3, pp. 20, 23, 39, 104, 234, 417. On the reception of Kautsky's ideas in Russia see Moira Donald. *Marxism and Revolution. Karl Kautsky and the Russian Marxists, 1900–1924* (Yale University Press, 1993).

57. Arthur Rosenberg. *A History of Bolshevism. From Marx to the First Five Years' Plan* (Oxford University Press, 1939), p. 123.

58. Quoted in Robert Conquest. *Lenin* (Fontana/Collins, 1973), p. 46.

59. Lenin. *Selected Works*, vol. 2, p. 475.

60. Brinton. *The Bolsheviks and Workers' Control*, p. 34; Lenin. *Selected Works*, vol. 2, p. 622.

61. See Alexandra Kollontai, 'The Workers' Opposition' [1921], in Alix Holt, ed. *Selected Writings of Alexandra Kollontai* (Allison & Busby, 1977), pp. 159–200.

62. Lenin. *Selected Works*, vol. 2, p. 371, vol. 3, p. 312; Tony Cliff. *Lenin* (4 vols., Pluto Press, 1975–9), vol. 2, p. 331. Solzhenitsyn, in *The First Circle* (1968), has Stalin say that 'A cook is a cook and his job is to get the dinner ready, whereas telling other people what to do is a highly skilled business' (quoted in Georg Lukács. *Solzhenitsyn* (Merlin Press, 1970), p. 52).

63. Quoted in Leonard Schapiro. *The Communist Party of the Soviet Union* (2nd edn, Eyre & Spottiswoode, 1970), p. 210. At this time about a third of 15,000 Party leaders were of proletarian origin. As late as 1927 fewer than 8 per cent had a secondary education.

64. Lenin. *Selected Works*, vol. 1, pp. 97, 365.

65. G. P. Maximoff. *The Guillotine at Work. Twenty Years of Terror in Russia: Data and Documents* (The Chicago Section of the Alexander Berkman Fund, 1940), p. 114; André Liebich. *From the Other Shore. Russian Social Democracy after 1921* (Harvard University Press, 1997), p. 77.

66. Maximoff. *Guillotine at Work*, pp. 260, 158.

67. Lovell. *From Marx to Lenin*, p. 188.

68. Lenin. *Selected Works*, vol. 3, p. 53.

69. Neil Harding. *Lenin's Political Thought. Theory and Practice in the Democratic and Socialist Revolutions* (2 vols., Macmillan, 1983), vol. 2, pp. 296–7.

70. Beatty. *Red Heart of Russia*, pp. 300–301. Countess Panina paid the money a few days afterwards and was released. She later emigrated, and lived until 1956.

71. Maximoff. *Guillotine at Work*, pp. 134–5.

72. Rosenberg. *History of Bolshevism*, p. 155.

73. Paul Avrich. *Kronstadt, 1921* (Princeton University Press, 1970), pp. 73–4.

74. Quoted in Walicki. *Marxism*, p. 310.

75. Quoted in Schapiro. *Communist Party of the Soviet Union*, p. 208.

76. D. J. Cotterill, ed. *The Serge–Trotsky Papers* (Pluto Press, 1994), pp. 162, 169.

77. Emma Goldman. *Living My Life* (2 vols., Duckworth, 1932), vol. 2, p. 886.

78. Quoted in Carr. *Bolshevik Revolution*, vol. 1, pp. 198–200.

79. Ibid., p. 199.

80. E. H. Carr. *The Russian Revolution. From Lenin to Stalin (1917–1929)* (Macmillan, 1979), p. 33; Brinton. *The Bolsheviks and Workers' Control*, p. 72.

81. Robert Vincent Daniels. *The Conscience of the Revolution. Communist Opposition in Soviet Russia* (Harvard University Press, 1960), pp. 126, 148.

82. V. I. Lenin. 'On Co-operation' (1923), in Lenin. *Collected Works*, vol. 33, pp. 467–8.

83. Victor Serge. *Memoirs of a Revolutionary* (Oxford University Press, 1963), pp. 80–1.

84. Quoted in Conquest. *Lenin*, p. 41.

85. Quoted in George Leggett. *The Cheka. Lenin's Political Police* (Clarendon Press, 1981), p. 54.

86. Service. *Lenin*, p. 322. Formally its name was 'The All-Russian Emergency Commission for Combating Counter-Revolution and Sabotage'.

87. Ibid., p. 365.

88. Serge. *Memoirs of a Revolutionary*, p. 80.

89. William Reswick. *I Dreamt Revolution* (Henry Regnery, 1952), p. 7. Dzerzhinsky's own statue stood in the square outside the Lubianka until 1991, when a crowd toppled it. There was an 'outrageously bad statue of Karl Marx' at the Smolny Institute in Petrograd as early as 1920: E. Sylvia Pankhurst. *Soviet Russia as I Saw It* (Dreadnought Publishers, 1921), p. 32.

90. Angelica Balabanoff. *My Life as a Rebel* (Hamish Hamilton, 1938), p. 209.

91. Lenin's *Materialism and Empirio-Criticism* (1909) was designed mainly to attack the 'idealist' faction amongst the Bolsheviks, led by Anatoly Lunacharsky and Alexander Bogdanov, who sought some accommodation between Marxism and religion. The British socialist George Lansbury, who met Lenin in 1920, later wrote that 'I still think of him as a man who would not willingly injure a single human being': *Looking Backwards – and Forwards* (Blackie and Son, 1935), p. 162.

92. O. B. *Red Gaols. A Woman's Experience in Russian Prisons* (Burns, Oates & Washbourne, 1935), p. 2.

93. Balabanoff. *My Life as a Rebel*, p. 206.

94. Reswick. *I Dreamt Revolution*, p. 11.

95. Maximoff. *Guillotine at Work*, p. 117.

96. Ibid., p. 146.

97. See V. I. Lenin, 'The Taylor System – Man's Enslavement by the Machine' [1914], in Lenin. *Collected Works*, vol. 20, pp. 152–4. At the end of the nineteenth century Frederick Winslow Taylor, the inventor of the efficiency system named after him, said the factory worker 'more nearly resembles in his mental make-up the ox than any other type' (quoted in Paul Mason. *Postcapitalism. A Guide to Our Future*, Allen Lane, 2015, p. 188). See Frederick Winslow Taylor. *Scientific Management* (1911) (Harper & Row, 1964). His methods are perhaps best known through Charlie Chaplin's satire on them in *Modern Times* (1936).

98. Price. *My Reminiscences of the Russian Revolution*, p. 283.

99. Lenin. *Selected Works*, vol. 3, p. 450; Maximoff. *Guillotine at Work*, p. 149.

100. Maximoff, *Guillotine at Work*, p. 240.

101. Alexander Berkman. *The Russian Tragedy* (Black Rose Books, 1976), p. 25.

102. Quoted in Bertram D. Wolfe. *An Ideology in Power. Reflections on the Russian Revolution* (Allen and Unwin, 1969), p. 172.

103. Reswick. *I Dreamt Revolution*, p. 54.

104. See E. A. Preobrazhensky. *The New Economics* [1926] (Clarendon Press, 1965); *From New Economic Policy to Socialism. A Glance into the Future of Russia and Europe* [1922] (New Park Publications, 1973). Preobrazhensky was shot by Stalin in 1937 with most of the rest of the Left opposition.

105. Lenin. *Selected Works*, vol. 1, p. 44.

106. Quoted in Conquest. *Lenin*, p. 28.

107. Ibid., p. 9.

108. Albert L. Weeks. *The First Bolshevik. A Political Biography of Peter Tkachev* (New York University Press, 1968).

109. Service. *Lenin*, p. 98.

110. Ibid., p. 202. Some think Lenin's habits of command and expectation of obedience derived in part from his noble background: Figes. *Revolutionary Russia*, p. 21.

111. Anatoly Vasilievich Lunacharsky. *Revolutionary Silhouettes* [1923] (Allen Lane The Penguin Press, 1967), p. 39.

112. L. Kunetskaya. *Lenin in the Kremlin. His Apartment and Study, the People He Met, the Books He Read* (Novosti Press Agency Publishing House, 1970), pp. 4–5.

113. Serge. *Memoirs of a Revolutionary*, p. 74.

114. Lenin. *Selected Works*, vol. 3, p. 461.

115. Kunetskaya. *Lenin in the Kremlin*, p. 57.

116. Balabanoff. *My Life as a Rebel*, p. 150.

117. Serge. *Memoirs of a Revolutionary*, p. 102.

118. Bertrand Russell. *The Practice and Theory of Bolshevism* (Simon & Schuster, 1964), pp. 32–3.

119. Bryant. *Six Red Months in Russia*, p. 137.

120. Pankhurst. *Soviet Russia as I Saw It*, p. 42.

121. H. G. Wells. *Russia in the Shadows* (Hodder & Stoughton, 1920), pp. 130–31.

122. Nadezhda Krupskaya. *Memories of Lenin* (2 vols., Martin Lawrence, 1935), vol. 1, pp. 11–14, 35, 119, 186–7; vol. 2, p. 81.

123. Quoted in Wilson. *To the Finland Station*, p. ix.

124. Figes. *Revolutionary Russia*, p. 23.

125. Trotsky. *Trotsky's Diary in Exile*, p. 44.

126. Lenin. *Selected Works*, vol. 3, p. 680.

127. Angelica Balabanoff. *Impressions of Lenin* (University of Michigan Press, 1964), p. 2.

CHAPTER 3: BOLSHEVIK LEADERS: BUKHARIN, TROTSKY, STALIN

1. Bertram D. Wolfe. *A Life in Two Centuries. An Autobiography* (Stein and Day, 1981), pp. 470–71. See in particular Stephen F. Cohen. *Bukharin and the Bolshevik Revolution. A Political Biography, 1888–1938* (Wildwood House, 1974).

2. Stephen F. Cohen. *Bukharin and the Bolshevik Revolution*, p. 205; N. I. Bukharin. *Selected Writings on the State and the Transition to Socialism*, ed. Richard B. Day (Spokesman Books, 1982), p. xiii.

3. Alexander Berkman. *The Russian Tragedy* (Black Rose Books, 1976), p. 41.

4. Bukharin. *Selected Writings*, p. xxii.

5. Nikolai Bukharin. *The ABC of Communism* [1919] (University of Michigan Press, 1967), p. 80.

6. Bukharin. *Selected Writings*, p. 13, 73, 78.

7. Nikolai Bukharin. *Historical Materialism. A System of Sociology* [1921] (University of Michigan Press, 1969), pp. 11, 49, 55, 61, 277.

8. The chief source is Isaac Deutscher's three-volume biography, *The Prophet Armed. Trotsky, 1879–1921*, *The Prophet Unarmed. Trotsky, 1921–1929* and *The Prophet Outcast. Trotsky, 1929–1940* (Oxford University Press, 1954–63).

9. Angelica Balabanoff. *Impressions of Lenin* (University of Michigan Press, 1964), p. 123.

10. Anatoly Vasilievich Lunacharsky. *Revolutionary Silhouettes* [1923] (Allen Lane The Penguin Press, 1967), pp. 65–6.

11. D. J. Cotterill, ed. *The Serge–Trotsky Papers* (Pluto Press, 1994), pp. 9, 11.

12. Leon Trotsky. *The Defence of Terrorism (Terrorism and Communism). A Reply to Karl Kautsky* (Labour Publishing Co., 1921), p. 101.

13. Quoted in Leonard Schapiro. *The Communist Party of the Soviet Union* (2nd edn, Eyre & Spottiswoode, 1970), p. 288.

14. John Reed. *Ten Days That Shook the World* [1919] (Lawrence & Wishart, 1961), p. 43.

15. See Isaac Deutscher. *Stalin. A Political Biography* (Oxford University Press, 1949); Robert C. Tucker. *Stalin as Revolutionary, 1879–1929. A Study in History and Personality* (Chatto & Windus, 1974); Robert C. Tucker. *Stalin in Power. The Revolution from Above, 1928–1941* (W. W. Norton, 1990); Simon Sebag Montefiore. *Stalin. The Court of the Red Tsar* (Weidenfeld & Nicolson, 2003); Simon Sebag Montefiore. *The Young Stalin* (Weidenfeld & Nicolson, 2007); Robert Service. *Stalin. A Biography* (Macmillan, 2004); Oleg V. Khlevniuk. *Stalin. New Biography of a Dictator* (Yale University Press, 2015).

16. Quoted in Boris Souvarine. *Stalin. A Critical Survey of Bolshevism* (Secker & Warburg, 1939), p. 66.

17. Other dates are often given: see Khlevniuk. *Stalin*, p. 11.

18. Sebag Montefiore. *Young Stalin*, p. 73. In films Stalin was invariably shown as considerably taller than Lenin.

19. Tucker. *Stalin as Revolutionary*, pp. 83, 72, 211.

20. Tucker. *Stalin in Power*, p. 3.

21. Khlevniuk. *Stalin*, p. 94.

22. Quoted in Service. *Stalin*, p. 226.

23. Quoted in Sebag Montefiore. *Stalin*, p. 4.

24. Quoted in Khlevniuk. *Stalin*, p. 5.

25. H. G. Wells. *Experiment in Autobiography* (2 vols., The Cresset Press, 1934), vol. 2, pp. 803–8.

26. Milovan Djilas. *Conversations with Stalin* (Rupert Hart-Davis, 1962), p. 59.

27. Victor Serge. *Russia Twenty Years After* [1937] (Humanities Press, 1996), p. 153.

28. Quoted in Service. *Stalin*, p. 241.

29. *The Letter of an Old Bolshevik. A Key to the Moscow Trials* (George Allen & Unwin, 1938), p. 16.

30. Leon Trotsky. *The Revolution Betrayed. What Is the Soviet Union and Where Is It Going?* (Faber & Faber, 1937), p. 99.

31. Kirov did have a more liberal view of the opposition than Stalin (*Letter of an Old Bolshevik*, p. 43).

32. Joseph Stalin. *Leninism* (George Allen & Unwin, 1928), pp. 15, 24, 33, 43, 45–6, 49, 51.

33. Ibid., p. 404.

34. Trotsky. *Revolution Betrayed*, p. 39.

35. Quoted in Service. *Stalin*, p. 272.

36. Quoted in Orlando Figes. *Revolutionary Russia, 1891–1991* (Pelican, 2014), p. 207.

37. Quoted in Max Nomad. *Aspects of Revolt* (Bookman Associates, 1959), pp. 29, 31.

38. Serge. *Russia Twenty Years After*, p. 132.

39. Two recent surveys are James Harris. *The Great Fear. Stalin's Terror of the 1930s* (Oxford University Press, 2016), and Jörg Baberowski. *Scorched Earth. Stalin's Reign of Terror* (Yale University Press, 2016).

40. Tucker. *Stalin in Power*, p. 444.

41. For further details see my *Dystopia. A Natural History* (Oxford University Press, 2016), pp. 128–76.

42. Figes. *Revolutionary Russia*, p. xvi. Hitler's long-term Generalplan Ost of course envisioned the enslavement of much of the population of the entire region, and the elimination of its educated classes.

43. Having shot his best commanders Stalin then ignored multiple warnings of Hitler's invasion plans, resulting in the unnecessary loss of vast amounts of men and equipment. The later myth of Stalin's military genius is thus sheer fabrication.

44. Ella Winter. *Red Virtue. Human Relationships in the New Russia* (Victor Gollancz, 1933), p. 17.

45. William Reswick. *I Dreamt Revolution* (Henry Regnery, 1952), p. 130.

46. Alexander Orlov. *The Secret History of Stalin's Crimes* (Jarrolds, 1954), p. 53.

47. Winter. *Red Virtue*, pp. 232–3.

48. Christian F. Ostermann, ed. *Uprising in East Germany, 1953. The Cold War, the German Question, and the First Major Upheaval behind the Iron Curtain* (Central European University Press, 2001), p. 36.

49. Winter. *Red Virtue*, pp. 121–2.

50. Quoted in E. H. Carr. *The Bolshevik Revolution, 1917–1923* (3 vols., Macmillan & Co., 1950–53), vol. 2, p. 188.

51. Quoted in Victor Serge. *From Lenin to Stalin* (Martin Secker & Warburg, 1937), p. 98. 'This contradiction is life,' Stalin said on another occasion, 'and it reflects completely the Marxian dialectic' (quoted in Merle Fainsod. *How Russia Is Ruled*, revised edn (Harvard University Press, 1963), p. 111).

52. Winter. *Red Virtue*, p. 28.

53. Elizabeth Lermolo. *Face of a Victim* (Arthur Barker, 1956), p. 19. Stalin agreed. Sylvia Pankhurst observed in 1920 that the Russians 'proceed on the theory, in spite of overwhelming evidence, that a man must be filled with disinterested and intelligent proletarian solidarity if he has been elected by a Shop Committee': *Soviet Russia as I Saw It* (Dreadnought Publishers, 1921), p. 50.

54. Trotsky. *Revolution Betrayed*, p. 94.

55. Serge. *Russia Twenty Years After*, p. 44.

56. Trotsky estimated that overall wage differentials in the 1930s were as high as a hundred times; while Serge put them at up to fifteen times within the working class (*Russia Twenty Years After*, p. 13). Eastman thought eighty-six times was typical (*The End of Socialism in Russia* (Martin Secker & Warburg, 1937), p. 33).

Differentials in the USA were perhaps fifty times in this period; they are now far greater.

57. An analogous law in France in 1850 was described by Marx as 'an excess of despotism' (10:578). In the USSR the rural population were not permitted to have internal passports until the 1970s and thus remained in a condition akin to serfdom.

58. Serge. *Russia Twenty Years After*, p. 68.

59. Ibid., p. 8.

60. Sidney and Beatrice Webb. *The Truth about Soviet Russia* (Longmans, Green & Co., 1942), p. 16.

61. Unto Parvilahti. *Beria's Gardens. Ten Years' Captivity in Russia and Siberia* (Hutchinson, 1959), p. 237.

62. Karl Kautsky. *Social Democracy versus Communism* [1933–4] (Rand School Press, 1946), p. 29.

63. Robert C. Tucker, ed. *Stalinism. Essays in Interpretation* (W. W. Norton, 1977), pp. 284, 293, 297.

64. See Gustav A. Wetter. *Dialectical Materialism. A Historical and Systematic Survey of Philosophy in the Soviet Union* (Routledge & Kegan Paul, 1958); Z. A. Jordan. *The Evolution of Dialectical Materialism. A Philosophical and Sociological Analysis* (Macmillan, 1967).

65. Bertrand Russell. *The Practice and Theory of Bolshevism* (Simon & Schuster, 1964), p. 70.

66. *Pravda* (Truth) was one of the two main Soviet papers, the other being *Izvestia* (News). So a contemporary saying ran that there was no news in the *Truth* and no truth in the *News*.

67. *History of the Communist Party of the Soviet Union (Bolsheviks). Short Course* (Foreign Languages Publishing House, 1939), pp. 9, 105–9, 268–9, 327.

68. E. H. Carr. *The Russian Revolution. From Lenin to Stalin (1917–1929)* (Macmillan, 1979), pp. 169, 187.

69. Quoted in Tucker. *Stalin in Power*, p. 539.

CHAPTER 4: AFTER STALIN, 1953–1968

1. V. I. Lenin. *Selected Works* (3 vols., Progress Publishers, 1977), vol. 3, p. 418.

2. Paul Mason. *Postcapitalism. A Guide to Our Future* (Allen Lane, 2015), p. 223.

3. On the post-war Soviet Union see Adam B. Ulam. *The Communists. The Story of Power and Lost Illusions, 1948–1991* (Maxwell Macmillan, 1992).

4. For example Leonard Schapiro. *The Communist Party of the Soviet Union* (2nd edn, Eyre & Spottiswoode, 1970), p. 627.

5. This was evidently gold-plated, or gold leaf, or perhaps painted with iron pyrite – 'fool's gold'.

6. Andrei D. Sakharov. *My Country and the World* (Collins & Harvill, 1975), p. 14.

7. See Fernando Claudin. *The Communist Movement. From Comintern to Cominform* (Penguin Books, 1975).

8. See Arthur Koestler et al. *The God That Failed. Six Studies in Communism* (Hamish Hamilton, 1950), for these cases.

9. Andrew Smith. *I Was a Soviet Worker* (Robert Hale & Co., 1937), pp. 21, 37.

10. Max Eastman. *The End of Socialism in Russia* (Martin Secker & Warburg, 1937), p. 9; *Stalin's Russia and the Crisis in Socialism* (George Allen & Unwin, 1940), p. 82.

11. Douglas Hyde. *I Believed. The Autobiography of a Former British Communist* (William Heinemann, 1950), pp. 228, 243, 303.

CHAPTER 5: WESTERN EUROPEAN MARXISM, 1920–1968, AND BEYOND

1. Quoted in David Caute. *The Fellow-Travellers. A Postscript to the Enlightenment* (Weidenfeld & Nicolson, 1973), p. 156.

2. Ibid., p. 10.

3. Unto Parvilahti. *Beria's Gardens. Ten Years' Captivity in Russia and Siberia* (Hutchinson, 1959), p. 65.

4. Quoted in Caute. *Fellow-Travellers*, p. 204.

5. See Georg Lukács. *Record of a Life. An Autobiographical Sketch* (Verso, 1983). Then, George Lichtheim. *George Lukács* (Oxford University Press, 1970); Andrew Arato and Paul Breines. *The Young Lukács and the Origins of Western Marxism* (Pluto Press, 1979); Arpad Kadarkay. *Georg Lukács. Life, Thought, and Politics* (Blackwell, 1991).

6. Kadarkay. *Georg Lukács*, pp. 195, 200, 214.

7. English edition, Merlin Press, 1971.

8. Lukács. *Record of a Life*, p. 77.

9. In Kadarkay's judgement (*Georg Lukács*, p. 270).

10. Georg Lukács. *Tactics and Ethics. Political Writings, 1919–1929*, ed. Rodney Livingstone (Verso, 2014), p. 48.

11. A very late work by Lukács, *Solzhenitsyn* (Merlin Press, 1970), actually takes its subject to task for not tackling the 'big political questions' in *A Day in the Life of Ivan Denisovich* (1962), and then promises 'a renaissance in Marxism' (p. 15).

12. Victor Serge. *Memoirs of a Revolutionary* (Oxford University Press, 1963), p. 187.

13. Kadarkay. *Georg Lukács*, pp. 461–3. A new edition of *Democratization* is *The Process of Democratization* (State University of New York Press, 1991).

14. Georg Lukács. *The Destruction of Reason* (Merlin Press, 1980). Three volumes of the 'Ontology', on Hegel, Marx and Labour, have been published by Merlin Press (1978–80).

15. On Gramsci see, John M. Cammett. *Antonio Gramsci and the Origins of Italian Communism* (Stanford University Press, 1967); Carl Boggs. *Gramsci's Marxism* (Pluto Press, 1976); Martin Clark. *Antonio Gramsci and the Revolution That Failed* (Yale University Press, 1977); Alastair Davidson. *Antonio Gramsci. Towards an Intellectual Biography* (Merlin Press, 1977); Roger Simon. *Gramsci's Political Thought. An Introduction* (Lawrence & Wishart, 1982); Paul Ransome. *Antonio Gramsci. A New Introduction* (Harvester Wheatsheaf, 1992); Antonio A. Santucci. *Antonio Gramsci* (Monthly Review Press, 2010). An English-language edition of Gramsci's key writings is Quintin Hoare and Geoffrey Nowell Smith, eds. *Selections from the Prison Notebooks of Antonio Gramsci* (Lawrence & Wishart, 1971).

16. Serge. *Memoirs of a Revolutionary*, p. 186.

17. Giuseppe Fiori. *Antonio Gramsci. Life of a Revolutionary* (NLB, 1970), p. 107.

18. Antonio Gramsci. *The Modern Prince and Other Writings* (Lawrence & Wishart, 1957), pp. 135–88.

19. Gramsci. *Selections from the Prison Notebooks*, pp. 245–6.

20. One example is Althusser's development of the concept of 'ideological state apparatuses': Louis Althusser. *Lenin and Philosophy and Other Essays* (NLB, 1971), pp. 121–73.

21. Galvano Della Volpe. *Rousseau and Marx* (Lawrence and Wishart, 1978), pp. 21–48.

22. See generally John Fraser. *An Introduction to the Thought of Galvano Della Volpe* (Lawrence & Wishart, 1977).

23. Karl Korsch. *Marxism and Philosophy* [1923] (NLB, 1970), pp. 47, 55; *Karl Marx* (Chapman & Hall Ltd, 1938), p. 169.

24. Douglas Kellner, ed. *Karl Korsch. Revolutionary Theory* (University of Texas Press, 1977), p. 15.

25. André Breton. *Manifestoes of Surrealism* (University of Michigan Press, 1969), p. 25.

26. Also translated as August Bebel. *Woman in the Past, Present and Future* (Modern Press, 1885). See Anne Lopes and Gary Roth. *Men's Feminism. August Bebel and the German Socialist Movement* (Humanity Books, 2000).

27. See Lily Braun. *Selected Writings on Feminism and Socialism*, ed. Alfred G. Meyer (Indiana University Press, 1987); Clara Zetkin. *Selected Writings*, ed. Philip S. Foner (International Publishers, 1984).

28. See generally, Martin Jay. *The Dialectical Imagination. A History of the Frankfurt School and the Institute of Social Research, 1923–1950* (Little, Brown, 1973); Trent Schroyer. *The Critique of Domination. The Origins and Development of Critical Theory* (George Braziller, 1973); Albrecht Wellmer. *Critical Theory of Society*

(Seabury Press, 1974); Susan Buck-Morss. *The Origin of Negative Dialectics. Theodor W. Adorno, Walter Benjamin, and the Frankfurt Institute* (The Free Press, 1977); Paul Connerton. *The Tragedy of Enlightenment. An Essay on the Frankfurt School* (Cambridge University Press, 1980); David Held. *Introduction to Critical Theory. Horkheimer to Habermas* (Hutchinson, 1980); George Friedman. *The Political Philosophy of the Frankfurt School* (Cornell University Press, 1981); Tom Bottomore. *The Frankfurt School* (Tavistock, 1984); Stuart Jeffries. *Grand Hotel Abyss. The Lives of the Frankfurt School* (Verso, 2016).

29. See Max Horkheimer. 'Traditional and Critical Theory' [1937], in Horkheimer. *Critical Theory. Selected Essays* (Seabury Press, 1972), pp. 188–243.

30. Buck-Morss. *Origin of Negative Dialectics*, p. xiii. See also Frederic Jameson. *Late Marxism. Adorno, or, The Persistence of the Dialectic* (Verso, 1990).

31. Walter Benjamin. *Illuminations* (Jonathan Cape, 1970), p. 262.

32. Walter Benjamin. *Moscow Diary* (Harvard University Press, 1986), p. 73.

33. Max Horkheimer. *The Dialectic of Enlightenment* (Allen Lane, 1973), pp. 120–67.

34. Ibid., p. 3.

35. Ibid., pp. 120–67. See further Theodor W. Adorno. *The Culture Industry. Selected Essays on Mass Culture*. ed. J. M. Bernstein (Routledge, 2003), pp. 98–106.

36. Jay. *Dialectical Imagination*, p. 57.

37. See Jean Baudrillard. *The Mirror of Production* (Telos Press, 1975).

38. Theodor Adorno and Max Horkheimer. *Towards a New Manifesto* [1956] (Verso, 2011), pp. 10, 14, 21, 23–4.

39. Adorno. *Culture Industry*, p. 188.

40. Herbert Marcuse. 'Liberation from the Affluent Society' (1967), in David Cooper, ed. *The Dialectics of Liberation* (Penguin Books, 1968), pp. 175–92. On Marcuse generally, see Robert W. Marks. *The Meaning of Marcuse* (Ballantine Books, 1970); Alasdair Macintyre. *Marcuse* (Fontana/Collins, 1970); S. S. Lipshires. *Herbert Marcuse. From Marx to Freud and Beyond* (Schenkman Publishing Co., 1974); Morton Schoolman. *The Imaginary Witness. The Critical Theory of Herbert Marcuse* (Collier Macmillan, 1980); Vincent Geoghegan. *Reason and Eros. The Social Theory of Herbert Marcuse* (Pluto Press, 1981); Douglas Kellner. *Herbert Marcuse and the Crisis of Marxism* (Macmillan, 1984).

41. Wilhelm Reich. *What Is Class Consciousness?* [1934] (n.p., 1973), p. 2. The attempt to combine Marxism with theories of sexual emancipation at an advanced theoretical level commenced with Wilhelm Reich, whose *The Function of the Orgasm* (1927) contended that the proletariat's suppressed sexual urges prevented it from achieving political consciousness. He was threatened with execution by some communists for introducing these issues.

42. Herbert Marcuse. *Negations. Essays in Critical Theory* (Allen Lane, 1968), pp. 159–200.

43. Herbert Marcuse. *Counterrevolution and Revolt* (Allen Lane, 1972), p. 3.

44. Herbert Marcuse. *Soviet Marxism. A Critical Analysis* (Routledge & Kegan Paul, 1958), pp. 18, 29, 32, 74–5, 81, 91, 112, 137.

45. Herbert Marcuse. *One-Dimensional Man. Studies in the Ideology of Advanced Industrial Society* (Routledge & Kegan Paul, 1964), pp. 3, 103, 254, 37.

46. Marcuse. *Negations*, p. xvii. Marcuse added, however, 'that freedom is only possible as the realization of what today is called utopia' (ibid., p. xx).

47. Herbert Marcuse. *An Essay on Liberation* (Allen Lane The Penguin Press, 1969), pp. viii–x, 3, 20.

48. See especially Jürgen Habermas. *Toward a Rational Society. Student Process, Science and Politics* (Heinemann, 1971); *Knowledge and Human Interests* (Beacon Press, 1972); *Theory and Practice* (Beacon Press, 1974); *Legitimation Crisis* (Heinemann, 1976).

49. Perry Anderson. *Considerations on Western Marxism* (NLB, 1976), p. 54. Anderson views the 'peculiar esotericism' of Western Marxism as an obvious weakness.

50. Jean-Paul Sartre. *The Problem of Method* (Methuen & Co., 1964), p. xxxiv. On Sartre's politics see Philip Thody. *Jean-Paul Sartre. A Literary and Political Study* (Hamish Hamilton, 1960), pp. 173–237; Wilfred Desan. *The Marxism of Jean-Paul Sartre* (Anchor Books, 1966). Lukács insisted that on 'crucial questions…Sartre remains an existentialist despite his flirting with Marxism' (Kadarkay. *Georg Lukács*, p. 447). On French Marxism more generally see David Caute. *Communism and the French Intellectuals, 1914–1960* (André Deutsch, 1964); George Lichtheim. *Marxism in Modern France* (Columbia University Press, 1966); Mark Poster. *Existential Marxism in Post-War France. From Sartre to Althusser* (Princeton University Press, 1975); Michael Kelly. *Modern French Marxism* (Basil Blackwell, 1982); Tony Judt. *Marxism and the French Left. Studies in Labour and Politics in France, 1830–1981* (Clarendon Press, 1986).

51. See Henri Lefebvre. *Marxist Thought and the City* (University of Minnesota Press, 2016).

52. See Richard Wolin. *The Wind from the East. French Intellectuals, the Cultural Revolution, and the Legacy of the 1960s* (Princeton University Press, 2010).

53. Karl E. Klare. 'The Critique of Everyday Life, the New Left, and Unrecognizable Marxism', in Dick Howard and Karl E. Klare, eds. *The Unknown Dimension. European Marxism since Lenin* (Basic Books, 1972), pp. 14, 20.

54. On their early collaboration see Elzbieta Matynia, ed. *An Uncanny Era. Conversations between Václav Havel and Adam Michnik* (Yale University Press, 2014). Charter 77 insisted on 'the sovereignty of moral sentiment' by contrast to 'the failure to use technology to create a morality': Erazim Kohák, ed. *Jan Patočka. Philosophy and Selected Writings* (University of Chicago Press, 1989), pp. 340–41.

55. Adam Michnik. *In Search of Lost Meaning. The New Eastern Europe* (University of California Press, 2011), p. 30.

56. See André Gorz. *Farewell to the Working Class. An Essay on Post-Industrial Socialism* (Pluto Press, 1982).

57. See André Gorz. *Ecology as Politics* (Black Rose Press, 1980); *Paths to Paradise. On the Liberation from Work* (Pluto Press, 1985); *Ecologia* (Seagull, 2010).

58. Gorz. *Paths to Paradise*, presents an early version of the 'income for life' argument which is today generally called a 'universal basic income'. For a later argument see, for example Nick Srnicek and Alex Williams. *Inventing the Future. Postcapitalism and a World without Work* (Verso, 2015); Rutger Bregman. *Utopia for Realists and How We Can Get There* (Bloomsbury, 2017).

CHAPTER 6: OTHER MARXISMS

1. Crucial here is Wallerstein's *The Modern World-System* (4 vols., Academic Press and University of California Press, 1974–2011).

2. On Mao see Edgar Snow. *The Long Revolution* (Hutchinson, 1973); Jonathan Spence. *Mao* (Weidenfeld & Nicolson, 1999); and, most importantly, Philip Short. *Mao. The Man Who Made China* (I. B. Tauris, 2017). A good general introduction to the period is Andrew G. Walder. *China under Mao. A Revolution Derailed* (Harvard University Press, 2015).

3. Edgar Snow. *Red Star over China* (revised edn, Victor Gollancz, 1968), pp. 90, 92–3.

4. Stuart Schram, ed. *Mao Tse-tung Unrehearsed. Talks and Letters, 1956–71* (Penguin Books, 1974), p. 282.

5. *Selected Works of Mao Tse-tung* (5 vols., Lawrence & Wishart, 1955–77), vol. 5, p. 33.

6. Ibid., vol. 1, p. 111.

7. Walder. *China under Mao*, pp. 65–6, 71.

8. Schram, ed. *Mao-Tse-tung Unrehearsed*, p. 126.

9. Nigel Harris. *The Mandate of Heaven. Marx and Mao in Modern China* (Quartet Books, 1978), pp. 52–3.

10. The lower figure is Short's, who also cites claims of 36 million (*Mao*, pp. 497, 501).

11. Snow. *Long Revolution*, pp. 19, 14–15.

12. Schram, ed. *Mao Tse-tung Unrehearsed*, p. 116.

13. Ibid., p. 203; Jerome Ch'en, ed. *Mao Papers. Anthology and Bibliography* (Oxford University Press, 1970), p. 100.

14. Ch'en, ed. *Mao Papers*, pp. 84, 96.

15. Schram, ed. *Mao Tse-tung Unrehearsed*, pp. 99, 277.

16. Snow. *Long Revolution*, p. 18.

17. See Stuart R. Schram, ed. *The Political Thought of Mao Tse-tung* (revised edn, Penguin Books, 1969); Stuart Schram. *The Thought of Mao Tse-tung* (Cambridge University Press, 1989).

18. *Selected Works of Mao Tse-tung*, vol. 1, pp. 282–338. The published versions of some of these speeches vary considerably from the originals. In the case of 'On Contradiction', for instance, criticisms of Stalin were deleted and warnings about excessive criticism inserted. See Walder. *China under Mao*, pp. 149–50.

19. Schram, ed. *Mao Tse-tung Unrehearsed*, pp. 108–110, 226.

20. Ibid., pp. 146, 150.

21. Ch'en, ed. *Mao Papers*, p. 38.

22. Schram, ed. *Mao Tse-tung Unrehearsed*, p. 169.

23. Harris. *Mandate of Heaven*, p. 289.

24. Schram, ed. *Mao Tse-tung Unrehearsed*, pp. 234–5.

25. Ibid., p. 164; Ch'en, ed. *Mao Papers*, p. 87.

26. Schram, ed. *Mao Tse-tung Unrehearsed*, p. 165.

27. Ch'en, ed. *Mao Papers*, pp. 51–2, 65; *Selected Works of Mao Tse-tung*, vol. 5, p. 297.

28. See Fidel Castro. *My Life*, ed. Ignacio Ramonet (Allen Lane, 2007).

29. Martin Kenner and James Petras, eds. *Fidel Castro Speaks* (Allen Lane The Penguin Press, 1970), p. 8.

30. Castro. *My Life*, pp. 99–102.

31. Ibid., pp. 105, 153.

32. Quoted in Nick Caistor. *Fidel Castro* (Reaktion Books, 2013), p. 57.

33. Castro, *My Life*, p. 181. It has been claimed that neither 'Marx's works nor any others are in any way the key to Castro's political behaviour': Andrés Suárez. *Cuba. Castroism and Communism, 1959–1966* (MIT Press, 1966), p. 16.

34. Castro. *My Life*, p. 257.

35. Ibid., p. 226.

36. Guevara's writings include Ernesto Che Guevara. *Episodes of the Cuban Revolutionary War 1956–58* (Pathfinder Press, 1996); John Gerassi, ed. *Venceremos! The Speeches and Writings of Ernesto Che Guevara* (Weidenfeld & Nicolson, 1968). Biographies include Jon Lee Anderson. *Che Guevara. A Revolutionary Life* (Bantam, 1997).

37. Castro. *My Life*, p. 307.

38. Frantz Fanon. *The Wretched of the Earth* (Macgibbon & Kee, 1965), p. 73.

39. Kwame Nkrumah. *The Autobiography of Kwame Nkrumah* (Thomas Nelson & Sons, 1957), p. 45.

40. Kwame Nkrumah. *Neo-Colonialism. The Last Stage of Imperialism* (International Publishers, 1965), p. xi.

41. Kwame Nkrumah. *Towards Colonial Freedom. Africa in the Struggle against World Imperialism* (Heinemann, 1962), p. xv.

42. Kwame Nkrumah. *Consciencism. Philosophy and Ideology for Decolonization and Development* (Heinemann, 1964), p. 101.

43. Ibid., p. 73. Nkrumah's writings also include *I Speak of Freedom* (1961), *Africa Must Unite* (1963), *Selected Speeches* (1997) and *African Socialism Revisited* (1967).

44. See Aimé Césaire. *Discourse on Colonialism* (MR Press, 1972).

45. Léopold Sédar Senghor. *On African Socialism* (Pall Mall Press, 1964), pp. 32–6, 46, 58, 91; Jacques Louis Hymans. *Léopold Sédar Senghor. An Intellectual Biography* (Edinburgh University Press, 1971), pp. 188, 193.

46. See Julius K. Nyerere. *Freedom and Socialism, Uhuru na Ujamaa. A Selection from Writings and Speeches, 1965–1967* (Oxford University Press, 1968); *Nyerere on Socialism* (Oxford University Press, 1969).

47. A general overview is Colin Mackerras and Nick Knight, eds. *Marxism in Asia* (Croom Helm, 1985).

48. See Pierre Brocheux. *Ho Chi Minh. A Biography* (Cambridge University Press, 2007); Sophie Quinn-Judge. *Ho Chi Minh. The Missing Years, 1919–1941* (Hurst & Co., 2003).

49. Quoted in Bernard Fall. *The Two Viet-Nams. A Political and Military Analysis* (Pall Mall Press, 1965), p. 82.

50. The key work is Lenin's 'On the National and the Colonial Questions' [1920], in V. I. Lenin. *Selected Works* (3 vols., Progress Publishers, 1977), vol. 3, pp. 372–8.

51. Quoted in Jean Lacouture. *Ho Chi Minh* (Allen Lane The Penguin Press, 1968), p. 22; Ho Chi Minh. *On Revolution. Selected Writings, 1920–66*, ed. Bernard B. Fall (Pall Mall Press, 1967), pp. 5, 41, 56; quoted in Brocheux. *Ho Chi Minh*, pp. 27, 50.

52. Quoted in Lacouture. *Ho Chi Minh*, p. 96.

53. This was literally true: Ho lived for a time in a cave, where he named a stalagmite 'Marx' (because its shape resembled him) and also a mountain, and a stream after Lenin (Brocheux. *Ho Chi Minh*, p. 70).

54. Ho Chi Minh. *On Revolution*, pp. 143, 225, 328, 353; Brocheux. *Ho Chi Minh*, pp. 83, 147, 162.

55. On Pol Pot see Philip Short. *Pol Pot. The History of a Nightmare* (John Murray, 2004).

56. See my *Dystopia. A Natural History* (Oxford University Press, 2016), pp. 219–35 for details.

57. David P. Chandler et al., eds. *Pol Pot Plans the Future. Confidential Leadership Documents from Democratic Kampuchea, 1976–1977* (Yale University Southeast Asia Studies, 1988), p. 128.

58. Ibid., p. 160.

MARXISM FOR THE TWENTY-FIRST CENTURY

1. Régis Debray. *Praised Be Our Lords. A Political Education* (Verso, 2007), pp. 15, 18.

2. Eric Hobsbawm. *How to Change the World. Marx and Marxism, 1840–2011* (Little, Brown, 2011), p. 13.

3. Eric Hobsbawm, ed. *The History of Marxism, Volume One. Marxism in Marx's Day* (Harvester Press, 1982), p. 234.

4. Leszek Kolakowski. *Main Currents of Marxism* (3 vols., Clarendon Press, 1978), vol. 3, p. 527.

5. Quoted in André Malraux. *Antimemoirs* (Hamish Hamilton, 1968), p. 389.

6. Thomas Sowell. *Marxism, Philosophy and Economics* (William Morrow, 1985), p. 203.

7. Angelica Balabanoff. *Impressions of Lenin* (University of Michigan Press, 1964), pp. 35, 137.

8. Bertrand Russell. *The Practice and Theory of Bolshevism* (Simon & Schuster, 1964), p. 101.

9. Roger Garaudy. *Karl Marx. The Evolution of His Thought* (International Publishers, 1967), p. 11.

10. Notably Herbert Marcuse. 'Repressive Tolerance', in Robert Paul Wolff, Barrington Moore, Jr, and Herbert Marcuse, *A Critique of Pure Tolerance* (Beacon Press, 1965), which describes toleration as 'an end in itself' (p. 82), and uses John Stuart Mill to support the argument.

11. Kolakowski. *Main Currents of Marxism*, vol. 3, p. 523; Georges Sorel. 'The Decomposition of Marxism' [1908], in Irving Louis Horowitz. *Radicalism and the Revolt against Reason. The Social Theories of Georges Sorel* (Routledge & Kegan Paul, 1961), p. 249. Sorel thought that, but for the 'historical accident' of the Russian revolution, it might have ended here around 1900 anyway (ibid.).

12. See David Harvey. *A Brief History of Neoliberalism* (Oxford University Press, 2005).

13. See generally David Harvey. *The Enigma of Capital and the Crises of Capitalism* (Profile Books, 2011).

14. Thomas Piketty. *Capital in the Twenty-First Century* (Harvard University Press, 2014), p. 27.

15. A good start here is Noam Chomsky. *Necessary Illusions. Thought Control in Democratic Societies* (Pluto Press, 1989).

16. For example Walter Scheidel. *The Great Leveler. Violence and the History of Inequality from the Stone Age to the Twenty-First Century* (Princeton University Press, 2017). For a survey of this theme see Pierre Rosanvallon. *The Society of Equals* (Harvard University Press, 2013).

17. See Adam Michnik. *In Search of Lost Meaning. The New Eastern Europe* (University of California Press, 2011).

18. Russell. *Practice and Theory of Bolshevism*, p. 11.

19. See Rutger Bregman. *Utopia for Realists and How We Can Get There* (Bloomsbury, 2017). Some types of transhumanism envision a merger of artificial intelligence and cyborg and organic additions that will greatly enhance human capability and longevity.

20. See Richard Wilkinson and Kate Pickett. *The Spirit Level. Why More Equal Societies Almost Always Do Better* (Allen Lane, 2009).

21. Gabriel Zucman. *The Hidden Wealth of Nations. The Scourge of Tax Havens* (University of Chicago Press, 2015), p. x.

22. John Gerassi, ed. *Venceremos! The Speeches and Writings of Ernesto Che Guevara* (Weidenfeld & Nicolson, 1968), p. 121.

INDEX

Gregory Claeys is a professor of history at Royal Holloway, University of London. Previously he taught at the University of Hanover, Germany, and Washington University, St. Louis. He is the author of eight books on the history of radicalism, socialism, and utopianism, including *Searching for Utopia,* and edited some fifty volumes of primary sources and essays. He lives in London.

The Nation Institute

NATION
BOOKS

Founded in 2000, **Nation Books** has become a leading voice in American independent publishing. The imprint's mission is to tell stories that inform and empower just as they inspire or entertain readers. We publish award-winning and bestselling journalists, thought leaders, whistleblowers, and truthtellers, and we are also committed to seeking out a new generation of emerging writers, particularly voices from underrepresented communities and writers from diverse backgrounds. As a publisher with a focused list, we work closely with all our authors to ensure that their books have broad and lasting impact. With each of our books we aim to constructively affect and amplify cultural and political discourse and to engender positive social change.

Nation Books is a project of The Nation Institute, a nonprofit media center established to extend the reach of democratic ideals and strengthen the independent press. The Nation Institute is home to a dynamic range of programs: the award-winning Investigative Fund, which supports groundbreaking investigative journalism; the widely read and syndicated website TomDispatch; journalism fellowships that support and cultivate over twenty-five emerging and high-profile reporters each year; and the Victor S. Navasky Internship Program.

For more information on Nation Books and The Nation Institute, please visit:

www.nationbooks.org
www.nationinstitute.org
www.facebook.com/nationbooks.ny
Twitter: @nationbooks